Caleb Everett
Linguistic Relativity

M000209949

Applications of Cognitive Linguistics

Editors
Gitte Kristiansen
Francisco J. Ruiz de Mendoza Ibáñez

Honorary Editor
René Dirven

Volume 25

Caleb Everett

Linguistic Relativity

Evidence Across Languages and Cognitive Domains

DE GRUYTER
MOUTON

ISBN: 978-3-11-048492-2
e-ISBN: 978-3-11-030814-3
ISSN: 1861-4078

Library of Congress Cataloging-in-Publication Data
A CIP catalog record for this book has been applied for at the Library of Congress.

Bibliographic information published by the Deutsche Nationalbibliothek
The Deutsche Nationalbibliothek lists this publication in the Deutsche Nationalbibliografie;
detailed bibliographic data are available in the Internet at http://dnb.dnb.de.

© 2013 Walter de Gruyter GmbH, Berlin/Boston
Typesetting: Meta Systems, Wustermark
Printing: Hubert & Co. GmbH & Co. KG, Göttingen
♾ Printed on acid-free paper
Printed in Germany

www.degruyter.com

Acknowledgements

By nature these sorts of things cannot be exhaustive, so I won't even attempt to thank all the people who were directly or indirectly instrumental in this work. Many of them are acknowledged through the discussion of their research in the pages of this book. To those whose work is mentioned, thanks for doing such fascinating stuff. Thanks are due as well to those at De Gruyter Mouton, and to an insightful and knowledgeable anonymous reviewer who offered helpful feedback.

I have the privilege of working at the University of Miami – a picturesque place and an ideal research context in innumerable ways. Many of my students have enriched my experience here immeasurably. (Two of them helped compile the references and index for this book – Amanda Capps and Navina DeLight.) Also, I'm grateful to my fellow faculty in the anthropology department, which is simply a great place to work. Many other colleagues at the UM College of Arts & Sciences have also helped foster a fantastic working environment.

As for family, what else is there? This book is dedicated to my wife Jamie and our son Jude – it is an unrivaled joy to share my life with such beautiful people. Like all my work, this volume is basically just something I did in between our times together.

I have two unique and gifted parents, Keren Madora and Daniel Everett, whom I consider myself fortunate to call friends. The rest of my extended family reads like a who's who of people I think are awesome: Shannon, Kris, BJ, Craig, Nate, Emily, Levi, Daniel, Madison, Abby, and of course Jim, Chris, Haley, Christopher, and Thomas. Friends warranting a shout out include Cory, Ange, Geninho, Helaine, Elivar (y keet), Marilena, Alexandre – that'll do for now. If I have "cirsumvrented" anyone, I apologize. (To quote one of my favorite scholars, Gob Bluth.)

This book owes itself in many ways to experiences I shared with four people along the verdant banks of the Maici, many years ago. For some time we lived a rustic existence along that clear, sinuous river, amongst a small tribe of people with a remarkable culture and language. All these years later that time continues to impact my life. And for that I am grateful.

Contents

1 Contextualizing the issues

1.1 Introduction

It's an old question. Does language affect how you think? The answer, in very broad terms at least, has been debated for centuries. A very closely related question has been the focus of intense scrutiny among linguists and other cognitive scientists for less time, on the order of decades: do patterns of thought vary in accordance with one's native language? Put differently, does there exist a sort of linguistic relativity, such that some aspect(s) of a person's cognition depends on, or is relative in accordance with, the language employed by that person? To many, this is a fascinating question, and some even spend significant portions of their careers trying to obtain a satisfactory answer to this and related questions. One of the reasons the question is so fascinating (to some at least) is that, apart from any actual evidence that may be brought to bear in formulating a response, people often posit very divergent answers based on their intuition. There are likely few questions in the cognitive sciences that elicit such disparate intuition-based responses. To some, the answer is clearly "yes" and such respondents may even find it puzzling that anyone might answer negatively. To others the answer is patently "no", and they may be equally perplexed by the opposing view. Given that personal experience and intuition are so clearly insufficient to arrive at a consensus vis-à-vis the answer to this question, empirical data are particularly crucial to generating an adequate response. Perhaps surprisingly, despite the deep historical roots of the question at hand, quality empirical data have only been arrived at somewhat recently. The purpose of this book is to introduce you to some of that data, acquired through the research of many linguists, anthropologists, cognitive psychologists, and others "ists" in related fields. Arguably, enough data have now surfaced in the relevant literature to arrive at some sort of satisfactory answer to this question. While the title of this book hints none too subtly at an affirmative answer, it is worth noting from the outset that careful examinations of the relevant data often suggest that more nuanced approaches to the answer (rather than a vociferous "yes" or "no"), and to the formulation of the question itself, may be warranted (see Malt and Wolff [2010:11]). Nevertheless, we will adopt the position that in some general sense the question must be answered positively, since the findings surveyed in this book are difficult if not impossible to reconcile with a negative answer.

The notion that thought patterns or cognition do vary in accordance with people's languages is referred to commonly and in this book as the "linguistic relativity hypothesis". This hypothesis was first articulated, or at least first quasi-cohesively articulated, in the work of two well-known linguists, Benjamin Whorf and his teacher Edward Sapir. (Though they never actually referred to their ideas on the topic as a "hypothesis".) For that reason, "linguist relativity hypothesis" is often employed interchangeably in the literature with "Sapir-Whorf hypothesis" or "Whorfian hypothesis". Such interchangeability appears to be falling out of favor, though, and probably should fall out of favor completely. After all, the linguistic relativity hypothesis in its current manifestation differs in some ways from the important ideas put forth by Sapir, Whorf, or any of their influential predecessors whose work helped inform current ideas on the topic. Given that the hypothesis is continually evolving in accordance with the ongoing acquisition of relevant findings, it is in some sense inaccurate to credit any particular scholars with the hypothesis. This is not to suggest that the work of some, in particular Whorf, was not seminal to the florescence of the current crop of ideas on the subject. It clearly was, as we discuss in some detail below. Nevertheless, in this book we are not particularly concerned with the history of the linguistic relativity hypothesis, nor with meticulously depicting the ideas of any one researcher or set of researchers who has weighed in on the issue. We are instead concerned with depicting the increasingly clear tableau of evidence that is finally allowing us to rely on experimental data, rather than intuitions and anecdotal evidence alone, in deciding whether and how one's cognitive processes are affected by his/her native language.

This introductory chapter serves several basic functions: One of these is to define the linguistic relativity hypothesis with sufficient clarity as to allow us to carefully survey the evidence for the hypothesis during the remainder of the book. This requires that some attention be paid to the history of work on linguistic relativity. What will (hopefully) result from this brief discussion of some well-known ideas in the literature is a crystallization of a more contemporary linguistic relativity hypothesis, one that is clearly related to the work of researchers such as Sapir and Whorf, but which is not married to any of their specific proposals. In attempting to define the hypothesis (or more accurately, set of hypotheses), we will consider some contemporary ideas that allow us to refine the notion of linguistic relativity by differentiating types of linguistic effects on cognition. We will also consider some common objections to the notion that linguistic differences impact thought, objections that vary considerably in merit. An ancillary aim of this chapter, taken up prior to the historically oriented discussion, will be to consider intuition-based arguments for and against linguistic relativity. This consideration should allow you to think about the issue from an experiential perspective, in case linguistic relativity is not something to which you have previously given much thought. Finally, the more pragmatic aim of this chapter is to outline the remainder of this book and to demonstrate how the themes of each chapter will be woven into a cohesive set of claims offering support for the existence of linguistic effects on nonlinguistic cognition across human populations.

1.2 Intuitions regarding linguistic relativity

It is likely that many or most of us have had personal experiences during which it was hard to transfer a thought from one language to another. Even if you speak two or more languages fluently, it is often difficult to translate ideas accurately between them, and frequently it seems that concepts are being missed even after careful deliberations over a given translation. There are clear motivations for the phrase "lost in translation". Even that phrase itself is difficult to translate into many languages. The 2003 film *Lost in Translation*, in which Bill Murray plays an American actor in Tokyo, befuddled at times by his surrounding culture and language, was given a number of different titles during its international release.

Have you ever tried to translate a joke from one language to another? This can be a difficult or even impossible task. So often, the foundational concepts of a humorous interaction cannot be accurately captured in a target language. If you have to explain a joke, after all, it generally ceases to be funny. This alone suggests that the humorous aspects to the meaning of any interaction cannot be completely translated, because translation so often entails the explanation of one set of lexical items in terms of a set of others. Take the following Chris Rock joke, selected from a random online joke generator: "I live in a neighborhood so bad that you can get shot while getting shot." A simple joke, one line long, based on simple premises. But my suspicion is that, should you try to convert it into another language, particularly one not closely related to English, you will quickly confront difficulties. For instance, while the construction "getting shot while X" is commonplace to speakers of American English and can be translated into other languages, the resultant translations may not convey a number of relevant connotations associated with the phrase. Significantly, these missed connotations are not simply a case of absent cultural cues. They relate at least in part to a grammatical phenomenon, namely a morphosyntactic construction ("getting shot while X"), that is present in English and absent in other languages. To cite another example of countless options, Woody Allen once observed that "Some guy hit my fender, and I told him, 'Be fruitful and multiply,' but not in those words." In this case, the humor results from an English phrase that has no exact analog in many languages, and furthermore is not even explicitly denoted in the quote. Is it possible to "think" this joke in another language? Can we really understand the joke in another language that does not utilize the crucial phrase that is only obliquely referred to in the English original?

Of course translation difficulties are not restricted to humor. If they were, they would have little to offer in the way of evidence of non-trivial cognitive effects dictated by crosslinguistic disparities. Often, though, translation difficulties reflect systematic differences in the way certain semantic domains are encoded in different languages. In these cases, intuition (and, again, we are not claiming that intuition is sufficient to resolve these issues) seems to point to very different associated patterns of thought. Systematic differences of the sort I am referring to surface for example when one language has more words at its disposal when referring to a particular semantic category. Perhaps the most famous example here is the oft-incorrectly-cited case of words for snow in Eskimo. It has been claimed that Eskimos have dozens if not hundreds of words for snow in their language, a claim that we will see is remarkably exaggerated. Yet there are innumerable less extreme yet analogous examples. We will offer a few taken from personal experience. You may very well have your own examples.

Let me start with an example that is at least somewhat systematic and clearly relates to the cultures of two different groups of speakers who enjoy, perhaps to varying degrees, the same game: soccer. The groups are Brazilian Portuguese speakers and American English speakers. Categorizing in a very coarse manner, it is fair to suggest that the soccer-playing characteristics of Brazilians differs dramatically from that of Americans, both in terms of style and success in competitions. Stereotypically anyway, Brazilian soccer players rely on flair and individual ability, while Americans rely on teamwork, athleticism, and less on individual technical ability. Such differences between American soccer subculture and Brazilian *futebol* subculture are reflected in lexical patterns. So, for example, consider the words for two types of dribbles carried out in an attempt to maintain possession of the ball at the expense of an opponent. One of these involves the ball-holder lifting the ball over the defender's head and retaining possession on the other side of the defender's body. The successful completion of this maneuver is most often called a *lençol* ('sheet') or a *chapeu* ('hat') in Portuguese. (These differ from a related dribble called the *lambreta* ['scooter']). The metaphorical bases for these terms are transparent, since both refer to items that can be pulled over one's head. In Brazil, if you are unfortunate to have an opponent give you a *chapeu* or *lençol* during play, you are likely to hear about it afterward. In pick-up games, discussion often ensues after the completion of such a maneuver as to whether in fact the ball cleared the opponent's head. In some contexts such a maneuver may be celebrated or talked about as much as the scoring of a goal. The point here is that there is often a significant amount of energy and discussion about whether a particular maneuver did or did not constitute a *chapeu* or *lençol*. Conversely, in my experience the attention paid to this maneuver is noticeably less among most American soccer players, quite possibly since this maneuver is not lexically encoded. That is, there is no common expression for this dribble in American English (though some Americans may on occasion adopt the Spanish term *sombrero*). Judging from intuition and personal experience only, it seems possible if not plausible that the absence of any relevant well-known terms for this maneuver has real consequences in terms of the conceptualization of the maneuver itself, and the degree of focus on it, by Americans. Since most American players lack a term for the concept to facilitate discussion of and verbally allow for emphasis of the act, it would be surprising to me if they thought about the maneuver in the same manner as Brazilian players (not impossible, just surprising). In other words, while the soccer cultures in question may play a role in emphasizing the dribble in question to varying degrees, the languages of the two cultures also seem to influence the extent to which the maneuver is conceptually reified.

Even in this very restricted domain of soccer playing across only two represented cultures, other examples could be purveyed. Another common dribble employed in soccer involves kicking the ball between a non-goalie opponent's legs. Here again American English speakers are at a lexical disadvantage. I am aware of only one common term for this maneuver in American English, *nutmeg*, while I have heard at least four terms for this dribble (or, more precisely, variants of it) in Brazilian Portuguese: *caneta* ('pen'), *rolinho* ('little roll'), *ovinho* ('little egg'), and *saia* ('skirt'). Some players seem more concerned with pulling off such maneuvers than scoring goals. More to the point, some Brazilian players insist there are clear yet minor disparities between some subset of these maneuvers, all of which involve the ball traveling through an opponent's legs and are represented via the same cover term in American English. So while Brazilian speakers may not have more words for snow than their American counterparts, it seems they have more words for varieties of soccer dribbles, which in some cases reflect nuanced distinctions between maneuvers and appear to have real consequences on the way the dribbles are conceptualized. Of course such experiential examples are useful for anecdotal purposes only, and I have not conducted any experiments to test for differences in the conceptualizations of these dribbles resulting from the manner in which they are described verbally.

Such cases from day-to-day life do hint at differences in vocabulary potentially generating differences in the attention directed towards, and the construal of, nonlinguistic features of our environment. Nevertheless, they also seem a bit trivial. They do not relate to major differences between languages, only to minor lexical disparities. And it would probably be a stretch to attribute pronounced thought differences to such minor differences in word inventories. But what about more systematic semantic differences between languages? If you have ever had the opportunity to investigate or learn a language that is completely unrelated to your own, you have likely uncovered such systematic differences. Consider an example from my own fieldwork among the Karitiâna, a group of about three hundred people who speak a Tupí language in southern Amazonia. When learning their language I was surprised to discover that the Karitiâna have no exact translation for 'monkey'. Instead there are numerous words for species of monkeys that are familiar to their ecology, including õrõm ('ateles paniscus'), pikõm ('cebus apella'), irõnh ('saimiri sciureus'), and ery ('callicebus callicebus moloch'). It is fair to say that most English speakers would be unable to provide names for these species, since monkey-species nomenclature is not a part of their vocabularies. In fact, when presented with pictures of the relevant species, English speakers typically refer to them via the cover term "monkey" that has no analog in Karitiâna. So what are we to make of this? Is this just a trivial linguistic difference? The Karitiâna have potential cultural motivations for lexically accentuating differences among these species, and not grouping them in the way English speakers do. For instance, some of these monkeys (particularly pikõm) are considered great ingredients for stew, and are coveted food items. Others are not. Crucially, all the experiential evidence (a type which has clear limitations, discussed in Section 1.4) I have is consistent with the notion that these terminological distinctions and the absence of a basic superordinate cover term for 'monkey' assist in the Karitiânas' discriminations of these monkey types. At the least, it is indisputable that there is no native concept for 'monkey' coded in the Karitiâna language, whereas myriad related concepts are coded in the language in a way that they are not for most English speakers.[1] Now of course Karitiâna speakers can learn a superordinate term and most are familiar with the Portuguese term macaco, just as an English zoologist may learn an even greater range of names of monkey species. But the point remains that such non-equiv-

---

[1] As research such as Berlin (1992) and Atran (1993) has demonstrated, in smaller non-industrialized societies the most basic ethnobiological terms, characterized by developmental primacy, tend to refer to more specific species-categorizations than basic terms in English. In other words, the pattern evident in Karitiâna monkey terminology is not aberrant.

alencies across this semantic category hint at very real distinctions in the manner in which the animals in question are construed by speakers of the two different languages. For any pair of languages, an assortment of such systematic or near-systematic disparities in the structures of lexical categories may be adduced. Often these disparities owe themselves to clear ecological factors (e.g. differences in the flora and fauna encountered in the daily lives of Americans and Karitiânas), or some more abstract cultural factor (e.g. soccer concepts shared by many Brazilians). To many, including myself, it seems plausible that such lexical disparities reflect and reinforce differences in the way speakers conceptualize the relevant entities, even in nonlinguistic contexts. The intuition of others may not accord with this relativistic interpretation, though, and they may remain unconvinced by such anecdotal data. They may even find it implausible that the Karitiâna taxonomy of monkey species reifies/ enforces greater conceptual distinctions between monkey types, even during nonlinguistic thought. They may suggest instead that, just because most English speakers lack the hyponyms for certain monkey species, this does not imply that the speakers do not recognize or conceptualize the differences between those species, at least once they have some experience with the monkeys in question. Conversely, some might suggest that just because the Karitiâna have no superordinate term for 'monkey', this does not imply that they do not, or do not typically, recognize a class of species that English speakers label with the term 'monkey'. I could offer more experientially based opinions and anecdotes based on time spent with the people, but these would not convince skeptics since opinions and anecdotes in and of themselves do not constitute objective data. After all, such intuition-based opinions may be subject to all sorts of biases on my own part, of which I may or may not be cognizant. As centuries of discussion on the relationship between language and cognition have demonstrated pretty clearly, anecdotes and experiential evidence alone will not resolve such debates.

The absence of complete correspondence of concepts across languages was first observed long ago. For instance, the 13th century English philosopher and friar Roger Bacon suggested that variances in semantic concepts across languages made loss-less translation impossible (Kelly [1979:9]). In this way his opinion diverged from another philosopher and clergyman who predated him by nine centuries, St. Augustine. For millennia believers of various faiths have struggled with the translation of their scriptures. It is a very onerous task, often taking decades, and many doubt that the resultant translations are in fact lossless. One of the many difficulties faced in such translation is the transfer of idiomatic expressions. Consider, for instance, translating a concept such as "lamb of God" into an Amazonian language. Just that phrase alone, which is found in English translations of John's writings in the Christian New Testament, presents a series of obstacles. An obvious one is that Amazonian cultures do not have sheep or lambs, and have often not typically been exposed to these species. Another is that shepherding is a foreign activity. These difficulties may seem more cultural than linguistic (assuming for now a simple division between culture and language), but other difficulties are not. The phrase itself relies on a metaphorical correspondence between animal sacrifice and other sorts of sacrifice, i.e. those required for spiritual salvation according to some believers of the scriptures in question. In other words, "lamb of God" indexes metaphors shared by speakers of English, while also indexing some major concepts (lambs and a monotheistic entity) that are foreign to many cultures. This phrase has been translated thousands of times into unrelated languages, but it would seem that in many cases there is some inevitable loss of meaning, however minor, across the translations. It serves as a useful illustration since it reflects the centuries with which people have been seriously struggling with representing the concepts denoted in one language in a language that does not share some crucial component concepts.

The difficulty of transferring concepts from one language to another is consonant with the notion of linguistic relativity. Such difficulty implies that, in some cases anyway, there are obstacles to thinking the same exact thoughts while utilizing different languages. In the light of such difficulty, it is not a stretch to think that different languages affect how their speakers think in general terms. But note that the latter claim is different than the former, and while the two are related the former cannot be offered as unequivocal support for the latter. The idea we are interested in here is whether different languages have demonstrable effects on the *nonlinguistic* cognition of their speakers. Difficulties in translation may provide intuitive support for this notion, but they do not directly impinge on the issue of nonlinguistic thought. Just because people speak in very different ways does not necessarily mean these speech differences yield disparities in how they think when they are not speaking. Furthermore, if real differences in thought are hinted at by differences in languages, this does not imply that the linguistic differences are themselves the shapers of those thought differences. After all, differences in conceptual and linguistic patterns may be due to some other underlying factor, perhaps broad cultural distinctions that yield affects on both language and thought. Regardless of the conceptual differences hinted at by challenges in translation, such challenges cannot establish a causal influence of linguistic disparities on thought, much as intuitions alone cannot. The inadequacy of such kinds of evidence has nevertheless frequently been ignored in the past, to the detriment of serious inquiries into linguistic relativity.

1.3 A brief history of the linguistic relativity hypothesis

The genesis and dissemination of the linguistic relativity hypothesis has a long and, in many instances, contentious history. The hypothesis is closely affiliated with other tenets in philosophy and the social sciences, and is sometimes mistaken for them. For instance, there is a long line of influential writers who at some point appeared to equate thought with language, to varying degrees. This list includes Plato (1892:252), Kant (1988[1798]:278), Watson (1913), Wittgenstein (1922), and Humboldt (1988[1836]). For instance, Humboldt noted that "Language is the formative organ of thought... Thought and language are therefore one and inseparable from each other." (1988:54) Now if language and thought are indistinguishable, it follows naturally that which language you speak will have a profound effect on your cognition more generally, assuming that differences across languages exist. In fact, the consequence of such an interpretation of the language-thought relationship is a sort of strong linguistic determinism, according to which your way of thinking is completely constrained and determined by the language(s) you speak natively. In the well-known words of Wittgenstein, "The limits of my language mean the limits of my world." (1922, proposition 5.6)

There are difficulties with the tack of equating language and thought. It seems clear, for example, that other species are quite capable of thinking, and often in sophisticated ways. Research on primates, for instance, is continually revealing new cognitive capacities of species ranging from capuchin monkeys to bonobos (see e.g. Tomasello and Call 1997). Research on dogs, dolphins and non-mammals, particularly a number of avian species, reveals frequently comparable results. Given that it is widely accepted that such species do not share language with humans, but clearly share a variety of cognitive abilities with us, it seems clear that language is not required for thought, and consequently should not be equated with it. Furthermore, studies with pre-linguistic infants suggests that they possess a variety of cognitive skills that one might assume requires language, but in fact precedes linguistic behavior ontogenetically. For example, infants are capable of some very basic arithmetic (Wynn [1992]).

Contra the simplified assumptions of some scholars (e.g. Pinker [1994]– see Section 1.5), however, contemporary work on linguistic relativity does not presume that language and thought are completely dissociable. Researchers who do this work are concerned with whether crosslinguistic dissimilarities yield dissimilarities in thought, and with establishing not only the existence but the magnitude of such potential dissimilarities. This very distinguishable issue has also received a fair amount of attention in the literature over the years, and it is worth tracing the trajectory of the idea, so that we can contextualize the contemporary work discussed in this text. I should stress that what follows is an extremely abbreviated discussion of the history of work on linguistic relativity. For more detailed treatments on this subject I refer the reader to works such as Aarsleff (1982) Koerner (1992), Lucy (e.g. 1992a, 1997, 2004), and Leavitt (2011).

There is a reason that the terms "linguistic relativity" and "Sapir-Whorf hypothesis" are often employed interchangeably, and further that the second term is often shortened to the "Whorf hypothesis". The reason is simple: more than any other researcher, Benjamin Whorf was responsible for formulating a coherent treatise on the effects of linguistic differences on thought. Whorf's work on the topic was clearly heavily influenced by his mentor, Edward Sapir, whose own work was colored by Franz Boas and other American ethnolinguists such as William Whitney. Whitney was, in turn, influenced by the renowned German linguist Wilhelm von Humboldt. The latter researcher's views were themselves affected by correspondence with linguists in America such as John Pickering and Peter Du Ponceau, not to mention some of the ideals that surfaced during the French enlightenment (see Aarsleff [1988]). In short, the lineage of influence on Whorf can be traced back to increasingly remote timedepths, and to some extent the cut-off point to such a tracing is arbitrary. Some, though by no means all, of the central components of a linguistic relativity hypothesis are evident in the work of scholars such Johann Hamman, Johann Herder, and even Ferdinand Saussure. In fact, the prevalent structuralism of the early twentieth century, which owed itself so much to the work of Saussure, was very compatible with the more explicitly relativistic views of Sapir and particularly Whorf (see Gumperz and Levinson [1996], Koerner [1992]). Structuralism suggests, after all, that components of semantic systems such as a particular morpheme are imbued with meaning only in the context of the oppositions they present to other components. In other words, the meaning of a particular morpheme or word can only be comprehended contextually, within a greater semantic matrix. Given the readily apparent divergences between semantic systems across languages, it arguably follows from structuralism that the meaning of a given word or morpheme, and the associated conceptualization of a given denoted entity, depends in large measure on the language being utilized. At the least, it seems clear that structuralism was not inconsistent with the notion of linguistic relativity.

Given the prevalence of ideas that were consistent with a linguistic relativity hypothesis of some kind during the latter part of the 19th century, the first part of the 20th century, and even earlier, it is difficult to definitively establish authorship of the hypothesis. Koerner (1992:174) makes the following pertinent observation: "As Christmann (1967) has shown, essential ingredients of the idea can be found in the writings of a number of 17th- and 18th- century thinkers, among them Vico and Herder, with the result that Justice (1987:56) spoke of a 'Vico-Herder-Humboldt-Sapir-Whorf hypothesis'."

Still, while the geneses of many hypotheses are difficult to pinpoint, there is often a clear stage at which an idea or set of ideas is more wholly developed and lucidly delineated, at which it has truly "arrived". In the case of linguistic relativity, it seems clear that this arrival only occurred with the work of Benjamin Whorf. Which is not to suggest that Sapir's work is not extremely important in this context. In fact, among other contributions, Sapir was the first author to co-opt the term "relativity" for linguistic purposes:

> It would be impossible to go on indefinitely with such examples of incommensurable analyses of experience in different languages. The upshot of it all would be to make very real to us a kind of relativity that is generally hidden from us by our naïve acceptance of fixed habits of speech as guides to an objective understanding of the nature of experience. This is the relativity of concepts or, as it might be called, the relativity of the form of thought. (1949 [1924]: 159)

It is important to stress, though, that Sapir still viewed humans as sharing an essential psychological common ground, or psychic unity, a perspective he shared with his mentor Franz Boas, the founder of American anthropology who stressed the psychic unity of mankind (see Lucy [1992a] for discussion). As noted in Sapir and Swadesh (1964[1946]:101): "All forms of linguistic expression are reducible to a common psychological ground, but this ground cannot be properly understood without the perspective gained from a sympathetic study of the forms themselves."

Another important view shared by Sapir and Boas was the notion that the influence of culture on language held more strongly than the converse influence. In other words, the relativity Sapir spoke of might best be termed "cultural relativity" rather than "linguistic relativity". Nevertheless he did suggest that one's language could directly constrain her/his thoughts, for example when he noted that "the 'real world' is to a large extent unconsciously built up on the language habits of the group." (Sapir [1949 (1929)]:162) However, in the same work Sapir spoke of language as operating as a "guide" to culture, and elsewhere his writings suggest that language serves to create a common understanding that constitutes culture. In short, while Sapir spoke of relativity of thought, his relevant work was predominantly oriented towards cultural disparity being the primary effector of relativity, with language serving as crucial symbolic guide to cultures. Furthermore, unlike Whorf, Sapir's discussions of the influences of language on thought, like the work of his predecessors, are somewhat devoid of specifics. He does not discuss in detail any cases or illustrations of the relativity he envisions, and his perspective on the relevant issues is more nebulous than that of his student. After all, Sapir was not attempting to draft some sort of testable linguistic relativity hypothesis. In touching on this issue, he was in large measure attempting (like Boas) to argue against a simplistic view of linguistic-cultural co-evolution that was so prevalent during his day, and which had been made prevalent in the work of previous influential researchers such as Humboldt. This perspective held, among other oversimplifications, that inflectional morphologies exhibited a positive correlation with more "advanced" cultural features, and was used by some to buttress the legitimization of the notion that some languages and cultures represented earlier evolutionary stages. This misappropriation of the tenets of evolution was objected to by Boas (1966[1911]) and Sapir, who stressed the need to actually examine the complex structural systems evident in indigenous languages, particularly those in the Americas they devoted much of their lives to documenting. In short, Boas and Sapir were both believers in the theoretical existence of a basic "psychic unity of mankind," who nevertheless apparently felt that fleshing out our understanding of this unity required clear documentations of the numerous complex languages in existence. The clear delineation of any relativity hypothesis seems to have been, at best, tangential to Sapir's aims. Some of his work is consonant with the subsequent formulations of the notion, though–most notably when he suggests that certain categories reflected in particular languages "are not so much discovered in experience as imposed upon it because of the tyrannical hold that linguistic form has upon our orientation in the world." (1964[1931]:138)

Only in Whorf's work is linguistic relativity formulated as a cohesive, or nearly cohesive, set of ideas regarding the influence of different languages on the thoughts of their speakers. Whorf addressed this issue with a greater deal of specificity than had been observed in the literature, and was the first author to develop concrete and specific examples of how features of particular languages putatively generated more widespread effects on the cognitive processes of their speakers (see Lucy [1992a, 1996]). Many of these examples have been the subject of criticism in the intervening years. Nevertheless, Whorf's ideas on the subject captured the fancy of many, and had a profound effect on the work of other researchers, including many contemporary ones whose work is the real subject of this book. So we will restrict the remainder of our discussion of the origins of linguistic relativity as a coherent concept to Whorf's work, bearing in mind the close relationship of that work to that of his immediate predecessors, most notably Sapir.

Whorf was a chemical engineer who, despite years of expressed interest in linguistics, only began formal studies on the subject (at Yale, with Sapir) at the age of 31, and who only lived another ten years beyond that point. Yet, contrary to the inaccurate characterizations sometimes offered, Whorf was not simply an "amateur" linguist. In fact, he was a remarkably productive scholar who published in major linguistic journals while contributing in important ways to a variety of linguistic sub-fields. A very influential collection of his work was published posthumously (Whorf [1956]). It is worth mentioning that much of this work was not related to the topic of linguistic relativity, and included extensive studies of Hopi and Nahuatl grammar, as well as work on Maya hieroglyphs. For an extremely comprehensive treatment of Whorf's work, as well as some important biographical background, see Lee (1996).

Among the most frequently cited selections from Whorf's work on the subject is the following, which represents the first clear formulation employing the term "linguistic relativity": "From this pact proceeds what I have called the 'linguistic relativity principle,'[2] which means, in informal terms, that users of markedly different grammars are pointed by the grammars toward different types of observations and different evaluations of externally similar acts of observation, and hence are not equivalent as observers but must arrive at somewhat different views of the world." (1956:221)

Lest one assume that the diversity of observations highlighted by different grammars was of a trivial sort, consider the following (also-well-known) excerpt: "Are our own concepts of 'time,' space,' and 'matter' given in substantially the same form by experience to all men, or are they in part conditioned by the structure of particular languages? Are there traceable affinities between (a) cultural and behavioral norms and (b) large-scale linguistic patterns?" (1956:138) Aside from the clear Einsteinian homage in the discussion of these ideas vis-à-vis a relativity of "time", "space", and "matter", what strikes one about this excerpt is the gravity of the relativity propounded by Whorf. He suggests that the perception of some very fundamental concepts may be influenced by language. Such a suggestion may seem extreme, and was uncorroborated in Whorf's work. However, that work hinted at ways in which corroboration might be achieved, and it is interesting to note that recent work has now provided data that are consistent with Whorf's ideas that even the conceptualization of space (see Chapter 4 of this text), time (Chapter 5), and matter (Chapter 8) are in fact affected by linguistic patterns. This is not to suggest that the

---

2 Note that Whorf did not refer to the linguistic relativity "hypothesis", as noted in Lee (1996) and Scholz, Pelletier, and Pullum (2011). Instead he discussed the "principle" of linguistic relativity. According to the analysis in Lee (1996), this principle was one of several crucial principles in Whorf's larger "theory complex" on the nature of linguistic thought. For a synopsis of the twelve major points in that complex, see Lee (1996:30–33).

relevant research has served simply to vindicate Whorf's claims, since his claims regarding the domains in question were not particularly concrete or specific.

Perhaps the most famous comments by Whorf on the matter are the following:

> The categories and types that we isolate from the world of phenomena we do not find there because they stare every observer in the face; on the contrary, the world is presented in a kaleidoscopic flux of impressions which has to be organized in our minds – and this means largely by the linguistic systems in our minds. We cut nature up, organize it into concepts, and ascribe significances as we do, largely because we are parties to an agreement to organize it in this way – an agreement that holds throughout our speech community and is codified in the patterns of our language. (1956:213)

These comments, it should be noted, have often been misinterpreted or over-interpreted in the intervening years. They have often been taken as being suggestive of a particularly strong sort of linguistic determinism, according to which speakers are incapable of loosing the linguistic handcuffs placed upon them during infancy. Such interpretations are generally inconsistent with the bulk of Whorf's work, however (see Lucy [1992a]), though when read in isolation these comments do not seem far afield from a strongly deterministic perspective. Regardless, we are interested in Whorf's perspective as it relates to the notion of linguistic relativity, i.e. the idea that systematic differences across languages lead to differences in nonlinguistic cognition, differences that are not necessarily impossible to overcome. We are not concerned with the notion of linguistic determinism, which is simply the idea that one's thoughts are completely governed by her/his native language.

By now it is hopefully clear what Whorf meant by linguistic relativity, at least in general terms. In the years since Whorf's work, the popularity of linguistic relativity has waxed and waned in large measure in accordance with the popularity of over-arching paradigms in the social sciences. So Whorf's work was met with initial enthusiasm at a time when behaviorism was prominent, and not surprisingly this enthusiasm dwindled with the rise of nativism, most notably the nativist Chomskyan paradigm in linguistics. (Though the Chomskyan framework is not necessarily incompatible with the Whorf's principle of relativity–see discussion in Scholz, Pelletier, and Pullum [2011].) The hypothesis was particularly prone to shifts in paradigmatic winds since little convincing evidence was presented on its behalf, either by Whorf or by any other proponents of the idea, prior to the last decade or so of the twentieth century. Which is not to suggest that Whorf presented *no* evidence in support of linguistic relativity. Next we briefly consider the most widely circulated exemplifications of relativity offered by Whorf, with the caveat that these examples are not being endorsed here as evidence for the hypothesis. They represent instead cases that may be taken to support the relativistic position on a less rigorous, more intuitive, plane. The examples fall into two broad types of relativistic effects according to which the divergent structures of semantic systems in contrasted languages supposedly influence their speakers' thoughts.

One type of evidence presented by Whorf related to the way in which languages "dissect nature differently" (1956:208). This sort of evidence was offered prominently in his papers entitled "Science and linguistics" (1940), "Language and logic" (1941), and "Language, mind and reality" (1941), all included in Carroll's compendium (Whorf [1956]). In "Science and Linguistics", he offers several cases not too dissimilar from the examples I offered above based on my own personal experience (and not much more rigorously either). In such cases, one language offers several lexical items or categories, including verbal and nominal ones, for a set of distinctions that are apparently not coded in another language. For example, Whorf notes that the Hopi have one noun for flying things besides birds, and that this noun can refer to insects, aviators, or airplanes. The assumption here seems to be that Hopi speakers conceive of flying entities in a dissimilar (more unified?) way than English speakers, perhaps like English speakers seem to conceive of certain soccer maneuvers in a different (more unified?) manner when contrasted with Brazilian Portuguese speakers. Note that no actual evidence was provided for either claim.

Another parallel example was employed by Whorf, and this example (perhaps unfortunately) came to be the poster child for linguistic relativity. Specifically, Whorf (in)famously contrasted the number of words for snow in English and Eskimo, a subject that had received some attention in Boas' work (1966[1911]:21–22). Whorf stated that:

> We have the same word for falling snow, snow on the ground, snow packed hard like ice, slushy snow, wind-driven flying snow – whatever the situation may be. To an Eskimo, this all-inclusive word would be almost unthinkable; he would say that falling snow, slushy snow, and so on, are sensuously and operationally different, different things to contend with; he uses different words for them and for other kinds of snow. The Aztecs go even farther than we in the opposite direction, with 'cold,' 'ice,' and 'snow' all represented by the same basic word with different terminations; 'iced' is the noun form; 'cold' the adjectival form; and for 'snow,' "ice mist." (1956:216)

There are several well-known issues with this claim, not the least of which is that Whorf makes claims about Eskimo nonlinguistic cognition based entirely on linguistic evidence. One gets the idea of the sort of cognitive disparity being hinted at, though, of the same ilk as that hinted at by the lexical disparities between Karitiâna and English vis-à-vis basic terms for "monkey" and its hyponyms.

We might call this sort of relativistic influence a "categorization" effect, according to which the way in which a particular semantic field is divided up in a given language impacts the ontological ratiocination of its speakers. Judging from Whorf's examples, one of the corollaries of this proposed effect is that speakers with a greater number of basic lexical items for a given semantic field construe that semantic field in more precise or discriminating ways than speakers lacking such terms. In the cited section above, for example, the explicit claim is made that Eskimos perceive falling snow and slushy snow to be "sensuously and operationally different." The only evidence presented in support of this claim is the fact that such concepts can be teased apart lexically with greater ease in Eskimo. The claim for divergent sensory and operational experiences of snow across the two groups in question is not further substantiated. Nevertheless, we get the sense of what Whorf is claiming regarding these "categorization" type effects, viz. that greater perceptual refinement is implied by more detailed lexical demarcations between portions of a given semantic domain.

Another well-known example of such a categorization type of relativistic effect is Whorf's claim that the means for coding temporal concepts are limited in Hopi, when contrasted with English. Here the categorization effect in question is grammatical, rather than lexical, but it nevertheless denotes a particular semantic domain that is split in different ways across the languages in question. According to Whorf, "Hopi may be called a timeless language" (1956:216), in large measure because "the Hopi verb gets along without tenses" (217). Setting aside Whorf's oversimplification of the ways in which Hopi speakers denote temporal deixis, the implication is that the types of categories evident in the English tense system affect its speakers' conceptions of time in a way that is unfamiliar to Hopi speakers. Among other distinctions, the three-fold "past", "present", and "future" distinction in English and other European languages helps to yield, according to Whorf, a greater objectification of time that enables speakers to imagine time as the occurrence of sequential "units" in ways not possible (or at least quite difficult) for Hopi speakers. (See Whorf [1956]:143–145, 216–218 for a more detailed account).

Another example of the sort of "categorization" effects offered by Whorf is the count-mass nominal distinction evident in some languages. As Whorf notes, in "Standard Average European" the distinction between count and mass nouns is evident in pluralization strategies, e.g. "mass nouns lack plurals, in English drop particles, and in French take the article *du, de la, des.*" (1956:140) Significantly, Whorf suggests, the division of matter into two broad categories of countable and non-countable entities does not actually reflect natural categories. Aside from a handful of cases such as air, sand, and water, "few natural occurrences present themselves as unbounded events" (1956:141). The net result of Standard Average European's rigid division between count and mass nouns is, according to Whorf, that this distinction is forced upon speakers' perceptions of types of matter. Conversely, Hopi speakers are free to perceive matter types without this particular enforcement of categories since their language "contains no formal subclass of mass nouns." (1956:141)

The preceding examples illustrate the sorts of categorization-type effects suggested by Whorf in his examinations of the ways in which disparate languages split various semantic fields, supposedly yielding correlated splits in conceptual patterns. There are issues with these particular categorization-type effects, as scholars have noted subsequent to Whorf's work. Nevertheless these sorts of examples did strike a chord with many readers, and continue to do so. And while Whorf's examples are largely unsubstantiated by the desirable nonlinguistic corroboration, research related to those examples is now being undertaken, for instance on the nonlinguistic classification of kinds of matter (see chapter 8).

The other principal sort of relativistic effect suggested by Whorf and discussed in detail in "The Relation of Habitual Thought and Behavior to Language", first published in 1941 and also included in Carroll's collection, might be termed an "analogy-based" effect. This type of relativistic effect can be further sub-categorized into lexical and grammatical analogies (see Lucy [1992a] for a detailed discussion). Whorf's most well known illustration of this sort of effect is a lexical analogy that putatively results in a perceptual effect for English speakers who use the word "empty".

During his employ with the Hartford Fire Insurance Company, Whorf analyzed hundreds of reports regarding the manner in which particular fires started. He believed these reports suggested that individuals were more careful around storage units labeled "gasoline drums" than those labeled "empty gasoline drums." (1956:135) Assuming Whorf's claim is correct (he provides no systematic analysis of the reports), this is a noteworthy correlation since it is plausibly explained by linguistic factors. In his words:

> Thus, around a storage of what are called "gasoline drums," behavior will tend to a certain type, that is, great care will be exercised; while around a storage of what are called "empty gasoline drums," it will tend to be different – careless, with little repression of smoking or of tossing cigarette stubs about. Yet the "empty" drums are perhaps the more dangerous, since they contain explosive vapor. Physically the situation is hazardous, but the linguistic analysis according to regular analogy must employ the word 'empty,' which inevitably suggests lack of hazard. (1956:135)

Now the word "empty" can be used in a strict manner that is synonymous with "null and void, negative, inert" (1956:135). It can also be used in a more colloquial manner, though, according to which something is empty but no claims regarding vapor are implied. If I say a barrel (or gas tank or suitcase or room...) is empty, for instance, there is typically no implication that the all gases such as oxygen have been vacuumed out. This duplicity of meaning leads to analogy-based behavior that would presumably not be observed in the behavior of speakers of other languages without the distinction. If a gasoline drum is labeled in a colloquial manner in which no implication of vapor absence is assumed, but encountered in another environment in which the label is interpreted strictly, the results are dangerous according to Whorf. The contents of the barrel are often perceived, by way of an analogy (or simply a misinterpretation) based on a slightly different definition of the word, as lacking all contents including hazardous ones. As a result, suggests Whorf, workers around "empty" gas drums behave carelessly at times, as though no vapors were contained in the drums. There is a prediction here: Workers who do not speak English or any other language that facilitates the sort of analogical reasoning characterized above might exhibit safer behavior in such contexts. The clear implication of such an example, and of other similar ones (see Whorf [1956:135], as well as Carroll [1956:29–30] for discussion), is that nonlinguistic behavior in such cases is conditioned in large part by one's native language.

Whorf presented numerous examples of analogy-type effects and categorization-type effects in his work. Those described above are illustrative of the sorts of relativistic effects he claimed to exist. In short, he believed that any language is systematically structured in its semantics, and that this structure has demonstrable effects on speakers' nonlinguistic categorization and perception. (Whorf 1956:252) This structuring is enforced by overt and covert linguistic categories, sometimes termed "phenotypes" and "cryptotypes", respectively. Even in the few examples of Whorf's discussed above, it is clear that such systematically structured categories could be lexical or grammatical in nature. Crosslinguistic dissimilarities in lexical or grammatical categories, according to his account, result in correlated behavioral and cognitive dissimilarity. It should be stressed that Whorf never suggested that these effects completely determine speakers' thoughts in a manner that results in cognitive incommensurability across populations (Kay and Kempton [1984:76–77]).

Whorf's work was crucial to the establishment of linguistic relativity as a viable concept, and there is much in contemporary research on the topic that owes itself to his relevant ideas. Yet it would also be inaccurate to see the current body of research as connected to that of Whorf in an unbroken fashion, or to see that work as being based primarily on Whorf's ideas. In fact, the current research differs dramatically from Whorf's, in large measure according to methodological parameters that will crystallize during the course of this book but might be pithily encapsulated as follows: the current crop of studies on this topic is based predominantly on experimental work involving nonlinguistic tasks and carried out with speakers of two or more languages. In contrast, Whorf did not conduct any experimental tests on human cognition or behavior. His work was foundational in offering up directions to be followed in future research, and presenting tentative examples that hinted at language-influenced habitual thought. These tentative examples went unsubstantiated in his work though. This is not meant as a criticism of Whorf (after all, he died shortly after drafting some of his original hypotheses), merely as a note on the history of this research.

Gumperz and Levinson (1996:24) summarize the linguistic relativity hypothesis, in its most schematic form, with the following syllogism:[3]

Given that:
(1) differences exist in linguistic categories across languages;
(2) linguistic categories determine aspects of individuals' thinking;
then:
(3) aspects of individuals' thinking differ across linguistic communities according to the language they speak.

Now if both (1) and (2) hold, then of course (*modus ponens*), (3) must also hold. This syllogistic reasoning is evident in Whorf's work, though not explicitly. Evidence for (3) is only now accruing, however, and the extent to which (1) and (2) hold remains a matter of some debate among linguists and others. Yet it is worth stressing that it is difficult to object to (1) and (2) in an absolute manner. Even the most ardent believer in a universal grammar must admit that *some* differences exist in linguistic categories across languages (even if they do not believe that these differences are particularly meaningful), and certainly it is difficult to avoid the conclusion, with even a modest amount of introspection, that linguistic categories determine *aspects* of thinking (even if one believes these to be superficial aspects of thinking that are only required for online linguistic processing). To a large extent, then, the question at hand is not whether (1) or (2) hold, but to what degree they hold. How significant are crosslinguistic differences? How impactful are such categories upon thought, and do they influence forms of thought beyond those directly related to constructing and deconstructing utterances?

---

3 This can be contrasted with the more specific formulation of the Whorfian hypothesis syllogism (Gumperz and Levinson [1996:25]).

Assuming (1) and (2) hold to some degree, however minor, our attention should naturally gravitate towards (3). How does individuals' thinking differ across linguistic communities? Is there evidence for very weak or trivial differences only? Or is there evidence for significant disparities in nonlinguistic cognition that can clearly be tied to the linguistic practices of individual communities? Or does the evidence fall somewhere in between these points? Surprisingly, in the several decades following Whorf's work there was remarkably little research undertaken to empirically address these questions, despite the fact that the acceptance of the relativistic hypothesis naturally hinges upon their answers. The absence of relevant research is particularly surprising given how popular Whorfianism became in some academic and non-academic circles, and also given how virulently it was opposed in other circles. As Levinson (2003) notes, it became a subject that many people were happy to weigh in on while vigorously attacking ideological opponents, while concomitantly adding little in the way of substantive data that could actually elucidate some of the relevant issues.

In many ways, empirical research on linguistic relativity was not taken up in earnest until the early-to-mid 1990's, most prominently in the work of John Lucy (1992b) and Stephen Levinson (1996). In this book, I take such influential works as the trigger for the explosion of serious inquiries into linguistic relativity. This is not to suggest that related research (e.g. Kay and Kempton [1984], Bloom [1981]) had not been carried out prior to that time. In fact, a number of relevant studies did surface in the linguistics and anthropology literature in the intervening decades, i.e. following Whorf's work and prior to the work of Lucy, Levinson, and a number of their colleagues mentioned in this book. With few exceptions, though, these works did not advance work on linguistic relativity empirically, and they most frequently did not generate much interest outside their specific sub-field. They often relied on linguistic data alone, and lacked data demonstrating cross-population differences in cognition, that is, they did not address point (3) in the above syllogism. Among these works, which were quite laudable in other respects, were Lee (1944) and Mathiot (1962). I refer the reader to Lucy (1992a) for a discussion of these studies as they relate to the relativity hypothesis. It is worth noting also that, during the latter part of the 20th century, cross-cultural psychology developed into a serious area of inquiry, with its flagship journal being founded in 1970. Unfortunately perhaps, most linguists remained unaware of related developments in this field and there was little cross-pollination of ideas between the fields. As a result, few studies in cross-cultural psychology impinged directly on the issue of linguistic relativity. Thankfully, that characterization is no longer accurate though it could be argued that linguistically motivated differences in psychology across cultures still receive insufficient attention.

The motivations for the decades-long delay in the start-up of the relevant research are multifarious. One significant development that contributed to the delay was the arrival of the generativist paradigm during this period. The acceptance of this paradigm seems to have played a role in leading many researchers to ignore the topic of linguistic relativity on theoretical grounds. Chomsky's (1965) influential work led many linguists to focus their attention on developing the most parsimonious theoretical treatments possible for "surface-level" crosslinguistic variation, reducing such differences to a limited set of features of a universal grammar. In some sense linguistic homogeneity became a greater focus than linguistic diversity. Practically, the universalist and innatist perspective allowed linguists to rely extensively on native-speaker elicitations, and arguably obfuscated the need for the methodological tools associated with other branches of the cognitive sciences, for instance the generation of experimental results and statistical tests on those results. (These sorts of tools are central to the works on relativity discussed in this book.) Furthermore, the belief held by many researchers that grammars are fundamentally alike seems to have devalued the need for detailed grammars of unrelated languages described on their own terms, i.e. without the encumbrances of a theoretical perspective that presumed some sort of deep-level uniformity across languages. Regardless, data on significant crosslinguistic variation (see Chapter 2), which were less and less amenable to a strong universalist account, continued to surface during the second half of the 20th century–particularly data gathered in areas such as Amazonia, New Guinea, the Caucasus, and Australia. These data contributed to numerous substantive shifts and splits in the universalist linguistic paradigm (e.g. Chomsky [1980], [1995], Pinker and Jackendoff [2005]), to the complete disenchantment of previous proponents of such an approach (e.g. Lakoff [1987], D. Everett [2005]), and to the waning influence of the universalist perspective evident today. Which is not to suggest that this perspective does not still maintain strong influence in some circles, as it clearly does.

Despite the theoretical obstacle of linguistic universalism, which gained strength shortly after the publication of Carroll's collection of Whorf's works, essential theoretical developments that were complimentary to the linguistic relativity hypothesis were also disseminated during this time, both in linguistics and in related fields. For instance, Vygotsky's (1962[1934]) influential work demonstrated the centrality of language in conceptual development. Similarly, work on semantics by authors such as Bowerman (1978) helped lead many researchers to re-focus on the semantic disparities across languages. Furthermore, linguistic anthropologists such as Silverstein (1979) and Hymes (1966) developed influential theoretical frameworks for the study of language, culture, and thought that invited rather than discouraged work on the issue, while addressing linguistic relativity at the theoretical level and demonstrating ways in which crosslinguistic variation impacts the indexical nature of communication. Within what might be termed by some "linguistics" proper, a number of very influential scholars remained devoted to exploring grammatical description and typology from a functionally and cognitively oriented perspective that did not assume universalism. These scholars include Givón (1984), Bybee (1985), Langacker (1991) and Comrie (1981).

All of these non-universalist strands of research ultimately contributed in one way or another to current inquiries into linguistic relativity, which were more directly triggered by the work of Lucy, Levinson, and their colleagues. This inquiry has been referred to occasionally as a "resurgence" of Whorfianism, or as "neo-Whorfianism". In many ways it is not a resurgence, however, but a re-envisioning of what work on this topic should consist of. The research described in this book is not modeled specifically after Whorf's, after all. It relates to some of the issues he drew attention to, but it is very non-Whorfian methodologically. Approaches to the subject are constantly evolving and being impacted by the work of numerous parties in related fields of the cognitive sciences. In this book we will avoid the association of research on linguistic relativity with labels bearing the names of particular researchers such as Whorf. Such terms increase the odds that the research will be judged not on its own merits, but on the merits of work from another era that differed in many significant respects. I will refer instead simply to work on "linguistic relativity", the hypothesis that crosslinguistic differences have *any* demonstrable effects on nonlinguistic cognition (Lucy 1997:295). More specific formulations of this general hypothesis are taken to be mutable, changing in accordance with our increasing understanding of the strength and pervasiveness, or lack thereof, of relativistic effects.

1.4 Motivations for criticisms of the hypothesis

There are many reasons that the linguistic relativity hypothesis failed to gain traction during the latter half of the 20th century, some of which were touched on in the preceding section. In many cases the relevant studies produced were susceptible to valid methodological criticisms, which our discussion has so far hinted at but not fully explored. Some of these criticisms have been crucial in shaping the research surveyed in this book. Other points have been less influential since, we will argue, they resulted from misperceptions of some relativistic claims.

Perhaps the most prominent problem characterizing work on relativity, particularly much of Whorf's work and a number of other studies in the subsequent decades, is simple circularity. This circularity is the by-product of the choice to employ one sort of linguistic data in support of a hypothesis based on another sort of linguistic data, all the while making claims about nonlinguistic behavior and thought (see discussion in Enfield [2000]). Consider Whorf's claims regarding numerous categorization-type effects, for instance the way in which water is thought of by Hopi and English speakers. English has a general word for 'water', whereas according to Whorf Hopi has two words for the relevant substance. One of these is employed for naturally occurring water (*pahe*), e.g. in lakes, waterfalls, rivers, etc., while the other is utilized when water is contained (*keyi*) in cups, bottles, ladles, and the like (1956:210). The different words for water are suggestive of differences in thought. Yet what evidence do we have for this difference of thought? We are offered nothing in this case beyond the linguistic data. If we want to convince skeptics that Hopi and English speakers actually think differently about water, however, we would need some correlation between the differences in linguistic taxonomy and actual behavior outside of language. In short, there must be testable predictions beyond the linguistic realm, and the reliance on data in the linguistic realm to support a hypothesis generated on those same linguistic data is patently circular. Furthermore, the utilization of linguistic data only runs the risk of ignoring parallel expressions that might reflect greater crosslinguistic similarity (see Kay 1996). In this case for, example, while there may be a basic cover term for 'water' in English there is also an assortment of other words that distinguish between types of water. I can, for instance, speak of "spring water" and "tap water". While both terms contain the cover term 'water', can we really be confident that English speakers do not distinguish kinds of water in fine-grained ways like that hinted at by the different terms for water in Hopi? The point here is not that they do or do not, but merely to illustrate how linguistic data alone offer insufficient support for such claims. Relativistic claims can only avoid circularity if we provide evidence for cognitive differences through some nonlinguistic behavior. Differentiated lexical encoding of a given semantic category does not reflect, *a priori*, differentiated nonlexical conceptualizations of the relevant category.

A second objection to the relativistic position is that it is particularly susceptible to confirmation bias. That is, researchers are more prone to interpret findings, even nonlinguistic data of some kind, in ways that confirm their hypotheses. Part of the reason claims related to linguistic relativity have been so susceptible to such a bias is that they have frequently been anecdotal in nature. For example, consider the example I offered above regarding the perception of monkey types by speakers of Karitiâna and English, respectively. Now the absence of a superordinate term for monkey in Karitiâna may reflect some important conceptual distinction between particular species of monkey types, and it may help to enforce that distinction in the minds of Karitiâna speakers in a way that English does not. Yet what nonlinguistic data do I have to support this claim? I mentioned above that there seem to be clear behavioral differences of the two populations vis-à-vis monkeys, and that Karitiâna speakers prefer the stew made out of some monkey types, for example. This sort of anecdotal data is problematic though since it is not systematically or objectively gathered, and as a result may be chosen, subconsciously or not, precisely because it supports my hypothesis. Maybe there are aspects of Karitiâna behavior that are consistent with the notion that *all* monkey types are conceptually grouped. I do not know of any, but I must admit the possibility that my attention is naturally drawn to the ways in which the Karitiâna clearly distinguish between monkey species because of the way I have interpreted the linguistic data, and therefore the possibility exists that I am paying less attention to behavioral data that may contradict my hypothesis. My claims are potentially susceptible to confirmation bias, no matter how strongly I feel about them based on personal experience with the people. In order to provide convincing evidence, such claims cannot rely on either linguistic *or* anecdotal evidence alone. It is worth stressing, though, that the same point holds for those skeptical of claims for linguistic relativity. Those believing that linguistic disparities do not impact nonlinguistic cognition must offer experimental, non-anecdotal, evidence for the absence of relativistic effects – at least if their position is to be defended on empirical grounds.

This brings us to the third and potentially the most serious criticism of this sort of work, which must be taken into account for claims on linguistic relativity to hold water. For lack of a better term, let me refer to this as the "apparent inextricability of linguistic influences on thought". Language is perhaps the most unique component of culture, the shared set of behaviors of a particular group of humans, and is crucial to the transmission and negotiation of many nonlinguistic components of culture. However prominent it might be, though, language does not represent the entirety of culture. There are aspects of culture that are clearly nonlinguistic, or that have rather tenuous ligatures to language. With this in mind, let us assume that we have established differences in some aspect of the cognition of two groups of humans, say a group of American college students and an aboriginal Australian population whose spatial orientation strategies differ markedly. Furthermore, let us assume that there are clear differences between the spatial orientation terms employed in the two groups' languages, and that these differences are consistent with the groups' demonstrated disparities in nonlinguistic spatial orientation. This is an interesting finding, one that is certainly consistent with a relativistic interpretation. But, bearing in mind the truism that correlation cannot be equated with causation, another interpretation remains. Perhaps the linguistic and cognitive data are consistent because of a more general cultural factor, one that is evident in nonlinguistic spatial orientation *and* also in the linguistic encoding of space. Now we might believe that linguistic behavior plays a major role in constraining the spatial orientation strategies of the two groups in question, but how do we extricate that role from a potentially more basic cultural factor that serves as a confounding variable? Methodologically, this is not a simple task. In some cases it may in fact be impossible. Yet as we will see there are ways this apparent inextricability of linguistic influence can be overcome, at least in large measure.

The three issues delineated above must be carefully taken into account in work on linguistic relativity, and are generally at least tacitly acknowledged by contemporary researchers. They have been addressed methodologically, with varying degrees of success, by many of the studies described in this book. They have not always been considered carefully, however, in discussions of linguistic relativity, and have therefore served as impetus for warranted criticisms of the hypothesis. In addition to these three substantive motivations for criticism of the hypothesis, there has been another more trivial (or more precisely, trivializing) motivation, namely exaggeration.

Some claims on linguistic relativity are based at least in some part on the exaggeration of differences between languages. Perhaps the most famous documentable case of hyperbole relates to the aforementioned disparity between number of words for snow in Eskimo and English. Pullum (1991:163) notes that Whorf's claim is based on an exaggeration of Boas's description of Eskimo words. According to Boas's (1966[1911]) description, Eskimo contains four words for snow, but Whorf "illicitly inflated" (1991:163) that number to seven (on Pullum's count) while also glossing over the varied sorts of words for snow in English (e.g. sleet, slush, snow...). In that sense Whorf was guilty of both the confirmation bias discussed above (by ignoring parallel translations in English), while also being guilty of exaggerating the actual Eskimo data. As Pullum humorously notes, however, Whorf's data then formed the basis of second-hand and third-hand (Eastman [1975]) discussions on the subject. The net result has been the popularization of claims that the Eskimos have "one hundred" (*New York Times*, Feburary 9, 1984) or more words for snow. Such claims are clearly apocryphal, though, and reflect a serious distortion of any actual linguistic data.

Judging from our discussion to this point, the motivations for criticisms of research on linguistic relativity are largely methodological. These issues must be taken into account if claims on the subject are to be taken seriously. It is worth underscoring, though, that the criticisms of many claims regarding linguistic relativity, both in the past and present, have often related in equal measure to aspects of the intellectual climate in which the research was or is received.

Many of Whorf's central points were initially accepted by a variety of social scientists, at least in part because of the common empiricist epistemology and behaviorism of the time. Shortly after the publication of the collection of Whorf's works (1956), however, there was a radical shift in the dominant ideology in linguistics, as discussed in the preceding section. The nativist linguistic theory popularized at that time appeared incompatible with the idea that linguistic disparities foster any sort of significant cognitive disparities. After all, how can such relativistic effects exist if there are no significant fundamental disparities across languages, that is, if languages share a universal grammar? More specifically, how can grammatical dissimilarities yield conceptual dissimilarities if all grammatical dissimilarities are ascribed to surface, non-"deep structure" phenomena only? Furthermore, if language is modular and detached from other cognitive processes in the way implied by the prominent nativism of the time, what extant mechanisms could allow language to influence nonlinguistic thought?

Significantly, the strong nativism that pervaded linguistics during much of the second half of the twentieth century (see discussion in Landau and Jackendoff [1993]) operated synergistically with some consonant contemporary developments in psychology. Some of the more significant strains of thought here were the nativist and modular approaches lobbied for in works such as Fodor (1975, 1983)[4], Piaget (1955, 1977) and more recently in Keller and Keller (1996). The details of the approaches characterized by such works are not altogether relevant here, though it is crucial to note that these influential frameworks are generally consistent with a unidirectional sort of influence of thought processes on language, rather than vice-versa.[5] Given a climate in which such nativism held sway, claims on linguistic relativity faced theoretical obstacles to serious consideration by many in the cognitive sciences. The skepticism towards relativity was in some cases voiced explicitly, for instance in Clark and Clark (1977) and Devitt and Sterelny (1987). It is somewhat surpris-

---

4 The modularity characterized in these works has given way to the massive modularity evident for instance in Pinker (2007), as well as weaker forms of the modularity hypothesis, e.g. Gibbs and Van Orden (2010). Note that Fodor himself does not advocate the massive modularity perspective (see Fodor [1998]).

5 Which is not to say that such perspectives admit no possibility of any relativistic effects. See e.g. Fodor (1975:389).

ing, though, that the universalist perspectives popular during much of this period were sometimes taken to be inherently anti-relativistic, since proponents of linguistic relativity do not maintain that *no* aspects of cognition or language might be universal or native. Even Whorf (1956:239) noted that language was "in some sense a superficial embroidery upon deeper processes of consciousness." Put differently, acceptance of significant linguistic diversity, along with associated cognitive effects of such diversity, does not imply the non-acceptance of universal aspects of human cognition. Given how much humans share genetically, most contemporary researchers presume a fair amount of universalism in human cognition. Many feel, however, that the extent of that universalism is an empirical matter that requires exploration. Proponents of linguistic relativity believe that this exploration will allow us to better establish which facets of human cognition are in fact susceptible to variance, perhaps due to linguistic influence. Socio-cultural and linguistic contexts of the acquisition of knowledge were to some extent de-emphasized by the popular nativist approaches mentioned above, and one of the by-products of this de-emphasis was that serious research on relativity was undervalued by many language researchers, some of whom were in fact theoretically adversarial to such work.

These various hindrances to work on linguistic relativity characterized much of the research climate of the latter half of the 20th century. They do not characterize the current climate, however, at least not to the same degree. Which is not to suggest that research on the subject does not face ideological opposition in some quarters. Much of this opposition doest not actually stem from familiarity with current work on linguistic relativity, but results instead from the wholesale association of the linguistic relativity hypothesis with the work of Whorf, which as we have noted is not immune to serious methodological criticisms. More troublingly, given the frequent exaggeration and distortion of some of Whorf's claims, work on linguistic relativity is sometimes characterized by distortions of Whorf's perspective itself, for instance in the oft-cited work of Pinker (1994). As Monaghan (2011:227) notes, the "ongoing distance between popular notions of Whorf and his legacy as seen from within linguistic anthropology is something members of the field continually attempt to correct." One could argue, though, that such attempts at correction represent a misappropriation of energies. That is, researchers in some cases have focused significant exegetical efforts on defending Whorf's actual intents. While it is disappointing to see any scholar's work grossly misinterpreted, though, in some sense Whorfian hermeneutics are immaterial to the contemporary discussions of linguistic relativity, which should be shaped not by his work but by the wealth of research presently being generated with an eye toward addressing the issues outlined above. As Deutscher (2010) notes, evidence against the strongest Whorfian claims has incorrectly been "taken as proof that people of all cultures think in fundamentally the same way." As the same writer points out, though, this is surely a mistake. So, rather than defending the original claims of Whorf, proponents of the linguistic relativity hypothesis might be best served by drawing attention to contemporary claims that are more well-grounded empirically. In doing so, perhaps some ideological opponents will engage more seriously with the topic of linguistic relativity.

Finally, in discussing issues that are troublesome to the linguistic relativity hypothesis, we should mention a political factor. As scholars have previously noted (Fishman [1982], Lakoff [1987:337]), admitting the possibility of cognitive disparities due to crosslinguistic factors allows for radical viewpoints according to which some linguistic features are seen as resulting in more complex/ advanced thought patterns. Such admission runs the risk of effacing cognitive similarities across groups of people, and exaggerating cognitive differences in simplistic terms. While most linguists and other cognitive scientists are not out to simplify and/or politicize their results, popular interpretations of such results may run that risk, as evidenced by claims regarding Eskimo words for snow. Exaggerated interpretations of data that distort the degree of cognitive dissonance across cultures are obviously not desirable. Yet it is worth noting as well that, from the perspective of many, linguistics and cognitive science more generally has suffered considerably from the superficial attention sometimes paid to profound kinds of linguistic diversity. If we are truly concerned with understanding human language and human cognition, surely we must by necessity be concerned with the evidence for diversity of these two phenomena across human populations. We need to better understand the observable ranges of these sorts of diversity, and any documentable correlations between them. Put differently, to advance our understanding of the role that language might play in "the mediation of culture and mind" (Lucy 2004:1), we must be willing to acknowledge the possibility of diversity in human cognition across populations. The acknowledgement of such diversity does not after all imply any simplistic conclusions regarding variant complexity or desirability vis-à-vis the diverse patterns in question.

1.5 Issues with some prominent criticisms

In addition to the warranted methodological and disputable ideological motivations for objections to linguistic relativity, some well-known objections are based on more tenuous motivations. More specifically, some objections are based on caricaturizations of the relativistic position.

Consider perhaps the best known attack on the relativistic position, Pinker's (1994) so-called "obituary" for linguistic relativity (see also his discussion of the "Whorfian hypothesis" in Pinker [2007:126–28]). Pinker (1994:57) posits that the hypothesis of linguistic relativity, which he defines as the notion "that differences among languages cause differences in the thoughts of their speakers" is "wrong, all wrong." This is a strong claim, yet in substantiating the claim Pinker fixates on an entirely different claim, one that is in fact objectionable: "The idea that thought is the same as language". In other words, he equates the latter Orwellian claim (see discussion in Casasanto [2008]) with the relativistic position. The caricaturization allows for a facile assault of the relativistic position. It is clear, after all, that thought is not isomorphic with language. Not even in Whorf's work is the claim made that thought and language are entirely dissociable, however, and certainly contemporary proponents of linguistic relativity do not adopt that position. As Casasanto (2008:65) notes, it is possible "that language can shape the way people think even if they do not think in language."

In many cases criticisms of the relativistic position have also pointed to Whorf's data and noted that his claims about other languages were inaccurate in various ways (e.g. Malotki [1983]). As noted above, these criticisms are fair as they relate to some of Whorf's work in particular, but they are not necessarily germane to discussions of much of the current research on relativity. One impetus for the current volume is that many skeptics of relativity still seem to operate under the assumption that Whorf's work represents the current state of the discussion on these issues.

In a similar vein, it seems that some of the ideological objections described above may be appealed to far too strictly. Much as strong deterministic claims equating language with thought are easily discarded, though, one can dispense with perspectives that completely ignore the potential for any sort of linguistic influences on thought. Such perspectives trivialize the profound variation in the semantic systems evident across languages by relying on universal approaches to meaning. Less radically, approaches such as Wierzbicka (1992) have suggested that the semantic concepts evident in crosslinguistic lexical variation can nevertheless be decomposed into atomistic units that are in fact universal, a conclusion that does leave open the possibility of some relativistic effects. Even such a decompositional universalist approach is considered by some untenable, however, since it may be difficult to reconcile with psycholinguistic data indicating that lexical concepts are activated holistically, not according to some series of semantic primes (see discussion in Levinson [2003]).

The notion that crosslinguistic semantic variation is somehow superficial and does not generate at least some variation in conceptualization is troublesome. Maintaining such a position on rigidly nativistic or modular theoretical grounds arguably does little to advance substantive debate on this important issue. An alternate position seems much more reasonable: As Vygotsky (1962[1938]) noted, "Thought is not merely expressed in words; it comes into existence through them." Or we might say that *some* thought seems to come into being through words. Words may relate to more basic concepts, but they are not simply mapped on to antecedent concepts, at least not in all cases. Instead they are tools that at least facilitate thinking about concepts. For example, terms such as "mortgage-backed securities" or "derivative-oriented hedge funds" help us think about financial instruments in new ways, just like *rolinho* and *caneta* might help some people think of soccer in new ways. The expansion of scientific knowledge correlates with lexical expansion, as people need to exchange concepts and combine concepts in novel ways. This is all common-sensical, but the point is that lexical variation must play some role in conceptual variation. Which is not to say that speakers of different languages cannot adapt to such variation. Again, this alternative position is not a deterministic one. It simply admits at least some role of lexico-semantic variation in conceptual representation, and this admission constitutes an admission of at least a weak form of linguistic relativity, given the evidence for lexico-semantic variation across languages. Much as we cannot simply equate thought with language, then, we must admit that we could not think in all the ways we do without language. Furthermore, if language is instrumental to certain kinds of thought, then it is far from unreasonable to consider the possibility that linguistic disparities impact nonlinguistic thought.

Another difficulty with some strong objections to the relativistic position is that they occasionally restrict their attention to a particular aspect of cognition. This is particularly true with respect to discussions of color perception. While initial work on the subject (Brown and Lenneberg [1954], Lantz and Stefflre [1964]) offered support for a relativistic position, subsequent work, most notably Rosch (1972) and Berlin and Kay (1969), seemed incompatible with a relativistic position. In fact such studies served as the death knell for the linguistic relativity hypothesis in some quarters. Setting aside for the moment the fact that numerous subsequent studies have now demonstrated linguistic effects on the perception of color (see Chapter 7), one wonders how the absence of evidence for linguistic relativity in one domain could be taken as evidence for its absence in all domains. To truly appreciate the possibility of linguistic influences on nonlinguistic cognition, we need to consider carefully acquired data for a number of cognitive domains. If we restrict our attention to one domain only while formulating general hypotheses on the matter, those hypotheses will likely be short-lived. Hopefully the evidence presented in this volume will allow those concerned with this issue, perhaps even some skeptics, the chance to consider pertinent evidence in a more holistic manner. If, after having considered such evidence, such skeptics are not persuaded, at least their decision will not be based on data associated with only one cognitive domain.

As noted in Section 1.4, one of the issues facing research on relativity is the challenge of extricating linguistic influences from nonlinguistic cultural influences on cognition. In conducting such work, it may be misleading to demonstrate that cognition varies across two tested populations, and then offer a strictly linguistic interpretation of such variation. After all, other nonlinguistic cultural variables may be at play in such variation. In short, the anti-relativists often accurately claim, sometimes implicitly, that correlation does not imply linguistic causation. Nevertheless, it is worth noting in this discussion of issues with some anti-relativist positions (more specifically, those that are recalcitrant vis-à-vis the existence of *any* linguistic influences on thought), that extensive correlation of the sort in question also cannot be ignored. We cannot discard inductive reasoning in our attempts to better understand these issues, after all. If numerous correlations are established between particular linguistic features and particular behaviors, for example directional term types and spatial orientation strategies (see Chapter 4), the consistency of such correlations may crucially inform hypotheses on the subject. Correlation may not establish causation definitively, but it often points to the most reasonable explanation of a series of observations, as evidenced for example by the mere "correlation" between cigarettes and lung disease.

Finally, it is worth addressing one other major complication confronting strong anti-relativistic positions. Some anti-relativists maintain that language may influence thought, but only by providing us with referable concepts (Devitt and Strerelny 1987:178), or only when we are thinking in relationship to language, i.e. they admit only some on-line processing effects such as the "thinking for speaking" effects discussed in Slobin's (1996) work. Yet an implicit assumption in this perspective is that the role of thinking for the specific purposes of language production and comprehension is somehow comparatively minor when contrasted to other forms of thought. This position is difficult to maintain completely, however, given how much language plays a role in our conscious experience. Consider for instance the results in Mehl et al. (2007) on the number of words American and Mexican college students produce per day. In that study, based on hundreds of participants, it was found that students produce approximately 15,000 words per day (irrespective of gender, contra popular assumptions). Now consider that most of these students must listen to and comprehend at least that many words, produced by their peers and others, on a daily basis. Consider as well what a large percentage of the students' lives is spent reading, writing, texting, or emailing, etc. The point is clear: Humans use language incessantly, for some large (though variable and admittedly undetermined) portion of their waking hours. So even if linguistic effects on cognition are restricted to the realm of language, a point that is vociferously disputed by proponents of linguistic relativity, it is worth stressing what a large realm that is! The activities of speaking, hearing, and otherwise engaging our language faculties comprise a sizeable chunk of our experience.

This, it would seem, is one of the problems with strong anti-relativistic positions: any admission of linguistic effects on cognition, even those associated with the processing of language only, forces one to consider just how pervasive such supposedly trivial effects may be. In addition, an actual consideration of just how experientially ubiquitous language is calls into question the notion that the systematic variations across "linguistic thought" does not bleed over into other aspects of thought. As Reines and Prinz (2009:1028) note, "linguistic behavior is so frequently rehearsed that it is likely to promote habits of thought that extend beyond language use." For instance, given the overwhelming frequency of pronouns, does it not seem at least possible that thinking "with" markedly divergent pronominal systems during speech would result in at least *some* disparate patterns of nonlinguistic thought related to the semantic categories that are relevant to pronouns? (See Chapter 9 for some tentative evidence for such a disparity.)

In sum, much as there are issues with simplistic positions of linguistic determinism, there are also issues with the strongest anti-relativistic positions. Not all of the relevant issues have been surveyed here, either. (See Levinson [2003], Lucy [2004], Boroditsky [2011], *inter alia*, for further discussion.) This is not to suggest that there are no reasonable objections to some claims regarding linguistic relativity. It is to suggest instead that the linguistic relativity hypothesis is also not susceptible to simple off-hand rejections. In fact, there is much about the hypothesis that strikes many language researchers as appealing and intuitive. As Levinson et al. (2002) note in addressing Li and Gleitman's (2001) critique of some work on relativity, "Resistance to this humble truth – linguistically-motivated categories pervade, change, and facilitate our thought – is puzzling."

1.6 Types of linguistic relativity

To this point, we have discussed the linguistic relativity hypothesis in the broadest manner, as the basic belief that differences across languages generate effects on nonlinguistic cognition. Prima facie, such a characterization may seem sufficient. Yet while it is a useful starting point, it is a bit too generic. It says nothing, for instance, about the potential strength or pervasiveness of the putative effects. Such a broad interpretation of the relativity hypothesis allows us to consider influences on nonlinguistic cognition that differ markedly from the strong sorts of deterministic influences unfortunately associated with the hypothesis (see Gordon [2010] for discussion). Aside from the magnitude of the supposed relativistic effects, our working definition is vague in another respect: It does not divide relativity into any categories of effect types. As various authors have noted (e.g. Lucy [1996], Reines and Prinz [2009], Wolff and Holmes [2011]), relativistic effects can be categorized according to the general manner in which they influence cognition.

Consider for example Lucy's (1996, 1997, 2004) basic categorization of "types" of relativity into three categories: "semiotic", "structural", and "discursive". The first sort of relativity relates to the question of whether language "fundamentally alters the vision of the world held by humans in contrast to other species" (1996:39). Semiotic relativity is a closer affine to the philosophical treatments of the subject which date back centuries, focused on the basic question of whether language and human thought are dissociable. Understanding semiotic relativity is an important goal, but one that does not necessarily require the clearer understanding of cognitive differences across human populations. The latter two sorts of relativity, structural and discursive, are related to such differences. Discursive relativity refers to the notion that variations in patterns in the *usage* of language may influence the thought patterns of particular speakers. Even within particular linguistic communities, usage varies across speakers for functionally oriented reasons (Hymes [1974], Gumperz [1982]), such as vocation, status, gender, etc. Such variation in usage may foster relativistic effects among speakers of the same language. While discursive relativity is a fascinating topic, it too is not the focus of this book. We are concerned with what Lucy terms structural relativity, which is taken here to be linguistic relativity proper. Structural relativity refers to the notion that "characteristics of specific languages have an impact on the thought or behavior of those who speak them" (Lucy 1996:41). Unlike the other two sorts of relativity, structural/linguistic relativity is inherently crosslinguistically focused. In investigating such structural relativity, researchers are generally concerned with the ways in which *systematic* disparities across languages influence nonlinguistic cognition. In this book we will assume, like most contemporary researchers of the topic, that the study of linguistic relativity is concerned with variations of *nonlinguistic cognition*, rather than mental processes directly associated with speech or speech acts, and rather than with other aspects of nonlinguistic behavior that are obviously tied to speech events or acts. More widely encompassing definitions of linguistic relativity are possible, however.[6]

The systematic linguistic disparities motivating relativistic effects may be grammatical or lexical.[7] Other relativistic topics associated with, for instance, variations in linguistic praxis within a given socio-cultural milieu, are interesting issues that are related to the topic of this book. But that topic is more narrowly defined so as to highlight a particular strand of research, that on linguistic relativity proper. Of course that strand is part of a larger fabric of work on language, culture, and thought, work that includes treatments of topics such as semiotic and discursive relativity.

Assuming one equates linguistic relativity with structural relativity, as we have done, the concept can still be further sub-divided. There are different approaches to this sub-categorization in the literature. Since there is significant overlap between certain characteristics of different kinds of relativistic effects, such categorization efforts imply a neatness of divisions between effect types that may not be entirely accurate. Nevertheless, they can serve as a usual heuristic, as we attempt to make sense of the potential ways in which linguistic relativity manifests itself. In Chapter 11 we present one such heuristic categorization, after surveying the various kinds of relativistic effects now evident in the literature.

In this book we maintain the traditional division between language and thought. It is worth noting, though, that this traditional dichotomy is a bit misleading. As Boroditsky (2011:65) notes: "What researchers have been calling 'thinking' this whole time actually appears to be a collection of both linguistic and nonlinguistic processes. As a result, there may not be a lot of adult human

---

6 Sidnell and Enfield (2012) suggest another alternative definition, according to which linguistic relativity refers to how the language one speaks may have "consequences for thought, and for social life more generally" (2012:302). They suggest three potential loci of relativistic effects. One of these is the topic of this book, the way in which language impacts nonlinguistic cognition. The other relates to the way in which linguistic disparities impact the indexical relationships of a speech act (see Silverstein [1979]). A third loci, according to Sidnell and Enfield, relates to the way in which social actions are given different local "spins" in accordance with the lexicogrammatical resources of a given language. Note that only the first of these loci actually pertains to the way in which language impacts thought outside of the context of speaking. For other research on such broadly defined relativity, involving facets of cognition more directly tied to discourse, see Niemeier and Dirven (2000).

7 Part of the reason we would not want to exclude systematic lexical differences is that, as much work on construction grammar (Goldberg [1995]) has demonstrated, the bifurcation of language into lexical and grammatical components is, from the perspective of many linguists at least, in some sense artificial.

thinking where language does not play a role." Rather than considering the ways in which language effects thought, we could frame our entire discussion in this book along different lines, for example: How *much* of thought is linguistic? How closely intertwined are linguistic thought and other thought types? Are linguistic facets of thought extricable from the greater web of thought? The standard convenient division between language and thought is utilized in this book, in large measure since this utilization facilitates interaction with the literature. Nevertheless, to some researchers at least, language represents one of many *types* of thought, and when we explore linguistic relativity we are essentially exploring the extent to which this type of thought interacts with others. Even if one chooses to frame the issue in this manner, however, the sorts of interactions between linguistic thought and other forms of thought cannot be stipulated *a priori* – we first need to look at the evidence across cognitive domains and languages.

1.7 The structure of this book

In this book some of the most crucial findings on linguistic relativity, uncovered primarily during the last two decades, are surveyed. The purpose of the survey is to represent the range and the depth of contemporary research on relativity in an easily digestible manner. To that end, we will consider the cognitive domains that have received the greatest amount of scrutiny. While the survey aims for comprehensiveness, it does not seek to be exhaustive. After all, much work on the subject is currently under way in this rapidly expanding field. Yet the remaining chapters of this book should at least familiarize you with the bulk of the significant recent research on this topic, while allowing you to come to your own conclusions regarding the evidence for different kinds of linguistic relativity.

It is worth stressing what this book is not. It is not a consideration of the cognitive mechanisms that allow for linguistic relativity, though some discussion of these mechanisms is offered in Chapter 11. It also does not address the social or political implications of linguistic relativity, or even whether such implications exist.

To more clearly depict where this survey will take us, it is worth encapsulating each of the following ten chapters. Chapter 2 serves as further background and considers the range of linguistic diversity that exists in the world. The discussion of such diversity is vital since relativistic effects crucially hinge on crosslinguistic diversity, and since many non-linguists are not familiar with the range of linguistic diversity actually in existence. We note in Chapter 2 that few (if any) meaningful linguistic universals have actually been found despite decades worth of field research. We point out that the 7,000 or so extant languages reflect a remarkable diversity of human experience and cultures developed during the course of their histories in diverse ecologies. We also discuss the existence of general cognitive diversity across human populations. In Chapter 3 we discuss how a causal link between linguistic and cognitive diversity might be established methodologically. We offer an overview of basic methods employed in contemporary research on linguistic relativity. In Chapter 4 the crosslinguistic, cross-domain evaluations of the linguistic relativity literature begin in earnest. The chapter consists of a survey of findings related to the construal of spatial relationships. We examine research on the effects of disparate spatial language features on speakers' spatial orientation strategies. We also consider work on the effects of various spatial adposition types on the perception of spatial relationships between objects. We devote the majority of our attention to providing overviews of several prominent studies, while also referencing numerous associated ones. This strategy of dwelling on some of the most noteworthy findings while indexing related ones is adhered to in subsequent chapters as well. Chapter 5 consists of an overview of research on crosslinguistic differences in temporal metaphors and their apparent influence on speakers' perception of time. In Chapter 6 we consider a seemingly extreme sort of linguistic relativity that has surfaced in studies on numerical cognition. We devote a significant portion of that chapter to work among anumeric populations, work that indicates a clear ligature between cross-group differences in numerical language and numerical thought. In Chapter 7 we discuss several studies on the discrimination of color. This domain is arguably the most studied in research related to the linguistic relativity hypothesis. Much of this work has been used to support the linguistic relativity hypothesis, and much has been used to support anti-relativistic positions. We consider the most recent evidence for linguistic effects on color discrimination. In Chapter 8 we survey findings gathered among speakers of languages with nominal classifier systems, findings that suggest speakers perceptually discriminate some objects in accordance with such systems, unlike speakers of languages without classifier systems. Similarly, we consider evidence that crosslinguistic differences in count-mass distinctions lead to real-world effects on the individuation of objects and substances. Chapter 9 consists of an overview of a number of studies on the demonstrable cognitive effects of systems of grammatical gender on the perception of inanimate objects and other non-gendered stimuli. In Chapter 10 we tackle several miscellaneous cognitive domains for which there is now a growing body of studies related to linguistic relativity, but which have received less attention than those focused on in Chapters 4–9. These domains relate to phenomena such as event discrimination, counterfactual reasoning, and the perception of agency. In the eleventh and final chapter, we draw some broad conclusions, based on the evidence surveyed in the other chapters. The most basic conclusion we will draw goes something like this: There is now strong evidence for some form of the linguistic relativity hypothesis, across a variety of cognitive domains and languages. The evidence for relativistic effects in some domains is particularly strong, in others less so. We offer suggestions as to why this might be the case. We also underscore that, while our understanding of linguistic relativity has been greatly refined by the research described in this book, more work is required in order to better establish the extent of the influence of particular features of languages on the thought processes of their speakers.

2 Acknowledging diversity

2.1 Introduction

The existence of linguistic relativity is clearly contingent on diversity. That is, if we are to accept that linguistic diversity helps to foster cognitive diversity of any sort or to any degree, we must first agree that there is evidence for both cognitive diversity and linguistic diversity across human populations. Furthermore, for the concept of linguistic relativity to merit exploration, we might expect these diversities to be non-trivial. The purpose of this chapter is to establish that cross-cultural cognitive and linguistic diversities are real and demonstrable, though they have arguably received insufficient attention in the cognitive sciences and linguistics more specifically. The bulk of this chapter will be occupied with exploring linguistic diversity, since a) there is a presumption among some that linguistic diversity is limited, and b) cross-cultural cognitive diversity receives greater attention during the remainder of the volume.

2.2 Cognitive diversity across human populations

Our understanding of the variance of cognitive psychology across human populations is in many ways inchoate. Yet the growing evidence being gathered on this topic suggests that, in ways that sometimes defy expectations, humans think in very different ways. Perusal of the *Journal of Cross-Cultural Psychology*, for instance, hints at both similarities and dissimilarities in certain facets of human cognition, and this despite the fact that much of the work in this venue focuses on western and/or industrialized societies. The extent of cognitive dissimilarities is unclear since careful inquiry into cognitive variance across human populations remains in its incipient stages. While numerous studies on cognitive variation across radically disparate cultures have been produced in recent years, their numbers pale in comparison to those of studies based on a much narrower range of the spectrum of culture types. Only now are we beginning to appreciate how the absence of a truly cross-cultural focus in the relevant work has potentially generated incorrect assumptions of uniformity of human cognition. This is not to suggest that uniformity of any sort does not exist, as we stressed in the preceding chapter. After all, humans share the same biology. This shared biology includes, however, massive cortical plasticity and other features that allow for adaptation to an assortment of ecologies. Furthermore a wealth of evidence points to cultural and biological co-evolution (Boyd and Richerson [2005], Boyd, Richerson, and Henrich [2011]) among humans, and the overwhelmingly shared DNA among human populations does not preclude variation in supposedly fundamental facets of human cognition, some of which may result ontogenetically from what are in fact culturally dependent factors. Establishing the universality of certain cognitive processes and associated behaviors, even some seemingly basic ones, remains in many cases an open-ended task necessitating cross-cultural and crosslinguistic approaches, only some of which are represented in this book.

As obvious as it may seem to some, it is important to reiterate that what is at issue here is the role of cultural factors, specifically language, rather than genetic ones. The comparatively limited role of allele variation in cognitive diversity is evidenced when pre-linguistic infants are transplanted from one culture to another. In such cases of cross-cultural adoption the children subsequently exhibit normal cognitive and social development. To cite one relatively uncommon sort of example, a friend of mine was born into a Tupían family in Brazil. Her native culture and language differ markedly from those of western industrialized societies in a number of respects. For a variety of reasons, including the death of her biological parents during her infancy, she was adopted by missionaries. Eventually she gained American citizenship, and presently resides with her American husband and children in the South. Her unsurprisingly typical cognitive development is evidenced by, among other things, a successful academic career including a college degree. Furthermore she is deeply ensconced in her current "southern" culture. While I am unaware of any other American Amazonian indigenes, her case is illustrative of a wider pattern, since humans native to one culture are frequently raised in another while exhibiting linguistic and cognitive development considered normal in their new culture.

Cross-population genotypic heterogeneity may play a relatively limited role in cognitive development, but nevertheless there is strong evidence for cross-population differences in cognition that result from socio-cultural, including linguistic, disparities across human groups. Since language-based motivations are the topic of this book, it is worth demonstrating that a number of nonlinguistically motivated variations in human cognition across human populations have already been detailed in the literature.

Consider the two horizontal lines (parallel to the text) in Figure 2.1. Which is longer, the one on the left or the right? If you are like most people that have been exposed to this pair of lines, you will select the one on the right though the lines are actually equal in length. The perception of these lines results in a well-known illusion, the Müller-Lyer (1889) illusion. This illusion was once presumed to result from some basic feature of human visual perception. Given

Figure 2.1: The Müller-Lyer illusion.

that it is a very low-level processing effect, certain accounts would seem to predict its universality, since according to them (e.g. Fodor [1975]), low-level basic cognitive processes are not predicted to vary across people groups. It turns out, however, that there is in fact extensive variation in the perception of paired lines such as those in Figure 2.1, in accordance with the culture of the perceivers. A team of cognitive scientists investigated this and other perceptual illusions across sixteen societies, representing a variety of cultural categories (Segall, Campbell, and Herskovits [1966]). Astonishingly to some, they discovered that this optical illusion varies to the point of non-existence in some cultures. For example, San foragers are not susceptible to this illusion and do not typically perceive the line on the left to be shorter than that on the right. Tellingly, of the sixteen societies tested, the pool of American participants demonstrated an extreme degree of susceptibility to the illusion. The next most-susceptible group was the European contingent of participants. The remaining societal groups varied in their susceptibility. To better understand the variance in the perception of these lines, Segall, Campbell, and Herskovits (1966) increased the length of the line on the left incrementally, in order to test at which length that line was perceived to be the same length as the line on the right. They referred to this modified length as the "point of subjective equality" or PSE. For over half the populations of the adults tested, the line on the left was only required to exceed the other line in length by six percent or less for the PSE to be reached. For two tested groups, PSE was reached with a one percent difference. The American undergrads tested comprised an outlier group, and the PSE was only attained for this group when actual length discrepancy neared twenty percent. In short, this illusion that was thought to instantiate a basic low-level perceptual characteristic of the human species turned out to be far from universal. Analogously variable results were obtained for some (though not all) of the illusions tested for in Segall, Campbell, and Herskovits (1966), including the Sander-Parallelogram and Horizontal-Vertical illusions.

It is unclear exactly what sort of cultural and ecological factors motivate the heighted susceptibility of Americans to this illusion, though Segall, Campbell, and Herskovits (1966) note that the repeated exposure to phenomena such as "carpeted corners" and other environmentally-contingent factors associated with American culture may play significant roles. As Henrich, Heine, and Norenzayan (2010) suggest, these results imply that the "visual system ontogeneti-cally adapts to the presence or recurrent features in the local visual environment."

Henrich, Heine, and Norenzayan (2010) discuss these results on visual perception in suggesting that the focus on Western, Educated, Industrialized, Rich, and Democratic (WEIRD) people in research on human psychology has led to an assortment of similarly erroneous assumptions regarding putatively universal cognitive processes. Much as linguistics has had a historical tendency to focus on "average European" languages, a tendency that Boas, Sapir, Whorf and other anthropological linguists labor(ed) against, psychology has had an unfortunate tendency to focus on subjects from WEIRD societies, according to Henrich, Heine, and Norenzayan (2010).[8] This conclusion is supported by Arnett's (2008) meta-analysis of major psychology journals, which suggested that between 2003 and 2007, 99% of the authors in the relevant journals were from Western industrialized nations, and that 96% of their samples came from such societies. This sample skewing results from practical considerations in most cases, and in many instances a more cross-cultural sample would not benefit the studies' aims. Nevertheless, the skewing is troublesome to the extent that some psychological processes are assumed to be universal when the studies that have uncovered them are based on a narrow and frequently non-representative cross-section of culture types. While no doubt many features of cognition are universal, many researchers believe such universality can only be established once those features have been uncovered in a wide-range of human cultures, including hunter-gatherer groups that are likely to more closely resemble in crucial respects the cultures shared by humans during the majority of the time in which our currently-shared neurophysiological apparatuses evolved.

Where cross-cultural sampling has been taken seriously in investigations into basic cognitive processes, some results have in fact suggested universal patterns. This is true, for instance, in work on the universality of certain basic emotions such as fear and joy (Ekman [1999]), the apparently universal belief in the autonomy of human mental and biological functions (Cohen et al. [2011]), or in the seeming universality of psychological essentialism discussed in Henrich, Heine, and Norenzayan (2010:69). (See also Gelman [2003], Astuti, Solomon, and Carey [2004])[9] In other cases, however, careful cross-cultural

---

8 In fact, research subjects typically represent a narrower segment of WEIRD societies, namely undergraduates. Results based on undergraduates often do not generalize to the other populations (Atran and Medin [2008], Medin and Atran [2004]).

9 Though see Prinz (2012) for an extensive critical discussion of much of the extant work on putative universals of human behavior, as well as a critical assessment of many of the universal features of human cognition posited by prominent evolutionary psychologists.

sampling has revealed variation where it might not have been expected. This is true in the case of some visual perception phenomena such as the Müller-Lyer illusion, but also in cross-cultural variations in folk-biological reasoning, self-evaluation processes, evaluation of others' behavior, and heritability of IQ.

Consider the case of folkbiological reasoning. Widely circulated work (Carey [1985]) has concluded that there is a crucial developmental stage, occurring between the ages of seven and ten, during which the perspective of humans vis-à-vis other biological entities is altered. Prior to this stage, children tend to anthropomorphize other biological phenomena, perceiving their characteristics in quasi-humanistic terms. Following this stage, the perception is generally reversed, to the extent that humans then perceive themselves as one of many kinds of biological entities in existence. While this transmogrification is interesting, it is unclear in fact how generalizable it is to the species as a whole. It turns out that the findings on which this conclusion is based have not been replicated in studies among smaller-scale societies indigenous to the Americas (Atran et al. [2001], Ross et al. [2003]). In fact, the transition appears to occur much earlier in non-urban societies in which humans interact more habitually and directly with a greater variety of flora and fauna. In some sense, the children in these less urban and industrialized societies exhibit less anthropocentrism in their reasoning concerning biological categories. Variant degrees of anthropocentric reasoning represent another non-trivial sort of cognitive difference. Yet this sort of variance can easily be missed or glossed over if assumptions of cognitive uniformity are made from the results obtained among one type of population. Such assumptions are particularly troubling since the populations they are based on, viz. western industrialized ones, are aberrant with respect to their members' familiarity with non-developed ecologies, and since non-industrialized cultures more closely resemble the cultures of humans residing in Africa prior to the scattering of the species into radically disparate environments. This presumed (relative) semblance between non-industrialized cultures, particularly hunter-gatherer tribes, and the original African cultures is due to shared features such as the absence of technologies like agriculture and writing, which have had profound effects on those cultures in which they have been adopted.

Another commonly held assumption of universality that is actually contravened by cross-cultural data relates to the notion of self-evaluation. It is commonly assumed that humans have a tendency to view themselves, on an individual level, in a positive light. The idea that "everyone is above average" is not merely shared by the fictitious citizens of Lake Wobegon. The tendency for people to have a comparatively positive assessment of self certainly surfaces in some western societies. People in such societies are often biased to perceived themselves and their behaviors in a more positive light than an objective assessment might warrant. This sort of perceptual narcissism is remarkably intuitive to many, perhaps since the positive valuation of self is inculcated in them from an early age. Certainly positive self-evaluation corresponds with the cultural values espoused in many media in contemporary American culture, for example. Yet, as you might have guessed given the course of the current discussion, it turns out that this tendency towards positive views of the individual self are far from universal. Studies among Native Americans (Fryberg and Markus [2003]), Fijians (Rennie and Dunne [1994]), and East Asians (Heine and Hamamura [2007]), *inter alia*, have demonstrated that there is extensive cross-cultural variation in the extent to which individuals are inclined to generally perceive themselves in a better-than-average sort of manner. One might even argue that some of these cultures exhibit a greater tendency towards self-objectivity. Regardless, what is clear is that such self-enhancing thought patterns are not universal, at least not in the manner sometimes assumed.

Just as there are cross-societal dissimilarities in aspects of how the self is perceived, there are dissimilarities in the manner in which others are perceived. Studies among Westerners have revealed an essentialist tendency according to which people perceive comportment to represent the nature or inherent disposition of a given person exhibiting the behavior in question (Jones and Harris [1967], Ross, Amabile, and Steinmetz[1977]). The behavior is assumed to represent some unwavering quality of the person in question, with less attention paid to mitigating situational factors. This pattern of attribution, though, turns out not to surface in studies of members of some societies. Studies among East Asians (Miyamoto and Kitayama [2002], Akiko et al. [1999]) and Russians (Grossmann and Varnum [2010]) suggest that members of these groups are more likely than Americans to attribute behavior to contextual constraints rather than to the essential disposition of the actors. In investigating the perception of personality across eight populations, Church et al. (2006) found that members of Western societies were more likely to judge personality traits to be stable concepts, less malleable by experiential factors, when contrasted to members of non-Western groups. The latter subjects were more likely to consider such traits poor descriptors of people, and more likely to perceive them as contingent on external factors. The variability in the perception of personality attribution strikes some Westerners as counter-intuitive. It is precisely because the results of systematic cross-cultural data collection are sometimes counter-intuitive, however, that such collection is crucial to the formulation of ideas on universal thought processes. After all, such ideas are typically promulgated by Westerners whose intuitions are, not shockingly, more likely to be matched by data gathered among other Westerners.

As a final example of cross-population variation in cognition, consider the example of IQ heritability. There is a strong assumption among some that measures of IQ are primarily determined by genetic factors rather than those associated with family environment. Even within American society, however, socio-economic status appears to play a significant role in the extent to which IQ is heritable. Turkheimer et al. (2003) present data on twins representing divergent socioeconomic statuses, and these data suggest convincingly that genetic factors play a much more prominent role in IQ variation among members of higher socioeconomic status, whereas factors associated with family environment play a comparatively greater role in those of lower status. The influence of socioeconomic status on heritability of IQ suggests that even cognitive processes with clear genetic influences remain susceptible to contextual influences and, more specifically, that IQ is affected by environmental factors within a western culture. The latter point is perhaps unsurprising but nevertheless worth stressing. If something like IQ, which is associated with an assortment of cognitive processes, can be affected by contextual factors within a given culture, it seems fair to assume that the cognitive processes in question would vary in accordance with the even-wider range of contextual factors evident in multiple cultures. After all, the differences between the childhoods of Americans from lower and higher socioeconomic statuses, respectively, pale in comparison to those between childhoods in western industrialized societies and, for example, indigenous tribal societies. (Rogoff, Morelli, and Angelillo [2003])

The aforementioned instances of cognitive variation, along with others surveyed in Henrich, Heine, and Norenzayan (2010) and elsewhere, have surfaced through the examination of data from a number of cultures, and have resulted from the recent surge in interest among cognitive scientists on the roles of culture and language in shaping cognition. As Bender, Hutchins, and Medin (2010) suggest, anthropologically oriented considerations of cultural influence on cognition are crucial for the future health of cognitive science and, more specifically, cognitive psychology. Such health is contingent on the recognition and exploration of cases of variation such as those mentioned here. Henrich, Heine, and Norenzayan (2010:78) make the following insightful claim regarding the potential motivations for such variation: "The causal origins of such population-level variation may be manifold, including behavioral plasticity in response to different environments, epigenetic effects, divergent trajectories of cultural evolution, and even the differential distribution of genes across groups in response to divergent evolutionary histories." To this manifold list of causal origins, we might add crosslinguistic variation, a causal feature that is potentially subsumed by "different trajectories of cultural evolution", yet merits explicit stipulation. In the next section we briefly survey the range of such crosslinguistic variation, in order to get an idea of how profound it is and how it too might help foster cognitive variation within our species.

2.3 Linguistic diversity across human populations

There are approximately 7,000 extant languages detailed in the most comprehensive listing of the world's languages, the *Ethnologue* (Lewis [2009]). This figure represents, somewhat closely anyhow, the number of mutually unintelligible languages in contemporary usage. Degree of intelligibility is a tricky notion though, and the decision to consider two speech varieties separate languages or separate dialects is not always easy, and is often informed by political rather than linguistic criteria. The decision to consider Mandarin and Cantonese 'Chinese' is largely political, as is the decision to consider Serbian and Croatian separate languages. In fact the former pair of languages are more dissimilar from each other on purely linguistic terms than the latter pair are from each other. In these cases linguistic criteria may suggest an alternate classification, but in some cases even linguistic criteria related to degree of mutual intelligibility are insufficient to arrive at such decisions since the division between "separate dialects" status and "separate languages" status is cline-like.

Regardless of the exact number of extant languages, what is clear is that there is a remarkable diversity in the linguistic practices of human beings. Some languages are manual, with dozens of signed languages in existence, and some of these, like American Signed Language, are spoken over enormous geographic areas. Not all languages involving manual signs are in the visual modality, either, as evidenced by the tactile signing of the deaf-blind. Most languages are conveyed via the vocal-auditory channel, but even these spoken forms can be represented in other modalities—via writing, Morse code, semaphores, etc. Given the limitations of human sensory and motor capacity, the diversity of forms that human language can take is remarkable.

Yet when we focus on speech only, the extent of linguistic diversity is no less impressive. About 100 spoken languages are isolates, with no known related languages. The remaining languages can be divided into 300 or so "stocks" or families of various sizes (Nichols [1992]), based on historical relatedness. Some areas of the world are particularly diverse in terms of the number of language families: There are approximately 50 language stocks in Amazonia alone (Everett [2010]), and even more in New Guinea. Since modern linguistics has been dominated primarily by native speakers of languages utilized in rich industrialized nations, in particular Indo-European languages, the vast majority of the linguistic enterprise has been focused on a very narrow band of the spectrum of linguistic diversity (i.e. one "stock").

Some things about speech are universal, at least to the extent that human groups share the same biological features that have been exapted for speech. These include vocal-auditory tracts with a lowered larynx that, paradoxically, facilitates both speech and choking. (Lieberman [2007]) The approximately 1:1 ratio of the lengths of the oral and pharyngeal portions of the supralaryngeal tract, which has resulted from the lowering of the larynx, is crucial to the production of disparate vowel types. Another universal biological feature that is crucial to speech is the cochlea in our inner ears, which is particularly sensitive to frequencies below 5,000 kHz, where most speech information is conveyed. The etiology of such universal features is a matter of some debate in current work on the evolution of language (Smith, Smith, and Cancho [2008]), yet computer-simulation-based studies suggest unequivocally that they predate the emergence of language itself (Christiansen, Chater, and Reali [2009]). Given the rapidity of linguistic and cultural change when contrasted to genomic change (see Atkinson et al. [2008]), it seems very plausible that such features were co-opted for linguistic purposes some time relatively recently, perhaps as little as 60,000 to 200,000 thousand years ago (see Kenneally [2007] for one survey of the relevant evidence). Language itself may well predate such co-opting, though, in non-spoken form.[10] Despite the universal nature of certain biological features co-opted for language by humans, the extant language stocks show remarkable diversity. This diversity is most easily understood within an evolution-oriented framework, so it is worth making a few relevant comments regarding the evolution of the only linguistic species.

The truth is, our understanding of human evolution is in constant flux. While it is clear, for instance, that hominids were bipedal as far back as Australopithecus, the bipedal status of our common ancestor with chimpanzees has become a topic of debate since the discovery of Ardipithecus (White et al. [2009]). The origins and motivations of bipedalism remain a source of discussion, as do the origins of other biological characteristics of our species such as our high encephelization quotient (E.Q.), i.e. the existence of our large, very calorie-consuming, brains (Schoenemann [2004]). Some research suggests that

---

10 In fact, one influential current strain of research on the evolution of language suggests that our biology was only exploited for speech well after the origin of language in the visual modality of gestures and signs (Corballis [2003], Arbib [2005]), after humans had begun demonstrating the ability to share attention and intentions with each other in ways that other primates lack even today (Tomasello [2008]).

our high E.Q.'s, like our relatively small gastro-intestinal tracts, may have bene-fited from the advent of cooking among our hominid ancestors, potentially as far back as 1.6 to 1.9 million years ago (Wrangham [2009]). In other words, cooking may be an example *par excellence* of culture influencing evolution.

While some of the motivations for our shared human biology are debated, though, findings on the development of our species point clearly to an African origin. These findings include countless fossil findings by physical anthropolo-gists, genetic evidence (e.g. Nei [1995]), and most recently (and much more controversially), linguistic evidence (Atkinson [2011], Jaeger et al. [2011]). The dispersion of our species from Africa occurred at least 50,000 years ago (Klein [2009] and probably much earlier). This point is crucial to our understanding of synchronic linguistic diversity, since relevant findings suggest that the first members of our species to exit the continent were already equipped with lan-guage and culture. This conclusion is supported by certain complex behaviors in human culture apparent around this time in the fossil record, for instance the complex glue-making processes evident at the Sibudu caves in South Africa, which would seem to have required language (Wadley, Hodgskiss, and Grant [2009]). In short, by the time we began our circum-ambulation of the world, we were equipped with the tools of culture and language; we were well adapted for adaptation.

This brief digression into the history of our species suggests then that the remarkable linguistic diversity that we see in the world today is primarily the result of processes that have occurred over dozens of millennia, during the transmission of language across social groups and across generations. In fact, linguists estimate that the current diversity on offer represents but a small segment of the diversity that has existed. Pagel (2000) posits the existence of over half a million human languages during the course of our species' history, or more than seventy times the amount currently in existence. The first lan-guage (or less likely, the small set of first languages) has changed in innumera-ble ways over the millennia, through processes such as grammaticalization (Hopper and Traugott [2003]) and phonetic change (Labov [2001]) that are still at work today. Rapid expansion helped foster rapidly diversifying language, which changed, at least in part, to meet local ecologies and cultural contexts. The net result was extreme synchronic linguistic diversity, to the point that few, some argue no, linguistic universals can be found in the world's languages today – which again only represent a fraction of the human languages that have been spoken since the African exodus.

As Evans and Levinson (2009) suggest in some detail, decades of research by linguistic fieldworkers and typologists have not yielded substantive linguis-tic universals of the sort many linguists in the mid-twentieth century expected to uncover. Instead, such research has yielded a phenomenal breadth of diversity in the forms and practices associated with language. Much as Henrich, Heine, and Norenzayan (2010) suggest that assumptions of universality vis-à-vis some human cognitive features are based unduly on findings among WEIRD populations, Evans and Levinson (2009) suggest that many expectations of linguistic universals were based in large measure on an over-reliance on European languages. This claim is familiar to many typologically oriented linguists, who have been making it in one form or another for some time. Put differently, an ever-growing number of linguists believe that assumptions of a "universal grammar" were inordinately influenced by the grammar of a small subset of the world's languages. As our knowledge of many non-Indo-European language groups has developed, it has been increasingly difficult to reconcile the relevant data gathered by linguists in the field with beliefs of grammatical homogeneity at any meaningful level. This has led to increasingly abstract formulations of what is universal to human languages (Chomsky [1995]). Hauser, Chomsky, and Fitch (2002) suggest that syntactic recursion is an exceptionless linguistic universal, yet even this feature is apparently not common to all human languages (D. Everett [2005, 2009]).

Members of all cultures have the capacity to learn language. Given the genotypic homogeneity of our species, this is not surprising. We all share common cognitive and perceptual capacities that facilitate the acquisition of speech. Our genes grant us certain features that allow us to learn language, but also to walk, and parse colors, and sounds, and generate various other behaviors that are common to our species. We share certain basic goals and needs as a species. We also share "exposure to salient discontinuities among entities that the world presents to the observer" (Malt and Wolff [2010:9]), for instance between water and earth, earth and sky, and the like. Yet, despite all that we share as a species, we are also a remarkably diverse one. In fact, some researchers have suggested that the most distinguishing characteristic of our species is its behavioral diversity. In the words of Prinz (2012:xi), for instance, "Human beings are genetically more homogenous than chimps, but behaviorally more diverse than any other species."

In the face of our genetic similarity, and the universal features of our environments, goals, and needs, it is perhaps not surprising that there are some basic commonalities shared by *many* languages. Also, relationships between languages and contact between unrelated languages have resulted in many other linguistic commonalities. In fact, given such motivations for linguistic similarity, the range of existing linguistic diversity is particularly noteworthy. After all, while there are certain statistical tendencies for "conditional" patterns in the world's languages (Greenberg [1966], Dryer [2003]), there are no uncontested "unconditional" linguistic universals. Furthermore, conditional or implicational patterns in the world's languages simply demonstrate that some linguistic features are more marked than others, and such markedness is often of a trivial sort. For instance, I could make the following true claim: "If a language has a word for the number seventeen, it must also have a word for the number one." This implicational universal holds true, but it is obviously vacuous. As Evans and Levinson (2009:438) suggest, once less vacuous conditional universals are examined, many are confronted with exceptions despite the fact that the vast majority of the languages that have ever existed are undocumented.

In those cases where implicational patterns are universally valid, they can frequently be explained by the greater processing cost of the antecedent with respect to the consequent (Haspelmath [2009]). For instance, with respect to the implicational universal just cited, it is more difficult to conceptualize "seventeen" than "one". More importantly, there are no substantive, non-implicational universals accepted by the all linguists. We cannot even claim, for instance, that all languages have vowels or consonants, since many languages are signed. We might claim that all spoken languages have vowels, but this illustrates another issue with some statements on universality: they are arguably tautological. If people use language in the vocal-auditory channel, then they must vibrate their vocal cords and open their mouths to be heard at most distances. So by necessity any language associated with this channel must have vowels – it would be pratically inaudible otherwise. Furthermore, some (though by no means all) implicational universals are based on such tautological expressions. Consider the following implicational, which is familiar to many linguists yet arguably meaningless:

"If a language has nasal vowels, then it has oral vowels."

Given that the consequent of this implication ("then it has oral vowels") is circularly exceptionless in spoken languages, any antecedent could be placed before it for the entire implicational to hold logically. For instance, these other candidate conditional universals are equally valid:

"If a language has forty-three adjectives, then it has oral vowels."

"If a language is spoken by agriculturalists, then it has oral vowels."

Ad infinitum.

In short, the search for meaningful universal aspects of the grammars of languages has been a largely frustrating one for linguists. Candidate universals such as constituency, recursion, and word order patterns are inevitably met with exceptions of various kinds (Evans and Levinson [2009], Croft [2001]). The absence of clear universals is particularly remarkable in the light of the sample of languages used to corroborate their absence: a very small percentage of the languages that *homo sapiens* has employed during its history. Furthermore, those in existence today have clearly affected each other in pervasive and demonstrable ways, resulting in some cases in linguistic tendencies that occasionally give the impression of universality with respect to some feature.[11]

Much as it is difficult to establish universal features of language, it is difficult to establish whether certain parts of the brain are genetically wired for linguistic tasks. While particular cortical areas such as Broca's and Wernicke's have long been known to correlate with certain linguistic abilities, people without these areas are capable of learning language, assuming the areas in question are removed very early during life–even in the extreme cases of hemispherectomies. Given the plasticity of the human cortex, many of its regions can be adopted for language usage. Furthermore, the results from neuroimaging studies paint a murky picture with respect to the cortical loci of language (Fedorenko and Kanwisher [2009]), and researchers are only now beginning to appreciate the importance of non-cortical anatomy, such as the basal ganglia, in linguistic functioning. (Lieberman [2007]) In a related vein, just as it is difficult to pinpoint areas of the brain specifically associated with language, it is also difficult to pinpoint particular genes associated with this human behavior. One oft-cited candidate "language gene" is FOXP2. While adaptations in the FOXP2 gene may have played a role in the development of language, though, this gene itself is common to many nonlinguistic mammals and its precise role in language production is far from clear.

Clearly it is difficult if not impossible to establish universal features associated with language, either in human speech or in human biology. Obviously, there are many universal aptitudes and capacities that relate to language, and there are certain common tendencies evident in the grammars of spoken languages. Such tendencies do not preclude the possibility of extensive linguistic variation, though, and as we focus increasingly on non-European languages, the visible wealth of diversity is impressive. Next we attempt to illustrate the sort of linguistic diversity that actually exists in the world's spoken languages. The illustrations given may be unfamiliar to non-linguists, some of whom have been led to believe that "the grammars and lexicons of all languages are

---

11 See for example the suggestions made by Dunn et al. (2011) vis-à-vis word order patterns. As the authors of that study note, lineage-specific tendencies point to socio-cultural and human-interactive factors determining linguistic structure in very real stock-dependent ways.

broadly similar." (Li and Gleitman [2002]) It is worth re-stressing that the ultimate goal of this entire discussion of linguistic diversity is to consider whether the typological data are consistent with the notion of linguistic relativity. After all, for the linguistic relativity hypothesis to even begin to hold water, there must be evidence for non-trivial variation in cognition and language across human populations.

Perhaps the most obvious way in which spoken languages diverge is through their sounds. At the coarsest level we can note that a language may have as few as eleven basic meaningful units of sound, for instance in the case of Pirahã and Rotokas. (Though these units may take different forms depending on their contexts, i.e. phonemes may exhibit extensive allophonic variation.) The phonemic inventories of these languages contrast markedly with a language such as !Xóõ, a Khoisan language with over one hundred phonemes.[12] (Maddieson [1984]) Admittedly these cases are statistical outliers, but they serve to illustrate the point that languages vary tremendously in terms of size of their sets of basic sounds. In many cases as well, languages differ in the way these phonemes are distributed. Some dialects of English, for example, have over twenty vowel phonemes and over twenty consonantal phonemes. While the overall number of phonemes in English is not particularly remarkable, the relatively high number of vowel types is.

Not only does the number of sounds vary from language to language, but the types of sounds used also vary. This range of sound types relates to every part of the human vocal tract, beginning with the vocal cords. As is well known, in many languages the fundamental frequency at which a speaker's vocal cords vibrate (pitch) can be used differentially to change meaning. In fact, over half the world's languages exhibit such tonality (Ladefoged and Maddieson [1996]). Yet to speakers of many languages, tone distinctions are notoriously difficult to learn. Furthermore, many languages require other kinds of vocal cord modulation in order to create meaning contrasts. For instance, the arytenoid cartilages in the larynx can be drawn closely together in order to create particularly tense vocal cords. This laryngealization causes the cords to

---

12 As Port (2007) suggests, the concept of the phoneme itself may be too heavily based on the Western tradition of segmenting sounds into letter-size units. According to Port, our alphabetic tradition gives the impression that such sounds are basic to language, an impression that is actually difficult to support with acoustic or experimental data. Syllables may be more meaningful units of sound to speakers of unwritten languages, or those with non-alphabetic traditions. After all, the difference between many plosives and fricatives are inaudible in the absence of adjacent vowels with characteristically influenced fundamental frequency harmonics known as vowel "formants" (Sussman et al. [1999], Everett [2008]). In other words, consonant-vowel clusters are difficult to tease apart perceptually and articulatorily.

vibrate more slowly than in cases of normal voicing, and creates a distinctive creaky sound. Such laryngealization is used to create meaning contrasts in some languages, for instance Danish, but is completely absent in others. The vocal cords can be used in other ways as well, for instance in "breathy" sounds. For a discussion of the range of ways in which vocal cord movement is altered across languages, see Ladefoged and Maddieson (1996).

Another very basic manner in which the languages of the world exhibit phonetic/sound-based diversity is in the range of airstream mechanisms they utilize. To create sound in the vocal tract, air must pass through it. The most natural way for an airstream to be generated would seem to be via compression of the lungs, and in fact an egressive pulmonic airstream is utilized for most sound types. Yet languages utilize three other airstream types also. In the case of the clicks of many sub-Saharan languages, for instance, air runs into the mouth after occlusion is created at two points in the oral cavity. This double occlusion results in a small chamber of air, whose size is then increased to reduce air pressure. When the occlusion closest to the front of the mouth is released, air rushes in to fill the chamber of lowered pressure, creating the popping or clicking sound. In the case of "ejective" sounds, found in many languages of the Pacific Northwest and elsewhere, air is ejected out of the mouth after pressure on an analogous chamber of air is increased rather than decreased. This chamber is created by closing the glottis at the same time occlusion is made at some location in the supralaryngeal tract. The glottis is then raised, the occlusion is released, and air is ejected from the mouth. Finally, implosives (common to Southeast Asia and found in other regions) are generated in a similar manner to ejectives, except in the case of the former sound type the glottis is lowered prior to the opening of the air chamber. The net result is a rush of air into the mouth. Spoken languages utilize an impressive variety of airstream mechanisms in their production, especially considering the clear physical bias towards using an egressive pulmonic airstream.[13]

We are beginning to get some sense of the phonetic diversity that exists in human languages, and we have not even considered the most obvious and significant way in which human languages vary according to this dimension: the manner in which people use their supralaryngeal articulators to make sounds. These articulators include the tip, blade, and root of the tongue, as well as the lips, teeth, and soft palate. The articulators are brought into contact or near contact with various parts of the vocal tract, and manipulated in other

---

13 Only the pulmonic airstream causes air to rush past the vocal cords in such a way as to create reduced air pressure across the vocal cords (via Bernoulli's effect), causing them to vibrate together in order to make the loud voiced sounds so crucial to language.

ways, in an as-yet-undefined number of ways. In other words, it is unclear how many sounds exist in the world's languages. A glance at the chart of the International Phonetic Association may give the impression that there is a fixed set of sounds in the world's languages, but this chart is merely a heuristic tool used to transcribe, sometimes approximately, languages' consonants and vowels.

Suffice it to say that, given that humans share tongues, alveolar ridges, teeth, soft palates, and the like, we appear to exploit this biology to the extent that is biologically permissible in the creation of dissimilar sounds. There are some crosslinguistic tendencies in the creation of meaningful sounds. These tendencies typically have clear articulatory or perceptual motivations, as evidenced by the commonality of contrasts between easily distinguishable vowels made with the tongue positioned in the back or the front of the mouth, respectively, and the commonality of sounds made with the lips or tongue tip. Despite such motivations for commonality, however, humans exploit their vocal tracts in a remarkable variety of ways during the production of speech. This variety is so extreme that the careful inspection of any one particular language often turns up uncommon or unique phonetic characteristics.

For an example of this, let me return to Karitiâna, an Amazonian language I have spent a fair amount of time investigating. One of the interesting things about the language, which is readily noticeable if you are attempting to transcribe it, is that certain words can be pronounced in very different ways from one utterance to another, by the same speaker. Some words with nasal sounds, produced with a lowered velum (soft palate), can vary in seemingly random ways. In particular, bi-syllabic words with nasals in the onset of the second syllable exhibit this variation. The word for 'thing', for example, can be produced as *kinda, kida,* or *kidnda.* The word for 'waist' can be pronounced as *senda, seda,* or *sednda.* Analogous examples abound. In most languages, such variation is impermissible. If you frequently pronounced an English word such as 'summer' as 'sumber' or 'submber', listeners would be puzzled. So why is such variation permitted in Karitiâna? Systematic acoustic analysis of many such words, produced by a number of speakers, suggests that the duration with which the Karitiâna lower their velum in such words is largely random. Basically the language does not insist on neat nasal sounds of a given duration. (Everett [2011a]) Since there are no other clearly documented cases of this sort of nasal pattern, Karitiâna may be unique in this respect. Crucially though, it is very non-unique in its utilization of a unique sound pattern. The point is that, whenever linguists look very carefully at the sound systems of relatively little-documented indigenous languages, they often uncover sound patterns that were previously unknown. It so happens that I have spent time analyzing the Karitiâna sound system. Had I spent time investigating some other indigenous language I might well be able to provide some unique feature of that language's sounds. The frequency with which field linguists uncover such unusual phenomena hints at the extreme diversity of sound patterns in the world's languages. In fact, many phoneticians are skeptical of the notion that there is some describable basic inventory of sounds in human languages. (Port and Leary [2005]) Many phonologists who have considered the wealth of data on sound diversity are equally skeptical that such a list could be generated (Pierrehumbert [2001], Bybee [2001]). In the most comprehensive survey of linguistic sounds to date, Ladefoged and Maddieson (1996:369) note that "the next generation of speakers... may even create sounds that have never been used in a human language before." In short, while humans share the same vocal apparatus, they exploit it in such diverse ways that it is impossible to place an upper limit on the kinds of sounds we make.

In illustrating the extremity of extant diversity in spoken languages, it makes sense to start at the lowest level, variation in the meaningful sounds produced and heard by humans. Physically at least, spoken language consists of sound waves transferred from the vocal tract of speakers to the inner ears of listeners. If extreme variation in the form of these acoustic signals exists, this variation may point to extensive variation at higher-level stages of language production and comprehension. Nevertheless, in principle this sound-pattern diversity could exist without concomitant variation at such higher levels. If linguistic variation plays a role in cognitive variation, though, there should also be evidence for significant crosslinguistic diversity in the semantic structures of lexicons, not to mention profound crosslinguistic diversity in morphological and syntactic patterns. In fact evidence for such diversity abounds. We will discuss several sorts of lexical variation during the course of this book. Suffice it to say that languages differ in how they demarcate many lexical domains including "color, space, body parts, motion, emotion, mental states, causality, and ordinary household containers" (Malt and Wolff [2010:5]). For now we survey some morphosyntactic variation via the consideration of some particularly salient examples of grammatical diversity.[14]

At the level of morphology, languages exhibit an impressive array of basic word structure types. Some languages allow words to consist of a long string of concatenated morphemes. Consider the following word from the aboriginal language Bininj Gun-wok (cited in Evans and Levinson [2009]): *abanyawoih-warrgahmarneganjginjeng*. This word is best translated with an entire clause

---

14 Interested readers unfamiliar with such variation may wish to consult typologically oriented surveys of morphosyntactic phenomena (e.g. Payne [1997], Givón [1984]).

in English: "I cooked the wrong meat for them again." The Bininj Gun-wok word is equivalent in meaning, but consists of a number of morphemes that cannot occur independently as in the English clause – this difference is not simply a matter of orthographic convention. Typologists refer to a language like Bininj Gun-wok as an extremely polysynthetic language, meaning that it allows words to consist of a large number of morphemes. English also allows words to have more than one morpheme, though not to the same extent. In the English translation just cited, the word 'cooked' has two morphemes, one denoting a type of event ('cook'), and the other indexing when that event occurred ('-ed'). Clearly, though, English is less polysynthetic than Bininj Gun-wok. Many languages allow even less morpheme synthesis than English. At the other end of the continuum of polysynthesis, when contrasted to languages like Bininj Gun-wok, are isolating languages such as Mandarin. In such languages, few if any words consist of more than one morpheme. In other words, seemingly basic categories such as tense and number, which English expresses via verbal and nominal suffixes, respectively, are not denoted via word inflections. So while some languages are particularly polysynthetic, others are isolating, and most fall somewhere in between. It is difficult to imagine how languages could vary more along this dimension.

In addition, languages allow morphemes to be attached to words in every way conceivable. The most common kinds of affixes are prefixes and suffixes, both of which are evident in an English word such as 'deconfigured'. It might seem that the beginnings and ends of words are the only places where affixes might be attached. It turns out, however, that languages also allow affixes to occur word-medially. This strategy is popular in particular among Austronesian languages. For example, in Bontok the word *fikas* means to 'be strong', while the word *fumikas* means to 'become strong'. (Payne [1997:30]) In other words, a *-um-* infix is employed to denote the transitional sense of the latter word. Languages also utilize morphemes that are comprised of two segments, one of which is obligatorily attached to the front of a root and the other of which is obligatorily added to the end of the root. The most well known example of a circumfix (to speakers of European languages anyway) is likely that denoting the past participle in German verbs such as *gespielt*. The root in this case is the verb *spielen*, 'to play', to which the circumfix *ge–t* is attached at both ends.

Clearly, there is extensive variation in morphological form across the world's languages. Some languages don't allow more than one morpheme per word, others allow a few, and others allow a large number. For those languages that allow the combination of multiple morphemes in one word, this combination may occur in a variety of ways. Some of these, such as prosodic combinations, have not even been touched on here.

Morphological diversity is not simply of matter of different kinds of forms, however. Such diversity also surfaces in a way that more obviously impinges on the issue of linguistic relativity, namely the variety of semantic and pragmatic categories denoted morphologically. Here the diversity is even more impressive. Consider a category as seemingly basic as tense. In English we have tense suffixes denoting whether an event occurred in the past, present, or future. It may be difficult to imagine verbs without such tense inflection. Yet tense inflection is much less basic than it may seem, and as many as half of the world's languages lack this morphological category (Bybee [1985]). Furthermore, those that do code for tense do so in myriad ways. Languages with past, present, and future distinctions are in the decided minority, and many languages appeal to a two-way distinction between future and non-future or past and non-past. In Karitiâna, for example, the future/non-future strategy is adopted. The word *ytakatat* means 'I went/am going' (though usually the former). When an *–i* future suffix is added, the resultant word *ytakatari* means 'I will go'. Verbs without a suffix denote events that are not in the future, and verbs with an *-i* suffix denote events that are. While there are only two tense distinctions in Karitiâna and many other languages, there are three in English, and even more in others. For instance, in Yagua there are seven tenses indexed morphologically (Payne [1997:236]).

Seemingly basic meaning categories such as tense and number vary significantly across languages, but the morphological instantiation of such categories is itself quite common, i.e. many languages have tense and number distinctions of some kind. There is another sort of morphological variation, though, variation in the kinds of categories to which individual languages appeal. Many category types only occur in a small subset of human languages. One sort of category that occurs in approximately a quarter of the world's languages is direct "evidentiality" (Aikhenvald [2004]). Evidential morphemes are used to denote the manner in which the information described in a clause was ascertained. For example, in the New Guinean language Fasu, a verbal circumfix must be used to denote information that was gathered visually. The word *a-pe-re* means 'I see it coming'. The root in this case, *pe*, means 'come'. The remainder of the meaning is conveyed via the visual evidential circumfix. (Loeweke and May [1980:71]) In the Muskogean language Koasati, on the other hand, an auditory evidential is often employed. The verb *aksóhka-ha*, for example, might be uttered when something nearby is charring. In this case the *–ha* suffix at the end of the word denotes the fact that the speaker can *hear* something charring. (Kimball [1991:207])

Many inflectional categories are less common than evidential affixes, for instance desiderative affixes. Such affixes are employed when speakers express someone's desire, likely their own, for a particular event to occur. In Karitiâna, for example, the verbal suffix *–wak* serves this function. So while the verb *pyt'y* means 'to eat', the verb *pyt'ywak* means 'want to eat'. Suffixes with similar functions are employed in languages such as Japanese and Sanskrit, yet desideratives are not particularly common.

More unusual categories are not hard to uncover either. One category that is familiar to linguists but is relatively uncommon is *mirativity*. Mirative morphemes are employed to denote events whose occurrence was somehow unexpected. In Turkish, for example, a suffix *–mIs* is attached to verbs in such cases. If it is attached to the verb root *gel* meaning 'to come', for example, the speaker is denoting an arrival that surprised them: *Kemal gel-mIs* means 'Kemal, surprisingly, came'. (Payne [1997:255])

The categories discussed here are of course just a sample of those evident in the morphologies of the world's languages. Numerous other morphological distinctions could be adduced, many of which would seem exotic to speakers of English. As linguists have begun to analyze data from a greater sample of the world's languages, they have confronted a greater range of morphological diversity. This is not to suggest that certain tendencies do not surface – as in the case of sounds they certainly do. For instance, more languages express tense distinctions than evidentiality distinctions. Languages utilize suffixes at a greater rate than infixes. And so on. Nevertheless, despite such tendencies, there is no clear upper limit on the number of morphological categories exhibited by the world's existing languages, not to mention the sum of all languages ever spoken.

A similar conclusion can be reached with respect to the last branch of phenomena treated in this brief survey of linguistic diversity: syntax. The most obvious syntactic sort of diversity evident in crosslinguistic surveys is the broad range of word orders permitted by the world's languages. If we take transitive sentences that consist of a subject, object, and verb,[15] for instance, the word order of English is typically S-V-O, e.g. "The jaguar ate the person." It is often difficult or impossible to establish the basic word order of a given language, though, and English is a particularly clear-cut case. Even if we restrict our attention to those cases where some sort of basic word order can be arrived at, there is remarkable variability across languages. (Dryer [1997]) It seems clear that, of the six orders in which S, V, and O can occur, some are more common than others. SOV ordering such as that evident in Japanese or Turkish is quite

---

15 Such terms are descriptively useful, but are not meant to imply universality. What is a subject in one language is not necessarily reified grammatically in another. See, for example, the discussions in Croft (2001).

common, as is SVO. VSO ordering is also not uncommon, and VOS has been attested for some time. Until the 1970's it was theorized that object-initial default word orders did not exist. As in so many other cases of claims regarding universal characteristics of language, however, such supposedly impermissible features eventually cropped up. In this case, several exceptions surfaced in Amazonia, most famously the Hixkaryana language (Derbyshire [1979]), whose most basic word order is O-V-S. In this language, the back-translation to a clause such as "The jaguar ate the person," would read something like "The person ate the jaguar." Hixkaryana speakers comprehend the last noun of the clause to represent the entity performing rather than undergoing a given action.

Equally extreme examples of syntactic variation, at least from the perspective of speakers of a language such as English that is characterized by rigid word order, are those cases in which languages permit words to come in any number of orders. Latin is perhaps the most famous case of such a "free word order" language. What is particularly remarkable about such languages is that their so-called constituents (like noun phrases or verb phrases) can be separated by other words. In clause (2.1) an adjective occurs at the opposite end of the clause with respect to the noun it modifies:

(2.1)	ultima	Cumaei	venit	iam	carminis	aetas
	last	Cumae	come	now	song	Age

'The last age of the Cumaean song has now arrived.' (Matthews [1981:255], cited also in Evans and Levinson [2009:441])

This clause represents just one of the many permissible orders in which these same words could be strung together. Such clauses were intelligible to Latin speakers since the language utilized an extensive case system to disambiguate semantic roles. In general, languages with extensive case systems are less reliant on conventionalized word orders for the expression of meaning.

Another major way in which languages exhibit syntactic diversity, and the last we will consider here, is through variation in the sorts of "pivots" they employ. The term pivot refers to a syntactic characteristic that typically correlates with the semantic agent and the pragmatic topic in a given clause. These attributes are often combined into a category called "subject", but in the case of a number of languages they are not. The syntactic pivot surfaces when a gap in a given clause refers implicitly to a preceding overt noun phrase. For example, in the clause "The woman slapped the man and Ø laughed," the gapped or implicit element (Ø) refers to the agent of the clause, the woman. Speakers of English omit the second occurrence of "the woman" and do not need to refer to her pronominally either. In Dyirbal (Dixon 1972), the translation of this clause would take the following form: *yibinggu yara bunjun Ø miyandanyu*. Here, though, the "gap" or omitted element refers not to the woman (*yibinggu*) but to the man (*yara*). In other words, the syntactic pivot in Dyirbal does *not* link an omitted element with the preceding agent, in this case the person doing the slapping. This sort of gapping strategy is part of a larger phenomenon known as ergativity (Dixon [1994]), a phenomenon that has caused many linguists to question whether the notion of "subject" is universal to all languages. At the least such examples have allowed linguists to realize that the syntactic pivots in some languages (e.g. English) are associated with agents, and in a much smaller number of languages (e.g. Dyirbal) they are associated with the entities that are undergoing an action (in the case in question, being slapped). In some languages, the syntactic pivot is unlike either that in English or Dyirbal, since it is not definitively associated with either the agent or the undergoer of an action. Karitiâna represents just such a case. When clauses are decontextualized the pivot is completely ambiguous. Consider (2.2):

(2.2) nonso   nakamit   taso   pyrypykynan   Ø
       woman   hit   man   ran   (gap)[16]
       'The woman hit the man and she/he ran.'

As we see in this example, the gapped element at the end of the clause may refer to either antecedent noun phrase, either the man or the woman. Karitiâna speakers rely on contextual cues to establish co-reference in such cases.

The syntactic pivot strategies utilized by languages clearly evince a profound sort of diversity. As in the case of object-initial word orders, the discovery of non-agentively-oriented pivots violated the expectations of many. This discovery, like that of unusual word orders, resulted from the careful description of lesser-known languages.

While we have only surveyed a few morphological and syntactic phenomena, the preceding examples serve to make our point: the diversity of morphosyntax evident in the world's languages is extreme, and often violates expectations based on centuries of careful examination of European languages. This extreme diversity is only apparent once unrelated languages in far-flung corners of the world are analyzed in detail. In the light of such diversity, the suggestion that linguistic diversity may play some role in cognitive diversity does not seem implausible. It seems quite possible, for instance, that Dyirbal speakers, Karitiâna speakers, and English speakers may conceptualize aspects of agency in different ways, given that their languages' syntactic pivots require

---

16 This is a simplified gloss, omitting morphemes that are irrelevant to this discussion.

them to index agency to varying degrees. While I have no experimental support for this suggestion, the idea does not seem particularly implausible in the light of the linguistic data.

There are common constraints on language production and comprehension shared by all humans, e.g. restrictions of short and long-term memory, limitations in the innervation of muscles used in articulation, biological constraints on the ability to perceptually discriminate certain acoustic signals, etc. Nevertheless, languages are so diverse that it is increasingly difficult for linguists to maintain once-commonly-held assumptions about many linguistic categories. One noted typologically oriented linguist describes the current state of affairs as follows:

> Thus, descriptive linguists still have no choice but to adopt the Boasian approach of positing special language-particular categories for each language. Theorists often resist it, but the crosslinguistic evidence is not converging on a smallish set of possibly innate categories. On the contrary, almost every newly described language presents us with some "crazy" new category that hardly fits existing taxonomies. (Haspelmath [2007:119])

Haspelmath's claims are made in the light of the extensive and ever-growing surveys of the lexical-grammatical structures of the world's languages, most prominently the *World Atlas of Linguistic Structures* (Haspelmath et al. [2011]).

In addition to the diverse practices associated with language acquisition across the world's cultures (Ochs and Schieffelin [1983]), and the diverse patterns associated with discourse, verbal play, and verbal art (Hymes [2001]), diversity in the *structure* of spoken languages clearly abounds. And of course linguistic diversity extends beyond spoken languages, as we have noted, since language can be produced with the hands, or heard in a series of beeps, or understood by touching a series of bumps, or read with ideograms, or read with sound-based symbols, etc. Perhaps the single most impressive feature of human language is in fact the diversity it exhibits.

2.4 Conclusion

In this chapter we have drawn attention to some of the variation in human cognition across cultures, and also to the extreme variation that characterizes extant spoken languages–which represent only a slice of the language pie that has existed to date. Based on the extent of these two broad sorts of variation, we conclude that the hypothesis that linguistic variation plays some role in fostering cognitive variation is not implausible. Nevertheless, it is a hypothesis that requires empirical substantiation, and the mere existence of cognitive and linguistic variation does not constitute substantiation.

3 Refining methodology

3.1 Methodological issues to be addressed

In this chapter we discuss some of the methodological implements currently available in the toolkits of researchers concerned with exploring a causal role of linguistic variance in cases of cross-cultural cognitive variance. These implements have been honed so as to address the issues sometimes associated with work on this topic, particularly the three primary issues outlined in the first chapter: "circularity", "confirmation bias", and the "apparent inextricability of linguistic influences on thought".

Well-established diversities of the sort discussed in the preceding chapter suggest that a relativistic account is not precluded by factors such as the putative universality of language, or the psychological homogeneity of humankind. Since such universality and homogeneity is still often presupposed, our first task was to dispel such notions. Nevertheless, even if one accepts the suggestion made above and elsewhere in the literature that significant cognitive and linguistic diversity exist across human populations, this acknowledgement does not necessitate the acceptance of meaningful linguistic effects on nonlinguistic cognition. It is possible after all that cultural-historical factors, aside from language, have helped foster both linguistic diversity and cognitive diversity, and that linguistic diversity has not played any role in promoting cognitive diversity.

How then do we establish that there exists a relationship between the two sorts of diversity we have delineated, particularly in the unidirectional sense we are concerned with here, i.e. how do we establish that linguistic diversity itself helps to promote cognitive diversity? This is actually a tricky question to answer definitively, and the truth is that there are clear methodological obstacles, some of which were outlined in Chapter 1, that must be circumvented in careful research on this issue. In his discussions of work on the linguistic relativity hypothesis, and in his re-envisioning of contemporary work on the subject, Lucy (1992a, 1997, 2004) presents a tripartite distinction of basic methodological strategies adopted in studies on the subject. According to Lucy, such strategies can be categorized as "structure-centered", "domain-centered", or "behavior-centered", and each of these approaches has characteristic strengths and weaknesses. This categorization serves as a useful starting point for our discussion of methodology (though not all studies surveyed in this book fit naturally into one of these categories), so let us address each in turn.

"Structure-centered" approaches are characterized by a focus on some set of differences between given languages. The assumption of those adopting this approach, traditionally at least, is that different semantic structures in two or more given languages implicitly reflect differences in the conceptions of their speakers with respect to relevant ontological categories. This approach characterizes Whorf's research, for instance his work on the construal of time among English and Hopi speakers. Whorf (1956) noted, for example, that English speakers treat temporal units as discrete substances via their denotation as nouns, e.g. days, months, years, etc. Hopi speakers, according to Whorf, construe time in a less discrete manner, judging from the way temporal events are indexed in Hopi. Accepting for the moment Whorf's claims on Hopi grammar, though, the limitations of a strict structure-centered approach are evident: As discussed in Chapter 1, in order to make claims about the nonlinguistic cognition of a language's speakers, we actually need evidence outside the linguistic realm. Claims for linguistic relativity based entirely on a language's structure are patently circular. Fortunately, the structure-centered approach has been refined and expanded. While still utilizing structural differences between languages as a point of departure, researchers adopting this approach now use relevant linguistic differences to generate hypotheses on nonlinguistic cognitive dissimilarities, and then test these hypotheses experimentally with nonverbal tasks. A variety of studies surveyed in this book could be considered structure-centered according to Lucy's taxonomy.

Rather than utilizing a given set of differences between languages as a point of departure, "domain-centered" studies are focused from the outset on a particular cognitive or experiential domain, for instance the categorization of color or the perception of space. Researchers survey the manner in which the given domain is encoded linguistically in a number of languages, in order to ascertain whether there is indirect linguistic evidence for differentiated conceptualization of the domain in question. One potential weakness of the domain-centered approach is the same as that noted for the structure-centered approach, namely that researchers may restrict their attention to the linguistic encoding of a particular domain, and draw conclusions on nonlinguistic cognition based on linguistic differences only. Ironically perhaps, the most notable misstep in the literature associated with this approach resulted in strong anti-relativistic claims. As we will see in greater detail in Chapter 7, a number of findings on color naming across the world's languages demonstrated that there were implicational universals in the way in which color terms are coded linguistically. These universal linguistic encoding strategies were taken as strong evidence that color perception does not vary across human populations. While some experimental work seemed to offer support for this claim (Rosch 1972), the claims on universal patterns of color construal were based primarily on the linguistic data associated with this domain. Once careful experimental work on the actual perception of color was undertaken, though, cross-group differences in color perception began to surface. It turns out these differences correspond with differences in color terms, despite the existence of common lexical patterns associated with the domain. The domain-centered approach has more recently been employed in dozens of studies on spatial orientation, some of which are discussed in the following chapter.[17]

The "behavior-centered" approach adopts a different tack, and is focused on explaining some noticeable difference in the behavior of two human populations by uncovering a linguistic source for the noticed behavioral difference. One example of this approach is Bloom's (1981, 1984) work on counterfactual reasoning, discussed in Chapter 10. Bloom began with the observation that Chinese speakers exhibited difficulty in answering questions requiring counterfactual or hypothetical reasoning. With this observation in hand, he sought a linguistic explanation, and concluded that the differentiated way in which counterfactuals are marked in English and Mandarin plausibly explained the poor performance of the Chinese respondents. To his credit, he provided experimental data in support of this conclusion, however the stimuli used in the experiments were subsequently shown to be problematic (Au [1983], Liu [1985]). Nevertheless, one gets a sense from Bloom's work of the form of the behavior-centered approach. This approach has been adopted in other work, but most contemporary work on linguistic relativity cannot be characterized as behavior-centered. Perhaps this is the case because the approach suffers from an over-reliance on post-hoc reasoning: If one is searching for a linguistic motivator for behavioral differences that have already been observed, *some* linguistic difference might surface as a viable candidate. Yet the selection of such a candidate on intuitive grounds does not preclude the possibility that a number of other cultural or linguistic factors might be involved. Most contemporary work takes a more subtle tack of beginning with linguistic differences, perhaps associated with a given domain only, and generating testable hypotheses on how such differences in language might foster differences in cognition. The choice to begin with behavioral differences runs the risk of generating more deterministic-like claims on the interaction of language and behavior, while potentially ignoring other factors that might motivate the behavioral disparities in question.

---

17 In this book categories of experiential and cognitive domains like color perception, quantity recognition, and the like, are treated separately. Structuring our discussions according to domains allows for us to consider the relevant work in cohesive chunks. It should be noted, though, that many of the individual studies considered are not "domain-centered" when considered in isolate.

The three broad approaches described by Lucy are useful starting points in a discussion of methodology, though like many heuristic taxonomies this tripartite grouping represents somewhat of an oversimplification. After all, many contemporary studies exhibit characteristics of more than one approach. For example, in our discussion of quantity recognition among speakers of the anumeric language Pirahã (in Chapter 6), we will see that the relevant studies are in some sense structure-centered, domain-centered, and behavior-centered. Much of the initial impetus for understanding numerical cognition among the Pirahã owed itself to outsiders' observations of their behavior. Later careful descriptions of the structure of terms for approximate quantities in their language further motivated experimental work on their quantity discrimination abilities, by several researchers (including myself). These careful descriptions were informed by other studies in the semantic domain of quantity representation, across numerous languages. So the studies on Pirahã numerical cognition could be considered structure-centered, domain-centered, behavior-centered, or some combination thereof.

Ultimately, studies on linguistic relativity should arrive at some similar place involving claims about the interaction between linguistic structure and nonlinguistic cognition, associated with a particular experiential domain and possibly with overt behavioral norms. With this similar end-point in mind we might think of the three suggested major methodological approaches as descriptions of starting points only, e.g. rather than characterizing a study as structure-*centered*, we might characterize it as structure-*motivated*. Differing initial foci may draw attention to potentially relativistic processes in divergent fashions, but once that attention is generated, the resultant studies should hopefully offer something for all concerned about the nexus of language and other types of cognitive processes.

It is by now clear that systematic investigations on linguistic relativity, whether motivated by structural or behavioral disparities, or concerned with better understanding a given experiential domain, are a recent innovation. Given the various ramifications of a careful understanding of linguistic influences on thought, this recency is perhaps puzzling. The motivations for the recency are in some cases theoretical, as discussed in the first chapter. They are also methodological, though. Ultimately careful examinations of potential cases of relativity entail both detailed linguistic fieldwork and the concomitant adoption of experimental tools and associated statistical analyses. These sorts of methods, the linguistic and the experimental, differ significantly in practice. The fact of the matter is that many linguists are well equipped for describing languages, but unfamiliar with the methods common to psychologists and others who commonly undertake experimental tasks on human cognitive processes. Conversely, many of the latter camp are unfamiliar with the detailed linguistic analysis that is foundational for some studies on the interaction of language structure and thought. This is somewhat inevitable, as it would of course be impracticable for all those interested in human cognition to be familiar with the minutia of morphosyntactic analyses. And extensive understanding of experimental and statistical methods would offer little payback to the research program of many field linguists. Whether or not this characterization holds going forward is another matter, however. Many graduate programs in linguistics now require students to take courses on experimental methods that are common to other branches of the social and cognitive sciences. Furthermore, there is an ever-growing reliance on quantitative approaches to linguistic analysis.[18] (Johnson [2008], Eddington [2009]) Despite the trend towards greater sharing of methods across fields in the cognitive sciences, though, for some time there has been inadequate cross-disciplinary interaction, and this inadequacy at least partially explains the recency of serious inquiries into linguistic relativity.

So how can experimental methods and traditional descriptive tools be utilized synergistically to arrive at a better understanding of the issues? The short answer to this question is that there are a number of ways, and these ways will only become sufficiently clear during the remainder of this book, as the strategies of various researchers are considered in turn. Still, we can sketch here some of the recurring strategies evident in the studies. First, researchers must establish the way in which two (or more languages) differ lexically or morphosyntactically. This is done via original fieldwork, or through the examination of previous reliable field studies. The challenges of linguistic fieldwork, particularly that carried out with little-documented languages in remote locales, are numerous. Once the onerously acquired results of such work are scrutinized, some significant differences between the described language and some other described language(s) (often a widely spoken Indo-European one) inevitably surface. These differences may relate to some other aspect of the culture in question, and ethnographic accounts may play a crucial role in establishing whether there is some behavioral feature of the society in question that correlates with the linguistic divergence. In some cases, though, researchers may be interested in a linguistic feature that would not be expected to

---

18 In some linguistic fields such as quantitative sociolinguistics (e.g. Labov [1966, 2001]) or experimental phonetics (e.g. Beddor and Strange [1982], Solé, Beddor, and Ohala [2007]), such methods were adopted some time ago. However in work on morphology and syntax, which more directly relates to the subject of linguistic relativity, this adoption has generally been more recent.

correspond to any overt nonlinguistic facet of the culture in question. Such a feature may in fact prove to be of particular interest, since its subsequent correlation with cognitive variation of some kind is less likely to be ascribable to general cultural factors.

Once the crosslinguistic differences are established, hypotheses may be generated regarding potential nonlinguistic cognitive effects of these differences. This is when the experimental methods prove handy. A nonlinguistic task, or an assortment of such tasks, must be designed and carried out among representative samples of speakers of the languages in question. The kinds of tasks that could be utilized are potentially limitless, but in practice they tend to fall into basic task categories that are familiar to cognitive scientists. These include reaction-time tasks, triad-discrimination tasks, tests of recall, and the like. Once the task or assortment of tasks is run with the populations in questions, the results obtained are quantified. Assuming a quantifiable disparity between populations results, this disparity is tested for statistical significance to establish that the results are not merely due to chance. For results to be considered significant, the odds of their being due to chance must be less than 5% ($p<0.05$) or, more desirably, 1% ($p<0.01$). The statistical tests adopted vary according to the structure of the experimental design, including the number of factors involved, and according to whether the resultant data are parametric or nonparametric. Frequently employed tests include Chi-square, Fisher's exact test, t-tests, analyses of variance (ANOVA's), logistic regression, and other procedures common to the social sciences.

Once a statistically significant disparity between populations is established for a given task or set of tasks, researchers have some evidence that the previously established linguistic disparity may in fact influence nonlinguistic cognition. At this stage, though, the strength of this evidence is debatable. After all, the correlation between a linguistic disparity and a particular nonlinguistic cognitive disparity may be due to some confounding variable. The sorts of potential confounding variables that need to be ruled out vary in accordance with the linguistic features in question, as well as the cultures of the populations being tested. How then do we establish the influence of a linguistic feature on a nonlinguistic feature, when all we have is correlation between the two for a particular task? There are various approaches to circumventing this "correlation" obstacle. One way is to introduce the speakers of one language with a linguistic feature from another, and to see whether this familiarization leads to changes in their nonlinguistic strategies. This approach is adopted for instance in Boroditsky [2001], discussed in Chapter 5. A newer approach is to present stimuli differentially (in a given task) to the two cerebral hemispheres. If the cross-population differences are more pronounced with respect to stimuli presented to the left hemisphere where language primarily resides in most people, this hemispheric effect hints that language disparities are most directly responsible for the differences in nonlinguistic cognition across populations. This approach is exemplified by Gilbert et al. (2006), discussed in Chapter 7.

Some cultural contexts are not amenable to such tactics, however, and in many cases all that can be definitively established is the correlation between a facet of the structure of a language and an aspect of nonlinguistic cognition. Nevertheless, if such linguistic-cognitive correspondence is established via multiple tasks, this correlation may infuse relativistic conclusions with a substantial degree of plausibility. While in theory correlation does not necessitate a causal relationship, the data might be most simply and directly explained via an account suggesting a causal role of language on nonlinguistic thought. In fact, there might be no plausible alternate accounts. The onus is on the researcher(s) in question, of course, to carefully consider and eliminate alternate explanations for their findings, and to convince readers of their interpretation.

Assuming that experiments have demonstrated (at least with some high degree of plausibility) the role of crosslinguistic disparities for a particular cognitive task, yet another lurking factor must be systematically taken into consideration: A linguistic feature could influence the results on a cognitive task, but only because speakers have appealed to language–perhaps as a last resort–to help them complete what may be to them an odd task. In other words, the results may be due to linguistic factors but not because the linguistic feature under investigation typically influences the speakers' nonlinguistic cognition. Instead, the results of the experiment(s) may simply say something about the strategies used by speakers during a given experiment. The adoption of such linguistically influenced strategies in experimental settings is not necessarily insignificant (as it does reflect the influence of language on thought), but it may offer little insight about speakers' day-to-day thought related to the cognitive domain being tested. One way this variable can be accounted for is by designing tasks so that participants cannot develop any one strategy for completing an experiment, or designing tasks so that their relationship to any relevant feature(s) of the participants' language is not transparent. Another way to account for this variable is through the usage of verbal interference during a particular task, in order to prevent respondents from relying on their language faculties simply to complete a given task. If differences across populations persist or are exacerbated during verbal interference, it is easier to make the case that the results are due to general cross-group cognitive differences that have become ingrained through previous linguistic practice, rather than through the use of language during the given task. If the differences disappear once participants are presented with a verbal interference task, however, this finding suggests that the cross-population differences are almost definitely due to linguistic factors. However, such a verbal-interference effect also suggests that the cross-population differences owe themselves to disparate online linguistic processing used during the experiment(s), rather than to deeper, more general cognitive disparities between the groups. The verbal interference method is used for example in Gilbert et al. [2006], examined in Chapter 7.

The methods characterizing this research will crystallize during the surveys presented in chapters four through ten. For now, though, it is worth illustrating the general approach being suggested through the discussion of a brief, hypothetical example. Recall that in the first chapter we noted that Karitiâna has no analog for the word "monkey". Rather than having a cover term for the range of species entailed by that term, speakers of this language use more specific terms for the animals in question, for instance *õrõm* ('ateles paniscus') and *pikõm* ('cebus apella'). We also suggested that certain aspects of the Karitiânas' behavior seem consistent with the notion that they think about these species in very distinct ways, compared to speakers of a language like English that groups them with the common term "monkey". Intuitively at least, the linguistic taxonomy seems to enforce or reenforce the given conceptual taxonomy. How might I investigate this potential linguistic-conceptual connection, though? More specifically, how would I explore the potentially causal role of the linguistic on the conceptual in this case?[19]

The first step, given that the relevant linguistic description is already at our disposal, would be to design a nonlinguistic task to be administered to speakers of Karitiâna and speakers of another language (or languages) with a commonly-appealed-to cover term for "monkey". Ideally this would be the language of another hunter-gatherer Amazonian tribe, allowing us to reduce some of the obvious conflating cultural variables such as degree of familiarity with the monkeys in question. What sort of task might we design to test for disparities in the conceptualization of monkey types? There are numerous candidates, so let me offer one: We could present a series of images of monkeys, perhaps via computer screen, to the two pools of experiment participants. Each speaker would be presented individually with several images at a time, of monkeys from a variety of relevant species familiar to the participants. Perhaps the images might depict portions of the bodies, or the bodies might be visually obstructed to increase confusability. For each presentation of images, one of

---

19 For a more comprehensive discussion of such linguistic-conceptual correspondences across cultures, I refer the reader to the introduction in Enfield (2004).

the images would represent one species, say *ateles paniscus*, and the remainder would represent a different species, say *cebus apella*. For each set of images, the speakers would be told to select the image that most differs from the others, though the images might differ in numerous ways besides monkey species. Now let us assume that, after repeated trials with dozens of image types and groupings, the Karitiâna speakers are found to more consistently discriminate (at a statistically significant rate) images according to e.g. the *ateles paniscus-cebus apella* distinction, while speakers of the other indigenous language(s) in question, with a cover term akin to "monkey", tend to exhibit greater perceptual confusability between the monkey types. Findings on categorical perception suggest unequivocally that people are more likely to confuse members *within* conceptually cohesive categories, so the greater relative confusability of the non-Karitiâna would suggest that those speakers tend to think of the relevant species in a more monolithic manner, when contrasted to the Karitiâna speakers. Put differently, the Karitiâna language might be responsible for its speakers' greater perceptual acuity vis-à-vis the monkey distinctions in question.

Assuming that we uncovered such a significant disparity for the cognitive task in question, how might we best establish that it is most likely due to the linguistic disparity between the two populations? One option might be to familiarize some Karitiâna (perhaps children) with a cover term for "monkey", and to see if their familiarity with such a term had a deleterious effect on their discrimination abilities. In fact, given that many Karitiâna are familiar with the Portuguese term 'macaco', the results based on speakers familiar with this cover term might be contrasted with those unfamiliar with the term. In addition, we might utilize verbal interference during this and other discrimination tasks to eliminate the possibility that participants are using linguistic clues merely as means to complete the unusual tasks in question. Ultimately, we may discover some cross-population differences in the conceptual discrimination of monkey species, and might be able to formulate a plausible account suggesting that the monkey taxonomy of Karitiâna enhances its speakers' species' discrimination abilities. Or perhaps the results may suggest nothing of the sort. It is quite possible in fact (and to some reading this, extremely likely) that no significant cross-population disparities would surface through such a task. Until such tasks are conducted though, we certainly have little to offer in the way of a concrete relativistic account.

This is a completely illustrative exercise, of course, and I have not conducted any experiments of the sort suggested here on monkey perception. If I were to do so I might encounter unforeseen methodological obstacles to the approach suggested. Nevertheless, one can begin to get a sense of the ways we can address the methodological challenges posed by this sort of research. There are a number of procedural steps that must be taken, and confounding issues that must be addressed. The relevant studies in the literature do so with varying degrees of success. In the remainder of this text we will focus on work that could be characterized for the most part as methodologically refined, conducted by researchers well aware of the sorts of concerns described above.

Finally, it is worth noting in this discussion of methodology that most of the studies in the literature on linguistic relativity are structured around experiments carried out with adult populations. This is due in large measure to the fact that controlled research with children in the non-laboratory contexts of many indigenous cultures faces serious methodological obstacles. While most (though not all) of the studies are adult-focused, though, there is a clear recognition by researchers interested in the issue of linguistic relativity that data gathered among children are likely to play a crucial role in our eventual heightened understanding of the association between linguistic diversity and cognitive variation. There are various ways in which such research will likely play a role. For instance, ongoing cross-cultural research on human ontogeny might help us to better understand what sorts of cognitive strategies are universal to humans. The documentation of these universal strategies will allow us to clarify the sorts of semantic structures across languages that do not clearly reflect these universal strategies, and will allow us to see whether the universal strategies in question fail to develop or atrophy among speakers of languages characterized by the structures in question. In a related fashion, detailed descriptions of the acquisition of unrelated languages may be complimented with experimental data gathered with speakers of those languages related to particular experiential domains, in order to more carefully explore the ontogenetic processes through which language may begin to constrain or facilitate thought. In short, our future knowledge of linguistic relativity will hopefully be informed by careful cross-cultural studies of the development of linguistic skills and other facets of cognition. While child psychologists have generated an ever-growing body of knowledge on the role of language in cognitive development, few studies with young children have specifically addressed the potential role of crosslinguistic disparities in the development of different cognitive strategies across cultures.[20] (Bowerman and Levinson [2001:14])

---

20 Work with other primates is also playing a role in growing our understanding of the influence of language on conceptual development (see Tomasello [2001]), though it is obviously limited in what it can tell us about the influence of crosslinguistic variation on cognition.

3.2 Conclusion

In our discussion of the common methodological approaches adopted in contemporary work on linguistic relativity, we have demonstrated how some well-established issues confronting such research can be handled. In the following chapters, the methodological approaches in question will come into focus more clearly, as they are exemplified in discussions of numerous explorations of the topic.

4 Space

4.1 Introduction

Here is a simple task that you can try, wherever you may be while reading this: Point north. Or point south. Or point in any other cardinal direction. Can you do this confidently, without consulting the GPS on your phone, a map, or some other external technology? My guess is that you cannot, at least not with a great degree of confidence. The truth is, most readers of this book would not be able to do so. On a number of occasions I have asked all of the students in a large lecture hall to point north. Inevitably, what results is a room full of hands pointed in a variety of directions, with seemingly all of the headings of a 360° arc represented. Certainly there is little-to-no correlation between north and any pattern in the pointing. If you are located in a grid-like city such as Manhattan, where the avenues run (roughly) north to south, and the streets run east to west, you might find this task more manageable. Even in such cities, though, most of us tend to have pretty meager direction-recall abilities once we are indoors, especially once we have made a series of turns. This is perhaps not surprising, and you might wonder why anyone would expect that people could perform this task accurately. As Boroditsky and Gaby (2010) note, however, some 5-year-old speakers of Kuuk Thaayorre, an aboriginal language in Australia, point in any number of directions requested of them with uncanny accuracy. Boroditsky (2011) notes that, while she has seen such children perform this task with relative precision, her experience with speakers of English at institutions such as Harvard, Princeton, and Stanford suggests that they cannot with any reliability. She is not the only one to make this observation either. In a series of experiments, a number of groups of people besides the Kuuk Thaayorre have been shown to excel at this sort of task. In this chapter we will discuss this and other related research, much of which has been conducted by Stephen Levinson and his colleagues at the Max Planck Institute for Psycholinguistics. The common thread of the research is a consideration of the ways in which systematic crosslinguistic differences in spatial language yield systematic disparities in nonlinguistic cognition associated with spatial reference and orientation. This subject that has received attention in books dedicated entirely to the topic (Levinson [2003], Levinson and Wilkins [2006], Dasen and Mishra [2010]), and also in numerous articles in widely circulated journals (e.g. Pederson et al. [1998], Levinson et al. [2002], and Haun et al. [2011]). Given the breadth and depth of the relevant work in the literature, a caveat is in order: This chapter does not exhaustively survey the literature on this topic. Instead, it focuses on some of the major findings presented in research on this cognitive domain, paying particular attention to the major experimental paradigms that have been implemented in the relevant investigations. Our primary goal will be to convey the state of the art of inquiries into this topic.

First, though, another illustrative task is in order, one that you could again undertake: Collect four objects within arm's reach. On my desk I have a pen, a book, a cell phone, and key ring. Now take the four objects and place them in a randomly sequenced linear array on some horizontal surface in front of you. Then memorize the order of the objects in the line. Even though there are only four objects, this may require a modest amount of focus since the order is arbitrary. Have you memorized the order? Now shuffle the objects, collect them, and turn around 180° so that you are facing the opposite direction. Place the objects back down on a flat horizontal surface now in front of you, the floor if necessary. Be sure and arrange the objects in their original order, i.e. their order in the first linear array. Are you confident in your recall abilities? What order are the objects now in? You might respond that they are in the "same" order, but what does that mean exactly? My guess is that you employed a strategy such as the one I did, in which I memorized the order of the objects relative to the left and right sides of my body. That is, when I initially placed the objects on the desk in front of me, the pen was to the left of the book, which was to the left of the phone, which was to the left of the key ring. After turning around, I kept the objects in what was to me the same left-to-right order. This array reformation is represented schematically in Figure 4.1.
This strategy seems intuitive to many, and may even seem like the "correct" answer. It is not the only strategy available, however. Consider Figure 4.2.
The orientation strategy described by Figure 4.2 is another "correct" option. On an informal basis, I have conducted variations of this task numerous times

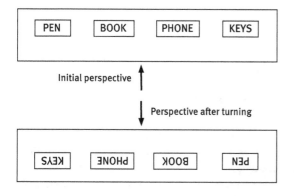

Figure 4.1: An egocentric/relative orientation strategy.

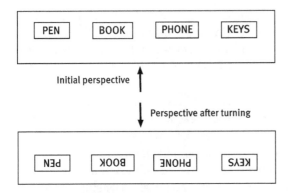

Figure 4.2: A geocentric/absolute orientation strategy.

with over a dozen speakers of Karitiâna. In all cases the strategy they employed is that depicted in Figure 4.2, not the one depicted in Figure 4.1. The Karitiâna are not special in this regard, either. Many tested populations use the orientation strategy in Figure 4.2 as a default strategy. Differences in approach to this sort of recall task point to cross-group variations in an aspect of nonlinguistic spatial cognition.

In this chapter we will consider evidence for cross-group variation in nonlinguistic tasks, including dead reckoning tasks of the "point-north" variety and rotation-based tasks of the sort just described. We will consider claims that such variation is most plausibly motivated by fundamental divides in the way spatial orientation and spatial frames of reference are structured in different languages. Prior to tackling these topics, however, we should address another major way in which languages have been shown to vary vis-à-vis spatial semantics: spatial topology.

4.2 Spatial topology

Not all spatial language relates to the linear orientation of objects or places with respect to each other or the human perceiver. In fact, much spatial language relates to notions of spatial topology, specifically those such as convergence, containment, connectedness, contiguity, and general proximity. For example, English particles such as "in", "on", and "under" denote spatial relationships of proximity, containment (in the case of "in") and vertical continuity ("on" and "under"). It has been suggested that such concepts correspond to extremely basic elements of neurocognition shared across the human species (Landau and Jackendoff [1993]), and this position would seem to predict the universality of the linguistic reification of such concepts. Such universality would also be predicted by suggestions in the literature that these seemingly basic topological notions are ontogenetically primitive (Piaget and Inhelder [1956]), i.e. that children have some innate set of basic topological notions such as "in", "on", and "under", which they bring to the table prior to the acquisition of their native language. According to such a perspective, children match the adpositional spatial terms of their languages early on (Johnston and Slobin [1979]) to pre-linguistic concepts of spatial topology. These predictions of universality confront serious challenges, though, upon careful consideration of the crosslinguistic utilization and acquisition of topological terms.

Perhaps the most well known way in which languages systematically vary in how they encode topological notions is the variety of means through which the path of a referent's motion is described. One way in which languages encode such concepts for event-path description is through adpositions, for instance the English prepositions "in", "on", "out", "over", etc., as in "He walked out". Germanic languages such as English, which tend to rely on adpositions for event-path descriptions, are often referred to as "satellite-framed" languages and contrasted with "verb-framed" languages (Talmy [2000]). In verb-framed languages, including Romance languages such as Portuguese, the path of the event (outwards in the example just cited) is typically denoted without reliance on an adposition, as in *Ele saiu* ('He went out'). The distinction between satellite-framed languages and verb-framed languages is far from dichotomous, and languages may have ways of expressing topological notions

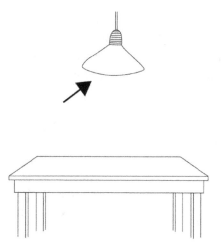

Figure 4.3: One of the situations describable via clause (4.1) in Karitiâna. Image taken from Topological Relations Pictures Series, Bowerman and Pedersen (1992).

through either strategy, for instance English can employ verbs to express "in" and "out" paths through Latin-based verbs such as "enter" or "exit", respectively. Nevertheless, this typological distinction gives us some sense of the sort of variability that exists in the grammatical realization of topological notions.[21]

Apart from the formal variation in the ways in which topological distinctions are conveyed, there exists a more profound sort of semantic variation of topological concepts. This variation is evidenced by the fact that some languages do not exhibit a distinction between "on" and "over", a distinction that is sometimes erroneously assumed to be universal. Consider clause (4.1), which was elicited from several Karitiâna speakers independently after they were asked to describe the scene depicted in Figure 4.3.

(4.1) *pyty-pa*   *okyp*   *nakaa-syp*   *bywo*
       eat-NOM   Vertical   be-PROG   lamp
       'The lamp is over/on the table.'

Crucially, the postposition *okyp* is used when an item whose location is being highlighted, the "figure" (in this case *bywo*, 'lamp'), is in a linear vertical relationship vis-à-vis another item, the "landmark" or "ground" (in this case *pytypa*, 'table'). While the figure is necessarily near the landmark, its position cannot be described with *okyp* if it is under the landmark or contiguous with the bottom surface of that landmark. It can be described with this term only if it is located above the landmark or contiguous with the top surface of that landmark. In other words clause (4.1) may refer to cases such as that depicted in Figure 4.3, but it also may be used when a lamp is found directly on top of a table. The word *okyp* is also elicited when Karitiâna speakers are presented with images such as that in Figure 4.4, which is describable via clause (4.2). In short, the concepts of "over" and "on" cannot be linguistically dissociated in the language, at least not via a simple adpositional distinction as in English.

(4.2) *pyty-pa*   *okyp*   *nakaa-syp*   *sey-pa*
       eat-NOM   Vertical   be-PROG   drink-NOM
       'The cup is over/on the table.'

In fact, many languages conflate topological distinctions that exist in other languages, while distinguishing topological notions that are conflated in others. Consider that English "on" conflates the Dutch distinction between *op* and

---

21 In fact, topological notions may even be represented in other parts of the clause, for instance via locative case markers. (See Levinson [2003:98–110] for a survey.)

Figure 4.4: Another spatial relationship describable with *okyp*. Image taken from Topological Relations Pictures Series, Bowerman and Pedersen (1992).

aan. The latter Dutch term is typically used to refer to situations in which the figure must counteract gravity to stay "on" the landmark, for instance a piece of fruit on a tree branch. Conversely, English makes a distinction between figures being "on" or "in" landmarks, while other languages may conflate these distinctions via the usage of one term, for instance the Spanish particle *en*.[22]

While crosslinguistic surveys of such distinctions are limited by the scarcity of quality data available, it seems clear from the extant surveys such as that in Levinson et al. (2003) that there are no topological concepts that are universally codified in the world's languages. This is not to suggest that there are no crosslinguistic tendencies related to spatial topology. In fact, Levinson et al. (2003) suggest that there are certain semantic "attractors", or topological notions that are frequently codified. One such attractor is the *okyp* ('on/over') spatial category evident in Karitiâna and many other languages. Other attractor notions are glossed in Levinson et al. (2003) as "in", "attachment", "near/ under", and "on-top". While such notions are common, they are hardly universal, as evidenced by the fact that "on/over", "attachment", and "near/under" are not coded as unitary concepts in English prepositions.[23]

The question that naturally arises in discussing such topological variability is whether this variability implies disparities in speakers' actual perceptions of spatial relationships between objects. For example, do Karitiâna speakers

---

22 English does not rigidly enforce the on/in semantic distinction. There are numerous idiomatic exceptions. Hence I can speak of being "on the bus" or "on the plane", or "in my chair".

23 Some are more likely to be codified in a given language than others, and Levinson et al. (2003:510) go so far as to posit an implicational hierarchy of topological notions, though they note that this hierarchy must be interpreted with caution.

perceive the relationships in Figures 4.3 and 4.4 to be more similar than English speakers do? Some evidence from language acquisition is at least consistent with the claim that the differentiated semantic structuring of topological notions has demonstrable effects on the manner in which some spatial relationships are perceived. Building on previous work on the acquisition of spatial terms (e.g. Bowerman [1994, 1996a, 1996b]), Bowerman and Choi (2001) contrasted the way in which English-speaking and Korean-speaking one-to-three year-olds verbally discriminate topological categories. Their results suggest that, as early as eighteen months, speakers of the two languages exhibit differences in their topological concepts. These differences relate to lexical distinctions such as *kkita* vs. "in". The former Korean word refers to a spatial relationship in which the figure is located in or on the landmark, but in a tight-fitting manner. The English word "in" makes no such requirement of tight-fittedness. Bowerman and Choi (2001) investigated whether young learners of these languages show signs of construing spatial relationships in accordance with such language-specific categories, or in accordance with some universal category. Put differently, they sought to uncover whether the construal of spatial relationships of each of the two groups of children was more similar to the other group's construal, or more similar to that of the adult speakers of their own language. One task the authors conducted was video-based. Children between the ages of 18–23 months viewed videos of objects coming into spatial relationships, for example a peg being inserted in a tight-fitting hole, a Lego being put in a box, or a book being inserted in a tight-fitting box. In some cases the viewing involved the audio presentation of a descriptive question including a relevant spatial term, e.g. "Where's she putting it *IN*?" or "Eti-ey KKI-e?" ('Where's [she] tight-fitting it?'). (Bowerman and Choi [2001:496]) When the spatial term in the audio stimulus matched the spatial relationship being witnessed visually, the young children stared longer at the visual stimulus. Given the crosslinguistic disparity, however, the actual stimuli stared at more intensively varied across the two groups. So, for example, Korean speakers had a tendency to stare longer at a video of Legos being put on other Legos in a tight-fitting way after hearing audio stimuli with *kkita*, while English speakers had a tendency to stare longer at a video of Legos being put in a box after hearing audio stimuli involving "in". 'Speakers' is a bit of misnomer here since the majority of experimental participants were unable to produce the relevant words in either language. Yet they clearly comprehended the words on some level, and their attention to the video and audio stimuli was demonstrably affected by the topological categories of the language they were in the process of learning.

While researchers do not doubt that there are universal facets of human perception of spatial-topological concepts, work such as Bowerman and Choi

(2001) implies that children do not bring a rigid set of topological concepts to the language-learning table. Were that the case, we might expect 18–23 months-old children to show similar orientation patterns associated with topological stimuli, regardless of differentiated linguistic stimuli. Instead, it appears that such patterns are shaped even before humans can appropriately produce the spatial terms in their language. From the moment we are able to observe such concepts in the behavior of children, they show signs of linguistic influence. Any universal biases that they do bring to language acquisition are apparently malleable. Topological notions take shape as children learn the relevant categories of their native languages.

Bowerman and Choi's (2001) findings, along with others on the development of spatial categories, do not constitute unequivocal evidence for linguistic effects on nonlinguistic processes of spatial perception since their tasks involved linguistic stimuli. Yet the findings are useful for framing discussions of such effects, since they demonstrate the way in which language helps shape orientation towards spatial concepts at an extremely young age. They suggest strongly that nonlinguistic conceptual categories associated with the domain of space are not as strong or inflexible as is sometimes assumed. As the authors note, "This outcome is particularly striking because, of all semantic domains, space is the one that has been cited most often in arguments for the critical role of children's autonomous concepts in early lexical development." (2001:497)

Given that linguistic influences on the development of topological concepts are not prevented by any putative autonomous concepts, it would not be altogether surprising to find that there exist linguistic influences on the nonlinguistic conceptualization of space. In the next section we consider the evidence for such influences on spatial "frames of reference", a facet of cognition that is more readily testable via nonlinguistic experimental inquiries.

4.3 Frames of reference

4.3.1 Experimental evidence

"Frames of reference" are basic ways to refer to coordinate systems when describing object positions (see Levinson [2003:24], Rock [1992:404] for more detailed definitions). For some time it has been known that speakers of some languages typically rely on an "absolute" (or "geocentric") frame of reference (FoR) when supplying descriptions of the spatial configurations of a set of objects. In others, such as English, speakers have a marked tendency to rely on a "relative" (or "egocentric") FoR. Consider again Figure 4.1. In this case, if

I were to describe the initial position of the phone on my desk, I might say that "the phone is to the left of the keys and to the right of the book," assuming that I am viewing the items from the initial (top) perspective described by the figure. This is a crucial point, though. To know whether my characterization of the location of the phone is correct, based on the description just given, I have to know something about my position when I viewed the items. Were I to view the same items from the opposite side of my desk, the characterization offered would be incorrect. In short, this sort of description is based on a relative FoR since it depends on viewer positioning. Suppose though that I described the position of the phone as follows: "The phone is to the north of the keys and to the south of the book." The FoR in this case is absolute, and this characterization would hold no matter which angle I viewed the items from. There is a long history of inquiry into types of frames of reference, in philosophy, psychology, and linguistics. (For a synopsis of that history, see Levinson [2003].) Various terminological choices have been made to discuss divergent frames of reference, but researchers on language and cognition seem to have settled on a basic set of terms. On the one hand, frames of reference can be referred to as egocentric or relative when they rely on the speaker's perspective at the time of description of the orientation of particular objects. On the other, they may be referred to as "allocentric", in which case the positioning of the objects is described via a more fixed feature of the environment. If they are allocentric, they may be further categorized as "absolute/geocentric" or "intrinsic".[24] An absolute or geocentric FoR utilizes some cardinal direction system, for instance as in the preceding description of the phone's northern position. An intrinsic frame does not rely on such a system, but relies instead on intrinsic features of the environment of the object. For example, say that I left my phone in class one day. If someone asks me where I left it, I might say I left it on the desk at "the front" of the class. Such a description does not rely on cardinal directions, but it is clearly not relative to my own position or orientation with respect to the phone. That description will be interpretable for anyone familiar with university classrooms: the desk in this case is next to an LCD screen and next to the lectern, i.e. the "front" of the class. This reference is based on the intrinsic shape of the classroom, some culturally shared 3-D model with a "front", "back", and "sides".

---

24 The three-fold categorization of orientation types is used as a basis for the discussion in this chapter, as it is in most recent work on the topic. It offers sufficient detail for a consideration of the work detailed here. It is worth noting, though, that orientation types can be categorized according to a related but more fine-grained six-fold categorization type. See O'Meara and Pérez Báez (2011:843) for a discussion of this classification.

For practical purposes, we can speak of a tripartite distinction between relative/egocentric, absolute/geocentric, and intrinsic frames of reference. It turns out that languages use these basic FoR's to varying degrees. Speakers of some languages rely extensively on relative descriptions, for example, while other speakers may rarely if ever utilize this sort of description. For a detailed analysis of the way in which the grammars of numerous languages rely on divergent frames of reference, see Levinson and Wilkins (2006). For now let us consider two well-known cases in which speakers tend to rely on absolute FoR's, Tzeltal and Guugu Yimithirr.

The Tzeltal of Tenejapa, who live in the Chiapas Highlands, use an absolute orientation system. This system is described in some detail in Brown and Levinson (1993). Crucially, the territory of these Tzeltal is characterized by a dramatic "uphill" slope, so that the (approximately) southern part of their territory has an altitude of about 1,700 meters (5,500 feet), while the (approximately) northern part of that land has an altitude of about 950 meters (3,000 feet). This altitude disparity results in pronounced effects on the environment, so that the uphill land is characterized by mountainous pine forests and the "downhill" land is more tropical. (Brown and Levinson [1993:49]) These diverse ecologies are exploited differentially in Tzeltal agriculture, and play a prominent role in the culture. This prominence is evident in the absolute frame of reference utilized in the language, since the location of objects is typically described with respect to the cardinal-like (but not quadrant-based) directions of being *ta ajk'ol*, 'to uphill', or *ta alan*, 'to downhill'. For instance, consider clauses (4.3) and (4.4), taken from Brown and Levinson (1993:55).

(4.3) *te lapsis*   *ay*   *ta*   *ajk'ol*   *yu'un*   *te limite*
       the pencil   EXIST   PREP   'uphill'   3E.RELN   the bottle
       'The pencil is uphill of the bottle.'
(4.4) *ay*   *ta*   *ajk'ol* *a'w-u'un/k-u'un*   *te lapis*
       EXIST   PREP   'uphill' of-you/of-me   the pencil
       'The pencil is uphill from you/from me.'

What is so remarkable about such a system, from the perspective of speakers of a language such as English, is that Tzeltal speakers do not rely on relative descriptors even when depicting the location of a small set of objects on a flat plane immediately in front of them, and even when in enclosed spaces when topographical or celestial entities are not visible. In other words, even in the absence of a shift in the vertical dimension between the relevant objects, their location can be denoted via horizontal reference that relies inherently on a topographical vertical shift of a much larger scale. Brown and Levinson (1993) present a series of anecdotes suggesting that the Tzeltal speakers in Tenejapa are constantly attuned to the locations of the "uphill" and "downhill" directions (as well as a "transverse" direction based on the other two). They note that in one case a Tzeltal-speaker agreed to be blindfolded, while being spun around in a darkened house. Even after being spun twenty times, he was able to point accurately to *alan*. Such a clear cognitive bias towards an absolute spatial orientation is plausibly engrained by the habitual linguistic reliance on the absolute FoR. As in the case of Korean children's acquisition of topological notions, Tzeltal children seem to have acquired their orientation of "uphill" and "downhill" by around two years of age (Brown [2001:518]). They do not apparently pass through a stage in which they first exhibit relative spatial orientation, only to have that orientation reconfigured in an absolute manner. This developmental fact suggests strongly that their spatial orientation is shaped by exposure to language at a young age, rather than their familiarity with more general facets of adult Tzeltal culture, e.g. a vocational reliance on cardinal directions. Below we consider some recent experimental evidence offered in support of the claim that adult Tzeltal cognition is impacted by spatial language.

In the Australian language Guugu Yimithirr, "rarely a sentence will pass without some morphologically specific form of a cardinal direction root, and virtually *all* location is described in such terms" (Haviland [1996:285]). This pervasiveness of cardinal direction reference characterizes Guugu Yimithirr spoken clauses, but it is also evident in accompanying physical gestures. Unlike Tzeltal directional reference, in this language the cardinal directions referred to correspond to quandrants that could be characterized as northern, southern, eastern, and western.[25] Speakers are constantly describing the location of referents with respect to these quadrants. Consider (4.5), a clause excised from naturalistic discourse, in which reference is made to the northern quadrant (*gunggaarr*).

(4.5)   ngayu nhangu bagay, eh... yarra gunggaarr nhaawaa
         'I poked him (and said), "Hey... look yonder there to the North!"'
         (Haviland [1996])

In this case, the speaker is recounting an experience in which he and another man swam some six kilometers through the ocean after being shipwrecked.

---

25 These quadrants are slightly askew, rotated slightly clockwise, of true north, south, east, and west. See Haviland (1998:5) for a precise description of the quadrants, which may be impacted by local environmental features such as the seasonal arc of the sun and the coastline near Guugu Yimithirr lands.

After arriving at the beach, he noticed a shark swimming in the waters to the north, and is describing to his interlocutor in (4.5) how he drew his shipwreck companion's attention to the shark. As he does so verbally, he also does so gesturally, by pointing north simultaneously. What is particularly remarkable about this case is that the event he is recounting occurred some thirty years prior to the time of the utterance of (4.5). Clearly the speaker's recollection of the spatial orientation of referents in the described event conforms to the absolute system found in his language, rather than a relative-type system.

Such cases provide strong ethnographic evidence that speakers of languages that utilize absolute FoR's almost exclusively have a tendency to spatially orient their environment in an absolute fashion. Building upon work by Haviland (1993, 1996), Levinson (1996a, 1997) conducted a series of experimental tasks among the Guugu Yimithirr, in order to better elucidate the effects of their default linguistic FoR on their nonlinguistic cognition. His working hypothesis was that speakers of this language must take the information they acquire through spatial perception and code it with absolute directions in order to be able to later describe the spatial relationships of items in a perceived scene. That is, if their language requires them to denote absolute directions, then at the time of perception they must be particularly attuned to those directions.

One of the basic experimental tasks employed by Levinson to initially test this hypothesis involved stimulus cards with color chips of different sizes pasted on them. These cards were similar to those depicted in Figure 4.5. (Though the cards in Figure 4.5 have clear fills surrounding grayscale chips, rather than black fills surrounding color chips as in the originals.)

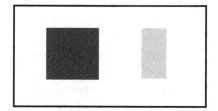 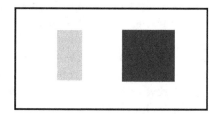

Figure 4.5: Grayscale reproductions of a pair of cards used as stimuli in Levinson (1997).

Subjects were presented with a pair of stimuli such as that in Figure 4.5, while facing north in a room, and were asked to select one of the cards. They then left the cards in place and were taken to a nearby room, identical in size, color, and furnishings. As they faced south in that second room, they were presented with a pair of stimulus cards identical to those witnessed in the first room.

They were then asked to select which of the cards they had just chosen in the other room. Crucially, the answer to this sort of question varies in accordance with the FoR employed. Say one employs a relative FoR. If s/he chooses the stimulus card on the left in Figure 4.5 while facing north, then while facing south s/he will choose the card that is then on the left (but represented by the right alternative in Figure 4.5), since when facing the opposite direction *that* card will now have the black square to the left of the gray chip. (You get a similar effect if you turn this book upside down, since the card on the right in Figure 4.5 will then be on your left, and will resemble the other card as viewed from the initial perspective.) Now say one employs an absolute FoR while selecting the card on the left, while facing north in the room. In such a case the black square will be recalled as being to the *west* of the gray rectangle. Now if one is turned 180°, s/he might assume the black square should remain to the west (not the left) of the gray rectangle in the selected card in the second room. In short, an absolute FoR will result in differentiated card selection vis-à-vis a relative strategy. In Levinson (1997), this basic experimental task was undertaken with 12 Guugu Yimithirr speakers and 15 Dutch speakers. The Dutch speakers employed a relative strategy overwhelmingly, in 44/45 cases, consistent with their language's reliance on relative spatial terminology. The Guugu Yimithirr speakers employed an absolute strategy overwhelmingly, in 27/34 cases. The cross-group disparity was significant at p=.0000 (Fisher's exact test), in the direction predicted (Levinson 1997:114).

Another task employed in Levinson (1997), and subsequently by others, involved the use of a "maze" of arrows such as the one presented in Figure 4.6. Task participants were presented with a maze-like array of connected black arrows on a white sheet, describing a series of directions. They viewed the arrows while facing South in one room. They were then moved to a second room, in which they were facing North, and asked to select, from a series of cards, the pattern of arrows that depicted the completion of the arrow maze, i.e. that described how the arrows might return to their point of origin. Given the reversal of their orientation, the selection from the three options in Figure 4.6 revealed the FoR they relied on cognitively during the task. Option 1 represents an absolute/geocentric strategy, since it only accurately describes the completion of the maze if one is employing an absolute FoR. Option 3, on the other hand, represents a relative/egocentric strategy, since once one's perspective is altered 180° that option will not describe the answer in absolute terms. As in the previous case, if you first look at Figure 4.6 rightside up, and next turn the page upside down, you might get a better sense of how the option selected reveals default FoR. Option 2 is a distractor option, utilized to ensure that the respondents comprehended the task. Selection of this option by any speakers would suggest task incomprehension.

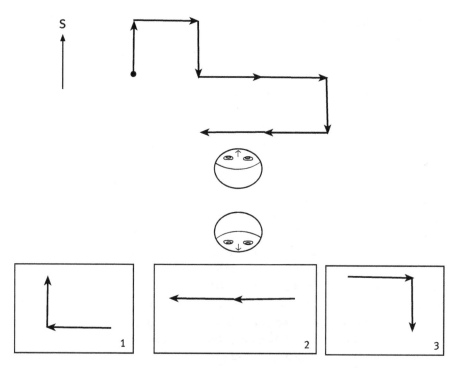

Figure 4.6: Reproduction of a maze task. (Adapted from Levinson [1997:119])

While several maze types were used for this task, there was a clear difference across populations. The twelve Guugu Yimithirr speakers employed an absolute FoR in a majority of cases (24/36), and only one of them consistently employed a relative strategy. In contrast, fifteen Dutch speakers employed a relative FoR in the majority of the cases (42/45). This disparity was significant (p=0.0000, Chi-square). In only one case was a distractor option selected, demonstrating that task comprehension did not motivate the disparity between the groups of speakers. In short, the patterns of solutions selected by the participants were strongly consistent with the default FoR employed in their native languages. This suggests quite plausibly that the subjects' native languages affected their performance on this nonlinguistic task, which presumably reflects their spatial orientation strategies more generally. Similar findings have been replicated with more elaborate maze tasks (and with speakers of other languages), for instance one in which participants watch a ball travel through a maze and then are asked to reproduce the path of the ball after being rotated 180°. (Levinson et al. [2002])

Recently I conducted the same basic arrows-maze task, with various stimuli such as that in Figure 4.6, with eight Karitiâna speakers. In most of the cases the Karitiâna selected options such as option 1 at the expense of those such as option 3. The disparity between their selection habits and those of the Dutch control group in Levinson (1997) were also significant (p=.0000, Fisher's exact test). While there are words for 'left' (*pon*) and 'right' (*he*) in Karitiâna, speakers do not systematically employ a relative FoR when providing directions or describing spatial relationships. Crucially, though, Karitiâna speakers also do not typically employ absolute/geocentric reference. The default linguistic FoR is an "intrinsic" one. I mention these results because they naturally draw us to a potential confound with the experiment types described by Figure 4.6: depending on the characteristics of the physical setting in which the stimuli are represented, the selection of option 1 may reflect an absolute/geocentric-oriented response *or* an intrinsic-oriented response. For example, the front of the room may be in the same direction as South, so if a participant chooses the first option they may be construing the arrows as returning South, *or* returning to the front of the room. While the results for the arrow-maze task and the color chip task used in Levinson (1997) are consistent with a relativistic account, then, the tasks used are open to criticism in that they do not distinguish clearly between all three FoR's. They are also susceptible to other criticisms. Perhaps the most obvious is that the stimuli employed in such tasks is much more familiar to individuals from western societies. For instance, two-dimensional mazes are surely less familiar to Guugu Yimithirr and Karitiâna speakers than they are to most educated westerners. It may seem implausible that conflating variables such as differing education experience could result in consistent disparities along the neat linguistic lines of the sort observed. After all, the indigenous speakers tested did not evince task incomprehension, but exhibited instead a consistent strategy matching that typically employed in their language. Nevertheless, the methodologies evident in Levinson (1997) were further refined and expanded in subsequent works, e.g. Pederson et al. (1998) and Levinson (2003).

The studies described in Levinson (2003) were conducted among numerous populations, representing an assortment of languages. These included languages with basic FoR's that were intrinsic, such as Mopan (Maya), relative/egocentric, such as Japanese or Dutch, as well as absolute/geocentric, such as Tzeltal and Guugu Yimithirr. The work was also conducted among speakers of languages in which more than one FoR was frequently employed, for instance in Kilivala (Austronesian), in which all three FoR's are commonly used. The crosslinguistic experimental work in question consisted primarily of five tasks, including two maze tasks, a "transitivity inference" task (see methodological discussion in Levinson [2003:163–165]), the task using color chips as in Figure 4.5, and an "animals in a row task". The latter task has become particularly influential, having been replicated and modified in more recent studies. Given its centrality to recent work on this topic, it is described next. It should be stressed though that all of these tasks are broadly similar and rely on the same methodological assumption: if speakers are presented with a set of stimuli and then rotated, their orientation to the stimuli in the rotated position will reveal whether the FoR they used to conceptually encode the stimuli matches the default FoR in their native language.

The most basic animals-in-a-row task is a simple performative task that does not merely require the participants to choose from a set of pre-selected options, as in the color chips task and the maze task described above. The task proceeds as follows: Subjects are presented with a transverse row of three toy animals, all of which are facing in the same direction. The toy animals are made of plastic, with an approximate width of 2.5 cm, a height of 3–4 cm, and a length of 5–7 cm. While only three toys are used for each trial in the case of the most basic version of the task, four toys are used during the course of the task: a pig, a horse, a cow, and a sheep. The toys in the stimulus array are located equidistant from each other. The task participant faces the three toy animals on a stimulus table, in the manner depicted in Figure 4.7. The subject is then rotated 180°, turning as s/he walks towards a second table located 4–6 meters away. At the "recall" table they are asked to reconstruct the original sequence of toys in accordance with the orientation of the animals in the memorized array of toys. More specifically, the subjects are asked to "Make it again, just the same". All instructions are carried out in the participant's native language, though no spatial or deictic terms are used during the instructions.

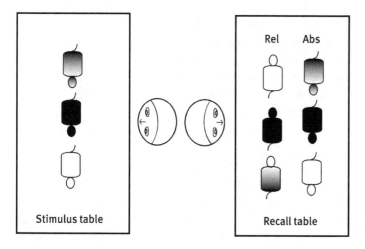

Figure 4.7: Abstract reproduction of the animals-in-a-row task. Adapted from Pederson et al. (1998).

As we see in Figure 4.7, the manner in which the subject reconstructs the array reflects their conceptualization of the original orientation, and an egocentric/relative conceptual encoding will result in a distinct reconstruction when contrasted with a geocentric/absolute coding. Note that this task also does not really distinguish between the utilization of intrinsic or absolute FoR's, however. The task must be modified, in the manner discussed below, for the reliance on either of these FoR's to be differentiated from reliance on the other.

The animals-in-a-row task has been conducted amongst a number of populations, in a variety of studies, with broadly consistent results of the sort predicted by a relativistic account. Speakers of languages that typically encode spatial information geocentrically tend to utilize the absolute/geocentric strategy for toy-array reconstruction, while speakers of languages that typically encode such information egocentrically more frequently employ the egocentric/relative strategy of array reconstruction. Levinson (2003:183–187) contrasts the results of the animals-in-a-row task obtained in numerous populations, among 85 speakers of languages with absolute coding strategies and 99 speakers of languages with relative coding strategies. The former group consists of speakers of Mparntwe Arrernte (Pama-Nyungan), Longgu (Austronesian), Belhare (Tibeto-Burman), Tamil (Dravidian), Hai‖om (Khoisan), and Tzeltal (Maya). The latter is comprised primarily of Dutch, Japanese, and English speakers. Members of the latter group evinced egocentric/relative reconstruction of toy sequencing in a vast majority of cases, while those of the former utilized apparently absolute (though possibly intrinsic) reconstruction in an overwhelming majority of task trials. In fact, nearly 60% of the speakers of "relative FoR" languages utilized relative reconstruction in 100% of the trials, while only a small fraction systematically did not. Conversely, nearly 60% of the speakers of "absolute FoR" languages employed reconstruction consistent with an absolute FoR in 100% of the trials, while only a very small fraction consistently did not. The difference between groups' reconstruction strategies was highly significant (Mann-Whitney U-test=1453, $p<0.001$), and clearly in the predicted direction. Similarly significant disparities were also observed for the other related tasks described in Levinson (2003).

Perhaps more interesting than these macro-level comparisons were the results of micro-level, pairwise contrasts between particular populations. For example, Mann-Whitney U-tests comparing the distribution of array-reconstruction strategies revealed significant disparities between the strategies of the speakers of Arrernte and Dutch ($p<0.001$); Arrernte and Japanese ($p<0.05$); Tzeltal and Dutch ($p<0.001$); Tzeltal and Japanese ($p<0.001$); Longgu and Dutch ($p<0.001$); and Longgu and Japanese ($p<0.001$). In fact, such differences were observed for any pairwise contrast between the results of a relative-FoR language's speakers and those of an absolute-FoR language's speakers. Furthermore, all pairwise contrasts between speakers with similar default linguistic FoR's revealed no significant disparities in array reconstruction. So, for example, speakers of Arrernte and Tzeltal tended to reconstruct the arrays in a non-egocentric fashion, and there was no significant disparity in the performance of the two groups. Conversely, there was no significant difference between the rate at which the Dutch and Japanese-speaking subjects utilized relative-type conceptual encoding strategies. In short, where we might predict task-behavior differences based on linguistic factors, such dissimilarity did in fact surface. Where we might predict task-behavior similarity based on linguistic factors, such similarity did in fact surface. Such language/task-behavior correlations, considered in detail in Levinson (2003), are particularly noteworthy in the light of the many cultural and ecological factors at work. While members of population pairs such as the Arrernte and the Tzeltal or the Dutch and Japanese differ according to numerous cultural criteria, their performance on the animals task, as well as the other tasks in question, can be predicted in large measure by linguistic factors alone. While the correlation between a particular set of linguistic features and a particular nonverbal behavior is insufficient in and of itself to make definitive relativistic conclusions (see discussion in Chapter 1), the correlation observed here is most easily explained via a relativistic account since the correlation holds across numerous cultures. (Though it should be mentioned that the English, Dutch, and Japanese speakers tested are all embedded in industrialized/urban cultures, a point returned to below.)

In addition to being supported by the language/task-behavior correlation observed across a number of diverse cultures, relativistic conclusions may be buttressed by studies within groups that share many cultural features. After all, if two groups of people are best characterized as representing the same culture while differing according to some linguistic parameter, the groups in question offer a particularly useful test case for relativistic hypotheses. In the case of potential linguistic influences on spatial cognition, one such case is that of two groups of Tamil speakers. As discussed in Pederson (1993, 1995), there are two primary groups of Tamil speakers in Madurai, Tamilnadu. One of these is rural and speaks a geocentrically oriented variety of Tamil, while the other is primarily urban and speaks an egocentrically oriented variety. According to the results in Pederson's studies, the orientation differences between the two groups of speakers, as ascertained from tasks such as the animals-in-a-row task, do pattern in the predicted direction. That is, those speakers of the geocentric variety tend to exhibit more geocentric patterns in their array reconstructions. It is important to stress, however, that the cross-group disparities in this case are not as significant as we might expect based on the rest of the literature so far surveyed. In fact, the disparities did not attain significance in the case of all tasks described by Pederson. The Tamil data are difficult to interpret, then, particularly in the light of the other factor involved, the urban vs. rural confound. While it is fair to say that the findings on Tamil are generally consonant with a relativistic position, they would hardly constitute convincing evidence, in and of themselves, to skeptics of such a position.

In a related fashion, findings among speakers of Australian English have demonstrated that speakers' performance on rotation-based tasks can vary, even in the absence of systematic linguistic FoR variation. Research conducted by David Wilkins (reported in Levinson [2003]) demonstrated that English speakers residing near the central Australian town of Alice Springs evince dissimilar results on such tasks, when contrasted with English speakers in Sydney. Crucially, though, the central Australian speakers tested had extensive contact with a geocentric-FoR language, namely Arrernte. In short, the results on the nonverbal tasks for the central Australians fall somewhere in between the results obtained for the Sydney English speakers and the Arrernte speakers. Again, these results might be interpreted as being congruent with a relativistic interpretation, to the extent that they demonstrate yet another instance of cross-group variability in spatial cognition, and to the extent that the speakers of English who have had more exposure to geocentric Arrernte speech (and gestures) exhibit more geocentric behavior. Furthermore, the results seem to suggest that the disparities between Arrernte and Sydney English speakers are not simply due to broad cultural factors, and that exposure to geocentric communication may help to re-orient the default FoR's of English speakers. In addition, the results appear to suggest that ecological factors (i.e. the difference between Sydney and the area around Alice Springs) are insufficient to account for the disparities in the task results between Arrernte speakers and Sydney English speakers. After all, even with extensive exposure to the Arrernte environment, English speakers do not completely adopt a geocentric conceptual coding. Nevertheless, it is also fair to say that these data are difficult to interpret, and could even be interpreted as being inconsistent with a strong relativistic position. After all, the data do suggest that there are spatial orientation disparities between central Australian English speakers and Sydney English speakers, though both groups technically speak a language with default egocentric FoR utilization.

In short, while the Tamil data and the Australian English data do not generally contravene a straightfoward relativistic position, they do not offer unilateral support for the position either. Perhaps they are most readily reconciled with a more nuanced relativistic position, according to which spoken language *and* other factors such as gesture and nonlinguistic facets of culture play associated roles in the development of basic spatial orientation strategies. Such a position is also buttressed by other recently collected data, for instance recent findings obtained among Yucatec Mayas on the role of gestures in spatial orientation strategies (see discussion below). It is worth stressing here that most contemporary advocates of the relativistic position are proponents of such a nuanced position, and do not suggest that speech is the *only* sort of habitual behavior or symbolic representation type that impacts spatial cognition. For example, speakers of a given language may have different degrees of exposure to symbolic technologies such as maps. Some English speakers may rely heavily on such technologies at inordinate rates during recurring activities, e.g. flying a plane or hunting large game. Such exposure may result in lessened reliance on the egocentric FoR characterizing most English speakers. Assuming that is the case, this reduced reliance does not contravene a relativistic position, it merely highlights another sort of influence on spatial cognition.

The work discussed to this point, carried out primarily during the 1990's and the early 2000's, relied heavily on the 180°-rotation experimental paradigm exemplified in Figures 4.5–4.7. While this paradigm has proven extremely useful and easy to apply, it suffers from the aforementioned inability of 180° rotation tasks to distinguish between geocentric/absolute and object-centered/ intrinsic FoR strategies. For instance, in Figure 4.7 the possible configurations employed after rotation can clearly distinguish only the egocentric strategy from the allocentric strategies (both geocentric/absolute and object-centered/ intrinsic). After rotation a subject might place a given toy in a particular location because it was e.g. the northern-most toy in the original array, or because it was e.g. closest to the "back" of the room in the original array. In order to better distinguish between absolute and intrinsic reconfiguration strategies, and in order to systematically address other potential pitfalls (such as carrying out the rotations within one room), the rotation paradigm has been altered in some recent studies. Haun et al. (2011) adopt a number of methodological innovations in their study of Dutch and Hai‖om speakers. For instance, rather than having the task participants rotate 180°, they had them rotate 90° (this innovation was first adopted in Levinson et al. [2002]). This rotation allowed the researchers to distinguish precisely which of the three potential FoR's were employed by the subjects during the task. In addition, Haun et al. (2011) tested the two populations in remarkably similar outdoor settings, depicted in Figures 4.8 and 4.9. In order to eliminate the potential exacerbating effects of varying amounts of schooling, the authors relied on Dutch and Hai‖om elementary school children 8–9 years of age. Hai‖om is a language spoken in Namibia with default geocentric FoR usage. While the researchers conducted four experiments, they all relied on the general rotation paradigm evident in Figure 4.8: While facing south outdoors and standing adjacent to their school building, students were presented with an array of toy animals on a table. They were then rotated 90° while moving to a second table on the other side of the building. Now facing west towards the school, they reconstructed the toy array per the instructions. Their reconstruction strategy then revealed whether they relied on an a) intrinsic/object-centered, b) geocentric/absolute, or c) egocentric/relative FoR during task completion.

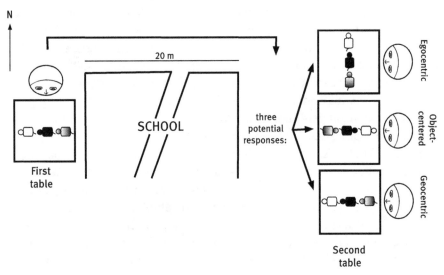

Figure 4.8: Depiction of the modified animals-in-a-row task. Adapted from Haun et al. (2011).

In the case of the first experiment involving an initial array of three toys, all twelve Dutch-speaking children used an egocentric FoR in the majority of cases, while ten of twelve Hai‖om speakers used a geocentric FoR. In the case of a second more complex task involving an array of six toys, all twelve Dutch-speaking children used an egocentric strategy, and all twelve Hai‖om speakers utilized a geocentric strategy (though errors surfaced for both populations). In other words, increased tax complexity led to increased reliance on the FoR most typically instantiated in the participants' native languages.

Some work (Li and Gleitman [2002], Li et al. [2011]) has suggested that cross-population differences in performance on the rotation-based experiments may simply reveal the preferences of speakers for task-completion only. In other words, differences in array reconstruction strategies may not reflect basic differences in FoR usage, but may point instead to the subjects' more trivial choice to use a particular FoR merely to complete the task—a choice that might

Figure 4.9: Two experimental subjects during task described by Haun et al. (2011). Copyright 2011 Elsevier BV, reprinted with permission.

be influenced by the desire to meet the researchers' expectations. This suggestion is difficult to reconcile, however, with the results in the third and fourth experiments in Haun et al. (2011). In the third experiment, Dutch children were explicitly instructed to utilize a geocentric strategy for array reconstruction, while Hai‖om speakers were explicitly instructed to employ an egocentric strategy. While some members of both groups were able to generally adhere to the instructions given to them, the number of errors rose and reconstruction of the six-toy arrays proved more difficult. In addition, about half of each set of respondents continued to rely on the characteristic FoR of their language, contra the instructions they received. Furthermore, the Dutch children more accurately reconfigured the array egocentrically (when they were not asked to choose a particular strategy), when contrasted with Hai‖om children even after the latter group was instructed to complete the task egocentrically. (This contrast was significant according to a Mann-Whitney-U-test, at $p<.0005$.) Conversely, the Hai‖om children more accurately reconfigured the array geocentrically (when they were not asked to choose a particular strategy), when contrasted with Dutch children even after the latter group was instructed to complete the task geocentrically. (This contrast was also significant according to a Mann-Whitney-U-test, at $p<.0005$.) These results demonstrate that strong cross-group disparities persist, even when subjects receive clear instructions on the FoR to be utilized.

It should also be stressed, though, that the results point to some plasticity in the strategies adopted. That is, a number of Hai‖om and Dutch children were clearly capable of adopting a strategy that is not ubiquitous in their language. Nevertheless, even when it did surface this counter-linguistic FoR transitioning had deleterious effects on the subjects' recall abilities. In a related manner, in the fourth experiment in Haun et al. (2011), it was found that Hai‖om speakers performed significantly better on the reconstruction task when explicitly instructed to complete the task geocentrically, compared to when they were explicitly instructed to complete it egocentrically. (The disparity across instruction conditions was significant at $p<0.05$, according to a Wilcoxon-test.)

In sum, there is now a robust literature on the correlation between basic linguistic FoR's and the default conceptual encoding of spatial relationships evident in rotation-based experiments. The findings in this literature suggest that, while other variables may play some role in establishing disparities in spatial cognition across groups, spatial language appears to play a particularly prominent role in creating such disparities. Of course the apparent existence of linguistic influences on FoR implementation does not imply that people are not capable of using FoR strategies that are not evident in or at least not common to their language. Most contemporary proponents of linguistic relativity do not presume such a simple deterministic interpretation. It is not surprising, for instance, that individual humans are capable of applying all three basic FoR's and transitioning between them. What is fascinating to those concerned with linguistic relativity is that these FoR's are not applied equitably across human populations, and that pervasive linguistic patterns apparently help to shape the default nonlinguistic strategies used by humans in their conceptualization of spatial relationships.

4.3.2 Some objections and other considerations

The spatial orientation research conducted by Levinson and colleagues has had a profound impact on the discussion of linguistic effects on nonlinguistic cognition. One of the ways in which this impact is evident is that those skeptical of relativistic effects for theoretical reasons, e.g. subscription to modular or quasi-modular approaches to grammar, are unlikely to simply discard the growing findings on this subject. A number have begun to seriously engage the relevant literature via their own experimental work among populations with disparate default linguistic frames of reference. In that sense, one of the greatest accomplishments of Levinson and colleagues has been to shift the onus of experimental corroboration in the treatment of this topic. The result of this shift is new studies on spatial cognition, some of which have a decidedly non-relativistic tone. Perhaps the most prominent studies produced by those skeptical of the claims of Levinson and colleagues are Li and Gleitman (2002) and Li et al. (2011).

Li and Gleitman (2002) question Levinson and colleagues' interpretations of their rotation-based experiments' results. They suggest for example that those results may owe themselves to contextual factors associated with the experimental settings, for instance whether the rotation experiments were carried out indoors or outdoors, or with window blinds up or down, rather than to crosslinguistic differences. Since Levinson et al. (2002) includes a point-by-point rebuttal of Li and Gleitman (2002) (noting, for example, that relativistic results are maintained whether experiments are conducted indoors or outdoors), we will focus here on some important points made in Li et al. (2011).

Via a series of tasks derived from those that have become standard to this line of research, Li et al. (2011) once again investigated the spatial reasoning of Tzeltal speakers in Tenejapa. The four tasks in that study differed in a crucial way from those reported in most research on this subject: all participants were required to choose one *correct* response from an assortment of options. In most of the work we have discussed so far, the tasks employed were open-ended, i.e. the speakers' predilections for particular FoR's were assessed based on their optional implementation of a default FoR strategy in experimental conditions–their hand was not typically forced.[26] While all of the particulars of the tasks in Li et al. (2011) are not altogether relevant here, for all four of their tasks a correct response could be attained in some cases via geocentric reasoning, and in others via egocentric reasoning. For example, in one of their experiments, speakers were presented with an evenly gridded, completely symmetrical, square maze on a table. A small ball was used to demonstrate the motion of a path through the maze. Tzeltal speakers witnessed the motion of the ball, and after being rotated 180° to face another table, were asked to recreate the path of the ball in *the same maze*. In some cases the speakers held the maze so that it was also rotated 180° (an egocentric condition), and in other cases

---

26 As we have already shown, this is not true in the case of Haun et al. (2011), however. This point goes unmentioned in Li et al. (2011), perhaps since the studies were nearly contemporaneous.

the maze was transferred to the second table without rotation (a geocentric condition). Surprisingly perhaps, Li et al. (2011:42) found that recall ability was significantly more accurate for this task in the egocentric condition. In general, for all four of Li et al.'s (2011) experiments, Tzeltal speakers were at least as accurate in those tasks requiring egocentric reasoning. This is an interesting point that suggests that the egocentric orientation capacities of these speakers may have been underestimated. Of course it requires replication, particularly given that there are potential confounding issues with the new methods employed by the researchers (some of which they discuss – see Li et al. 2011:42).

Assuming for the moment that Li et al.'s (2011) results would hold for the many other populations that have now been shown to rely on default geocentric orientation strategies (an important assumption that goes unmentioned in their study), it appears that speakers of languages with absolute/geocentric FoR strategies are capable of accurately utilizing egocentric concepts in nonlinguistic tasks, whenever egocentric reasoning is required.[27] This point is inconsistent with a strong deterministic approach according to which spatial language alone shapes spatial reasoning. It is far from inconsistent, however, with the relativistic claim that *tendencies* in one's spatial language foster *tendencies* in one's spatial cognition. In fact, open-ended tasks of the sort frequently relied upon by Levinson and colleagues could be considered particularly crucial to our understanding of linguistic FoR influence on nonlinguistic cognition, when contrasted with tasks with definitive answers. Open-ended tasks seem to reveal the default cognitive orientation of speakers,[28] and allow for ease of contrast of default FoR utilization across linguistic groups.

While Li et al.'s (2011) findings are important to our understanding of Tzeltal spatial reasoning, demonstrating that Tzeltal egocentric abilities surpass what is sometimes assumed, the authors' conclusions are arguably overextended. They claim that, because Tzeltal speakers are capable of accurately performing egocentric tasks, spatial language must not shape spatial reasoning in any profound way. The biggest issue with this claim stems from a basic methodological issue with their study (discussed in broad terms in Chapter 1 of this book): the lack of a control group of speakers of a language without

---

27 Note that the Hai‖om data in Haun et al. (2011) suggest that such capacities may be reduced by reliance on geocentric language, unlike the Tzeltal data in Li et al. (2011).

28 Li et al. (2011) suggest that subjects in open-ended tasks may simply be choosing the strategy that they believe the experimenter would like them to employ. The problem with this claim is that there is a wealth of ethnographic data suggesting that the strategies adopted in open-ended tasks are consistent with the patterns observed in everyday life. In other words, the consistency of reconstruction strategies is clearly not simply experimental artifact.

default geocentric FoR. In other words, while Li et al.'s data are crucial for improving our understanding of Tzeltal spatial cognition, some of their conclusions are difficult to evaluate without knowing, for example, how English or Dutch speakers would do on the same tasks they employ. It is possible and in fact quite plausible that the performance of the Tzeltal speakers in the geocentric condition (for the aforementioned maze task) far exceeds that of such control groups. If so, this point would corroborate the finding described in Haun et al. (2011) vis-à-vis Hai‖om and Dutch speakers: subjects that typically use geocentric FoR's in speech do relatively well at tasks requiring geocentric reasoning. To more substantively buttress their conclusion that language does not shape spatial cognition, Li et al. (2011) could have provided data with control groups consistent with their position. The absence of such control data is in fact puzzling given the strength of their conclusions. This is particularly true in the light of much anecdotal data that suggests that most speakers of English, for example, struggle with many tasks that rely on geocentric reasoning. For instance, perhaps like me you have often observed people, used to giving and being given directions in relative terms, turning maps to an egocentric perspective in order to make sense of their immediate surroundings.

Li et al. (2011:51) also claim that different linguistic strategies for frames of reference may essentially be epiphenomenal, owing themselves to "differences in the circumstances that populations find themselves in", presumably topographical features. Such an interpretation glosses over the well-known observation that geocentric language does not correlate with any particular environmental factor, and has now been documented for numerous populations living in radically disparate ecologies. What *has* been demonstrated for these various populations is that they all share geocentric language, and furthermore that they all share default geocentric spatial orientation in various spatial reasoning tasks. This central finding is certainly not vitiated by the Tzeltal speakers' abilities to accurately employ egocentric reasoning in non open-ended tasks. Furthermore, while Li et al. (2011) downplay the results in open-ended tasks, one could defensibly posit that such tasks are more indicative of the kinds of tasks faced by individuals in day-to-day living. Many if not most spatial reasoning tasks (e.g. generating directions to a destination, picturing one's home, envisioning a future furniture configuration, etc.) are open-ended, allowing people to choose whichever strategy they see fit. In some sense, we may be most interested in the results of open-ended tasks, then, and most curious about the default orientation strategies of various populations. The now strong correlation between default orientation strategies and particular linguistic FoR's remains a robust finding that requires explanation. The most straightforward explanation seems to be that proposed by Levinson and colleagues: linguistic practice helps to shape the default spatial orientation strategies that are so common to human cognition and experience. No viable alternative explanation for this correlation has emerged.

Not only does linguistic FoR correlate with default cognitive FoR according to the measures devised by Levinson and colleagues, it also correlates with patterns of gestures that co-occur with spoken language. For example, in languages in which the absolute FoR is basic, absolute-type gestures accompany stories in the language (see discussion in Majid et al. [2004]). This was evident in our consideration of some Guugu Yimithirr data above, for instance. Given that gestures potentially serve as a window into online cognitive processes, this correlation arguably supports the conclusion that linguistic FoR's impact such processes. A note of caution is in order here, however. It has frequently been assumed in the literature that spatial language motivates gestural patterns, e.g. that Guugu Yimithirr speakers point in cardinal directions because of the absolute FoR common to their language. While this is a common assumption, there is at least one documented case in which a FoR surfaces in the gestures of speakers to a more marked degree than it does in their spoken language: Yucatec Maya.

Unlike the Tenejapan Mayas, Yucatec Mayas do not rely predominantly on a geocentric FoR in speech. Bohnemeyer and Stolz (2006) suggest that the speakers of this language deploy all three FoR's fairly equitably in speech elicitation tasks. In naturalistic recordings, though, descriptions of object locations are generally conveyed without utilization of any of the three FoR's, and instead Yucatec speakers overwhelming employ deictic terms such as *te'(e)l*, 'here/there', and *way*, 'here', at the expense of terms associated with the three FoR's (Le Guen [2011:912]).[29] Le Guen (2011) sought to better delineate Yucatec speakers' awareness of their somewhat infrequently employed geocentric FoR via an elicitation task in which participants were asked to point to cardinal directions such as *chik'in*, 'west', by being prompted with the appropriate term. Surprisingly perhaps, Le Guen found that knowledge of these directions was modest for the eleven male speakers tested. These speakers only pointed accurately to the "south" and "north" in a slight majority of cases, though their accuracy for "west" exceeded 80% and for "east" exceeded 90%. Even more interestingly, the nine females tested struggled with this task, and were generally unable to accurately point to any of the cardinal directions when prompted with a given term. In other words, female Yucatec speakers are generally unfamiliar with the basic *terms* for cardinal directions in their language. Signifi-

---

29 For a detailed examination of the system of deixis in Yucatec Maya, I refer the reader to Hanks (2005).

cantly, though, both male and female speakers consistently employed an absolute/geocentric FoR when gesturing in a "location" task. For the task in question, speakers were asked to describe the location of a store with respect to a gas station. Both the store (the "figure") and the gas station (the "ground") in this task were located about 30 km from the experiment's setting. While geocentric terms were rarely employed by any of the twenty task participants (they once again relied almost exclusively on deictic terms), the co-speech gestures they utilized were overwhelmingly consistent with a geocentric FoR. In short, the twenty speakers tested did not employ geocentric spoken language, and the females were even unfamiliar with the meanings of the relevant geocentric terms, yet they did evince geocentric gestural patterns.

Le Guen (2011) also conducted a nonverbal 180° rotation task involving toy animals, like that described above by Figure 4.7, with 31 speakers. Surprisingly, perhaps, he found that participants employed a geocentric strategy in 85% of the trials. Most significantly, there was no significant difference between the rates at which males and females selected this strategy ($t(29)=0.28$, $p>0.05$), despite the fact that female speakers were generally unfamiliar with geocentric terms. Given the consistent geocentricity evident in the Yucatec gestures and in their problem solving, but the absence of geocentricity in their spoken language, these results suggest that default FoR usage in synchronic speech does not motivate the patterns in the Yucatec experimental data.

Whether one views Le Guen's findings through a relativistic lens depends in large measure on one's definition of language, and whether that definition subsumes co-speech paralinguistic gestures. To anthropologically oriented linguists, gestures accompanying speech are very much a crucial part of the linguistic system that also includes information coded in the vocal-auditory channel. (See for instance Hanks' [2005] influential work on deixis, as well as Enfield [2009].) There is now an extensive body of evidence suggesting that the advanced gestural communication of humans is crucial, both ontogenetically and phylogenetically, to the development of spoken language in our species (Tomasello [2008]). In some cases gestures have been shown to reflect cognitive processes associated with co-occurring spoken language, for instance in the case of certain metaphors and in the conception of time (Núñez and Sweetser [2006]). Nevertheless, the gestures in Yucatec Maya do not correlate neatly with spoken language, at least not to the extent that they do in Tzeltal Maya (see Levinson [2003:244–279]), and so any influences on cognition they might have are largely independent of synchronic speech.

Le Guen's (2011) results are surprising to the extent that they imply that gestural patterns may influence cognition even in those cases when default gestural FoR is not matched by default FoR in speech. This finding implies that dissociations between gestures and spoken language must be carefully accounted for in future work. To establish more clearly the influence of speech on nonlinguistic spatial cognition, researchers will need to tease apart the role of gesture from accompanying speech. Clearly not all cases are similar to that of the Guugu Yimithirr, for instance, for whom FoR patterns in gesture and speech so closely align.

These findings on the correlation of gesture and spatial cognition could be interpreted as evidence that gesture and speech merely reflect underlying facets of spatial cognition that vary cross-culturally. A natural question, then, is how we establish that linguistic patterns, including gestural ones, motivate the cross-cultural variation in spatial cognition that has now been so extensively documented. The following comments from Levinson (1997) are pertinent:

> It may be objected that the whole system of absolute orientation, the associated gesture and interaction system, is much more than merely a linguistic phenomenon... Why not, for example, reverse the argument and claim that the cognitive system of absolute spatial conception drives the language? The answer is that there is no obvious way in which a community-wide cognitive practice of this sort could come to be shared except through its encoding in language and other communicative systems like gesture (see Haviland 1993). (Levinson [1997:125])

Levinson claims that language *and* gesture offer the most plausible sources of cross-group disparities in orientation strategies, and this claim seems prescient in the light of Le Guen's (2011) data. In the case of Yucatec speakers who do not regularly employ cardinal direction terms, geocentric cognitive processes are apparently shared across the community because they are systematically encoded in a communicative manner, namely gesture.

It is worth noting also that even in the case of the Yucatec Mayas, the patterns evident in orientation tasks may owe themselves indirectly to patterns in spoken language. As Le Guen (2011:931) notes, adult men who rely on geocentric references in their speech may play a crucial role in maintaining the reliance on geocentric FoR in the gestures of others, resulting in the default geocentric orientation strategies evident among Yucatec Maya speakers. Put differently, patterns in speech may impact nonlinguistic cognition, only in a very indirect manner.

We should also point out that the shared geocentric gestures of Yucatec Mayas could be construed as a communicative vestige, owing themselves to ancient patterns in speech. Given the relative pervasiveness of geocentric FoR's in the speech of numerous Maya groups, there is a distinct possibility that such geocentric language was present in proto-Maya. Presuming momentarily that that was in fact the case, the existence of geocentric gestures in Yucatec communication is unlikely to be a recent innovation, and is more likely due to inherited features of their speech still evident in the language of older males. Under such an interpretation, the current patterns of spatial orientation, which apparently owe themselves in large measure to gestural language, may also owe themselves diachronically to spoken language. This is not a possibility considered in the literature, but one that merits some attention. If language can potentially impact nonlinguistic spatial cognition through vestigial co-speech gestural forms, then some sort of "diachronic relativity" might be at work. The mere existence of this possibility illustrates once again the complexity of the issues involved in comprehensively exploring the manners in which language can impact nonlinguistic cognition.

Ultimately the findings from studies like Le Guen (2011) underscore the fact that various factors may be involved in impacting spatial orientation strategies. Judging from the robust correlation between the FoR's used in language and in nonverbal experiments, across numerous cultures, patterns in speech are indeed one such factor. Yet co-speech gestures may also play a role. Furthermore, factors such as schooling and literacy, as well as other cultural and ecological factors, may play roles in some cases as well (see discussion in Dasen and Mishra [2010]), though they have been considered and ruled out in others (see Levinson [2003]). For example, there is a weak correlation between relative linguistic FoR's and urban cultures. This is not to suggest that relative language does not play a role in the preponderance of relative cognitive strategies in nonverbal tasks in such cultures, but that some other factor such as linear writing may also help to rigidly inculcate a default relative FoR in some speakers' conceptualization of space. The challenge that remains in this still-nascent area of inquiry is to better tease apart the roles of various factors, including default FoR's evident in discourse, in impacting nonlinguistic spatial cognition. There are many ways that this work can be refined going forward, and future work will hopefully more clearly establish how speech shapes spatial orientation *in association* with other factors such as patterns of gestural communication. For now, though, we must be satisfied with the rapidly accruing evidence that spoken and gestural language does influence the nonlinguistic selection of spatial FoR's, across a number of documented settings in an assortment of cultures.

4.4 Dead reckoning

As was mentioned in the introduction to this chapter, a fair amount of anecdotal data suggests that members of different populations vary significantly in terms of their abilities to point in particular cardinal directions when prompted to do so. College students and faculty in western university settings tend to struggle with such tasks. On the other hand, speakers of languages that are heavily reliant on geocentric FoR's have been shown to comparatively excel at such tasks. The anthropological and linguistic literature is replete with relevant anecdotes on way finding and dead reckoning abilities. In and of themselves, such anecdotes are inadequate support for the claim that geocentric language facilitates geocentric spatial orientation. Other factors, such as the physical environment in which the anecdotes are collected, may play a role. Say for example that some riverine indigenous group relies heavily on absolute directional terms analogous to "upriver" and "downriver", and that directions are typically provided with reference to these abstracted geocentric terms, which are absolute though not cardinal directions in the traditional sense. Now assume that speakers of this language are generally able to point in these "upriver" and "downriver" directions, even when surrounded by jungle and not near the river in question. We could confidently observe that such speakers have the ability to point to a particular geocentric direction on cue, in a way that most English speakers do not. Yet perhaps the heightened pointing abilities of the indigenous speakers would disappear if they were transported to a remote city. Given that the contexts in which speakers' performances are contrasted vary so significantly, the implication of language as a causal factor may be specious. In the example given earlier in the chapter, it was noted that Tzeltal speakers excel at pointing in specific cardinal-like directions. Yet again, though, some might claim that it is impossible to informatively contrast the dead reckoning/pointing behaviors of Tzeltal and English speakers, since the environments familiar to these speakers vary so significantly. Put differently, while English speakers may struggle with pointing in requested cardinal directions in the Tzeltal context, Tzeltal speakers might similarly struggle with such tasks in a completely foreign context. In short, while it is tempting to ascribe explanatory power to linguistic factors, various other contextual and experiential factors may play a role in fostering such disparate performance.

This line of reasoning, according to which cross-cultural disparities in dead reckoning skills are explainable largely in terms of environmental factors, is difficult to maintain in the face of more systematically gathered data. Levinson (2003:225–245) summarizes the results of a series of dead reckoning studies conducted among speakers of languages with geocentric FoR's and egocentric FoR's, respectively. The former group was comprised of Tzeltal (Brown and Levinson [1993]), Guugu Yimithirr, and Haiǁom (Widlock [1997]) speakers, while the latter consisted of Dutch, British English (Baker [1989]), and Japanese speakers. Participants were transported from their normal environments to a novel location. They were unaware that their dead reckoning skills would be tested. After being transported to locations at least two kilometers (and typically much more, as far as 350 km) away, they were asked to point in the direction of unobservable landmarks including a "home" landmark. In the case of the studies among the speakers of geocentric languages, visibility was heavily restricted at 40 meters or less. Numerous trials were conducted for each of the members of the six populations. The local ecologies varied significantly, as each of the six environments differed qualitatively in some respect from all of the others. For instance, only the Guugu Yimithirr speakers were tested in a rain forest, while only the Hai‖om speakers were tested in desert-like conditions. None of the participants were allowed to rely on maps, which in any case would have been unfamiliar to some.

The directions pointed to by the numerous task participants were coded according to heading (from 0–360°). This heading was then contrasted with the actual heading of the requested landmark, ascertained via GPS and other tools. Levinson (2003) describes the results obtained for the populations. It was found that the speakers of the three geocentrically biased languages consistently outperformed members of the other three groups, as evidenced by reduced angular deviation from the correct heading. More significantly perhaps, the speakers of such languages exhibited remarkable accuracy in the directions they pointed to for "home". Using "circular statistics" (Batschelet [1981]), Levinson (2003) calculated the "mean vector length" of the responses for each population. This metric quantifies the consistency of headings utilized by the speakers. The figure ranges from a minimum of zero, representing randomly selected headings, to a maximum of one. This maximum is only achieved when there is 100% similarity in the dead reckoning gestures of a group's respondents. For speakers of the three geocentric/absolute-biased languages, the mean vector lengths ranged from 0.858 (Tzeltal) to 0.95 (Guugu Yimithirr). For speakers of the egocentric/relative-biased languages, the mean vector lengths ranged from 0.2585 (Dutch) to 0.55 (English). Pairwise contrasts across linguistic FoR types revealed significant disparities, and in the predicted direction: speakers of languages with default geocentric FoR demonstrated much more homogeneity in their response patterns. That is, for each pairwise contrast the mean vector length of the speakers of a language with default geocentric FoR was significantly greater than that obtained for the speakers of a language with a default egocentric FoR.

Li et al. (2011:33) essentially discard the results of such dead reckoning experiments since the testing situations "varied between the comparison groups," putatively making the results impossible to interpret. This dismissal is perhaps a bit disingenuous, though. After all, while it would be impossible to completely control all the factors in a testing situation that includes such large geographic areas, many aspects of the testing situations were in fact controlled. In addition, the geographic variety represented by the studies in question potentially supports the idea that geocentric FoR usage in speech facilitates dead reckoning. That is, bearing in mind the diverse ecologies of the Guugu Yimithirr, Tzeltal, and Hai‖om speakers, their similar mean vector lengths are all the more remarkable. In sum, the data so far considered on this subject suggests that speakers of languages with default geocentric FoR's excel at dead reckoning tasks. A very plausible motivation for this tendency is that speakers of such languages are forced to think geocentrically by their habitual usage of absolute spatial language. Note that this interpretation, which admittedly would benefit from further substantiation among a greater assortment of cultures, does not imply that one cannot excel at dead reckoning if s/he does not speak such a language. As Levinson (2003:243) notes, fluency in such a language is not a necessary condition for excelling at dead reckoning. Judging from the results obtained to date, however, it is a sufficient one.

It is still possible that geocentric language and dead reckoning skills correlate positively because of some other confounding cultural variable. For that reason it is crucial that more data, from a much wider variety of cultures, be collected. Nevertheless, it is worth stressing that the cultures with geocentric-biased languages, in which relevant studies have so far been conducted, differ according to a variety of major parameters such as subsistence type and basic ecology. As of now, then, no viable alternative to geocentric-biased language has been presented as a possible motivator of the heightened dead reckoning abilities of such people. Regardless of one's belief in or agnosticism regarding the facilitating effects of geocentric language on wayfinding, however, the dismissal of cross-cultural variation in dead reckoning skills appears unwarranted. After all, in addition to the relevant experimental evidence on offer, there is also extensive anecdotal and ethnographic evidence for such cross-cultural variation.

4.5 Discussion and conclusion

It seems clear that the habitual symbolic representation of space impacts non-linguistic spatial cognition. While this symbolic representation is typically spoken, other communicative practices such as shared modes of gesture also seem to play a role in affecting spatial cognition. While there is now a rich literature on the interaction of language and spatial cognition, not all of which has been surveyed here, more work is required to better dissociate the influences of spoken language from those of other related facets of human cultures. Future methodological advances should catalyze the refinement of hypotheses regarding the correlation between crosslinguistic variation in spatial language and variations in performance on nonverbal tasks. New methodologies are already evident in some recent work on the topic, for instance Danziger's (2011) study of Mopan Maya spatial orientation strategies, in which tasks based on the three-dimensional manipulation of pieces of LEGO's yielded results consistent with a relativistic interpretation.

In a related vein, research advances should better inform our understanding of the mechanisms through which spatial language affects spatial cognition. Recent studies suggest such advances are already taking place. For instance, neuroimaging data (Dils and Boroditsky [2010]) suggest that processing motion language results in consistent motion "aftereffects" similar to the effects of motion-envisioning events. Given the close association between motion language and spatial language, alluded to in the discussion of "verb-framed" and "satellite-framed" languages in Section 4.2, such neurological effects of motion-language processing hint at analogous effects of spatial-language on neurocognitive processes. At the least the potential for such effects merits exploration. Future imaging studies may result in a clearer understanding of the neural mechanisms through which spatial language can affect the conceptualization of space.

Perhaps more pressingly, continued experimental work among children should hopefully play a crucial role in refining our understanding of the ways in which spatial language facilitates certain kinds of spatial cognition. For example, a recent study by Shusterman, Lee, and Spelke (2011) has helped illuminate the way in which language exerts influence on the spatial orientation strategies of 4-year-olds. That study demonstrated that a modest amount of verbal expression enables children to more accurately rely on landmark information while searching for an object after being disoriented, suggesting strongly that language affects the children's conceptual representation of their environment. While the study does not address variation in spatial cognition across populations, it sheds light on the way in which spatial language can impact cognition at an early age. Future studies among child speakers of numerous languages, differentiated by a typology of spatial language features, might elucidate the processes through which divergent language fosters divergent spatial cognition.

The strength and pervasiveness of linguistic effects on spatial cognition remains a matter of debate, and will likely remain so for some time. Majid et al. (2004) suggest for example that language plays a significant role in "restructuring" this domain. Whether one accepts this strong characterization or not, what seems uncontestable is that default strategies associated with the construal of topological concepts and FoR's differ significantly across cultures, and that these strategies correlate neatly with linguistic factors. Contra the suggestions of some work on this topic (Gallistel [2002]), it does not appear to be the case that languages simply differentially encode basic FoR's that are still utilized in some fundamentally equivalent way by their speakers (even if all FoR's may be accessible to all people). It also is not apparently the case that spatial cognition is fundamentally egocentric, contra the claims of some prominent studies, e.g. Wang and Spelke (2002). At least the cross-cultural ontogenetic data do not seem to support this position. After all, preferences for particular FoR's in language and behavior surface at a very early age, and there is no evidence that the egocentric FoR is acquired earlier or more easily than allocentric FoR's (see Majid et al. [2004]).

With all these points in mind, though, it remains an open question just how much language actually restructures the fundamental domain of spatial cognition. As work such as Dasen and Mishra (2010) demonstrates, other cultural factors such as schooling differences can also play a strong role in re-orienting patterns of spatial reasoning. Levinson and colleagues (and others working on this topic) do not claim that language is the *only* major factor to play a role in shaping habitual spatial cognition. It is certainly a pervasive one, though, and the only attested ubiquitous factor that consistently aligns with the behavior of subjects' in nonverbal spatial-reasoning tasks. This alignment is now attested in a variety of cultures and culture types. For all of the cultures with documented default geocentric strategies of spatial reasoning, their one easily uncovered commonality is the habitual engagement of geocentric language. Work on spatial language and cognition has now been carried out among cultures that vary according to a wide number of major parameters, including literacy, dwelling type, subsistence pattern, degree of individualism or collectivism, and ecological zone (see Majid et al. [2004:112]). Levinson and Wilkins (2006) consider data on numerous predominantly absolute-FoR languages, including Arrernte (Pama Nyungan), Balinese (Austronesian), Belhare (Tibeto-Burman), Guugu Yimithirr (Pama Nyungan), Haiǁom (Khoisan), Longgu (Austronesian), Tzeltal (Maya), and Warwa (Nyulnyulan).[30] Given the range of cultures and ecologies represented by these languages, the consist-

---

30 That study also includes studies on languages that rely heavily on multiple FoR's, namely Ewe (Niger-Congo), Kgalagadi (Bantu), Kilivila (Austronesian), Tamil (Dravidian), Tiriyó (Carib), and Yucatec (Maya). It includes as well studies on predominantly intrinsic-FoR languages, namely Jaminjung (Australia), Mopan (Maya), and Totonac (Totonacan)–not to mention studies of the predominantly relative-FoR Dutch, English, and Japanese languages.

ency of the correlation between geocentric language and geocentric behavior, at least in the nonverbal tasks so far implemented, is clearly not an ecologically motivated aberration.

While broad correlations between spatial language features and nonverbal cognition exist, it is worth reiterating that such a broad correlation does not imply that other ecological and socio-cultural factors (besides speech and gesture) play no role in impacting spatial cognition. Nevertheless, attempts to uncover other consistent influences on spatial cognition, such as gender roles, literacy rates, and age, have yielded mixed results. While such factors do correlate with spatial cognition strategies in a modest number of investigated cases (see Dasen and Mishra [2010], Polian and Bohnemeyer [2011][31]), they appear to have limited explanatory power in others (see discussion in Levinson [2003:193–197]). In short, no strong and consistent correlation between nonlinguistic factors and spatial reasoning types has surfaced, apart from the aforementioned modest tendency for cultures in urban environments to rely more heavily on relative FoR's. The absence of such a clear correlation, taken in concert with the clear linguistic FoR/spatial-cognition-strategy correlation, suggests strongly that language is a major player, probably the biggest player, in shaping habitual spatial cognition in open-ended tasks. Whether it completely restructures spatial cognition is another matter, and more studies such as Li et al. (2011), across a number of populations, may help to shed light on this issue. Recall that that study demonstrated that the habitual usage of geocentric language does not completely inhibit the Tzeltals' egocentric reasoning. Even in such a case, though, the frequent usage of geocentric language may facilitate geocentric reasoning more than it inhibits egocentric reasoning, and may help to restructure spatial cognition to the extent that geocentric cognition is enhanced in such groups, at least in contrast to speakers of languages that do not frequently appeal to absolute FoR's. As Gentner (2007:193) notes with respect to linguistic influences on spatial orientation, "The neo-Whorfian debate should not be on whether language forces one unique conceptual system on its speakers but on whether it privileges some systems over others."

---

31 This study was part of larger ongoing project entitled *Spatial language and cognition in Mesoamerica* (*MesoSpace*). A series of investigations made through this project are discussed in a 2011 issue of *Language Sciences*. While the findings in the studies vary, the results obtained among speakers of ten Mesoamerican languages are by and large consistent with a relativistic interpretation. O'Meara and Pérez Báez (2011:850) note that, with respect to the idea that patterns in these languages correlate with a "bias against the relative FoR", support is offered by data from "all languages in the MesoSpace sample".

Another issue that requires further exploration is the extent to which spatial reasoning is shared among hominidae. Perhaps surprisingly, the evidence on offer suggests that children and great apes are more likely to utilize allocentric reasoning for some basic tasks. (Gentner [2007], Haun et al. [2006]). In a series of experiments involving the basic rotation paradigm discussed above, Haun et al. (2006) discovered that four-year-old German children, as well as orangutans, gorillas, bonobos, and chimpanzees, performed better when the task entailed allocentric orientation than when it entailed egocentric orientation. Significantly, though, for eight-year-old German children the pattern was reversed. This finding accords well with the general conclusions of Haun, Levinson, and others that language serves to privilege certain forms of spatial cognition during development.

The effects surveyed in this chapter suggest habitual linguistic choices serve to spotlight or more quickly enable certain kinds of nonlinguistic thought, in this case related to spatial cognition. Geocentric language apparently augments basic geocentric spatial reasoning possibilities, allowing facilitated access to geocentric solutions to spatial reasoning problems. The data we have discussed are difficult to reconcile with agnosticism regarding the existence of *any* linguistic influence on nonlinguistic spatial cognition.

5 Time

5.1 Introduction

The odds are good that at some point you have spoken to someone about events that are going to happen in the days "ahead of" you. (Or in the weeks, months, or years ahead of you.) You might also have referred at some point to some challenges "in front" of you. Maybe you have talked about potential future events that you can see "on the horizon". Conversely, you likely have referred frequently in your life to occurrences that are now "behind" you since you have already "gone through" them. Given that the future is not actually a visible entity in front of your body, and the past is not some object or place that is behind it, such expressions are clearly metaphorical. In fact, there are several prominent metaphors that surface in English language about time. One of these might be termed TIME PASSING IS MOTION (Lakoff [1993]), evident for example when speakers talk about "going to" do future actions or when they mention "coming" events.[32] Another related prominent metaphor evident in English temporal language might be termed THE FUTURE IS IN FRONT/THE PAST IS BEHIND (see discussion in Lakoff [1987]). This specific spatial metaphor surfaces in a vast number of languages besides English. It is not a linguistic universal, however. In fact, there are languages in which the metaphor is not appealed to in any systematic fashion. In Aymara a diametrically opposed metaphor is evident, namely THE FUTURE IS BEHIND/THE PAST IS IN FRONT. This metaphor may seem counterintuitive, but in some respects it more directly correlates with reality. After all, we are unaware of what will transpire in the future, much like we cannot see what is behind us. Conversely, we are aware (or at least more aware) of what has happened in the past, much as we can see what is in front of us. Even the Aymara metaphor for time represents an egocentric perspective though, according to which linear time "passes through" the speaker. Another extant metaphor for time is seemingly even more exotic in that it eschews this sort of linear approach. Among the Yupno of New Guinea, the past is referred to as being downhill and the future is denoted as being uphill. (Nuñez et al. [2012]) This topographic metaphor for time is reflected during co-speech gestural patterns, regardless of the direction in which Yupno speakers are faced while speaking.

---

32 This metaphor can be further sub-categorized into related but distinguishable metaphors according to which ego moves through time, or in which time moves towards ego. See the relevant discussion in Núñez and Sweetser (2006).

One question that naturally arises in the light of such metaphorical variation across languages is whether it generates different conceptualizations of time across populations. Recent research has sought to address this issue, and in this chapter we consider some of the interesting findings that have resulted from that research.

5.2 Spatial metaphors and temporal conceptualization

The more general metaphor at work in both English and Aymara could simply be labeled as TIME IS A LINE. The common linear model of time surfaces not just in language but in a variety of nonlinguistic phenomena such as two-dimensional representations of time, for instance calendars in which days and other temporal units are represented via adjacent figures (often squares) as part of a linear array. In many languages like English, there is more than one linear metaphor for time available. (See footnote 31.) The commonality of linear metaphors for time is indicative of the pervasive manner in which people are apt to use the spatial domain as a source for references to the temporal domain. (Clark [1973], Gentner [2001]) The spatially oriented conceptualization of time so common to linguistic expressions appears to be motivated by the fact that people often rely on metaphors from physically concrete domains to refer to more abstract areas of experiences (Clark [1973], Lakoff and Johnson [1980]). The fact that space is fundamental to analogical reasoning associated with other domains such as time was even noted by Whorf, who stated that "our idea of space has also the property of acting as a surrogate of nonspatial relationships." (1956:159) Such "surrogate" metaphorical functioning is reified linguistically through numerous interrelated idioms that govern how we talk about time.

Given that space-based metaphors for time exist, we might speculate whether the disparate default patterns of spatial orientation evident across cultures result in divergent conceptualizations of time. Some recently collected evidence suggests that they do. Boroditsky and Gaby (2010) present some fascinating data on this topic, gathered among Pormpuraawans, members of an Australian aboriginal community in the Cape York Peninsula. Several indigenous languages are spoken in the community, all of which share an absolute-type system of spatial description. One of these languages is Kuuk Thaayorre, whose speakers (as mentioned in the last chapter) excel at cardinal-direction recall.

Boroditsky and Gaby (2010) conducted two simple tasks in order to test whether the absolute spatial representation so characteristic of these aboriginal languages and cultures impacts the representation of time among Pormpur-aawans, when contrasted to a control group of American English speakers. In the first task, subjects were presented with several sets of cards, each of which contained a series of images depicting a "temporal progression". For example, one set contained images of the same man at four different stages of his life. Subjects were individually presented with shuffled sets of cards, and upon each presentation were asked to correctly order the set on the ground in front of them. In the second "dot-drawing" task, speakers were presented with a dot on the ground in front of them, and asked questions such as: "If this here is today, where would you put yesterday? And where would you put tomorrow?" They then placed dots on the ground in response. For both tasks, each speaker was tested while facing in two directions, separated by 180° or 90°.

As expected, American English speakers placed earlier events in both tasks closer to their left side, and later events closer to their right. That is, their strategy towards the tasks revealed a left-to-right linear conceptualization of temporal progression, in 100% of the trials. This egocentric conceptualization is likely motivated in part by linguistic factors and/or by its specific congruence with the left-to-right orientations of writing and calendric representations of time in American culture. Crucially, the results obtained for the fourteen Pormpuraawans tested were strikingly divergent. While many of their picture and dot placements were oriented in a rightward fashion (i.e. with later events further to the right), many were oriented in a leftward manner. Furthermore, some of the placements were aligned sagittally, either leading away from or towards a subject's body. From an egocentrically oriented perspective, they might have seemed to be in disarray. However, when cardinal directions were considered, it was found that the Pormpuraawan responses tended to reflect a westward orientation. In other words, later events were placed further to the west in the linear arrays. While this tendency was far from exceptionless, it was significant. The westward orientation was utilized significantly more frequently than any other possible orientation. (By-participant and by-item t-test contrasts were significant at $p<0.01$ and $p<0.001$, respectively, when "westward" was contrasted with each of the three other vectors.) The general westward orientation of the Pormpuraawans also surfaced after they were rotated, demonstrating unequivocally that they were not relying on an egocentric orientation. Clearly, then, the strategies adopted by the two populations differed. One plausible motivation for the Pormpuraawans' strategy is that their temporal-progression orientation in such tasks reflects a spatial metaphor for time, based on the absolute orientation evident in their speech and co-speech gestures. This metaphor might be labeled THE PAST IS EAST or THE FUTURE IS WEST. There is an obvious physical motivation for this metaphor, since the sun rises in the east and is in the eastern part of the sky earlier in the day. Nevertheless, such reasoning is clearly analogical in nature. The extent to which it relies on language for its reification is unclear, however. The findings in Boroditsky and Gaby (2010) are consonant with an interpretation according to which spatial language helps to motivate cross-population differences in temporal conceptualization. It is quite plausible such linguistic differences play some role in fostering these differences, much as left=past/right=future calendric orientation likely plays a role as well. Ideally the specific role of purely linguistic factors could be explored by, for example, contrasting the results obtained among monolingual and bilingual Pormpuraawans. (Those participating in Boroditsky and Gaby [2010] were bilingual, fluent second-language speakers of English and familiar with western Australian culture.) Setting aside our uncertainty of the extent of linguistic influence on such findings, it is clear that the results reveal cross-cultural disparities in the way space is employed in analogical reasoning about time.

Space clearly serves as a natural foundation for analogical reasoning related to abstract aspects of human experience, like time. After all, the perception of time is much less tangible – its very conceptualization is fostered in fundamental ways by the reliance on analogy to space. In fact, for most of the world's people it is likely difficult to represent temporal conceptualization linguistically without relying on some sort of spatial metaphor. Implicit in some research on the topic is the assumption that such metaphors are universal to linguistic depictions of time (Casasanto [2008]). While this assumption is grounded on numerous analyses of temporal language in a wide variety of genetically unaffiliated languages, there are some apparent exceptions to this nearly ubiquitous pattern. Nuer (Evans-Pritchard [1939]) and Ainu (Ohnuki-Tierney [1973]) do not typically rely on spatial-based metaphors since they utilize event-based, non-calendric time systems. As Evans-Pritchard (1939:197) notes, the "Nuer have no abstract numerical system of time-reckoning based on astronomical observations but only descriptive divisions of cycles of human activities." Put differently, Nuer temporal language is seasonally influenced but socially oriented, and does not reflect an easily quantifiable approach towards time. Perhaps for this reason Nuer temporal language is not readily amenable to space-based analogical reasoning. A similar assessment could be made of Ainu, since time is also not quantified in that language. Speakers of that language "rarely or never reckon time intervals numerically" (Sinha et al. [2011:146], Ohnuki-Tierney [1973]). In the recently documented case of Tupí-Kawahib (a language related to Tupí-Karitâna and spoken in the same Brazilian state), there is also no evidence of quantified time or space-based metaphors for time.

Sinha et al. (2011) provide absorbing data on Kawahib. In an elicitation task, they found that there are no words in the language for "time", "year(s)", "week(s)", and "month(s)". Aside for names for two seasons ("dry" and "rainy"), as well as basic sub-divisions of these seasons and terms related to the diurnal cycle, there are apparently no temporal nouns in the language.

More interestingly perhaps, a simple experiment described in Sinha et al. (2011) suggests speakers of Kawahib (alternatively called Amondawa) do not conceive of time in a linear or, more generally, a spatial manner. The experiment was similar to the basic dot-placement task conducted by Boroditsky and Gaby (2010) among the Pormpuraawans. Four Kawahib speakers, out of a total population of 115, were tested individually. Each was provided with a number of paper plates. They were then asked, in their native language, to "make a map of time in Amondawa with them" (Sinha et al. [2011:150]), so that each paper plate would represent one unit of Amondawa time, for instance the *kuaripe*, or 'dry season'.

Sitting on the floor, the speakers placed the plates in front of themselves. A consistent pattern emerged across the four respondents. Each of the speakers placed the plates in a curvilinear pattern directly in front of themselves. There was no evidence of any sort of cyclic depiction of time, since no speakers placed the plates in a circular or approximately circular configuration. Furthermore, there was no evidence of a clear linear representation of time, since no speakers placed the plates in an approximately straight line. Most tellingly, the speakers did not utilize a default left-right or right-left strategy. That is, there was no evidence that they conceive of time in some directional sense, as has been observed in populations as diverse as Americans and Pormpuraawans.

In a second iteration of the task, the Amondawa were asked to use the paper plates to describe the temporal sequence of parts of the diurnal cycle for which there are names in Kawahib. The results were identical, to the extent that all participants organized the plates in a curvilinear fashion, one that revealed neither a linear nor cyclical conceptualization of time. In short, the data in Sinha et al. (2011) suggest that speakers of Kawahib, which exhibits a paucity of temporal nouns and which lacks any spatial metaphors for time, do not apparently conceive of time in a linear or cyclical fashion. Furthermore, they apparently do not conceptualize earlier events as originating to the "left" along some axis (as English speakers often do), nor to the "east" (as Pormpuraawans often do). The findings in Sinha et al. (2011) are modest to the extent that the paper plate task they describe was only conducted with four Amondawans. Given the consistency of those four speakers, though, and given the striking pattern evident in those speakers' responses, there are several implications to the study. Most relevant for our purposes, the results provide experimental evidence that the common spatial basis for temporal language is not universal. As the authors note, "The widespread linguistic mapping ... between space and time, which is often claimed to be universal, is better understood as 'quasi-universal'." (2011:165) More specifically, in this case of aspatial temporal language, there is no evidence for a cyclical or linear representation of time in the minds of speakers. The mapping between space and time is absent at the linguistic level, but is also apparently lacking at a basic conceptual level.

The Amondawa findings help us to better frame the results obtained among populations such as the Pormpuraawans and Americans. As radical as the differences of temporal conceptualization appear to be between these latter two groups, both groups still utilize spatially oriented conceptualizations of time, much as both groups speak languages with divergent spatial language that seems to impact the way time is conceived. The Amondawa data suggest that, when spatial language is not accessed for the purposes of temporal reference, the conceptualization of time may be more divergent still.

As Sinha et al. (2011:166) themselves stress, their findings on the Amondawa require more extensive testing among a larger number of Kawahib speakers, as well as among speakers of other languages that may exhibit such aspatial temporal reference. Future work with members of the Amondawa culture may demonstrate for example whether those who have more experience with spatial temporal language in Portuguese are less likely to depict time with a curvilinear pattern and are more likely to shift to a linear representation. Such results might help to distinguish the extent to which the differing conceptualization of time among the people is due to linguistic or more general cultural factors (in the manner evident in other work on the topic, see Section 5.3). After all, it is possible that the cross-group variation in temporal conceptualization evident among English speakers, Pormpuraawans, and Amondawans, may result partially or entirely from nonlinguistic cultural disparities (e.g. disparate calendric-representation traditions, or lack thereof). Nevertheless, the findings described in Boroditsky and Gaby (2010) and Sinha et al. (2011) are noticeably consistent with an account suggesting that linguistic spatial-temporal metaphors, or their absence, impact speakers' performance on nonlinguistic tasks.

Bearing in mind exceptions such as the case of Kawahib, it is fair to say that spatial-temporal metaphors are nearly universal in the world's languages. Furthermore, in the many languages in which such metaphors have been documented, one metaphor surfaces recurrently: THE FUTURE IS IN FRONT/THE PAST IS BEHIND. (While strictly speaking these are two separate metaphors, we refer to them as a unit given their clear inter-dependence.) As mentioned above, though, this particular linear orientation towards time does not surface in all languages. As is discussed in detail in Núñez and Sweetser (2006),

Aymara systematically indexes a metaphor that they term FUTURE IS IN BACK OF EGO/PAST IS IN FRONT OF EGO. The motivations for this typologically unusual metaphor likely stem from another metaphor that is common to the world's cultures, namely KNOWLEDGE IS VISION (Lakoff and Johnson 1980). That is, since speakers know which events have occurred in the past, by metaphorical extension they can see those events. On the other hand, events in the future are "unseen" (see Miracle and Yapita [1981]). Regardless of the motivation for this analogical orientation towards time, its existence in Aymara is documentable in both speech and co-speech gesture. In fact, Aymara is the only well-documented case in which this metaphor has been shown to exist,[33] though there is limited evidence that it might be found in other Andean languages (Núñez and Sweetser [2006]).

Linguistic evidence for this metaphor is not difficult to uncover in Aymara, and revolves primarily around two words, *nayra* and *qhipa*. The former means 'eye', 'sight', or 'front', and also is used in temporal expressions referring to past events. The latter means 'back' and is also used in temporal expressions referring to future events. The terms are polysemous, then.[34] Examples (5.1)-(5.4) contain expressions in which these two terms are used for deictic time references. These clauses are taken from Núñez and Sweetser (2006:415,416).

(5.1)	*nayra*		*mara*		
	eye/sight/front		year		
	'last year'				
(5.2)	*ancha*	*nayra*		*pacha*	*-na*
	a lot	eye/sight/front		time	in/on/at
	'a long time ago'				
(5.3)	*qhipa*		*uru*		
	back/behind		day		
	'a future day'				
(5.4)	*aka*	*-ta*	*qhipa*	*-ru*	
	this	from	back/behind	to,towards	
	'from now on'				

These and other examples that could be adduced indicate pretty clearly that the FUTURE IS IN BACK/PAST IS IN FRONT metaphor surfaces in Aymara

---

33 There are some suggestions in the literature that this metaphor surfaces in languages such as Classical Greek, Maori, Toba, and Malagasy. See Núñez and Sweetser (2006:413) for a reassessment of these claims.

34 In the case of *nayra* this polysemy is based in part on a metonymic link, wherein the 'eye' denotes a part of the 'face' and more generally the 'front' of ego.

speech. One might object, however, that such expressions are not directly comparable to English expressions such as the "those days are behind me" or "the holidays are ahead of us" since the Aymara expressions do not refer to the first person. Put differently, it is not immediately clear from these expressions whether the metaphor at work in Aymara actually references the location of events with respect to the speaker's body, as the metaphor in English (and so many other languages) clearly does. Co-speech gestures in Aymara suggest unequivocally, however, that speakers are in fact denoting the metaphorical location of events with respect to their own bodies.

Metaphoric gestures often accompany metaphoric speech. Furthermore, patterns in such co-speech gesture have offered numerous important insights into subconscious patterns in cognition (Goldin-Meadow [2003], McNeill [2005]). The "window into cognition" such gestural patterns afford is evident, for example, in Le Guen's (2011) study of spatial reference among Yucatec Mayas, discussed in the previous chapter. In that case it was found that co-speech gestures were crucial to the elucidation of communicative influences on a facet of nonlinguistic cognition. The same could be said of co-speech gestures in Aymara, though in the case of Aymara the gestures in question are more obviously tied to spoken data such as those in (5.1)–(5.4).

Núñez and Sweetser (2006) conducted interviews with 30 Aymara individuals in Northern Chile, between the ages of 38 and 84. Most of these individuals were fluent Aymara speakers, though most also spoke Spanish with varying degrees of fluency. A handful were members of the Aymara community but spoke only Spanish fluently. The older individuals tended to have higher rates of Aymara fluency and lower rates of Spanish fluency. The interviews generally lasted from 20 to 50 minutes, and were video recorded. The authors then analyzed the resultant video (approximately 20 hours), in order to uncover patterns in the co-speech gestures related to temporal reference. Here we are concerned with the gestural patterns they uncovered for the sagittal plane, in which speakers pointed in front of themselves or in a rearward direction during instances of temporal deixis.

The most basic finding evident in the analysis of the video recordings was that Aymara speakers pointed frontwards along the sagittal plane when referring to past events, and pointed rearward when referring to events in the future. This tendency was mitigated by the degree of fluency in Spanish, however. Those Aymara speakers who did not speak Spanish (and were older) used a past=front/future=behind system of co-speech gesture in four of four cases. Conversely, the Aymara who only spoke Spanish (and were younger) used a past=behind/future=front gestural system in five of six cases. This disparity was significant according to a one-tailed Fisher's exact probability test ($p=$

0.024). In the words of the authors, "fluency in Aymara relates to frontward gestures referring to the past, whereas fluency in Spanish relates to backward gestures." Conversely, fluency in Aymara correlated with backward gestures used to refer to the future, while fluency in Spanish related to frontward gestures to refer to the future. For instance, in one case an Aymara speaker utilized a backward ipsilateral thumb movement at the moment he uttered the phrase *quipa timpun*, 'future time' (2006:433).

The consistency between the Aymara spoken and gestural data vis-à-vis temporal deixis suggests that there is a linkage between language about time and wider cognitive processes, much as data from Amondawa and other cultures have suggested. This does not imply necessarily that the linkage is causal, though, i.e. that language disparities create cognitive disparities. But such linkages do demonstrate that these linguistic metaphors are not just diachronic residue, i.e. that they do not merely have some etymological association with a conceptual metaphor. Given that the relevant verbal expressions do not represent recent innovations, it seems plausible that the relevant patterns in temporal language help to motivate synchronic cognitive patterns that surface in, and are likely reinforced by, patterns of co-speech gesture. Alternatively, one might conclude that the gestural patterns are more likely to individually motivate the relevant cognitive patterns. As mentioned in Chapter 4's discussion of gesture in Yucatec Maya, however, co-speech gestures are not entirely dissociable from spoken language. After all, "Finding after finding has confirmed that gestures are produced in synchronicity with speech, that they develop in close relation with speech, and that brain injuries affecting speech production also affect gesture production." (Núñez and Sweetser 2006:419)

With respect to the current discussion, it seems unlikely that gestural patterns alone motivate the orientation towards time among fluent Aymara speakers. Instead, these gestural patterns seem to offer a window into a particular way of conceiving time, one that has been passed on from generation to generation of Aymara speakers through the only systematic semiotic means capable of playing such a role in the culture: speech. As McNeill (1992) and others have noted, co-speech gestures vary crosslinguistically, and are subject to language-specific modulation. They are typically unconscious, and do not result from overt extrication of language-consistent patterns. For that reason, studying them yields insights into cognitive patterns below the level of consciousness, and the Aymara data are plausibly interpreted as doing just that.[35]

---

[35] One ancillary question that arises in the discussion of Aymara is why the temporal metaphor evident in the language is attested at all given that it has not been documented outside Andean cultures. Núñez and Sweetser (2006:419) offer one interpretation: In Aymara, the description of an event is grammatically required to denote whether the event was seen or unseen. It is a crucial distinction in the Aymara (and more generally, Jaqi languages') system

The Aymara data in Núñez and Sweetser (2006) were all excised from speech events. So while the gestural and spoken data coincide, it is possibly the case that these patterns only surface during online language usage. In other words, a skeptic might suggest that the patterns only surface because Aymara speakers must encode their gestures in a way that is consistent with their native language, and that these patterns (even if subconscious) do not necessarily point to fundamental differences in *nonlinguistic* temporal cognition between Aymara speakers and, say, English speakers. Even if we were to consider these results merely side effects of online linguistic processing, however, it is difficult to argue that they are somehow trivial. After all, the spatial metaphor for time evident in Aymara speech and gesture is ubiquitous in Aymara communication. Even if one were hesitant to accept the (at least) plausible claim that the speech and co-speech gestures in question reflect a remarkable *nonlinguistic* conceptualization of time, one cannot ignore the pervasiveness with which this metaphor surfaces in Aymara behavior.

A strict "online" interpretation of the Aymara data is also difficult to reconcile with a subtle point evident in Núñez and Sweetser (2006). In several of the video-recorded excerpts containing elderly Aymara speakers gesturing, they gesture frontwards while referring to the past, even when speaking in Spanish. The Aymara speakers in question do not change their gestural patterns (at least not in the cases in question, see Núñez and Sweetser [2006:430–432]) when they translate their speech into Spanish. For instance, as one speaker produces the word *antiguamente* 'long ago, in the past', he uses his index finger to point frontwards. In another case, when an elderly speaker is referring to *tiempo futuro*, 'future time', he gestures "across his body and pointing backward, contralaterally over his left shoulder." (2006:432) The fact that front=past/behind=future gestures are employed even during the utilization of another language suggest that these co-speech gestures reflect deep cognitive processes rather than "merely" linguistic processes that result from the online engagement of a specific spatial metaphor for time.

The results in Núñez and Sweetser (2006) are similar to other findings in the literature that have provided evidence for metaphorical influences on cognitive processes associated directly with language utilization, for instance in Gentner (2001) and Gentner, Imai, and Boroditsky (2002). The latter study dem-

---

of irrealis/realis evidentiality. So the importance of seeing (realis) or not seeing (irrealis) events in the language correlates neatly with the grammaticalization of *nayra*, 'front' (seen/realis) as a past tense marker, and of *quipa* 'behind' (unseen/irrealis) as a future marker. This correlation does not predict that all languages with similar evidential systems should have similar patterns of temporal deixis, it merely assists in better understanding the case of Aymara.

onstrated that the usage of conflicting metaphors results in extra processing costs when speakers are asked to read or hear a series of sentences about the relative timing of events, as evidenced by delays in their temporal inferences regarding the sequencing of events in question. Such results demonstrate effects of conventionalized metaphors on thought, though the effects in question are clearly tied to the engagement of language faculties. Other studies demonstrating the close linkage between spatial thought and temporal language include Boroditsky (2000) and Boroditsky and Ramscar (2002), which have demonstrated the influence of spatially focused thoughts on the interpretation of ambiguous questions about time. For example, in the latter study participants were asked to think about themselves moving through space, or about an object moving through space. They were then prompted with a question: "Next Wednesday's meeting has been moved forward two days. What day is the meeting now that it has been rescheduled?" There are two possible answers here, of course, either Monday or Friday. The answer selected by the respondents depended in large measure on whether they were first thinking about themselves moving forward (in which case the answer was more likely to be "Friday"), or about something else moving forward (in which case the answer was more likely to be "Monday"). In other words, if they thought of themselves (ego) moving forward, moving a day of the week "forward" meant moving it further from themselves.

In a related study, Matlock, Ramscar, and Boroditsky (2005) found that even instances of so-called fictive motion through space impacted thoughts about time. Fictive motion surfaces in linguistic expressions involving words for motion, even though no physical motion is actually entailed, as in "The highway runs along the coast". In one of the experiments described in the study, 142 Stanford undergraduates were presented with sentences that involved fictive motion (e.g. "The tattoo runs along this spine") or did not involve fictive motion (e.g. "The tattoo is next to the spine"). They were asked to draw images based on these sentences and were then presented with the same question mentioned above, utilized in the other related studies ("Next Wednesday's meeting..."). The responses to this question varied in accordance with whether or not they had drawn an image for a sentence with fictive motion or one without fictive motion. In cases with fictive motion, participants were more likely to respond "Friday" than "Monday", when contrasted to cases without fictive motion ($p<0.01$ based on a Chi-square test). These results suggest that the interaction of motion language and temporal thought is extensive. After all, the mere utilization of such language resulted in subconscious effects on the question-response patterns, even though the motion presented in the stimuli sentences was fictive rather than literal.

Findings such as those in Boroditsky and Ramscar (2002) and Matlock, Ramscar, and Boroditsky (2005) demonstrate effects of spatial metaphors for time on the construal of the sequencing of events. Such clear linkages between spatial and temporal language could still be interpreted as online "thinking for speaking" effects, though, since the tasks in these studies involved linguistic responses. Nevertheless, given the ubiquity of language it seems plausible that such effects associated with online linguistic processing could impact other completely nonlinguistic cognitive processes.

Recent research has sought to more definitively establish whether or not metaphors evident in temporal language have demonstrable effects on speakers' nonlinguistic cognition. Some work has demonstrated that the presentation of certain linguistic stimuli result in nonlinguistic behavioral effects. Other work has demonstrated that such effects surface even without linguistic priming, i.e. in completely nonlinguistic contexts. Let us consider first some of the work on the former sort of phenomena, in which linguistic priming yields effects on nonlinguistic behavior.

Miles, Nind, and Macrae (2010) demonstrate one way that the temporal and spatial domains are linked in human behavior. Specifically, they address the phenomenon of "chronesthesia", the subjective motion through imagined time that is characteristic of our species (Suddendorf and Corballis [2007]). They examine whether the metaphorical associations of past=behind and future=forward impinge on body posture during temporal thought. Twenty individuals were tested individually in the study. Each participant was blindfolded and had a motion sensor attached to the side of their upper left leg. This motion sensor was capable of measuring body sway. Participants, who were unaware of the goal of the task, stood in a pre-designated spot, and were told to imagine two scenarios while standing in place. In the first of these scenarios, they were asked to remember what their everyday life had been like four years prior, and to imagine a typical day during that time. In the case of the second scenario, they were told to envision what their life might be like four years in the future, and to imagine a typical day during that time. Motion data conveying the amount of forward and backward sway by the participants were collected, for a total of 15 seconds after the presentation of each set of instructions. The authors found that when participants imagined events four years prior to the experimental setting, they tended to sway backwards in a nearly imperceptible manner. Conversely, when they envisaged events four years in the future, they tended to sway forwards. Furthermore, this cross-condition discrepancy was exacerbated by the duration of the testing. Body sway increased incrementally during the 15 second testing segment, though in opposite directions depending on whether participants were asked to envision the past or the future. Positive and negative sway generally ranged from two millimeters forward to two millimeters backward. Linear regression equations were used to depict the patterns of body movement, along the anterior-posterior sagittal plane. In the case of trials involving future imagery, the slope of the equation ($y=0.14x+0.82$, $r^2=.64$) was positive, indicating the increased forward leaning as a function of time spent imagining the future. In the case of trials involving past imagery, the slope of the equation ($y=-0.08x-0.17$, $r^2=.37$) was negative, indicating the increased backward leaning as a function of time spent imagining the past. The difference in body postures across the two conditions was found to be significant ($p<.05$) according to several mixed ANOVAs.

Miles, Nind, and Macrae (2010) do not specifically address the possibility that an aspect of English metaphors for time, which does not surface in all languages, may motivate their findings. Nevertheless, one suspects that such patterns of chronesthesia would not be observed among Amondawa and Aymara speakers, for example. Regardless, the results in the study reveal a remarkable way in which construing the future as being towards ego's front and the past as towards ego's back yields effects on a nonlinguistic facet of human behavior.

In a similar vein, Casasanto and Boroditsky (2008, 2003) have demonstrated the existence of nonlinguistic cognitive patterns consistent with spatial metaphors for time in English. Crucially, though, the results in Casasanto and Borodtisky (2008), which we will focus on here, were not based on any sort of linguistic priming. In other words, the authors conducted a completely nonlinguistic task whose results hinted at underlying linguistic influence on the cognitive patterns in question. In six related experiments with MIT undergraduates, they demonstrated that the visual spatial displacement of a stimulus impacts the perceived duration with which viewers are presented with that stimulus. Interestingly, variations in duration of stimuli did not impact their perceived visual displacement. The authors suggest that the most plausible motivation for this asymmetric effect is the pervasiveness of spatially grounded metaphors for time evident in the English language, namely the "time as distance" analogy evident in expressions such as "long time" or "short time". To more clearly represent what is meant by this spatial effect on the nonlinguistic construal of time, let us examine one of the experiments described in the study.

Nine English speakers viewed growing lines on a computer screen. These lines varied in their final displacement/length (200 to 800 pixels) and also varied in terms of the duration for which they were presented (one to five seconds). There was not a direct correspondence between actual duration of presentation and actual visual displacement. For example, some lines became relatively long in a short amount of time. The authors were interested in whether, in such cases, speakers would (for instance) perceive the duration to be greater merely because the length of the visual displacement was greater, or whether in cases of less displacement perceived duration would be reduced. They were also concerned with whether variations in duration would affect the perceived lengths of the lines. A total of nine lengths and nine durations were employed, for a total of 81 stimuli types. Each participant viewed 162 line tokens, from a normal viewing distance. After witnessing each token, they were asked to reproduce the amount of visual displacement (i.e. the physical length) of the line on the screen via movement of a mouse, or alternatively to reproduce the duration for which the line had been presented, by clicking a mouse twice. Interestingly, the researchers found that the length of a line affected the perception of the time for which the line was visible. Lines that grew longer were more likely to be perceived as having been displayed for a longer duration, though this perception was not always accurate. Lines that were shorter were more likely to be perceived as having been displayed for a shorter duration. The results demonstrated that visual information in the spatial domain impacted the perception of qualities in the temporal domain. The reverse relationship did not hold, however. That is, the duration of a displayed line did not impact its perceived visual displacement.

In order to more precisely quantify the effects of visual displacement on duration, the authors formulated linear regressions of the data. Estimated duration of stimuli, in milliseconds, was charted according to amount of actual visual displacement, in pixels. The correlation evident in this regression ($y=0.63x+2503$) was positively sloped and remarkably strong, at $r^2=0.94$. Estimated visual displacement was also charted according to amount of actual duration. In this case, the regression ($y=0.003x+440$) was nearly flat, and the correlation was extremely weak, at $r^2=0.05$. Casasanto and Boroditsky (2008) present the results of five other related experiments. In all cases the resultant regressions revealed a positive correlation between actual visual displacement and perceived duration, with r^2 values ranging from 0.72 to 0.94. In all cases as well, the resultant regressions revealed very little correlation between actual duration and perceived displacement, with r^2 values ranging from 0.03 to 0.29. In short, their data suggest strongly that temporal perception of English speakers varies in accordance with spatial factors. It is worth noting that, setting aside the spatial effects on the perception of duration, the participants' judgments of visual displacement and duration were both quite accurate overall. So the results do not owe themselves to some inherent difficulty in the task vis-à-vis duration assessment. They owe themselves instead to an asymmetrical interaction between spatial information and cognitive processes associated with the perception of time. The asymmetrical dependence of the latter on the former suggests that the findings are the result of space-based metaphors for time in the English language, rather than some more general interaction between thought about space and thought about time. (Casasanto and Boroditsky [2008:589]) The results are suggestive only, though, since the study in question considers only data from English speakers. In research considered in the following section, Casasanto, Boroditsky and other researchers more directly address the possibility that the different metaphors for time evident in languages result in cross-population differences in the conceptualization of time.

Taken one by one, the sorts of "metaphorical" effects described so far in this chapter for a variety of languages do no necessitate a causal role of linguistic metaphors in shaping nonlinguistic thought about time. Were we to consider the results obtained among English speakers in isolate, for instance, we might merely conclude that all humans' conceptualization of time is spatially oriented, and that this orientation towards time happens to surface in language. Taken in concert, however, the above studies are irreconcilable with such an account. After all, the cognitive patterns in question vary significantly across the cultures and associated languages examined individually in the respective studies. Clearly humans vary in the way they map time onto space (or, as the Amondawa data demonstrate, *whether* they may time onto space). Nevertheless, one could argue that these cross-cultural differences, while correlating remarkably well with crosslinguistic differences, do not necessarily imply a causal role of language in nonlinguistic cognition since the patterns may be due to other cultural disparities. While such a perspective is potentially defensible, it suffers from a weakness that is generally symptomatic of radically skeptical perspectives towards linguistic relativity: How are such cross-cultural differences in thought transmitted and maintained across generations except through the utilization of the associated linguistic factors? Thought processes are not transmitted genetically, of course, and language is the most natural candidate for the cross-generational transmission of such cognitive processes. Predictably, in cases such as that of the Aymara in which the language is being lost, the nonlinguistic conceptual orientation towards time hinted at by the language is also atrophying – replaced not coincidentally in that case by the conceptual orientation evident in the spatially based temporal metaphors in the replacement language, Spanish.

One of the recurring points of the studies thus far considered is that there are differences across languages in the sort of spatial metaphors that are employed for the denotation of the sequencing of time. The studies have also demonstrated that patterns in temporal language do surface in facets of nonlinguistic cognition. While the findings surveyed so far are consonant with a relativistic position, though, none of the individual studies surveyed has explicitly demonstrated that a given *crosslinguistic* dissimilarity in temporal language yields an associated dissimilarity in nonlinguistic thought. Some recent studies have directly addressed this point via the controlled contrast of populations speaking different languages. Next we consider some of the more noteworthy findings from such work.

5.3 Crosslinguistic studies on temporal perception

The findings in Casasanto and Boroditsky (2003, 2008) suggest that English speakers' perception of time is impacted by the space-based metaphor evident in expressions such as "long time". If this interpretation is correct we might predict that, for speakers of languages in which this metaphor is less prevalent and in which other metaphors are more prevalent, experimental inquiries into their perception of duration should yield disparate results from those evident in Casasanto and Boroditsky (2003, 2008). For instance, it is well known that some languages rely primarily on spatial metaphors for time of a different sort than the linear "time as distance" metaphor so common in English. Consider examples (5.5)-(5.8), taken from Casasanto et al. (2004), which contain instantiations of the "length" metaphor in English, along with their closest equivalent translations into Greek.

(5.5)   long night
            megali nychta 'big night'
(5.6)   long relationship
            megali schesi 'big relationship'
(5.7)   long party
            parti pou kratise poli 'party that lasts much'
(5.8)   long meeting
            synantisi pou diekese poli 'meeting that lasts much'

As we see in these examples, English phrases relying on the length-based "time as distance" analogy for time are translated into Greek without reliance on that metaphor. Instead a "time as quantity" metaphor is used to express duration in these cases. This metaphor is spatial, but clearly three-dimensionally oriented unlike the English metaphor in question. Given the pervasiveness of the "time as quantity" metaphor in Greek, we might predict that the behavior of Greek speakers in experiments such as that in Casasanto and Boroditsky (2008), described above, would differ from the behavior of English speakers.

Casasanto et al. (2004) sought to test this prediction by undertaking a series of tasks with speakers of Greek and English. They also conducted the tasks with speakers of Indonesian, a language that, like English, relies heavily on the "time as distance" metaphor, and Spanish, a language that, like Greek, relies heavily on the "time as quantity" metaphor.

Prior to reviewing the experimental results in Casasanto et al. (2004), it is worth noting that the authors conducted web-based searches to demonstrate the prevalence of the relevant metaphors in the aforementioned languages. For example, they searched via Google for the expressions "long time" and "much time" and found that the former English expression was nearly three times as common as the latter. Similar results obtained for Indonesian, for the phrases *waktu panjang*, 'long time', and *waktu baynak*, 'much time'. In the case of Spanish and Greek however, phrases relying on the quantity-based metaphor were much more common than phrases relying on the distance-based metaphor. In the case of Greek, *poli ora*, 'much time', was about four times as common as *makry kroniko diatstima*, 'long time'. In the case of Spanish, *mucho tiempo*, 'much time', was almost nine times as common as *largo tiempo*, 'long time'. These search results are consistent with native speaker intuitions regarding the prevalence of the metaphors in the languages, though they are based on coarse corpus analysis methods.[36]

Casasanto et al. (2004) conducted the same experiment described above from Casasanto and Boroditsky (2008, 2003), with 65 speakers of all four languages. As predicted, they found that the interaction between visual displacement and perceived duration was asymmetrical in the case of English and Indonesian speakers. These speakers' perceptions of durations correlated positively with the length of the observed line on the computer screen. Linear regressions charting perceived duration (in ms) along the y-axis vs. actual vis-

---

36 For instance, the authors only consider one exemplar from each of the metaphors in question, for each language. There are other English expressions besides "much time" that rely on a quantity-based metaphor for time. These include "in a little while" or "a lot of time", which are hardly infrequent. Using the same Google-based methods used in Casasanto et al. (2004), searches I ran recently yielded 475 million cases of "long time" and 390 million cases of "a lot of time". Another search yielded 52 million cases for the pluralized "lots of time". Surprisingly the total number of hits for each of the two expressions ("long time" vs. "lot(s) of time") is quite similar (475 vs. 442 million). This sort of result suggests that the disparity between the rates at which the relevant metaphors are used in English may be exaggerated by the methods in Casasanto et al. (2004). It is worth stressing, then, that though one can use the word "long" to refer to the duration of any event, as in "long lunch", "long discussion", "long tv show", etc., the phrase "a lot" cannot be used in an analogous fashion. This fact, better than the internet frequency of "long time", reflects the entrenchment of the "time as distance" metaphor in English.

ual displacement (in pixels) on the x-axis had very positive slopes in both cases. The correlations were quite strong, at r^2=0.98 for English speakers and r^2=0.80 for Indonesian speakers. Significantly, this sort of space-on-time influence was not evident when the Spanish and Greek speakers' perceptions of duration were tested. The resultant regressions in the latter cases were only weakly positive, with non-significant correlations (r^2=0.33 for Greek speakers, r^2=0.13 for Spanish speakers).

What of the influence of the "time as quantity" metaphor on temporal perception? If language impacts the nonlinguistic perception of duration, shouldn't speakers of Greek and Spanish have their perception of time influenced by quantity-oriented (rather than length-oriented) visual stimuli? Furthermore, wouldn't we expect such an asymmetric influence not to surface for English and Indonesian speakers? To test these associated predictions, Casasanto et al. (2004) also conducted an experiment with all four groups of speakers that tested specifically for this sort of quantity-on-time influence. The experiment was quite similar to that described above from Casasanto and Boroditsky (2008), differing in one crucial respect. Unlike the visual displacement task, participants did not view a line that grew incrementally on a computer screen. Instead, they were presented with depictions of abstract "containers", 600 pixels high and 500 pixels wide. They were told to imagine the containers were filling with water, and the depictions showed the containers "filling" with pixels, one line at a time. The durations for which the containers were displayed varied, as did the amount of pixels filled into the containers. A total of 162 container-fill image sequences were presented to the participants. As in the case of the analogous visual-displacement task, participants were asked to click a mouse twice to represent the duration for which they had witnessed each container. The prediction in this case was that images depicting greater "fill" amounts would result in increases in the perception of their duration, for speakers of Spanish and Greek. Also, given the relative weakness of the "time as quantity" metaphor in English and Indonesian, it was predicted that speakers of these languages would not be impacted vis-à-vis their duration perceptions. Fascinatingly, both predictions were met by the data. Linear regressions charting perceived duration (in ms) vs. actual fill volume (in pixels) had very positive slopes for both the Spanish-speaking and Greek-speaking test populations. The correlation between factors was quite strong, at r^2=0.95 for Greek speakers and r^2=0.97 for Spanish speakers. Such quantity-on-time effects did not surface for the English-speaking and Indonesian-speaking test groups. In both cases, the resultant regressions were only marginally positive, with lower r^2 values (r^2=0.18 for English speakers, r^2=0.51 for Indonesian speakers). In addition to these results, Casasanto et al. (2004) provide linear regression analyses that demonstrate a significant and positive correlation between the frequency of "time as distance" and "time as quantity" metaphors in subjects' native languages and the degree of visual-displacement and quantity-fill interference, respectively, in those subjects' estimations of stimuli durations (2004:3).

In sum, the differences that surfaced among the four populations tested in Casasanto et al. (2004) are exactly in line with a relativistic account. Speakers of languages with a more heavily entrenched "time as distance" metaphor are apparently influenced by this linguistic factor when perceiving the duration of the relevant stimuli. Conversely, speakers of languages with a more entrenched "time as quantity" metaphor are influenced by that linguistic factor when observing the duration of the stimuli used for these tasks. While these results are remarkable, it is worth emphasizing that the tasks in Casasanto and Boroditsky (2003, 2008), Casasanto et al. (2004), and Casasanto (2005) are all based on the same experimental paradigm. The extent to which that paradigm captures pervasive facets of nonlinguistic cognition is unclear. Hopefully future work with a much more diverse set of tasks will be undertaken in an effort to replicate the interesting results obtained through this research.

Finally, in discussing the work of Casasanto and colleagues it is important to stress that the results surveyed here are not easily ascribed to general cross-cultural factors that surface in both the languages in question and in the duration-estimation patterns observed. As Casasanto (2008:75) notes, in the case of one experiment English speakers were trained with/exposed to the somewhat unfamiliar "time as quantity" metaphor for around half an hour. Consistent with a relativistic account, after repeated linguistic exposure towards this metaphor, their performance in the subsequent experiment on duration estimation was more similar to that of Greek speakers. That is, as they perceived greater amounts of container "fill", they were more likely to estimate longer durations of the container stimuli. This result suggests that the cross-population differences between English/Indonesian speakers and Greek/Spanish speakers is most appropriately ascribed to linguistic disparities rather than general cross-cultural factors. Consonant results obtained with a wider array of languages and cultures would of course further buttress this interpretation. It is fair to say, though, that the results of such research are at least highly suggestive that "Beyond influencing how people think when they are required to speak or understand language, language can also shape our basic, nonlinguistic perceptuomotor representations of time." (Casasanto [2008:75])

Much of the recent crop of research regarding linguistic influences on the perception of time owes itself to some influential initial work by Lera Boroditsky (2000, 2001). In Boroditsky (2001), she examined the role of spatial metaphors in the temporal cognition of English and Mandarin speakers, respectively. While there are some potential methodological points of contention with Boroditsky (2001), points that have been addressed in the author's subsequent work, the study has influenced the agenda of much research on this topic. For that reason, it is worth considering the major findings evident in that work.

As has already been mentioned, English is replete with tokens of horizontal metaphors for time, most notably the FUTURE IS FRONT/PAST IS BEHIND. While cases of this basic horizontal metaphor are not difficult to uncover in Mandarin, that language also makes use of a vertical metaphor for time, one that is rare in English (though vertical temporal orientations surface when we speak of things being "passed down" through generations, or of an event "coming up"). In Mandarin, this metaphor is pervasive and is reified in large measure through the terms *shàng*, 'climb' and *xià*, 'descend' (Chun 1997). The former term is employed to refer to events nearer the past, and the latter to events nearer the future. According to this vertical metaphor, then, "up" is associated with the past and "down" is associated with the future. With this information in mind, Boroditsky (2001) conducted a series of reaction time experiments on the construal of time, with speakers of both English and Mandarin. In all of the experiments, speakers responded to true/false question pairs. In the case of each pair of questions, the first question was based on an image that was either vertically or horizontally oriented. For example, subjects were presented with an image of an abstract black worm-like figure crawling in front of a white (otherwise identical) worm-like figure. They then evaluated the veracity of the statement "The black worm is ahead of the white worm". (Boroditsky [2001:7]) In the case of the "vertical" images, speakers were presented with an image such as a black ball located above a white ball, and asked to evaluate the truth of the statement "The black ball is above the white ball". Each horizontal and vertical priming image and associated description was then followed by a true/false question about time, for example "March comes *earlier* than April".[37] The true/false assessment involved the progression of months in all cases. Reaction times for all true/false assessments were calculated and contrasted across the groups of speakers. Significantly, all written materials were provided in English only.

The results of the cross-group contrasts of reaction times were noteworthy. English speakers were generally faster at answering a true/false question about time after horizontal primes, e.g. the "worm" example, then after vertical primes, e.g. the "ball" example. Their reaction times improved around 200 ms

---

37 Some of these time questions utilized spatial metaphors, but here we are concerned with the results pertaining to those that did not.

(about 2200 ms vs. 2400 ms.) in the former condition. The opposite effect was observed for the Mandarin speakers, though, who made true/false judgments more quickly after vertical primes, by around 150 ms (about 2350 ms vs. 2500 ms). The disparity between conditions was significant for each language cohort ($p<0.05$), but in the opposite direction. This finding suggests that the presence of the vertical metaphor for time in Mandarin results in differentiated temporal processing for Mandarin speakers, vis-à-vis English speakers, after visual priming. The results are fascinating in part because the study was carried out entirely in English, ruling out the possibility that Mandarin speakers were merely "thinking for Mandarin" during the task.

An important methodological innovation in Boroditsky (2001) was the use of bilingual Mandarin English (ME) speakers of varying degrees of proficiency in Mandarin. For one of the experiments, only ME speakers were considered, and these speakers varied in terms of the age at which they began acquiring English. It was observed that there was a positive correlation between that age and the amount to which reaction times were reduced following vertical priming. In other words, the longer speakers had spoken only Mandarin, the more characteristically "vertical" their approach to time was, at least judging from their reduced reaction times in such cases. This finding suggested the results were due specifically to linguistic factors, rather the other cross-cultural factors. In order to further support this assessment, Boroditsky (2001:17) also conducted the experiments with English speakers who were familiarized with a vertical metaphor for time, via exposure to phrases such as "Monday is *above* Tuesday". As predicted, when speakers were trained in this manner, their performance on the true/false temporal judgments began to resemble those of Mandarin speakers, to the extent that they judged temporal statements more quickly following vertical primes. This latter result suggests that the cross-group differences between Mandarin and English speakers are due specifically to linguistic factors. It also hints that the reaction-time patterns in question are quite malleable, though, and are not strongly determined by life-long familiarity with one particular linguistic metaphor for time.

Boroditsky (2001) generated significant discussion regarding the potential influences of language on temporal cognition. Not all of this discussion was positive, however. While the methodological innovations evident in the study were welcome, some grew skeptical of the relativistic conclusions as the results were not replicated in subsequent research on temporal cognition. Chen (2007) replicated Boroditsky's (2001) methods but obtained divergent results, to the extent that English speakers' reaction times were reduced following *vertical* priming. It should be noted that the speakers tested in Chen (2007) differed significantly from those in Boroditsky (2001), though, since a relatively small number of English speakers were tested and since all were residents of Taiwan. Nevertheless, the failure to replicate was puzzling. In a similar study, January and Kako (2007) also failed to replicate Boroditsky's (2001) findings. They found that there was generally no difference in the reaction times following horizontal priming and vertical priming for English speakers. In the case of one experiment, horizontal priming resulted in *longer* reaction times for English speakers, contra the findings in Boroditsky (2001). January and Kako (2007) appears to have been plagued by several fundamental operational issues, however. As a result of bugs in the experimental program used for that study, the true/false questions regarding time were not properly counterbalanced with the appropriate vertical and horizontal stimuli, a serious blunder that in and of itself could have yielded specious results. (See discussion in Boroditsky, Fuhrman, and McCormick [2011:29].)

Other attempts at replicating the findings have also been unsuccessful, however. These attempts include Tse and Altarriba (2008) and work with inconsistent results in Boroditsky's own lab (Boroditsky, Fuhrman, and McCormick [2011:24]). Such inconsistencies resulted in the refinement of the experimental paradigm in Boroditsky (2001). This refinement included the utilization of tasks that were completely nonlinguistic, that dissociated sagittal (front-back) and transverse (left-right) horizontal metaphors for time, and that tested for patterns in the construal of time over numerous duration units, not merely months as in Boroditsky (2001). The net result of these methodological refinements includes two widely circulated studies, Boroditsky, Fuhrman, and McCormick (2011) and Fuhrman et al. (2011). Both of these studies focused again on speakers of Mandarin and English, and both offer even stronger support for the claim that crosslinguistic dissimilarities in spatial metaphors for temporal reference yield associated disparities in nonlinguistic temporal cognition. Next we consider the principal results obtained in these studies.

Boroditsky, Fuhrman, and McCormick (2011) again relied on English speakers (n=118) and on ME bilinguals (n=63). The speakers participated in a reaction time experiment. For each trial of the experiment, participants would see an image of an object or person on a computer screen for two seconds, followed by an image of the same object or person at a different moment in time. For example, they saw a picture of Woody Allen followed by another picture of Woody Allen at a younger stage in life, or at an older stage. A total of 114 images were used in the trials. The time differences implied by the image sequences ranged from years (e.g. in the case of Woody Allen) to seconds (e.g. in the case of depictions of coffee being poured). After image presentation, speakers chose whether they thought the second image represented an "earlier" or "later" time. This choice was made by pressing a corresponding button on a keypad. If the second image was perceived to be earlier than the first, a black button was pressed. If it was perceived to be later, a white button was pushed. These buttons appeared in a linear array. Crucially, the orientation of this array of keys was varied. For a number of participants (51 English speakers, 26 Mandarin speakers), the keys were arranged horizontally, so that the "earlier" button was located to the left of the "later" button (the canonical arrangement, consistent with a left-to-right orientation of time) or to the right of the later button (the non-canonical arrangement). The keypad was placed parallel to the surface of the table where testing occurred. For the remaining participants, the keypad was presented vertically, perpendicular to the table surface. The "earlier" button in such cases was located either above the "later" button (the canonical arrangement, consistent with the top-to-bottom orientation towards time evident in Mandarin) or below the "later" button (the non-canonical arrangement).

The results obtained for the English speakers revealed important disparities across the two keypad-orientation conditions, with a significant interaction with the canonical/non-canonical arrangement status. In the case of the English speakers, correct responses took an average of 1108 ms (after the presentation of the second image) when the keypad was placed horizontally and when the keys were arranged in a canonical fashion. When the keys were arranged in a non-canonical horizontal fashion, the reaction times of English speakers averaged 1396 ms. In other words, the conflict between the key orientation in such non-canonical cases (right=earlier) and a prominent metaphor for time in English (left=earlier) resulted in significant interference. This interference was significant according to an ANOVA ($p<0.001$). This pattern was also observed for the Mandarin speakers, since reaction times were greater in the non-canonical horizontal condition (1682 ms) than in the canonical horizontal condition (1450 ms).[38] The interference pattern observed in both languages is consistent with the presence of a left=earlier/right=later horizontal temporal metaphor, which exists in both languages. It is also consistent with the left-to-right orientation of writing familiar to both sets of participants (the Mandarin speakers who participated were literate in left-to-right script).

What about the vertical-keypad condition? In the case of English speakers, reaction times were significantly slower than in the canonical left-right horizontal condition (1108 ms). In the canonical "up is earlier" vertical condition, their reaction times averaged 1362 ms, while in the non-canonical "down is

---

[38] Overall, English speakers' reaction times were lower across all conditions. The authors suggest this difference may be due to the heightened familiarity of the English participants with these sorts of experimental tasks.

earlier" condition, their reaction times averaged 1345 ms. In this case, canonical status yielded a higher average reaction time, though the differences between "up is earlier" and "down is earlier" conditions were minor. In contrast, Mandarin speakers' reaction times benefited tremendously when the canonical vertical key arrangement was employed. In the "up is earlier" condition, their reaction times averaged 1475 ms, while in the "down is earlier" condition, their mean reaction time was 1645 ms. This disparity was significant according to an ANOVA ($p<0.001$).

In short, native Mandarin speakers showed a "canonicality" effect in both the vertical and horizontal keypad conditions, while the English speakers evinced such an effect only in the latter condition. This finding is exactly in keeping with the linguistic predictions for these nonlinguistic tasks, since Mandarin frequently utilizes a "left is earlier" metaphor *and* a "top is earlier" metaphor, while English only utilizes the former metaphor. It should be noted as well that the interaction between language and canonicality effects in each vertical/horizontal condition was observed for all duration types tested, i.e. whether the sequential images represented times that were separated by seconds, months, years, etc. These results demonstrate that, when speakers make time-based choices along a spatial orientation that is incongruent with a dominant linguistic spatial-temporal metaphor, interference effects surface. Spatial language impacts the nonlinguistic temporal reasoning required of the task.

Similar interference effects were uncovered in Furhman et al. (2011). Two experiments were employed in that study. The first resembled that in Boroditsky, Fuhrman, and McCormick (2011), though it differed in some crucial respects. Most relevant for our discussion, different populations were used in the study. Fifty-nine English speakers from Stanford participated, as did 75 students at two universities in Shanghai. The Mandarin speakers were native to China and had limited familiarity with English, having never resided in an English-speaking country like the Mandarin speakers tested in Boroditsky, Fuhrman, and McCormick (2011). The instructions to the task were provided in the speakers' native languages. Once again, participants were presented individually with sequences of two images and asked to evaluate whether the second image came earlier or later than the first. Their reaction times were calculated based on the speed with which they pressed buttons on a keypad, configured much as they were for the Boroditsky, Fuhrman, and McCormick (2011) study.[39] All speakers were exposed to all task configurations (unlike

---

39 In Furhman et al. (2011), three basic keypad orientations were used. One was vertical, as in Boroditsky, Fuhrman, and McCormick (2011), but two (rather than one) were horizontal. Fuhrman et al. (2011) employed both a sagittal (front-back) orientation of the earlier/later keys, as well as a transverse (left-right) orientation. Only the latter orientation was utilized in Boroditsky, Fuhrman, and McCormick (2011). The results obtained for the sagittal orientation

Boroditsky, Fuhrman, and McCormick [2011]). A total of 168 images were used in the study, involving 56 temporal sequences such as a banana being eaten or Julia Roberts aging.

The patterns observed in the experimental results were exactly in keeping with those in Boroditsky, Fuhrman, and McCormick (2011). First, the canonicality effect in the transverse horizontal condition surfaced again. Responses of English and Mandarin speakers were characterized by significantly reduced reaction times when the "earlier" key was located to the left of the "later" key. In the case of English speakers, the mean reaction time in this canonical condition was 936 ms, while the mean reaction time was 1045 ms in the "right is earlier" condition (paired by-items t tests, $p <.0001$). In the case of Mandarin speakers, the mean reaction time in the canonical horizontal condition was 1675 ms, while the mean reaction time was 1793 ms in the non-canonical horizontal condition (paired by-items t tests, $p <.01$). Speakers' responses were faster when the keypad was oriented in a manner consonant with the left-is-earlier horizontal spatial-temporal metaphor used in both English and Mandarin.

Once again, the canonicality effect in the vertical condition only surfaced for the Mandarin speakers. Their reaction times in the "top is earlier" condition averaged 1609 ms, significantly faster than the reverse condition's mean reaction time of 1853 ms (paired by-items t tests, $p <.0001$). In contrast, the English speakers' mean reaction times in the "top is earlier" condition averaged 974 ms, which was only marginally faster than the reaction time in the reverse condition, 993 ms (paired by-items t tests, $p =.98$). As in Boroditsky, Fuhrman, and McCormick (2011), then, English speakers' reaction times were not significantly affected by either of the orientations of time in the vertical condition, while Mandarin speakers benefited from a "top is earlier" orientation on the response keypad. In sum, the nonlinguistic experimental paradigm evident in both Boroditsky, Fuhrman, and McCormick (2011) and Fuhrman et al. (2011) has now yielded strong evidence for linguistic effects on the nonlinguistic recognition of temporal sequences in observed images.

Fuhrman et al. (2011) provide another sort of compelling evidence for the impact of temporal language on temporal thought. That evidence is based on a separate experiment type, in which task participants represent time via gestures. Standing next to the task participant, an experimenter gestured in space to an area about one foot directly in front of the participant's chest, via a palm-up, fingers-together motion. The experimenter then asked a question such as

---

are not discussed here, in part because there was not a clear pattern found in those results (and no clear pattern predicted by linguistic factors either).

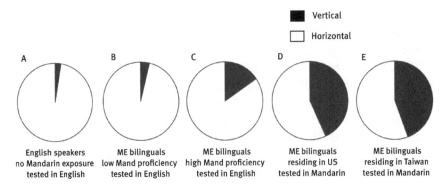

Figure 5.1: Ratio of vertical and horizontal temporal gestures, in accordance with language proficiency and language of testing. Taken from Fuhrman et al. (2011:1319). Copyright 2011 Wiley-Blackwell, reprinted with permission.

"If this here is TODAY, where would you put YESTERDAY?" (or "tomorrow"). The questions related to three temporal units, either days, as in the preceding example, or months, or meal times (i.e. locating dinner or breakfast with respect to lunch). The experimenter then tabulated whether the participant responded to the question by gesturing above the highlighted location, or to the left of the location (from the participant's perspective), or in some other location. The linguistically oriented expectation was that English speakers would tend to gesture towards the left of the denoted location when pointing to earlier events, and to the right of the location when pointing to later events. Conversely, the expectation was that Mandarin speakers would, in a fair amount of cases at least, gesture towards a location above the denoted space when describing earlier events, and below the space when pointing to later events.

One hundred and thirty four English speakers participated in the study, as well as 196 ME bilinguals who resided in the USA or Taiwan. Crucially, the latter group consisted of speakers that varied significantly in terms of their fluency in Mandarin. This allowed the experimenters to test for differentiated patterns of gesture in accordance with degree of fluency in Mandarin. The results obtained were remarkably consistent with the linguistically based predictions. English speakers' gestures reflected a horizontal orientation to time in 94% of the cases. (In 88%, this orientation was "left-is-earlier".) ME speakers with the highest degrees of fluency in Mandarin (ranked "four" or "five" on a five-point scale) exhibited a remarkably divergent distribution, with their gestures reflecting a vertical orientation in many cases. The ratio of vertical and horizontal gestures used by the task participants is depicted schematically in Figure 5.1. Two points evident in the figure are worth highlighting. First, it is apparent that the amount of vertical gesturing increases in accordance with fluency in Mandarin, and decreases with higher degrees of familiarity with/ exposure to English. The second striking point is that the rate at which speakers utilized the vertical gestural orientation for time varied in accordance with the language of testing. The former point is suggestive of completely nonlinguistic differences in temporal orientation, dependent on language fluency. That is, more fluent Mandarin speakers are simply more likely to conceive of time vertically. The latter point is suggestive of nonlinguistic differences in temporal orientation that are more superficial, affected by the immediate linguistic context. These latter sorts of differences could be construed as "thinking for speaking" effects, reflecting the fact that the utilization of a given language primes people to think in certain ways only while using the language in question. The demonstration of both of these sorts of effects on cognition in a single study conveys well the possible co-existence of these two kinds of linguistic influences. In the words of Fuhrman et al. (2011:1322), "Temporary and chronic effects of language are not mutually exclusive."

The existence of differences in the performance of Mandarin and English speakers on a variety of time-based experiments has now been demonstrated repeatedly in the literature. While the cross-population disparity is clearly tied to metaphors evident in the speech of the two groups, this does not preclude the possibility that other factors may also play a role in the construal of time. One factor that appears to play such a role is orthography, specifically direction of writing. In an experiment testing for differences in the spatial arrangement of temporal sequences, Chan and Bergen (2005) uncovered differences between Taiwanese Mandarin and mainland Mandarin speakers. For that study, subjects were asked to arrange five sets of three temporally sequenced pictures (e.g. tadpole/young frog/adult frog) in an array. English and mainland Mandarin speakers tended to arrange the pictures from left to right, with earlier images being towards the left. Some mainland Mandarin speakers used a top-to-bottom orientation. Taiwanese Mandarin speakers' responses were more heterogeneous, with left-to-right and top-to-bottom distributions equally represented, and with a number of right-to-left sequences. Chan and Bergen (2005) suggest that this heterogeneity is best explained by factors associated with writing, namely that Taiwanese Mandarin can be written in all three orientations, whereas English and mainland Mandarin (at least for the last fifty years or so) are restricted to left-to-right horizontal writing. In a similar vein, Fuhrman and Boroditsky (2010) provide compelling evidence that Hebrew speakers and English speakers think about time differently. For example, when asked to arrange images of temporal sequences in physical space, Hebrew speakers, who write right-to-left, are likely to do so with a right-to-left orientation. Based on such results, it seems that writing systems play a role in cross-cultural differences in temporal orientation. This is an important point in the context of the current discussion. To be clear, the claim made in recent work on language-mediated temporal cognition is not that all cross-cultural differences in this cognitive domain owe themselves to differences in speech. Other factors may also play a role, including writing system dissimilarities, different calendric representations, and any other systematic semiotic differences associated with the representation of time. At the core of the linguistic relativity hypothesis is the belief that habitual experience with dissimilar symbolic representations can yield differences in nonlinguistic thought. While a variety of kinds of symbolic representations of time may impact its nonlinguistic conceptualization, however, the results we have examined suggest strongly that linguistically instantiated metaphors for time play a role in the creation of cross-cultural differences in the construal of time.

5.4 Discussion and conclusion

The findings discussed in this chapter provide evidence for relativistic effects in the domain of temporal cognition. While the effects in question are not necessarily as radical as some of those documented vis-à-vis other domains, for instance spatial orientation (see Chapter 4) or numerical cognition (see Chapter 6), they are based on experimental work in which confounding factors, such as research setting and broad cultural differences across test groups, have arguably been more controlled for. This control is due in part to the languages that have received the closest scrutiny in this work, particularly in the work of Boroditsky and colleagues: English and Mandarin. Since speakers of these languages can easily be tested in laboratory environs, unlike many indigenous tribal groups around whom discussions of linguistic relativity often revolve, the role for confounding variables can be reduced. Another strength of the studies described above is that their frequent focus on Mandarin and English has particularly broad implications since these are the two most widely spoken languages in the world today, with hundreds of millions (maybe as many as two billion) of native and second-language speakers.

Given that systematic inquiry into linguistic effects on temporal cognition is relatively young, some major areas must still be addressed methodologically. While it is noteworthy that several of the languages so far considered in this research (including Indonesian and Greek) are spoken by millions, it remains the case that the experimental work described above has only been conducted with speakers of a handful of languages. It seems likely that future work will adopt and perhaps expand the methods in the studies described in this chapter, and implement those methods among a wider array of cultures. For instance, recall the findings in Miles, Nind, and Macrae (2010) with respect to chronesthesia. In that study it was observed that, as English speakers think about the future, they sway forwards almost imperceptibly. Conversely, when they imagine the past they sway backwards. It would be fascinating to see what sorts of results would be obtained among speakers of a language like Aymara in which the dominant spatial metaphor for time depicts past events as being in front of the speaker and future events as behind the speaker. It would be equally fascinating to find out what results would obtain in a chronesthesia study among the Amondawa, whose language apparently does not use spatial metaphors for time. Granted, there are numerous methodological roadblocks that would need to be circumvented for such research to take place. But the possibilities remain for such intriguing experimental work on temporal cognition.

In a related manner, future work may address different kinds of linguistic effects on temporal cognition. The research surveyed in this chapter is strikingly metaphor-focused. While languages clearly differ markedly in the sorts of spatial-temporal metaphors they rely on, they also differ profoundly in other ways through which time is indexed. For example, the tense and aspect systems evident typologically differ markedly. (See e.g. Comrie [1976, 1985]). For example, as mentioned in Chapter 2, Yagua has seven tenses (Payne [1997:237]). English utilizes only three, but some languages utilize fewer. Karitiâna has only two tenses, future and non-future. Future research on the conceptualization of time could explore the potential effects of such marked grammatical disparities on temporal cognition.[40]

The results obtained in the studies of Boroditsky and her colleagues are not consistent with a strong deterministic perspective. As noted above, it was found in Fuhrman et al. (2011) that ME speakers' experimental behavior varied

---

40 Interestingly, recent unpublished work by an economist makes claims for large-scale relativistic effects of tense systems on the way in which speakers think about time and, as a result, the way in which they save and spend money. More specifically, Chen (n.d.) suggests that speakers of languages with "strongly grammaticalized future time reference" think of future events as being more remote, when contrasted with speakers of languages without a clear future tense. As a result, Chen claims, speakers of the former sort of languages (including English, Spanish, and French) are more prone to save less, invest less, and be obese, when contrasted to speakers of the latter sort of languages (including Flemish and German). Chen documents this correlation even within single countries, for instance Switzerland. Nevertheless, there are numerous issues with his study, which have been addressed in several online venues such as *Language Log*, and such a strong deterministic claim is unlikely to be accepted without significant evidence beyond that which he presents.

somewhat in accordance with the language in which they were tested. Further-more, in studies such as Boroditsky (2001) and Casasanto et al. (2004) it was observed that, after being familiarized with spatial-temporal metaphors not common to their native languages, speakers' performances on the experimen-tal tasks changed rather easily. Such findings are incompatible with the exis-tence of deep-seated linguistically motivated ontological disparities in cogni-tive temporal categories. They suggest instead that language serves to induce certain kinds of temporal thought, rather than dictate such thought in a force-ful manner. In a related vein, it should also be noted that the mere existence of divergent metaphors for time in any given set of contrasted languages does not *necessarily* imply the existence of nonlinguistic differences of thought. It has previously been observed that, at least in the case of some entrenched, conventionalized idioms with metaphorical origins, the metaphorical bases do not seem to be accessed cognitively (Glucksberg, Brown, and McGlone [1993]). To demonstrate cross-cultural disparities in temporal cognition, then, it is not sufficient to highlight differences in the temporal metaphors in the languages associated with the cultures in question. Nonlinguistic tasks such as those discussed in this chapter must be carried out. It is fair to say that the extent of the effects of language on temporal cognition remains for now an open-ended issue. Nevertheless, the mere existence of such effects seems now to be beyond contestation.

Spatial and temporal cognition are closely associated neurologically (Oliv-eri et al. [2009]). Perhaps it is not surprising then that habitual exposure to a particular spatial way of speaking about time should affect nonlinguistic thought about time. Given that languages clearly offer divergent levels of expo-sure to various sorts of spatial-temporal metaphors, it is furthermore not par-ticularly shocking that speakers of different languages should exhibit different tendencies in the conceptualization of time.

The physical reality of the passing of time is in some sense immutable, and the cerebral architecture involved in the perception of time, and in reason-ing about time, predates the dissemination of peoples, cultures, and languages around the globe. So it is to be expected that there are fundamentally universal facets of human temporal cognition. Yet this fact does not preclude the possi-bility of some variability in this domain. This lack of mutual-exclusivity between universality and variation in temporal cognition is echoed by Casas-anto (2008:75), who suggests that "conceptual mappings from space to time may be given in essentially the same form via correlations in physical experi-ence to everyone and then *also* conditioned by the languages we speak."

In the cases surveyed in this chapter, variability in temporal cognition corresponds with predictive linguistic factors. Regardless of the extent of this variability, which remains unclear, its mere existence has profound effects on our understanding of human temporal cognition. As Boroditsky, Fuhrman, and McCormick (2011) note, "Evidence demonstrating crosslinguistic differences in how people mentally represent time requires that we include patterns in language and culture as a central ingredient in the human conception of time." In sum, while much more work is required to establish the pervasiveness of cross-cultural variation in temporal cognition, as well as the extent to which such variation owes itself to linguistic factors, the evidence now available suggests clearly that such variation does in fact exist, and is created at least in part by crosslinguistic disparities.

6 Quantities

6.1 Introduction

The introduction of new mathematical concepts into cultures can fundamentally alter facets of the relevant societies. This introduction is made possible at least in large measure through the lexical reification of those concepts. Prior to the utilization of a word for "zero" in Europe, introduced long after it had been utilized in India and Arabia, the associated concept was not evident in European mathematics. In a related manner, the spread of calculus was made possible by words for concepts such as "derivative", "limit", "integral", and so on. Once such words are introduced into a language, they allow people to think in new ways, impacting how they construe mathematical relationships. In this way, the claim that language about numbers affects how people think is self-evident. The distillation of mathematical concepts into labels serves as a clear conceptual tool, enabling or at least facilitating certain kinds of thought. Yet, while some languages clearly lack terms like derivative or limit, their speakers' general nonlinguistic cognition is not plausibly impacted by that absence. In other words, such terms may assist people when they are performing very specific kinds of problems, but they do not likely affect how the speakers generally think about quantities, or relationships between quantities. The influence of such crosslinguistic lexical disparities on thought would seem to be marginal.

But what of more basic linguistic distinctions associated with numerical thought? What if, for instance, you spoke a language that had no words for concepts like "one" or "two" or "three"? Would that affect the way you generally think about quantities? Would it inhibit your ability simply to contrast different quantities? If such an effect existed, it would be far from marginal, and would relate to the general nonlinguistic ability to recognize quantities precisely, even in cases that were far removed from the implementation of advanced math skills. Recent research regarding linguistic effects on numerical cognition has directly addressed such questions. In this chapter we will focus on some of the principal findings of that research, as we consider the ways in which crosslinguistic differences in the encoding (or lack thereof) of numerical concepts can potentially impact thought.

These sorts of questions may themselves seem odd, since many assume that all languages have words for numbers. This assumption of universality is natural. Nearly all documented languages have numbers, and certainly all widely spoken languages have them. Furthermore, numbers have been used by humans for millennia, and possibly tens of millenia. The archaeological record speaks to this. For example, in 1960 archaeologists discovered a bone on the Congo-Rwanda border. This bone, known as the Ishango bone (de Heinzelen [1962]), is a 10 cm long baboon tibula. There are three arrays of engravings on the bone that display quantities of 48, 60, and 60 marks, respectively. The marks appear in groups, a number of which represent prime numbers. While there is debate about the meaning of these marks, it seems pretty clear from the Ishango bone that whoever carved the markings was capable of, at the least, counting. Whatever language they spoke, it most likely had number words. Fascinatingly, carbon dating suggests the Ishango bone was carved about 22,000 years BCE (Brooks and Smith [1987]). In other words, this bone provides archaeological evidence for the existence of mathematical reasoning and, indirectly, numeric language at least twenty-four millennia ago. If humans have had numbers at least that long, it may strain credulity to suggest that any contemporary languages could be completely anumeric. Yet human cultures have lost (or never acquired) seemingly basic technologies, including fire, throughout their history (Boyd, Richerson, and Henrich [2011]).

There are occasionally claims of anumericity in contemporary descriptions of indigenous languages, but these claims are not always borne out by systematic analysis. To cite one recent example, Dixon (2004) suggested in a comprehensive grammatical description that there are no native words for numbers in Jarawara, an Arawá language of Amazonia. Given that I was fortunate enough to spend some time with a number of Jarawara speakers on a recent field trip to Amazonia, I was anxious to better understand this aspect of their language. To my surprise, however, it turns out that the language actually does have a native number system, one that is similar to that evident in descriptions of other Arawá languages. (See Everett [2012a] for a delineation of the number system in Jarawara and other Arawá languages.) In addition, the Jarawaras have an interesting traditional tally mark system, no longer in systematic use, in which numbers are carved in a narrow piece of wood.

As the Jarawara case illustrates, uncontested cases of anumeric language are exceedingly rare. One comprehensive typological survey of number systems (Hammarström [2010]) suggests that there are only two documented cases of anumericity in the world's languages: Xilixana Yanomami and Pirahã, unrelated Amazonian languages. The former case is less clear, however, since the linguistic description on which claims for anumericity are based is less detailed, and since there have been no experiments undertaken to demonstrate anumericity among the Xilixana. In contrast, there has been substantial work demonstrating that Pirahã is in fact anumeric, lacking any precise number words and even lacking the grammatical category of number, i.e. lacking a singular vs. plural (or dual or trial) distinction. We discuss the case of Pirahã in Section 6.3.

While completely anumeric languages may be rare, however, languages vary widely in the amount and kinds of number words they utilize. A number of languages only have precise number terms for smaller quantities, for example "one" and "two", or one, two, and "three". In many others such as English, the number of terms for quantities is limitless, and it is permissible to iteratively combine base terms to form terms for larger quantities, in an open-ended manner. Not surprisingly, most cultures in the world today have access to such a limitless number system, either in their own language or in the language of a culture they have come into contact with. Anumeric languages are undoubtedly rare in large measure because humans are apt to borrow numbers once confronted with them. They are an extremely convenient "cognitive technology" (Frank et al. [2008]) or "conceptual tool" (see discussion in Everett and Madora [2012]).

The number systems of languages vary along other dimensions besides the range of quantities they are capable of precisely denoting. Most notably, they differ significantly in terms of the bases they employ. In English and many other languages the number system used is a decimal one, in which "ten" serves as a recurring unit for larger numbers. Decimal systems are particularly common typologically since humans have ten fingers that are naturally used in counting. Human biology offers up other natural number bases, though, including a vigesimal base. After all, we have a combined twenty manual and pedal digits. Given that human toes are exposed in so many cultures, a vigesimal-based system seems natural as well, and it is in fact attested in languages such as Maya and Nahuatl. Binary-based number systems also surface in the world's languages, and these may also be motivated by anatomical factors such as the presence of two eyes, two ears, or two nostrils on the human head. Human anatomy has played a prominent role in shaping number systems (see Heine [1997]). In some cases the foundation of a number system on human anatomy is less straightforward. For example, among the Yupno (Wassmann and Dasen [1994]), ordinal numbers are associated with particular parts of the human body. Terms for 1–20 correspond to fingers and toes, but other parts of the anatomy are also relied on. For example, the terms for 21 and 22 correspond to the ears, and 26 and 27 to the left and right nostrils. Other number systems evident in the world's languages include base-six or senary (Plank [2009]) and base-eight systems. In many cases, languages may utilize one base for smaller numerosities and a different base for higher numerosities. Not all number bases are derived from human biology, either. For instance, the Nadahup languages of Amazonia have an interesting number system whose base relates to the marital patterns in the local cultures (Epps [2006]). For recent surveys of number system and counting system types, see Hammarström (2010), Bender and Beller (2011), and Epps et al. (2012).[41]

Clearly there exists a remarkable diversity in the types of number systems evident in human languages. But does such diversity foster variation of any kind in numerical cognition? This question has been dealt with in the recent literature, most notably in work carried out among speakers of anumeric languages or nearly anumeric languages. Prior to our examination of the relevant studies, it is worth providing some background context on the current understanding of numerical cognition more generally. There is after all an enormous literature on this topic, in psychology and other related fields. A few points merit our attention now, since they turn out to be particularly relevant to the discussion below.

First, the evidence suggests that pre-linguistic infants are capable of some types of math. More specifically, they are able to recognize differences between numbers from one to three. This point was demonstrated in a series of innovative tasks such as those described in Wynn (1992), which entailed the presentation of stimuli to five-month-old infants. For example, the infants watched as one or two mouse-like puppet figures were presented to them and then covered up behind an opaque screen. They then watched as another figure was added by being visibly slid behind the screen, or watched as a figure was taken away visibly. The experimenter could also take away or add figures behind the screen, without the infant witnessing that manipulation. After this manipulation, the screen was removed and the infants could see how many figures remained. For example, in one case the infants saw two figures that were then covered by the screen and visibly joined by another figure. However, one figure was removed while the screen covered the figures (out of view of the babies), so when the screen was removed two figures still remained. This sort of situation clearly violates a basic mathematical expectation: 2+1 = 3. A variety of such manipulations were conducted, all involving quantities from 1–3. Wynn found that infants stared longer when the number of figures presented after the screen was uncovered violated basic arithmetically based expectations. In other words, babies realized that 1+1=2, 1+2=3, 2–1=1, and so on. Other studies have revealed similar patterns. For instance, Feigenson, Carey, and Hauser (2002) demonstrated that, given the choice of 1–3 crackers, infants choose the larger quantities. They are clearly capable of discriminating between one, two,

---

41 In this latter work the authors document a weak correlation between subsistence type and numeral complexity. More specifically, they describe a correlation between hunter-gatherer cultures and limited number systems.

or three crackers, but struggle with accurately discriminating quantities beyond that range. So, for example, when given a choice between three and two crackers, they choose the former amount. Perhaps surprisingly, though, when given a choice between four and two crackers, or six and three crackers, they choose randomly. In other words, their ability to exactly discriminate quantities is limited to sets smaller than four items. Given that the infants in such studies are pre-linguistic, the results imply that such basic arithmetical ability does not rely on language. These and other relevant data supporting this conclusion are surveyed in, for example, Feigenson, Dehaene, and Spelke (2004).

In a similar vein, much work has demonstrated that other primates and more phylogenetically removed species are capable of differentiating between quantities equal to or less than three. In a similar study to Feigenson, Carey, and Hauser (2002), Hauser, Carey, and Hauser (2000) tested the ability of rhesus monkeys to choose between quantities of 1–3 apple slices. The monkeys consistently chose the larger quantity. With quantity choices such as four or eight apple slices, though, the monkeys chose randomly.

Given that non-speaking babies and other species are capable of exactly recognizing smaller quantities, we can be confident that this ability is language-independent. There is another "number sense" (Dehaene 1997) that is language-independent as well, since it too surfaces in other species. Specifically, various species are capable of approximating larger quantities. They can recognize the difference between really large quantities and much smaller quantities. Accuracy of discrimination correlates positively with an increase in the ratio between the relevant quantities. This sort of "fuzzy" math is characterized by analog estimation, in which the magnitude of errors of responses increases in tasks as the quantities involved increase. So, for instance, when rats are trained to push a lever down a certain number of times, their accuracy decreases as the requisite number increases. But the responses are not random, rather the number of times they push the lever is normally distributed, with the means of responses corresponding relatively closely to the actual target number (Platt and Johnson [1971]). The evidence for this cognitive ability in other species is surveyed in Feigenson, Dehaene, and Spelke (2004). Crucially, this second phylogenetically basic sort of numerical cognition does not allow for the exact representation of large quantities. Other species cannot, for example, consistently differentiate between six and seven items. The larger the discrepancy between two numbered sets, the more likely species are to differentiate between them. This point holds for human infant cognition as well. This ratio dependency is evident for instance in the findings in Xu and Spelke (2000), who found that six-month-old infants can discriminate between quantities of 8 and 16 dots, or 16 and 32 dots, in which cases the ratio between quantities is 1:2. Infants cannot accurately discriminate between quantities when the ratio falls to 2:3, however, for instance when choosing between 8 and 12 dots or 16 and 24 dots.

In short, non-speaking babies and other species are capable of exact quantity differentiation with quantities from 1–3, and of approximating quantities beyond that range. Given that they are not phylogenetically restricted and are even shared by some non-mammals (see e.g. Scarf, Hayne, and Colombo [2011]), it is extremely likely that these abilities are homologous and have been in the human lineage for tens of millions of years. The abilities are certainly genetically endowed, and are served by distinguishable regions of the human cortex (Dehaene et al. [1999]). Nevertheless, humans are clearly capable of numerical cognition that is disparate from either of these innate senses for number. In particular, humans are capable of exactly recognizing and manipulating quantities greater than three. Most of us can, for example, differentiate eight items from nine items with ease. Other species cannot do this, though, and neither can pre-linguistic humans. This has led to the suggestion that language may play a fundamental role in fostering this sort of more advanced numerical cognition. Specifically, it has been suggested that number words and counting may allow humans to link up the two genetically endowed neurophysiological capacities for exactly recognizing smaller quantities and for approximating larger quantities (see Spelke and Tsivkin [2001], Condry and Spelke [2008]). If this account is accurate, this linkage is what then allows humans to apply exact recognition to quantities beyond three. The question that must be addressed in the context of the current discussion is whether there are crosslinguistic and cross-cultural data supporting this assessment. More specifically, do speakers of languages with few or no number words struggle with exactly recognizing and manipulating quantities greater than three? Such data are crucial to our understanding of the potential effects of language on a fundamental sort of numerical thought, and to our understanding of numerical cognition more generally.

In the next section we examine some of the work carried out with speakers of a nearly anumeric language. In Section 6.3 we address recent work with speakers who do not have access to number words of any kind. It should be stressed from the outset that all the speakers described below are normal adults without any documented neurological or cognitive impairments. They are all well adapted to their local ecologies, and have successfully maintained their cultures without reliance upon (many) number words.

6.2 The case of nearly anumeric language

Mundurukú is a Tupí language spoken by about 7,000 people in the southern region of the Brazilian Amazonian state of Pará. The language has words for five numbers, 1–5. Pica et al. (2004) describe an elicitation experiment corroborating this assessment. Speakers were presented with a number of objects, ranging from 1–15, and asked to name them. For numbers 1–5 there was a fair amount of consistency in the names offered, though for higher numerosities a variety of vague terms were used. For example, when two items were presented, the term *xep xep* was utilized in 100% of the cases. Consistency of responses declined for 3–5 items, and also did not reach 100% for one item. This suggests that the number terms in Mundurukú are used to refer imprecisely to such quantities, much as English speakers may sometimes use terms like "a couple" or "a dozen" in an imprecise manner even though such terms are clearly based on specific quantities.[42] This point is explored more fully in Pica and Lecomte's (2008) elaboration of Mundurukú numbers. Since there are terms clearly associated with 1, 2, 3, 4 and 5 in the language, Mundurukú is considered a nearly anumeric, rather than completely anumeric, language.

Speakers of Mundurukú have been the subject of two widely circulated studies on numerical cognition, both published in *Science*. (Pica et al. [2004], Dehaene et al. [2008]) In one of these studies (Pica et al. [2004]), the quantity recognition skills of the people were assessed via a simple experimental paradigm. The other study focused on the mental number scales utilized by Mundurukú speakers when representing numerosities in a linear fashion. Since the findings in Pica et al. (2004) relate to a basic cognitive ability that has also been examined in studies with anumeric speakers (considered in Section 6.3), we will focus our attention on the results from that work.

Pica and colleagues conducted two basic sorts of tasks, each of which had two variants. The first sort of task assessed the capacity of Mundurukú speakers to perceive differences in numerosity between two large quantities. For one variant of this task, the 55 Mundurukú participants and 10 French controls were presented with two sets of dots on a computer screen. These sets ranged in size from 20–80 dots. The participants merely had to point to the larger cluster of dots. Mundurukú speakers responded above chance level, regardless of whether they were monolingual, bilingual (speaking at least some Portu-

---

42 One wonders how common such imprecision actually is in languages with limited number systems. In only a handful of such cases has the precision of such terms been explored via systematic elicitation/experimentation. Given that anthropologists' and linguists' native languages have exact number terms, it seems possible that inaccurate assumptions of numeric precision, biased by researcher intuition, could easily be made.

guese), adults or children, and regardless of whether they had received any formal education. Their performance was worse than those of the French controls, perhaps because of the novelty of this sort of experimental task, but only differed in a modest manner. Crucially, for both French speakers and Mundurukú speakers, accuracy decreased and response time increased as the ratio of the quantities of the two sets of dots decreased. When one set was twice as large as the other, accuracy was high and response time low. When this ratio of 2:1 fell to 1.5:1, or 1.3:1, or 1.2:1, accuracy and response time suffered in the predicted direction for all groups. In short, the French speakers and Mundurukú speakers were subject to a "distance effect", though both groups were generally quite adept at approximating large quantities of dots. This is in keeping with the claim discussed above that such approximation abilities are found in all human cultures and also in other species.

In contrast, the tasks testing Mundurukú speakers' exact recognition of quantities revealed dramatic differences between them and the control population of French speakers. One such task, depicted in Figure 6.1, required the participants to view a subtraction process. They witnessed animations in which dots were placed into a can, and then a number of dots were removed from the can. They were then asked to point to an image of a can containing 0, 1, or 2 dots, in order to test whether they exactly recognized the difference in quantity between the numerosity inserted into the can ($n1$) and that removed from the can ($n2$). The size of $n1$ and $n2$ ranged from 0–8. So, for example in the scenario represented in Figure 6.1, a speaker would witness five dots being inserted (visually) into the image of the can, and four dots being removed. They would then be expected to point to the right middle image of a can to demonstrate their recognition that $n1$ and $n2$ differed by only one dot.

What Pica and colleagues found was that the French speakers were adept at this task regardless of the magnitude of $n1$. In sharp contrast, the Mundurukú speakers struggled with this task when $n1$ exceeded four. In fact, the larger the quantity of $n1$, the more inaccurate their responses were. This pattern was consistent with a strategy of analog estimation, since the Mundurukú speakers' responses were characterized by a correlation between $n1$ magnitude and degree of imprecision. This pattern was observed for all native speakers of the language, though bilingual and educated participants did exhibit greater rates of accuracy for this and the other related task testing exact quantity recognition. The latter task was identical, except that speakers were asked to name $n3$ (the difference between $n1$ and $n2$), rather than point to it. Crucially, for both exact quantity recognition tasks, there was a gross disparity between the results obtained with French and Mundurukú speakers. As the authors note: "The Mundurukú's [sic] failure in exact subtraction was not due to misunder-

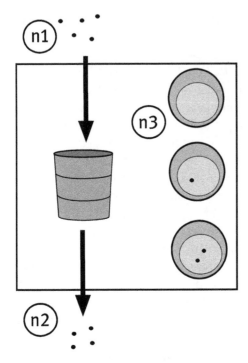

Figure 6.1: Sample task from experiments conducted among the Mundurukú.
Adapted from Pica et al. (2004).

standing of the instructions, because they performed better than chance (indeed, close to 100% correct) when the initial number was below 4." (2004:502)

In short, the data in Pica et al. (2004) are consistent with the claim made in the literature on numerical cognition, outlined in Section 6.1, that number words are crucial to allowing humans to precisely recognize exact quantities greater than three. Nevertheless, the data do not allow us to completely rule out other confounding variables. It is possible, for example, that the performance of the Mundurukú on the tasks in question was affected by more general cultural factors. For instance, it is possible that a culture may resist the utilization of number words *and* other associated practices that help to enable exact number recognition. As has been repeatedly stated in this book, in order to clearly establish the causal role of language in such cases, data from a variety of cultures are necessary.

Some Australian aboriginal languages are also characterized by having few number-related morphemes. For example, Warlpiri and Anindilyakwa have no ordinal number words (e.g. "first", "second", "third") and no clear cardinal number terms (e.g. "one", "two", "three"). Crucially, however, these languages have nominal classifier systems according to which items must be categorized according to number. So, in the case of Warlpiri, there are singular, dual, and trial classifiers. In the case of Anindilyakwa, there are four classifiers: singular, dual, trial, and plural. Through a series of quantity-matching experiments, Butterworth et al. (2008) investigated the role of this limited numeric classifying on thought. They compared the performance of groups of child speakers of English, Warlpiri, and Anindilyakwa on basic numerical tasks. Unexpectedly in the light of the Mundurukú data, they found that the performance of the aboriginal children did not differ markedly from the monolingual English speakers'. Based on this finding, Butterworth et al. (2008) offer up some strong anti-relativistic claims.

We mention the findings in Butterworth et al. (2008) here since they were claimed to impinge on the issue at hand. We do not discuss them in much detail, however, because they are not, we believe, directly contrastable with the results gathered in the other studies discussed in this chapter. This is true for several reasons. First and foremost, the aboriginal languages' classifier systems frequently draw speakers' attention to precise disparities between quantities, representing small numbers in an exact manner. In languages with such classifier systems, the classifiers are ubiquitous in speech, causing numerosity to be indexed whenever nouns are produced. So, while strictly speaking such aboriginal languages have few number terms, they are radically disparate from languages like Mundurukú and Pirahã, in which speakers are not forced to make exact numerical distinctions of any sort since the languages lack a grammatical number system and since the few number terms that exist (in Mundurukú) are imprecise. In addition, Warlpiri and Anindilyakwa speakers have borrowed number words from English, and it is unclear how much the children in Butterworth et al. (2008) had been exposed to such number words. In short, while Butterworth et al. (2008) present important data on aboriginal numerical cognition, it remains unclear at present how or if these data are relatable to the present discussion of the influence of anumeric language or nearly anumeric language on numerical cognition.

The clearest relevant data on offer regarding the speakers of a language with limited number terms and no nominal grammatical number, Mundurukú, are remarkably in line with the claim that number words dramatically benefit basic numerical cognition. In the following section we consider pertinent data from two other groups of speakers. These speakers do not have access to any number terminology.

6.3 The case of anumeric language

Pirahã is a language spoken by approximately 700 monolingual Amazonian indigenes. The people live on a reserve in the southeastern portion of the Brazilian state of Amazonas, along the Maici river, a tertiary tributary of the Amazon.

Pirahã is an unusual language in a variety of respects, and has engendered a serious amount of discussion among linguists in the last few years. Much of this discussion has centered around D. Everett's[43] documentation of numerous typologically anomalous features in the language, for instance the lack of recursion evident in Pirahã syntax. (D. Everett [2005, 2009]) D. Everett (2005) also claimed that there are no number words in the language. While it had previously been suggested that there are terms for 'one' (*hói*), 'two' (*hói*), and 'many' (*baágiso*), D. Everett (2005) claimed these terms were not in fact number words, but vague expressions for ranges of quantities. Judging from these claims, the terms are even less precise than the terms for numbers in Mundurukú, since at least in the case of those numbers the terms are clearly associated (though non-exactly) with specific numerosities.

Frank et al. (2008) conducted two word-elicitation tasks that corroborated D. Everett's (2005) claims that the three terms in question are not in fact number terms, and do not precisely relay numerosities. One of these was an "increasing-quantity" elicitation task. Pirahã speakers were presented first with one spool of thread, and asked to provide a number term for the quantity provided. The researchers then added spools of thread to the presented array, one at a time, and after each spool was added participants were asked to identify the new quantity. For this task the speakers did use *hói* in all presentations of a singular spool of thread, and *hoí* in all cases in which two spools of thread were presented. However, they also used the latter term to refer to as many as seven spools of thread. They employed *baágiso* to refer to quantities ranging from three to ten spools. Significantly, in a "decreasing-elicitation" task, responses were even more dispersed. Pirahã speakers were presented first with ten spools of thread, and asked to name this quantity. In most cases they provided *baágiso*, though they also used *hoí* in some cases. The researchers then subtracted spools of thread one at a time, and after each spool was subtracted asked the participants to identify the new quantity. *Baágiso* was used for quantities ranging from seven to ten spools, *hoí* was used for four to ten spools, while *hói* was utilized for one to six items. These findings are summarized graphically in Figure 6.2, adapted from Frank et al. (2008). Given that

---

43 Full disclosure: He is my dad.

the terms in question are used to denote such ranges of quantities, it seems clear that these terms are approximate only, somewhat like the phrase "a few" is approximate in English. (Of course, English has no term that can be used for "one" or "a few", as *hói* apparently is.) Significantly, these are the only quantity-associated terms in the language, and the language completely lacks number distinctions elsewhere in its grammar, even in its pronominal paradigm. Pirahã is simply the most anumeric well-documented language.

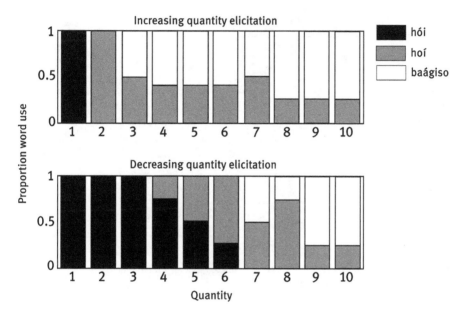

Figure 6.2: Results of a word-elicitation task with the Pirahã. Adapted from Frank et al. (2008:820).

Piqued by the language's anumericity, researchers have investigated the numerical cognition of speakers of Pirahã in order to better understand the role of language in numerical thought. Without cases like this it would be impossible to assess this role with a normal adult population. While there is a lot of important research on the ontogeny of numerical cognition (e.g. Sarnecka and Gelman [2004]) among children, adult speakers of numeric languages who lack proficiency with number words generally have other cognitive or developmental abnormalities. Given that there are no documented cognitive abnormalities among the Pirahã, their numerical cognition naturally drew the attention of researchers concerned with this aspect of human psychology.

The first study to experimentally assess Pirahã numerical cognition was Gordon (2004), which was published in the same issue of *Science* as Pica et al.

(2004). In a series of tasks conducted over two summer research trips, Gordon conducted eight basic quantity recognition tasks with seven adults. One of the tasks was similar to that depicted in Figure 6.1 above, used among the Mundur-ukú. In the case of that task, Pirahã speakers witnessed the experimenter plac-ing nuts in a can. The experimenter then withdrew the nuts one by one, and the participant stated whether or not any nuts remained in the can. The results of the task are depicted in Figure 6.3.

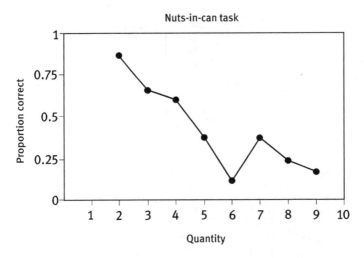

Figure 6.3: Results of the nuts-in-can task conducted among the Pirahã. Adapted from Gordon (2004:497).

As can be judged from the figure, the Pirahãs' performance on this task was generally inaccurate. The proportion correct only exceeded 50% when 1–3 nuts were placed in a can. In general, their ability to differentiate between quanti-ties suffered when the number of stimuli grew. The deleterious affect of larger numerosities was even noticeable in a series of five tasks that entailed the mere recognition of one-to-one correspondences between sets of numbers. Three of the tasks merit special attention, since they have subsequently been replicated in Frank et al. (2008) and Everett and Madora (2012). These are the basic "one-to-one" matching task, "hidden" matching task, and the "orthogonal" matching task. In the case of all of these tasks in Gordon (2004), stimuli (AA batteries) were placed in front of Pirahã participants in a linear array. The participants were then asked to match the array with their own array, equal in quantity. In the case of the basic one-to-one task, all the participants had to do was place one battery next to each of the batteries in front of them. In the case of the hidden task, the target arrays were hidden after being presented for several seconds, so that when the Pirahã attempted to match the relevant quantity the initial array was no longer visible. In the case of the orthogonal matching task, the initial array remained visible throughout the task, but it was presented at an approximately 90° degree angle to the matched array. That is, the target array was presented in line with the participants' sagittal plane, on a surface directly in front of themselves, while they were asked to match the array along their transverse plane, on the same surface. Put differently, this latter task required the participants to spatially transpose the viewed quantity.

In the case of the orthogonal matching tasks and hidden matching tasks, the Pirahãs' performance once again deteriorated for higher numerosities. They accurately recognized arrays of one or two items in 100% of trials, and approximately 75% of trials involving three items. Performance continued to decline for quantities beyond four. Most fascinating, however, was the people's performance on the basic one-to-one task. The results to that task are depicted in Figure 6.4.

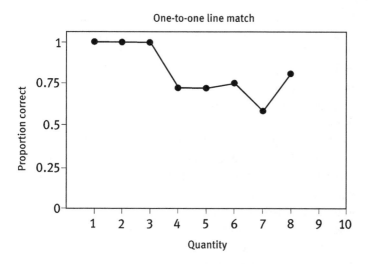

Figure 6.4: Results of the one-to-one matching task. Adapted from Gordon (2004:497).

Speakers were only 100% accurate at matching arrays of 1–3, with errors creeping in for all other tested quantities. In addition to the drop-off in accuracy for tested quantities greater than three, another pattern was observed. Much as in the Pica et al. (2004) study, the magnitude of errors increased in proportion to the quantity tested. This proportional increase was represented by Gordon via a "coefficient of variation", which is simply the standard deviation of the responses divided by the mean of the responses, calculated separately for each target number. What Gordon found was that this coefficient averaged 0.15 for all the Pirahã responses in the one-to-one task. A coefficient of this magnitude surfaces when participants employ analog estimation in numerical cognition tasks, per Weber's law (see Whalen, Gallistel, and Gelman [1999]). In other words, the data did not suggest that the Pirahã were completely guessing for higher numbers, or that they did not understand the task. The patterns in the responses suggested instead that, for quantities greater than three, they were using imprecise estimation rather than exact recognition of one-to-one correspondence.

The results in the basic one-to-one matching task in Gordon (2004) suggested that numeric language enables basic numerical thought. That is, number words are seemingly required for humans to precisely recognize one-to-one correspondences for quantities greater than three. This finding was consistent with the findings in Pica et al. (2004) for Mundurukú, but was even more dramatic since no subtraction was required in most of the tasks conducted by Gordon.

While many researchers were fascinated with the data offered in Gordon (2004), some remained skeptical of his interpretation of those data. They questioned, for example, whether the difficulties faced by the Pirahã when matching quantities were causally motivated by their language. As Casasanto notes (2005:1721), "In the absence of any environmental or cultural demand for exact enumeration, perhaps the Pirahã never developed this representational capacity – and consequently, they never developed the words." This point relates of course to one of the common valid criticisms of much work on linguistic relativity. How do we extricate linguistic effects on cognition from more general cultural effects? In a related vein, how can we be sure that cases of anumeric language are not due to general cultural factors that also motivate the cognitive patterns in question? As outlined in Chapter 3 of this book, there are various methodological tacks that can be adopted to dissociate potential linguistic effects from potential nonlinguistic cultural influences. As Casasanto (2005) points out, one way to do this is to contrast the results obtained among groups like the Pirahã with other control groups that are similar in culture but differ according to the relevant linguistic feature. While a nice ideal, however, in practice this approach is not easy to implement. Contrasts between the results obtained among the Pirahã with results obtained among indigenous tribal groups with number words may face limitations.

Let me offer a brief example hinting at such limitations. Recently I conducted research on the numerical cognition of speakers of another Amazonian language, Jarawara, and replicated the three tasks just described from Gordon (2004). The Jarawara, who are also a relatively isolated tribe of Amazonian hunter-gatherers, excelled at these tasks. As mentioned earlier in this chapter, during the course of this research I also uncovered a native Jarawara number system (Everett 2012a). Given that the Jarawara are another hunter-gatherer Amazonian tribe that *does* have number words and excels at exact quantity recognition, then, it is possible to interpret the results as being consistent with those of Gordon (2004), and consistent with a relativistic interpretation. Yet, while Jarawara culture is more similar to that of the Pirahã than my own, the cultures differ in many crucial respects. For example, the Jarawara have more eagerly embraced aspects of Brazilian culture. So it is quite likely that the results obtained in the brief study on their numerical cognition (Everett [2012b]) are due to other factors such as the Jarawaras' trading patterns with Brazilians. In actuality the Jarawara data offer only modest insight into the Pirahã findings, given the existence of other potential explanations for the cross-group disparities on the tasks in question. In short, contrasts of the Pirahã data with those obtained in any one other indigenous culture that has number words do not necessarily eliminate the role of cultural confounds. Other kinds of cross-cultural data do turn out to be vital to a better understanding of the findings on Pirahã numerical cognition, though, as we will see below.

In another study on Pirahã numerical cognition, Frank et al. (2008) replicated the three experiments described above from Gordon (2004), namely the basic one-to-one matching task, the hidden matching task, and the orthogonal matching task. They conducted their work with fourteen adults, in a different village from the two in which Gordon worked. The study also differed from Gordon's in terms of the stimuli used. Instead of AA batteries, Frank et al. (2008) presented the participants with arrays of spools of thread, placed vertically on a table in front of the participants, who were once again tested individually. The participants were provided with empty rubber balloons to match the number of presented spools of thread. These stimuli types were chosen in part because the people are very familiar with them.

With respect to the orthogonal matching task and the hidden matching task, the results in Frank et al. (2008) did not differ significantly from those in Gordon (2004). That is, the Pirahã speakers excelled at matching quantities from 1–3, but struggled to exactly match quantities beyond that range. The proportion of correct responses fell precipitously when higher quantities of stimuli were tested.

Significantly, however, the findings in Frank et al. (2008) differed significantly from those in Gordon (2004) vis-à-vis the basic one-to-one matching task. What they found was that the speakers were, by and large, able to exactly recognize one-to-one correspondences between sets as high as ten. Only two

errors, made by the same individual, surfaced in this task. Paired by-participants t-tests contrasting the proportion of correct responses revealed that the
Pirahã performed significantly better on the one-to-one matching task than
they did on either the hidden matching task or the orthogonal matching task.
($p<0.001$ in each case) The results of the latter two tasks did not differ significantly from each other, however. For both of these tasks, the coefficient of
variation hovered around 0.15. In other words, the speakers tested in Frank
et al. (2008) used analog estimation strategies when they had to mentally
transpose or remember the stimuli. When they simply had to match a given
quantity, though, they used exact recognition (except in the case of one participant). The authors concluded that number words are an important "cognitive
technology" required for the recall and mental transposition of quantities, but
that they are not necessary for the mere exact recognition of correspondences
between sets of quantities. Put differently, according to the authors the presence of number words in a language enables certain kinds of thought about
numbers, but does not influence numerical thought in the very fundamental
way suggested by Gordon (2004). (Note that Frank et al.'s [2008] claim is still
relativistic in nature, though in a weaker manner.)

Upon first reading Frank and colleagues' important study, I was fascinated
yet puzzled by the discrepancy between their results and Gordon's vis-à-vis the
one-to-one matching task. They suggest in their article (2008:822) that the poor
performance of the Pirahã for the one-to-one matching task in Gordon's study
was due to the stimuli he used, AA batteries. These batteries rolled in some
trials, potentially complicating the task. Yet this explanation is difficult to reconcile with the fact that Gordon conducted numerous test trials with other
stimuli, with similar results. Some of these test trials were video recorded, and
these recordings reveal incorrect responses on the basic one-to-one matching
task even when stimuli are not moving at all. In order to better understand
the discrepancy between the studies, I consulted Keren Madora, one of only
two fluent non-native speakers of Pirahã. Madora has decades of experience
among the Pirahã.[44] While Madora was unfamiliar with the results in Frank

---

44 Full disclosure again: She is my mom. Some personal history is relevant to this discussion.
My parents went to the Pirahã in the late seventies, at the time working as missionaries. They
have maintained contact with the people since that time. As a child I spent a lot of time,
intermittently, living in Pirahã villages, along with my two sisters. Our family's time there is
documented in part in my father's book, *Don't Sleep, there are Snakes* (D. Everett [2008]).
During our first years among the people, it became clear that they faced difficulties with
mathematical tasks, even when conducted in their own language. Descriptions of these
difficulties helped motivate Gordon's research. It should be stressed again that the people are
by all accounts not neurocognitively impaired and, of course, are extremely well adapted to
their environs.

et al. (2008), she was aware of when the research had taken place, and in which village – one named Xagiopai. She offered a crucial insight: In the months leading up to the research conducted in Frank et al. (2008), she had worked extensively with all of the adult members of that village, attempting to teach them basic math skills. While previous attempts had been unsuccessful, she felt she had made some progress at Xagiopai once she began introducing number-word neologisms into Pirahã. Many previous attempts to teach the people basic math had been unsuccessful, so it seems quite plausible that the results at Xagiopai reported in Frank et al. (2008) were due to the familiarity of those speakers with number words such as the innovated term *xohóísógió* ('four'), meaning "all the sons of the hand".

In order to resolve the important discrepancy between Gordon (2004) and Frank et al. (2008), I traveled with Madora to the Pirahã tribe in order to once again replicate the relevant tasks. We visited a different village whose members had never been exposed to number neologisms, much like those Pirahã tested in Gordon (2004). We replicated the one-to-one matching task, the hidden matching task, and the orthogonal matching task, using the exact stimuli employed in Frank et al. (2008). Fourteen adults participated in our study. Our findings are detailed in Everett and Madora (2012). A few points are worth highlighting here. First, with respect to the orthogonal matching task and hidden matching tasks, the results obtained were statistically indistinguishable from those in Frank et al. (2008). The Pirahã clearly understood the tasks, but attempted to resolve them via analog estimation, failing to exactly recognize quantities greater than three. Figure 6.5 depicts the completion of one trial of the basic one-to-one matching task.

The results of the hidden matching task are presented in Figure 6.6, where they are contrasted with the similar results from Frank et al. (2008). The similarity of the results is readily apparent. See Everett and Madora (2012) for a contrast of the similar orthogonal task results obtained across the two studies.

Most significantly, with respect to the pivotal results on the one-to-one matching task, the results in Everett and Madora (2012) were similar to those in Gordon (2004), not Frank et al. (2008). Figure 6.7 contains a contrast between the results in Everett and Madora (2012) and those in Frank et al. (2008), for the relevant task. In Frank et al. (2008), 54/56 responses for this task contained the correct response, while in Everett and Madora (2012) only 32/56 responses were accurate. The disparity between results across the studies, for this task only, was significant according to a paired by-participants t-test contrasting the individuals' proportions of correct responses ($t[13] = 6.62$, $p = .000$).

Results from other quantity recognition tasks are also discussed in Everett and Madora (2012) and Everett (In press). The results of all these tasks, includ-

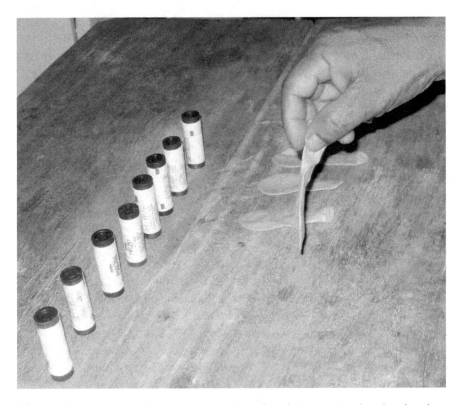

Figure 6.5: Picture of a one-to-one matching trial conducted for Everett and Madora (2012).

ing those conducted in different modalities, suggest the majority of Pirahã speakers struggle with the exact recognition of quantities beyond three, much as the results in Gordon (2004) did. The only Pirahã speakers who excel at the basic one-to-one matching task had previously been familiarized with innovated number words based on Pirahã morphemes. These speakers include those represented in Frank et al. (2008) and also include two speakers discussed in Everett and Madora (2012). The latter two speakers that were tested by us were visiting the village in which we conducted our research, but were from Xagiopai. They also excelled at the task, like the other Pirahã tested at Xagiopai, and this seems unlikely to be a coincidence.

Given the results of these three studies carried out among four Pirahã villages, it is clear that the people struggle with recognizing exact correspondences between quantities. This is particularly true when mental transposition or memorization of quantities is required for tasks. Most significantly perhaps, the people generally use analog estimation when attempting to simply recognize quantities over three. (Coefficient of variation for this task hovered around

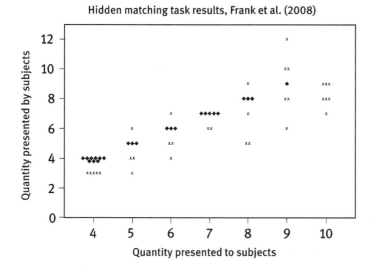

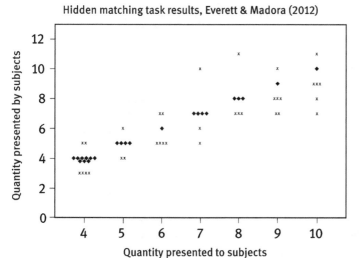

Figure 6.6: Results of the hidden matching task in Frank et al. (2008) and Everett and Madora (2012). Values along the x-axis represent the target number, presented in arrays to the Pirahã. Values along the y-axis represent the responses, i.e. the quantity of the array used by the participants in their matching attempts. Incorrect responses are charted with an "x", correct responses with a black diamond. Responses are staggered along the x-axis so that each trial can be presented separately.

0.15 in Everett and Madora [2012]). The exceptions to this latter pattern have only surfaced with Pirahã that had been systematically exposed to number words. This intra-cultural variation is one of the most important bits of data

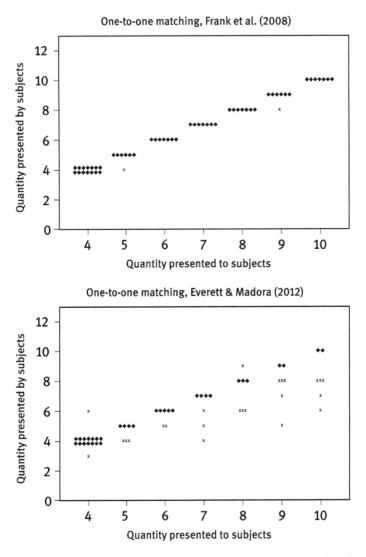

Figure 6.7: Results of the one-to-one matching task in Frank et al. (2008) and Everett and Madora (2012).

on this group's numerical cognition. It demonstrates that the Pirahã are not prevented from learning exact quantity recognition by other factors, either cultural or genetic, and implies that the acquisition of number words plays a key role in enabling such recognition. At the least, this interpretation seems the most plausible one in the light of the data so far gathered. The relevant data from Everett and Madora (2012) are summarized graphically in Figure 6.8. Note

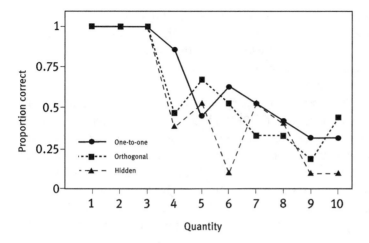

Figure 6.8: Composite results for the three relevant tasks in Everett and Madora (2012).

how quantity recognition clearly deteriorates for quantities beyond three, for all three tasks.

What seems indisputable at this point is that the Pirahã, despite being normal adults who have excelled in their current environment for centuries, struggle with basic quantity recognition tasks. This fact is most plausibly motivated by their anumeric language, particularly in the light of the fact that their quantity recognition ability seems to improve after they are familiarized with novel number words. Nevertheless, the findings on this fascinating case are limited to the extent they represent only one culture. Ideally these Pirahã data could be contrasted with other normal adults without number words. Thankfully, findings gathered among a completely unrelated culture do offer the possibility of fruitful contrast.

Recently a study was undertaken on the quantity recognition abilities of Nicaraguan homesigners, who are deaf individuals that communicate with an elaborate gestural communication system. This system lacks symbols for numbers, and is not classified as a language. Unlike the Pirahã, the homesigners are embedded in a numerate culture. Since it has previously been claimed that the Pirahã and Mundurukú results may owe themselves to general cultural factors, the case of Nicaraguan homesigners drew researchers' attention since the signers clearly have no cultural obstacle precluding their acquisition of quantity recognition. This conclusion is supported by the fact that the signers can preferentially discriminate denominations of the local currency, and by the fact that they use their fingers to communicate about quantities. These points are established in Spaepen et al. (2011), a study that investigated whether the numerical gestures of the homesigners represent exact numbers, and which sought to elucidate the quantity recognition abilities of the signers. In the study, the performance of four homesigners on a variety of quantity recognition tasks was contrasted with two control groups: one of unschooled hearing Nicaraguans, and the other of Nicaraguans fluent in a numeric sign language (American Sign Language).

One of the tasks described in Spaepen et al. (2011) was a "card task" in which participants were presented with cards that had depictions of a quantity of some item. The quantity depicted varied from 1–20. Participants were told to report how many items were on each card. Through training the researchers revealed they were interested in the exact rather than approximate quantity of the items. For this simple task, respondents were given unlimited time to convey their responses. The control populations' results contained almost no errors, as they simply counted the presented stimuli and reported the number. In contrast, the homesigners' results contained numerous errors. The magnitude of these errors increased in accordance with the quantity of the target stimuli, as evident in Figure 6.9.

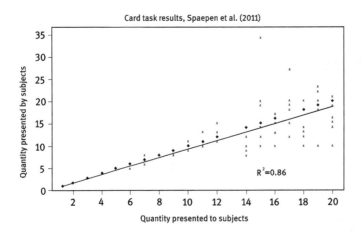

Figure 6.9: Results for a quantity recognition task in which homesigners were asked to report the number of items on cards they were shown. Each correct response is denoted via a diamond, each incorrect one via an "x". Adapted from Spaepen et al. (2011).

It is evident in Figure 6.9 that, though the homesigners use gestures to denote quantities, they do so in an imprecise manner. This imprecision is not random, however, revealing instead a pattern of analog estimation similar to that evident in the Mundurukú and Pirahã data. Responses for lower numerosities tend to be accurate, while those for higher numerosities are characterized by fewer correct responses and a greater deviation in the responses.

Among the other tasks conducted by Spaepen et al. (2011) were two that have also been carried out among the Pirahã: the one-to-one matching task and the hidden matching task described above. (Termed "covered" and "uncovered" tasks, respectively, by Spaepen and colleagues.) Homesigners and members of the control groups were presented with arrays of white poker chips, and asked to match those arrays with their own quantity of white poker chips. In the case of the hidden matching task, the target array of poker chips was covered once the participants began creating their matching array. Training trials were conducted to demonstrate that the requisite matches should be exact in number.

For the basic one-to-one matching task, homesigners' response arrays did not deviate dramatically from the target arrays, but a large percentage of cases did contain errors. The signers used their fingers to attempt one-to-one correspondence with the target arrays, and then used their fingers again to establish quantity semblance of their response array. This strategy appeared to benefit their accuracy, since magnitude of errors did not increase significantly with target number for this task. For the other tasks, including the hidden matching task, magnitude of errors did in fact increase with target number. When the homesigners could not directly match their fingers with the target, then, they relied on analog estimation. They could not, for example, accurately count a number with their fingers. The homesigners faced difficulties specifically when attempting to provide exact responses for quantities greater than three. Crucially, this was true even in the case of the one-to-one matching task. For that task, 100% of the trials involving arrays with 1–3 items contained correct responses. For numbers greater than 3, however, that ratio of correct responses fell to 61%. Fascinatingly, these proportions are very similar to those found in Everett and Madora (2012) for the Pirahã, vis-à-vis the basic one-to-one matching task. (See discussion in Everett [2013a].) Close inspection of the data in that study reveals that 100% of the trials for 1–3 were correct, and that the ratio fell to 59% for quantities greater than three.

In the case of the hidden matching task, the Nicaraguan homesigners' responses were accurate in 100% of the trials for 1–3 items, with accuracy falling to 50% for quantities beyond that range. Again, these patterns are strikingly similar to those observed in Everett and Madora (2012) for the Pirahã. Tabulation of the correct responses in the hidden matching task in that study reveals that the Pirahã responses were 100% correct for quantities from 1–3, but only 41% correct for higher numbers. Another parallel between the studies is that the homesigners' responses reflected a pattern of analog estimation, with the magnitude of errors increasing with target number for the hidden matching task.

The findings on Nicaraguan homesigners' quantity-differentiation capacities are summarized as follows in Spaepen et al. (2011):

> However, despite the fact that homesigners use their fingers to communicate about number, they do not consistently produce gestures that accurately represent the cardinal values of sets containing more than three items. Moreover, they cannot reliably make the number of items in a second set match the number in a target set if the sets contain more than three items.

Spaepen et al.'s (2011) conclusions are consonant with those arrived at in another study among deaf Nicaraguan adults, Flaherty and Senghas (2011). Through a series of matching tasks with thirty deaf speakers of Nicaraguan sign language (not homesigners), Flaherty and Senghas (2011) demonstrate that deaf Nicaraguans very familiar with number symbols outperform those who are less familiar with such symbols. They conclude that, to be fully numerate, one must possess a "memorized sequence of number symbols", and that immersion in a numerate culture alone is insufficient for one to acquire full numerosity.[45]

The data on offer suggest that speakers of a nearly anumeric language (with apparently no *precise* number terms), the Mundurukú, and members of two groups without number terms, the Pirahã and deaf Nicaraguans, face remarkably similar difficulties when recognizing quantities. All three groups struggle with the exact discrimination of quantities exceeding three. Furthermore, all three groups utilize analog estimation when attempting to match such numerosities, rather than resorting to some random guessing strategy.[46] Members of all three groups seem to lack awareness of two fundamental principles of mathematical reasoning: the clear recognition of one-to-one correspondences between equal sets of quantities greater than three, and the "successor principle" stipulating the regularity of such quantities when they are increased by one unit (i.e. that every natural number n has a successor that is equal to $n+1$). The absence of evidence for the successor principle is less surprising perhaps, given that these people do not have counting routines. The fact that these groups seem to lack the exact recognition of one-to-one correspondences (for higher quantities) is more remarkable. It is worth stressing,

---

45 The results in Flaherty and Senghas (2011) are not directly contrastable with those obtained among the Pirahã, since all the Nicaraguan participants in their study, unlike those relied on by Spaepen et al. (2011), could produce some number signs for at least the numbers "between one and five". (Flaherty and Senghas [2011:430])

46 This latter point is particularly important, since it demonstrates that the results of the aforementioned studies are not simply due to participants' task incomprehension or disinterest.

though, that members of all of these three groups excel at the recognition of one-to-one correspondences for numbers less than four. This point offers dramatic support for the claims in Condry and Spelke (2008) and elsewhere that numerical language serves a profound role in uniting the two innate mathematical "senses" discussed above: the exact recognition of small quantities and the approximate recognition of large quantities.

6.4 Other kinds of effects

To this point we have considered studies of speakers of anumeric or nearly anumeric languages, given the important implications of such work on the role of numeric language in enabling numerical thought. Such studies offer evidence for one of the most radical kinds of linguistic relativity present in the literature. For that reason they have attracted significant attention in the social sciences. There are other less radical potential relativistic effects associated with numeric language, however. Some of these have yet to be investigated. For instance, one potential area for research is the role of number bases in quantity discrimination. As we noted at the outset of this chapter, many languages use decimal systems, while others may use quinary, or vigesimal, or binary systems, or systems with other bases. Does this crosslinguistic variation yield disparities, however subtle, in quantity-grouping strategies in nonlinguistic tasks? I am unaware of any research on this topic. At least two milder sorts of potential relativistic effects in this domain have been considered, though. Next we briefly consider these two in turn.

One potential sort of effect relates to the way in which numbers are named. As discussed in Seron and Fayol (1994), for example, French dialects differ in the terms for some numbers. For example, in Belgian and Swiss French the word for 'seventy' is *septante* and the word for 'ninety' is *nonante*. In France, the analogous terms are *soixante-dix*, 'sixty-ten', and *quatre-vingt-dix*, 'fourscore-ten'. Another difference between these dialects is that in France the numbers for 71–79 are based on the term for 60 plus a term for a teen number. Also, in France the numbers for 91–99 are based on the word for 80 plus a term for a teen number. Seron and Fayol (1994) provide data suggesting that children in France face certain difficulties in processing numbers in these ranges (when contrasted with Belgians), plausibly because of the manner in which they are encoded in their dialect of French.

Researchers have also sought to explore whether differences in number-naming patterns help children understand number terms at different rates. For example, in many European languages including English, the terms for teen numbers are non-transparent and irregular, for instance "eleven", "twelve", "thirteen", "fourteen", whereas in a number of widely-spoken Asian languages, the comparable terms would be glossed as 'ten one', 'ten two', 'ten three', 'ten four', with more transparent additive meanings. Also, in a language such as English multiples of ten have non-transparent names such as "twenty", "thirty", and "forty", whereas in the relevant Asian languages the terms might be glossed 'two ten', 'three ten', and 'four-ten', with more transparent multiplicative meanings. Miura et al. (1994) provide evidence that speakers of Korean, Japanese, and Chinese outperform French, English, and Swedish-speaking children in tasks requiring them to match multi-digit numbers. They suggest that these disparities are due to the just-mentioned linguistic disparities between these groups of languages. While such results are consistent with a relativistic interpretation, though, there are other potential explanations for the findings since clearly the cultures vary along other dimensions, including pedagogical ones.

Other evidence on the role of number-term-naming in cognitive processing is offered in Brysbaert, Fias, and Noël (1998). The authors of that study contrasted the behavior of French and Dutch speaking individuals in addition tasks. These subjects were chosen since their native languages differ in terms of the order in which tens and units occur in numbers. For example, the order of units for 24 in Dutch is 'four and twenty' rather than 'twenty four'. Brysbaert, Fias, and Noël (1998) investigated whether this sequencing strategy might influence the manner in which Dutch speakers add numbers, when contrasted with French speakers. They tested the addition abilities of these groups (both verbally and visually) with a variety of types of problems, for instance 3+45. In verbal presentation, the Dutch speakers would be adding 'three' and 'five and forty' (glosses of the actual expressions) as opposed to 'three' and 'forty-five'. Since the smaller units in such a problem ('three' and 'five') are adjacent and more obviously tied together in Dutch, it seemed possible that the Dutch system would foster faster response times in such cases. This was in fact the case. Dutch speaker reaction times were lower, at least when the stimuli were presented verbally and their responses were verbal. Crucially, though, this cross-population difference disappeared when the subjects provided responses via typing. This lead Brysbaert, Fias, and Noël (1998) to conclude that the initial cross-populations differences were not due to differences in cognitive processing during mathematical addition, but were instead caused by different strategies required of the linguistic output for each language, after the mathematical processing occurred. In other words, Brysbaert, Fias, and Noël (1998) posit that their data provide negative evidence for a relativistic effect, despite the cross-population differences that surface for their verbal-response task. Brysbaert, Fias, and Noël's (1998) results could be interpreted as providing evidence for a "thinking for speaking" effect only, though the authors do not frame their results in this manner.

Before concluding this section another cross-cultural finding on number-processing should be mentioned, since it relates to written language. This finding is based on an observation about the SNARC effect. The SNARC effect refers to the spatial-numerical association of response codes. Dehaene, Bossini, and Giraux (1993) found that, when asked to classify the magnitude of single digits, participants responded more quickly with their left hand sides when the numbers in question were smaller than five. With numbers greater than five, though, the subjects responded more quickly with their right hand side. This SNARC effect has now been documented for a variety of tasks (Wood et al. [2008]). Crucially, though, the left=smaller/right=larger association of space and numbers is stronger with subjects who write from left-to-right. In fact, the SNARC effect is actually reversed for speakers of languages written from right-to-left (Zebian [2005]). Most radically, the SNARC effect actually reverses for the same subjects when they switch from a language with left-to-right writing to one with right-to-left writing, as shown in Shaki and Gevers' (2011) work with Hebrew-English bilinguals. Clearly the writing direction associated with particular languages interacts with the SNARC effect, creating an indirect linguistic influence on this facet of numerical cognition.

In sum, the selection of studies considered in this section hints at opportunities for uncovering more modest, though perhaps more crosslinguistically pervasive, relativistic effects on numerical thought. Some of these studies already offer evidence for subtle cross-cultural differences in numerical cognition, and provide tentative evidence that these differences may be due to patterns associated with language (e.g. orthographic convention) or actual linguistic patterns (e.g. regularity of words for multiples of ten). Future work may more clearly dissociate the effect of linguistic patterns from other possible cultural confounds such as disparate pedagogical traditions.

6.5 Discussion and conclusion

The findings surveyed in this chapter, particularly those on speakers without numbers or with a small set of imprecise numbers, are consistent with the psychology literature suggesting that humans are endowed with two core systems of numerical cognition. One of these enables us to exactly discriminate small quantities, and the other allows us to inexactly estimate larger quantities. Nicaraguan homesigners, Mundurukú speakers, and Pirahã speakers are of course genetically equipped with these number senses. What they appear to lack is the ability to systematically connect these two capacities in order to exactly recognize larger quantities. The remarkable similarity between the findings gathered among these three populations suggests quite strongly that language plays a pivotal role in enabling very basic numerical thought. This interpretation is consistent with ontogenetic data that have led researchers to the same conclusion (Condry and Spelke [2008]).

The gross similarity of the findings obtained among the three groups most focused upon in this chapter is significant in another respect: it helps to rule out cultural confounds. While both are autochthonous Amazonian groups, the Mundurukú and Pirahã cultures differ markedly in numerous respects. Clearly they each also differ from the urban culture of the Nicaraguan homesigners. Despite these cross-cultural disparities, and despite the fact that the homesigners live in a numerate society, the findings discussed above show that the quantity recognition abilities of the members of these groups are very much alike. The clearest causal factor motivating this similarity is that of anumeric language. Furthermore, given the consistency of this linguistic explanation with the developmental and neurophysiological literature on the subject, the data suggest even more strongly that numeric language plays a fundamental role in allowing humans to recognize, recall, and manipulate quantities greater than three. This interpretation is further supported by the fact that anumeric speakers who were familiarized with numeric terms, the Pirahã at Xagiopai, exhibited enhanced capacities for quantity recognition.

Assuming this plausible account is accurate, it remains unclear which aspect of numeric language plays a role in enabling exact quantity recognition. Is the presence of precise number words sufficient, or must speakers have access to a counting routine? The influence of counting routines in numerical cognition is well known (Carey [2009], Hurford [1987]), but the magnitude of this influence remains a relevant open-ended issue that is being explored with cross-cultural work (Dowker, Bala, and Lloyd [2008]).

In a similar manner, ongoing work may help to tease out other less dramatic effects of numeric language on numerical cognition, for instance the sort pointed to by the research highlighted in Section 6.4. In fact, research of this sort may in the long run prove more fruitful. After all, there are only a few cases of anumeric or nearly anumeric languages, and even fewer in which the speakers of these languages are monolingual. Even in such cases, rates of monolingualism are falling. So research on the role of anumeric language in thought may soon face insurmountable obstacles.[47]

---

47 Even in the case of the Pirahã, western culture is being introduced into some villages in a radical manner. Recently the Brazilian government has constructed large western structures

The evidence presented in Sections 6.2 and 6.3 suggests that numeric language has a major augmenting effect on nonlinguistic numerical cognition. Numeric language appears to serve as a crucial "conceptual tool" (Gentner [2003], Gordon [2010]) that enables a fundamental shift in our capacity to think about quantities. As I have suggested elsewhere, numeric language serves as "ground-floor conceptual scaffolding for much of human numerosity" (Everett [2013b]), since it apparently allows children and adults to recognize quantities in an exact manner. This latter point is worth stressing, since the findings on adult speakers of anumeric or nearly anumeric languages may be incorrectly interpreted in strong deterministic ways. Speakers of such languages may have radically different ways of referring to and thinking about quantities, but there is little reason to suspect that these differences cannot be compensated for via the acquisition of number terms and counting. The Pirahã, Mundurukú, and Nicaraguan homesigners are clearly endowed with the same basic number senses that are shared by humans in all cultures. In this way the findings in this chapter point once again to both variation *and* universality in human cognition. It just so happens that the cognitive variation engendered by anumeric language is of a seemingly dramatic sort.

Finally, it is worth pointing out that the findings discussed in this chapter may have indirect implications for our understanding of human history. If exact quantity recognition for quantities greater than three relies on numeric language, this implies that many ancient material technologies that required such quantity recognition must have also relied indirectly on such language (Everett [2013b]). The innovation and diffusion of numerical language appears to have created a fundamental shift in the way in which our species conceptualized quantities, and this shift doubtlessly played a pivotal role in the shaping of many human technologies and, therefore, in the more general shaping of most human societies.

---

on the reservation, including clinics and even a school. For the first time in over two centuries of contact with outside cultures, there are signs that some of the people may be adopting more than a few aspects of Brazilian culture.

7 Color

7.1 Introduction

Quickly answer the following two questions: What color is the sky on a clear day? What color are the leaves of a palm tree? Most likely, you responded "green" to the second question and "blue" to the first. Yet speakers of many languages would use the same word to answer both of these questions, since many languages utilize a 'grue' category that encompasses the portion of the color spectrum subsumed by English "green" and "blue". One question that has long fascinated those curious about the effects of language on thought is whether such disparate representations of the color spectrum impacts the actual perception of such colors, so that speakers of languages with a 'grue' category actually do not distinguish between blue and green hues in the same manner that speakers of other languages do. In an attempt to answer such questions, researchers have provided experimental and anecdotal data from a host of cultures. As it turns outs, the investigation of the existence of such language-mediated perceptual effects has played a major role in the more general investigation of linguistic effects on nonlinguistic cognition. Much of this work is contentious and has paradoxically resulted in some of the strongest claims for *and* against the presence of linguistic effects on low-level cognitive and perceptual processes.

It is in some sense puzzling that debates surrounding color terminology and color discrimination came to play such a prominent role in discussions of relativistic effects, since color terminology plays a rather peripheral role in grammar. While crosslinguistic data suggest that nearly all languages have terms dedicated to color reference, color is not generally a category indexed in morphological paradigms. This is in sharp contrast to the semantic domains discussed in the preceding chapters, namely those associated with spatial, temporal, and numerical distinctions. Morphological systems are generally replete with affixal and adpositional resources for specifying things like the location or orientation of referents, the time at which an event occurred, or whether the number of referents being discussed is singular or plural. Such systems do not, however, provide means to systematically denote the hue of given referents. There is for example no suffix denoting "purple" in the world's languages. Given the lack of centrality of color to the world's grammars, some have suggested that color terms have played an outsized role in the literature on linguistic relativity (Lucy [1997]).

Much of the literature on the interaction of language and color perception has been based in one way or another on Berlin and Kay's (1969) famous study on basic color terms, and has focused on recurrent crosslinguistic patterns in the way in which colors are named. While this naming research is undoubtedly significant, most of it actually provides little experimentally based insight into potential effects of language on color perception. Given this fact, and given that such work has rightfully been discussed in innumerable works in the anthropological, psychological, and linguistic literature, our attention to this naming research will be relatively abbreviated. In Section 7.2 we provide a concise overview of such work, detailing some of the major claims made vis-à-vis the ways in which colors are named across languages, in addition to considering some of the criticisms in the literature pertaining to the general research paradigm utilized in such work. In Section 7.3 we will focus on a series of intriguing recent experimental studies on the actual perception of color. We will see that the experimental work in question offers some fascinating and nuanced evidence for linguistic influences on the categorical perception of colors. In Section 7.4 we offer some concluding remarks on the research surveyed.

7.2 Color categories across languages

Berlin and Kay's (1969) seminal work on color categories in the world's languages was motivated in large measure by skepticism towards relativistic claims. More specifically, the authors were skeptical of some claims in the literature that the spectral referents designated by color terms were essentially arbitrary, varying unpredictably from language to language. Such strong claims of variability had clear implications for the study of language and cognition, since some interpreted them as meaning that people's low-level perceptions and groupings of color types were determined by arbitrary linguistic conventions that varied in an undetermined manner. In addition, some psychological research of that era (Brown and Lenneberg [1954], Stefflre, Vales, and Morley [1966]) suggested that the colors encoded in a given language are more readily recalled by its speakers. This claim imbued greater import to the notion that color terms vary unpredictably across languages. Berlin and Kay's (1969) skepticism was motivated in large measure by their first-hand experience with some unrelated languages, experience which suggested to them that color terms were too easily translatable for such extreme claims of variability and determinism to be accurate.

In order to more systematically address this issue, Berlin and Kay (1969) elicited color terms from speakers of twenty languages, and examined semantic data gathered by field researchers in an additional seventy-eight languages.

Their linguistic sample was not immune to subsequent criticisms, for instance that it relied too heavily on written languages in industrialized societies. Other criticisms included the suggestions that the language sample was not sufficiently diverse in terms of represented linguistic families, that the colors were elicited from bilingual speakers familiar with English colors, that the interviewers were not fluent in the target languages, and that the samples were not obtained *in situ* but in an urban American setting. (Kay, Berlin, and Merrifield [1991]) These particular criticisms have been addressed in subsequent work for the World Color Survey (Kay et al. [2009]), which began in 1976 and sought, with the help of linguists from the Summer Institute of Linguistics, to document color terms in 110 languages in their natural contexts, with at least twenty-five representative speakers in most cases. This work has generally supported, with some refinements, the original claims offered in Berlin and Kay (1969), so it would be unfair to say that the claims associated with this work are not based on a sufficient sample of geographically and genetically unaffiliated languages. (This does not mean the World Color Survey has been immune to all criticisms, however, as we will see below.)

The two principal claims in Berlin and Kay (1969) that have also been buttressed by research in the intervening decades are as follows: A) There is actually a restricted universal set of color categories in the world's languages, and crosslinguistic variations in color term reference adhere to tight constraints once linguistic data are carefully considered. B) The basic color term inventories of language develop in a predictable manner, i.e. color systems evolve in a predictable fashion as they increase in terms of the number of basic color terms. This evolutionary pathway was explicitly delineated for the first time in Berlin and Kay (1969) and developed further in other work (Kay, Berlin, and Merrifield [1991]), though it should be noted that the general hypothesis that color term systems evolve from simpler to more advanced kinds was actually quite popular in the nineteenth century.

Before the implications of such claims can be addressed, some methodological considerations are in order. It is important to consider how the relevant findings were arrived at, and what exactly is being discussed when researchers speak of "basic color terms".

Like researchers before them such as Lenneberg and Roberts (1956), Berlin and Kay (1969) relied on a series of color chips developed by the Munsell Color Company, originally intended for marketing that company's color system developed for commercial uses. The array of Munsell chips represented 329 colors. These colors varied incrementally in terms of both hue and lightness, and were maximally saturated. Forty variations in hue, each with eight variations in lightness, were presented in a single continuous array depicted as a

Mercator projection of a color "cylinder". In addition to these 320 colors, nine neutral colors, varying only in darkness, were also presented. In their initial work, Berlin and Kay (1969) presented the array as a whole unit to the study's participants, but in subsequent elicitation work the chips of the array were presented individually to the participants. In the array, hues vary along the horizontal axis, while lightness varies along the vertical axis.

In Berlin and Kay (1969), speakers of the various languages were asked two questions after being presented with the array. First, they were asked to point to all of the chips that could be denoted via a given basic color term. Second, they were asked to select the clearest or most prototypical example of the basic color term in question. By using this simple method with multiple speakers, the researchers were able to map the boundaries between the colors denoted by the terms, while also ascertaining the best exemplars or focal points of each color category indicated by the terms.

This method relied on a simple understanding of what the basic color terms were in the participants' languages. These basic terms were arrived at via elicitation with the languages' speakers. In order to be considered "basic", each color term was required to meet several criteria: it had to be monolexemic, so that the meaning was not transparent (as in e.g. "firetruck red"), the color denoted by the term could not be encompassed by another term, the color had to be widely applicable to any sort of object, and it had to be clearly salient to the speakers of the language in question. In addition, the term in question was required to have the same morphosyntactic distribution as other established basic color terms. Furthermore, it could not be a recent loan word. (Berlin and Kay [1969:6]) In the case of English, the application of this set of criteria results in the following list of basic color terms: white, black, red, green, yellow, blue, brown, purple, pink, orange, and grey. Terms such as the following do not make the list: chartreuse, mauve, salmon-colored, cherry red, gold, blond, etc.

As mentioned above, the Munsell chips have now been presented to speakers of well over one hundred languages. All of the data gathered with the chips do point to crosslinguistic variation in basic color terms, but concomitantly suggest that this variation is constrained in a predictable fashion, as discussed in, for example, Kay and Maffi (1999). While the number of basic color terms in a given language ranges from two[48] to a putatively optimal maximum of eleven (but potentially twelve – see Davies and Corbett's [1997] analysis of Russian), these terms appear to demarcate the chips of the Munsell array in a

---

[48] Ignoring for the moment Pirahã, which D. Everett (2005) suggests lacks color terms altogether.

governed manner. For example, no languages have only three basic color terms that denote chips that are green, yellow, and blue, respectively. Instead, if a language has three basic color terms we can be confident that those terms will denote chips that would be glossed as 'white', 'black', and 'red' in English.

The major claims made via the color chip elicitation paradigm are as follows: First, color terms evolve in a predictable sequence. That is, languages add words to their inventory of basic color terms in a way that demarcates the color spectrum in an increasingly detailed but constrained way. Second, all languages have at least two basic color terms, and languages with only two color terms represent the first "stage" of color-term evolution. Third, the foci or best exemplars of color terms are located in predictable loci within the color spectrum, with only a minor amount of variation observed across languages. These findings all strongly suggest that color term variation is limited by some universal governing factor, generally assumed to be the commonality of human neurophysiological perception. Kay and McDaniel (1978) suggest in fact that there are six basic "neural response" categories: red, green, black, white, blue, and yellow, and that basic color terms denote these categories or a limited set of composites of these categories. This interpretation has since been called into question. For instance, Robserson et al. (2000:394) note that, while neurons respond selectively to particular light wavelengths, or combinations of wavelengths, there is no evidence that such selectivity parallels color categorization patterns across languages.

Given the robust literature that already exists on the type of color term research first promulgated in Berlin and Kay (1969), we do not wish to belabor the major results here. We should note however that the resultant implicational scale governing the usage of basic color terms can be pithily summarized as follows: If a language has two basic color terms only (so-called Stage I languages), those terms will separately denote white and black chips.[49] If a language has three basic color terms, they will separately denote white, black, and red chips (so-called Stage II languages). If a language has four basic color terms, white, black, and red will still be indexed separately, as will green (or a 'grue' composite of green and blue) or yellow chips (Stage III languages). If a language has five basic color terms, we can predict that this inventory will offer distinct terms for white, black, red, green (or 'grue') *and* yellow chips (Stage IV languages). In languages with six basic color terms, these five terms will be joined by a term separately denoting blue chips (Stage V languages). If

---

49 Note that this does not imply that the color terms are the same as English "white" and "black", since they encompass wider ranges of the color spectrum. A similar caveat applies to all other stages.

there are seven basic color terms, the seventh term added will denote brown chips (Stage VI languages). Finally, if there are eleven basic color terms, we can predict that the additional four terms will distinguish between purple, pink, orange, and grey chips (Stage VII languages). In short, the data gathered by Kay, Berlin and colleagues suggest that basic color terms do not reflect unlimited variation, and that they are quite constrained by universal factors. The universality of the implicational scale they offer has been interpreted as clear evidence that all human speakers are biased to focus on certain neuro-physiologically salient colors. According to such an interpretation, as languages develop more color terms, the bias towards such salient colors becomes more readily apparent. Those categories that are permissibly grouped into composite categories, such as 'grue', become linguistically differentiated in accordance with a universal bias towards certain foci – in the case of 'grue' the clearest exemplars of green and blue. Accordingly, the boundaries and foci associated with basic color terms will always be governed by the immutable salience of particular colors, and color term systems will not develop in accordance with some set of capricious linguistic or cultural factors.

The universalist conclusions offered in Berlin and Kay (1969) and much subsequent work on this topic were taken by many to represent clear evidence against the linguistic relativity hypothesis. In some sense this is understandable, since linguistic relativity can be interpreted in a strong manner, according to which the low-level processing of physical phenomena (such as portions of the visible light spectrum) is governed by highly variable crosslinguistic disparities. Yet in another vital sense, the strong anti-relativistic interpretation by some of Berlin and Kay (1969) and other related work is puzzling. After all, this research points out quite vividly that, while color term systems vary in constrained ways, they do vary. It is possible, for example, to have languages with only two basic color terms, and others with eleven. Furthermore, the boundaries between basic color terms are not isomorphic across all languages, even according to the methods used in such research. In short, even if linguistic variation vis-à-vis color terms is constrained by universal factors, that variation nevertheless exists. The natural question is whether the linguistic variation that does exists impacts the nonlinguistic processing of color terms. Surprisingly perhaps, given how Berlin and Kay's (1969) work was sometimes championed as the death knell for linguistic relativity, until recently few attempts were made to systematically address this question. In one sense the strong dichotomization between universal and relativistic perspectives appears to have hindered experimental work on this topic. As has been stressed in this book, the acceptance of the existence of some form of linguistic relativity by no means precludes the acceptance of universal aspects of human cognition.

As we saw in the preceding chapter, for example, some facets of numerical cognition vary in accordance with linguistic factors, while other facets appear to be governed by the human genome.

A notable exception to the general absence of experimental studies on this topic in the years following Berlin and Kay (1969) was the work of Rosch (1972, 1973). Her experimental investigations related directly to Berlin and Kay's (1969) universalist findings, and addressed the implications of such findings vis-à-vis human cognition. Rosch conducted a series of recall-based experiments with speakers of a New Guinean language, Dani, in which only two color terms are used to refer to the entire Munsell array. With Berlin and Kay's (1969) conclusions as backdrop to her work, Rosch hypothesized that speakers of this language might exhibit greater facility recalling focal colors associated with the eleven supposedly basic color terms, even though the two color terms in Dani, *mili* and *mola*, clearly do not distinguish between all eleven colors. In short, her work did suggest that the foci associated with these eleven basic color terms were more easily recalled than other colors. Her work also suggested that Dani speakers learned novel color terms more easily in accordance with the universal implicational scale established by Berlin and Kay (1969). That is, her work suggested that color terms associated with "earlier" stages in their implicational scale were more easily acquired by Dani speakers. Setting aside for the moment some possible criticisms of Rosch's methods (see Lucy and Shweder [1979, 1988], Saunders and van Brakel [1997] for some discussion), her work moved the discussion of color terms and cognition forward to the extent that it placed a greater emphasis on actual experimentation on the cross-cultural perception of color terms. Nevertheless, few other contemporary researchers adopted this sort of experimental approach. Regardless, it was generally assumed in many quarters that the research of Berlin and Kay (1969) had demonstrated the absence of relativistic effects on thought, despite the existence of few substantive studies on the role of color term variation on actual nonlinguistic thought.

Despite its influence on the field, Berlin and Kay (1969) and subsequent related work was open to critiques, and in fact spawned a secondary literature of such critiques. These include MacLaury (1997), Saunders and van Brakel (1997), Lyons (1995), and Wierzbicka (2008), along with others. Next we would like to draw attention to some of the more noteworthy criticisms of this influential work on the semantic domain of color.

One criticism has already been alluded to, namely that the demonstration of constraints on color naming does not imply that the extant naming variation plays no role in color term construal and perception. While universal neurophysiological constraints on color term reference may exist, they offer evidence only for psychophysical effects on color terms. As Levinson (2001:7) notes, a strong anti-relativist position requires that one "investigate the reverse effect, not of psychophysics on language, but of language on psychological coding or reaction." With few notable exceptions such as Rosch (1972, 1973) and Kay and Kempton (1984), this sort of investigation went lacking for many years following Berlin and Kay (1969).

Another criticism of work in the Berlin and Kay (1969) mold is that it is not linguistically detailed. Lucy (1997) suggests that the morphosyntactic properties of color terms are not detailed in sufficient depth for this approach, so that in many cases the grammatical category of the basic color terms uncovered is unclear. As Lucy (1997) and others point out, conducting careful linguistic inquiries into a given semantic domain generally requires that the researcher first establish the structural and distributional properties shared by a certain category of words in a particular language. In doing so, researchers insure that the category's very existence is supported by language-internal considerations, rather than by assumptions based on language-external factors such as the researcher's intuitions derived from years of speaking an unrelated language. The tools of the color-term research promoted by Berlin and Kay (1969) are essentially too blunt according to scholars such as Lucy (1997). As he notes, *"You do not need to know anything about languages or linguistics at all to read this literature or even conduct research within the tradition...* You cannot generate a typology of 'color systems' across languages without establishing that such systems actually exist as identifiable 'systems' in those languages." (1997:330) The net result of such an approach, according to skeptics like Lucy, is that uniformity of color term categories is imposed on the data collected in different languages.

In a related vein, the work in question assumes a definition of basic color terms (offered above) that is based on the set of basic color terms in English, but may not point to substantive lexical categories in a given target language. The assumption of the very existence of such lexical categories sharing the properties of basic color terms in English could potentially bias investigators into perceiving the terms they hear/transcribe during the Munsell description tasks as "basic" color terms, when the terms in question may best be described in another manner. In some languages, for instance Yélî Dnye, the distinction between putatively basic color terms and other color-associated lexemes is not clear-cut and there is significant intra-speaker variation in the utilization of the supposedly basic color terms (see Levinson [2001]). The potentially basic color terms in that language are not monomorphemic, either, and are reduplicated forms based on terms for tangible referents associated with certain hues. For example, the word *mtyemtye* is glossable as 'red' and is based on the term for a red parrot species called *mtye*. Analogously, the term *mgîdîmgîdî* is glossable as 'black, dark', and is based on the term for 'night', *mgîdî*. (See Levinson [2001:10] for other forms.)

As an alternative strategy to focusing on basic color terms, linguists could simply exhaustively describe the semantics of terms associated with colors in the world's languages, without relying so intensively on the Munsell array or a notion of basic color terms derived from English. Only then, according to Lucy (1997) and others, would we be able to fruitfully and independently contrast the associated semantic concepts across languages, while offering unbiased contrasts of the way in which these concepts are encoded. For an example of the way this approach might be applied to the description of basic color terms in one given language, see Levinson (2001). When such an approach is adopted, it becomes clear that careful consideration of an assortment of language-internal criteria may result in the less clear-cut establishment of an inventory of basic color terms. In the case of Yélî Dnye, morphosyntactic criteria point to an inventory of four forms serving as basic color terms. The closest counterparts to these terms in English are 'black', 'white', 'red', and 'dark-red'. Other terms are more frequently employed in color-naming tasks, though, and seem to be more salient to the Yélî Dnye speakers. This is true in particular of terms denoting green hues. To complicate matters further, the colors that are most consistently named by Yélî Dnye speakers would be glossed in English as 'black', 'white', and 'green'. In short, Levinson (2001:39) suggests that, while a traditional survey in the World Color Survey model would suggest Yélî Dnye is a language with three unproblematic basic color terms ('white', 'black', and 'red'), i.e. that it is a "Stage II" language, this assessment would misrepresent in crucial respects the actual color terminology of the language.

In addition, another interrelated criticism of the Munsell-chip naming research is that the methodology characteristic of this paradigm does not typically result in the careful consideration of all the semantic features actually associated with the terms elicited. Given the nature of the stimuli used in such tasks, they are restricted to eliciting terms related to hue and lightness. Yet is has been demonstrated that terms associated with lightness and hue are often associated with other semantic features, for example luster, degree of reflection, and luminosity. According to this criticism, the selection of Munsell chips as exclusive elicitation stimuli biases the data towards a hue-and-lightness orientation that reduces important crosslinguistic disparities and results in the overestimation of similarity in basic color term inventories. Consider the case of Hanunóo, delineated in Conklin (1964). Conklin's data suggest that there are four basic color terms in the language, best glossed as 'black', 'white', 'red', and 'light green'. Such a system seemingly fits neatly into the implicational scale offered by Berlin and Kay (1969). As noted in Lucy (1997:324), however, this interpretation obfuscates some crucial aspects of Hanunóo semantics:

> First, there is the opposition between light and dark... Second there is an opposition between dryness or desiccation and wetness or freshness (succulence) in visible components of the natural environment which are reflected in the terms *rara'* ["red"] and *latuy* ["green"] respectively. This distinction is of particular significance in terms of plant life... A shiny, wet, brown-colored section of newly-cut bamboo is *malatuy* ["green"] (not *marara'* ["red"]).

In short, were we to examine Hanunóo terms associated with color simply by presenting speakers with a Munsell array, we would likely miss the fact that hue, lightness, and saturation are interwoven with the concepts of wetness and freshness, in a way that we would never predict based on familiar color term systems.

An additional potential issue with the Munsell-based methodology for assessing color term denotation is that many of the colors in the Munsell array are completely foreign to the ecologies of some cultures. In some cases, task participants' first exposure to a given combination of hue and lightness may have been during the elicitations conducted for the World Color Survey. Given that they had previously not been exposed to such stimuli, such participants may have differed in their willingness to apply native terms to the unfamiliar colors. In fact, some participants have not been comfortable naming the stimuli in the requisite manner (MacLaury [1997]). In addition, Roberson and Hanley (2010:190) note that, when participants are presented with chips that are not all maximally saturated, cross-cultural differences surface in their willingness to apply otherwise similar color terms to varyingly saturated forms.

Such criticisms are worth bearing in mind and do suggest that the degree of universality in the semantic domain of color is often overestimated. It seems quite possible that the basic color terms gathered via Munsell elicitations only partially represent the semantic domain associated with color in many languages. Nevertheless, proponents of the Berlin and Kay (1969) paradigm might point out that they are particularly interested in understanding the way in which languages denote degrees of hue and lightness, and that other associated meanings fall outside the purview of their goals and approach. Furthermore, there is no reason to expect that languages should exhibit universal patterns of demarcation of the Munsell array simply because other facets of color-term semantics may be glossed over by this approach. In fact, there seems to be general consensus in the field that the findings gathered via the approach first promulgated in Berlin and Kay (1969) (and subsequently employed in Kay and McDaniel (1978), Kay et al. (2009), *inter alia*) do point to, at the least, common tendencies in the ways in which languages differenti-ate hue and lightness reference. It seems implausible that the patterns observed are mere methodological artifact. As Regier et al. (2010) note, for all the criticisms of the general Berlin and Kay (1969) paradigm, it is certainly not the case that subsequent work has demonstrated that terms denoting hue and lightness are unconstrained across languages. We can in fact make predictions about the referents of color terms in languages, at least vis-à-vis hues denoted in color chips, based on the tendencies observed in other languages. Such predictions do not completely, or even adequately in many cases, describe the semantic structures associated with color terminology in the target languages. Yet they are hardly vacuous either, and point to important cross-population patterns in hue discrimination. These patterns do have exceptions, though (Regier et al [2009]). Perhaps future work that addresses some of the criticisms noted above will more comprehensively elucidate the full range of color sys-tems in language, as opposed to addressing patterns in Munsell chip denota-tion.

Recent work by Kay and colleagues has offered additional evidence for universalist claims regarding hue and lightness denotation in the world's lan-guages, but points to a shift in the sorts of universalist claims made by the researchers. The studies in question apply computational methods to the color naming data in the World Color Survey data set. In Kay and Regier (2003), the authors investigated the extent to which the color categories evident in the World Color Survey surfaced due to chance, as might be predicted (according to the authors of that study) by a non-universalist account according to which color categories result from non-innate linguistic factors. In order to do this, Kay and Regier (2003) located the centroid of each of the basic color categories in the 110 languages, within the Munsell array. The centroids were arrived at by calculating the point representing the "center of gravity" of the naming responses for chips of each basic color type. Via these centroids, they estab-lished the "cross-language dispersion" of categories as follows: Each centroid's location was contrasted with the most comparable centroid in each remaining language (e.g. the centroid for 'red' in one language was contrasted with the location of the centroid for 'red' in other languages). The total distance between all of these centroids was tabulated, thereby yielding the metric of dispersion. If this total distance was relatively small, it would suggest relatively small crosslinguistic variation for a given color category. The question Kay and Regier (2003) ultimately sought to answer was whether the "cross-language dispersion" of each of the color categories was less than or greater than what might be predicted by chance. The universalist hypothesis would predict that this dispersion would be significantly less than that predicted by chance, presumably due to some neurophysiological bias towards certain color category centroids. (Note that the authors do not address other possible non-neurophysiological motivations for such universal patterns.)

In order to evaluate the "cross-language dispersion" values, Kay and Regier (2003) contrasted them with those values arrived at via 1000 iterations of a randomly rotated color cylinder, based on the Munsell array,[50] rotated along the dimension of hue. When contrasted to these randomized values, the authors observed that the actual "cross-language dispersion" values evident in the color categories in the World Color Survey is significantly lower than those of any of the randomized datasets of color systems. This finding offered further support for the claim that the centers of color categories evident in the world's languages are not arbitrarily distributed, and lent greater evidence for the universalist perspective on color discrimination.

This perspective was supported as well by a related study, Regier, Kay, and Cook (2005). The authors of that study examined the best exemplars of basic color categories, as selected by native speakers of all 110 languages of the World Color Survey. They then aggregated these exemplars and considered the quantitative patterns in the aggregated best-exemplar choices across languages. They observed that certain regions of the Munsell array were significantly more likely to represent best-exemplar choices, and furthermore that these regions corresponded relatively closely to the best exemplars of basic color terms as established by an English speaker in Berlin and Kay (1969). This finding offers support for the claim that there are universal foci, or attractors of focus, within the Munsell array. According to Regier, Kay, and Cook (2005), these universal foci result in the observed crosslinguistic commonalities evident in the World Color Survey.

While clearly there are crosslinguistic differences in color category boundaries evident in the World Color Survey survey, Regier, Kay, and Khetarpal (2007) claim that the basic color terms in languages nevertheless reflect approximately optimal partitions of the color grid. They suggest, as other researchers have (see Jameson and D'Andrade [1997]), that certain areas of the color spectrum are natural attractors of focus due to the specific interactions of hue and lightness, for instance the area associated with bright red and another with bright yellow. Such attractors are putatively most dissimilar psychologically,

---

50 Recall that the actual array used in elicitations is a Mercator projection of this "cylinder". In actuality, when saturation is factored into the Munsell array, along with hue and lightness, the 3-dimensional projection of the array is closer to spherical than cylindrical. Yet it is also asymmetrical, so not exactly spherical either, and is therefore sometimes referred to as the Munsell "tree".

and this dissimilarity would predict, according to Regier, Kay, and Khetarpal (2007), that color categories would be structured so as to reinforce this dissimilarity. In other words, color boundaries in the world's languages should typically be maximally well-formed in terms of demarcating boundaries that preserve linguistic disparities between psychologically dissimilar parts of the hue/lightness continuum. Regier, Kay, and Khetarpal (2007) employed simulations to generate the color systems that would be predicted by a concerted effort to maximally distinguish between salient dissimilar colors, which were selected prior to the simulations. These simulations resulted in theoretically optimal color space divisions for systems involving 3, 4, 5 or 6 color terms. The authors then contrasted these "theoretical optima" with the actual boundaries between color terms in the languages of the World Color Survey. They tested whether the actual boundaries paralleled closely those established to be theoretically optimal, when contrasted with systematically rotated versions of these boundaries (for each language tested), shifted along the hue dimension as in Kay and Regier (2003). Assuming that the authors initial assessments of which colors are most psychologically dissimilar were not biased by their awareness of the distributions of color terms in the world's languages, the contrast between theoretical optima and the actual distribution of color term boundaries across the world's color naming systems could provide further evidence for a universalist perspective. In fact, Regier, Kay, and Khetarpal (2007) observed that, in the majority of cases, the 110 languages represented in the WCS exhibited color naming systems that corresponded relatively closely to the theoretically optimal compartmentalizations of the color spectrum. This was true even in the case of supposed exceptions to color naming universals including Berinmo, Pirahã, and Warlpiri. The authors do note that there are exceptions to this pattern, however, in which languages exhibit color boundaries that do not generally conform to expectations based on theoretical optima. In such cases the actual color naming systems are less ideal vis-à-vis such optima when contrasted with systems that are identical in the shape of their delimitation of the Munsell array, but rotated along the hue dimension. One such exception is Karajá, an Amazonian language in which the term *ãrè* denotes color chips that are yellow, green, blue, and purple. Another exception is Waorani, another Amazonian language that is thought to be typologically unique in having one term that covers white and yellow chips, and a separate term covering red chips.

According to Regier, Kay, and Khetarpal (2009), the universal tendencies in color naming, as well as exceptions to these tendencies, are best explained by the physical characteristics of color and human perceptions of those characteristics. In their words (Regier, Kay, and Khetarpal [2009:892]):

The color solid is a warped blob. Some hue-lightness combinations achieve greater saturation, hence presumably greater salience, than others. The resulting irregular landscape,
coupled with simple principles of categorization, accounts both for universal tendencies
of color naming, and for some deviations from those tendencies – thus reconciling the
traditionally opposed 'universalist' and 'relativist' views of color naming (Jameson and
D'Andrade 1997, Regier, Kay, and Khetarpal 2007).

These claims hint at an important common thread in much of the recent
research of Kay, Regier, and colleagues: the reconciliation of universalist and
relativist views on color discrimination and naming. This thread will be
returned to later in this chapter as we consider recent experimental work by
these researchers, work that provides significant evidence for linguistic effects
on the nonlinguistic discrimination of colors.

Studies such as Kay and Regier (2003), Regier, Kay, and Khetarpal (2007),
and others with similar results (e.g. Lindsey and Brown [2006]), attempt to
reduce researcher bias in the demonstration of universal tendencies in color
naming, by applying computational methods to the description of crosslinguistic patterns of color naming. Yet this attempt may not completely appease
those skeptical of their general approach to color terminologies across languages. The motivation for this is simple: While this recent work applies new
methods to the problems at hand, it still relies on data gathered for the World
Color Survey via the Munsell-chip paradigm. As we have already noted, a number of scholars have voiced their dissatisfaction with the Munsell-chip based
methods, and studies such as Kay and Regier (2003) and Regier, Kay, and
Khetarpal (2007) are also not immune to the relevant criticisms. After all, if
one is convinced that the data in the World Color Survey are predisposed to
represent color naming systems in a manner that is biased towards the color
naming system of English, s/he would be unsurprised to find that computational analyses of these same data would result in the conclusion that color
naming systems tend to partition the color spectrum in a near-optimal manner,
much as, crucially (and not coincidentally to such critics), the English system
does.

Setting aside such strong objections, it seems clear that numerous widely
circulated studies have adequately convinced most concerned with the linguistic denotation of color that the now well-known crosslinguistic tendencies in
color reference merit explanation. No extensive crosslinguistic studies of color
naming systems have presented a serious alternative motivation to the patterns
offered in such work (aside from potential bias towards English), and no studies have presented data from numerous languages systematically demonstrating that color terms are in fact unconstrained. Furthermore, the patterns hinted
at by the work of Kay, Berlin, and others are seemingly most parsimoniously

explained by appealing to humans' neurophysiological commonalities. The existence of such commonalities in the perception of color should not be particularly unexpected given how little variation there is in the human genome, and it might be more startling to find that color terms are unconstrained vis-à-vis hue and lightness reference. Nevertheless, accepting that there are in fact crosslinguistic tendencies in color term naming, it is *possible* these tendencies could be explained via alternative, non-neurophysiological interpretations (see discussion in Roberson and Hanley [2010]). Several other factors could in fact motivate these patterns. These include patterns in the arrays of colors represented by commonly eaten fruit, or commonly contacted vegetation. Furthermore, naturally occurring dyes do not equitably represent all of the chips of the Munsell array, potentially biasing members of many cultures towards certain focal colors. And while not all cultures have access to such fruit or dyes, the associated colors and color terms can easily be transferred from language to language as cultures come into contact. The net result of such ecological factors could be cross-cultural patterns that give the appearance of cognitive universals in the domain of color discrimination, but owe themselves to less fundamental similarities across people groups (Lyons [1995]). At the least such factors should be considered along with the possibility that similarities of color-term inventories reflect genetically motivated neuro-cognitive commonalities.

Regardless of one's perspective regarding the motivations for the universal tendencies in color naming, the common patterns in question should not prevent us from examining the crosslinguistic variation that does exist, and from considering whether that linguistic variation yields disparities in the nonlinguistic conceptualization of the visible color spectrum. After all, even if we conclude that crosslinguistic variation in focal hues and category distinctions is insignificant (which seems an imprudent step) or, more modestly, that such variation is universally constrained (which seems plausible), such conclusions do not constitute evidence for the absence of disparate nonlinguistic conceptualizations of color categories across populations. As always, experimental data on actual perceptual and cognitive processes, gathered among speakers of different languages, are required. It turns out that a significant amount of recent innovatively acquired experimental data, much of it gathered by Kay and colleagues, provides evidence that crosslinguistic variation in color terminology does in fact yield disparities in the perceptual discrimination of color categories.

7.3 Evidence for disparate discrimination of color categories

7.3.1 Categorical perception effects

Rosch's (1972) work among the Dani of Irian Jaya offered initial support for the hypothesis that speakers of languages with only a few color terms (two in the case of the Dani) nevertheless more easily recall focal colors not represented in their language, presumably because humans are biased towards such basic color categories. As noted above, however, with the exception of Rosch's research, few related experimental inquiries were produced in the three decades following Berlin and Kay (1969). Two notable exceptions to this trend were Lucy and Shweder (1979) and Kay and Kempton (1984). The latter two studies offered some evidence for relativistic effects on the categorical perception of colors. In fact, the phenomenon of categorical perception, which refers to the fact that cross-category stimuli are more easily discriminated from each other when contrasted to within-category stimuli, has played a prominent role in the literature on color discrimination. In the case of Kay and Kempton (1984), for example, the authors presented experimental data demonstrating that speakers of English exhibit categorical perception effects at the green/ blue boundary, i.e. that they more easily perceive minor disparities between colors that are differentially categorized as "green" and "blue". Such minor disparities were less easily perceived by speakers of Tarahuma (Uto-Aztecan), a language in which the relevant colors are lexically grouped in the same 'grue' category. Significantly, Kay and Kempton (1984) observed that verbal interference reduced the categorical perception effect evident in the English speakers' responses.

In just over the last decade, there has been a surge in the number of studies on the role of color term variation on the nonlinguistic categorization and recall of colors. In 1999 Jules Davidoff, Ian Davies and Debi Roberson published a short but influential study in *Nature*, on the discrimination of colors among speakers of Berinmo, a Melanesian language indigenous to Papua New Guinea. Berinmo has five basic color terms. Davidoff, Davies, and Roberson (1999) replicated Rosch's (1972) experiments with speakers of Dani, also a Melanesian language. Contra Rosch (1972), however, Davidoff, Davies, and Roberson's (1999) results provided strong evidence for relativistic effects on the discrimination of colors. This evidence pertained to recall abilities associated with particular color categories.

The five basic color terms of Berinmo are *mahi, wap, wor, nol,* and *kel*. While the *nol* color category denotes Munsell chips that are denoted with "blue" and "green" in English, the *wor* category denotes chips that are denoted with "yellow" and "green" (in the lighter green range) in English. In other words, there is a *nol* vs *wor* category boundary where none exists in English color terms, since all relevant chips are classified as "green" by English. Conversely, there is a "yellow" vs "green" category boundary in English where none exists in Berinmo, since all relevant chips are classified as *wor* in that language. (Davidoff, Davies, and Roberson [1999:203])

Davidoff, Davies, and Roberson (1999) asked participants to recall color chips over a period of 30 seconds and 5 seconds. Subjects were presented with chips of a particular color, and, following the relevant interval, asked to select the color they had witnessed from two alternatives. The incorrect alternate was sometimes from the same linguistic category and sometimes not. For example, the speakers could be presented with a chip that was classified as *nol* or green. The incorrect alternate in the choice pair might also be green according to English speakers, but classified as *wor* in Berinmo since it was a lighter variety. That is, the choices represented two linguistic categories in Berinmo but only one in English. Conversely, in other cases the choices represented two linguistic categories in English but only one in Berinmo. What Davidoff, Davies, and Roberson (1999) observed was that there was a significant disparity in the recall patterns of the English-speaking and Berinmo-speaking populations. Berinmo speakers were more likely to correctly choose from the pair of choice colors when the alternate color represented a different linguistic category in Berinmo, i.e. when the *nol-wor* boundary was crossed. Their selections were less accurate when the alternate colors represented different linguistic categories in English but not Berinmo, i.e. when the "green"/"blue" or "yellow"/ "green" boundaries were crossed. English speakers, on the other hand, were more likely to recall the correct choice when the alternate crossed an English color term boundary, but not when it crossed the *nol-wor* boundary. In short, Davidoff, Davies, and Roberson (1999) provided compelling evidence that disparate categorical effects in color recall result from disparate lexical reifications of the color spectrum. Apparently when colors are represented with separate color terms they are easier to recall, regardless of whether the colors represent putatively universally distinguished categories such as blue and green. This finding suggests at the least that color terms can be used as a cognitive tool to enable better recall of perceived stimuli, and Davidoff and colleagues interpret the finding to mean that the actual perception of colors is impacted by linguistic factors. Davidoff, Davies, and Roberson's (1999) results and a related set of findings are described more fully in Roberson, Davies, and Davidoff (2000). In that study the authors conclude that "Our present results demonstrated, in a variety of tasks with quite different instructions, that Categorical Perception was consistently more closely aligned with the linguistic categories of each language than with underlying perceptual universals." (2000:393)

The basic finding offered in Davidoff, Davies, and Roberson (1999) and Roberson, Davies, and Davidoff (2000), namely that color names affect stimuli recall patterns, was replicated in a study on the color discrimination abilities of speakers of Himba, a Namibian language with five color categories (Roberson et al. [2005]). These categories have similar central foci but crosscutting boundaries when contrasted to the five categories of Berinmo. The Himba-speaking and Berinmo-speaking populations differ markedly in terms of size, since there are tens of thousands (rather than hundreds) of Himba speakers, and ecologies, since the Himba live in an desert environment (rather than a tropical one). These cultural disparities helped serve as an impetus for experimental work among the Himba.

Roberson et al. (2005) conducted a number of tasks among the Himba, contrasting the results obtained among that population with those obtained among the Dani (Rosch [1972]), the Berinmo (Roberson et al. [2000]), and English speakers. Here we will focus our attention on two of the experiments described in Roberson et al. (2005). In one task, 24 monolingual Himba speakers were tested for their ability to recall particular color chips, much like the Berinmo speakers were tested in Roberson, Davies, and Davidoff (2000). As in Rosch (1972), the researchers tested recall vis-à-vis best exemplars of particular colors (red, yellow, green, blue, orange, purple, pink, and brown) along with 16 Munsell chips that have been shown to be more difficult for English speakers to identify. These 16 chips included ones that were previously classified by Rosch as "boundary" chips, meaning they occupy spaces near the periphery of supposedly basic color categories in the Munsell array. They also included so-called "internominal" colors, which fall on the border of the supposedly basic categories. In choosing such colors, the authors allowed for the contrast of their results with previous studies of English and Berinmo speakers. Based on the rate at which some colors are consistently named by speakers of a given language, the so-called "naming agreement" rate (arrived at via previous tasks), Roberson et al. (2005) were aware of which colors were considered "focal" best exemplars for English, Berinmo and Himba speakers. These naming agreement data suggested in fact that some of the focal categories conflicted so that, for example, some of the Himba focal colors were actually internominal categories in English. This conflict allowed the researchers to test whether variance in "focal" status across languages is reflected in color recall patterns across the languages' speakers.

The target colors were tested as follows: Himba speakers were shown the Munsell array, which was then covered. The speakers were then shown individual target chips, each of which was one square inch in size, for a period of five seconds. The target chip was then removed, and the participants were asked to select, from the Munsell array, the target chip they had just witnessed.

The ratio of correct responses was tabulated and transformed into a metric called a d' score, which helped to account for patterns of random guessing in the data. The relevant feature of this d' score is that higher values denote greater accuracy of color recall. Clear variations in these d' scores were found. For instance, for the putatively universal focal colors, Himba speakers' mean d' score was 1.50 (standard error: 0.23). This score differs markedly from the 2.47 (0.24) obtained with English speakers. In contrast, for the so-called boundary colors, Himba speakers' mean d' score was 1.80 (0.07), while English speakers' mean d' score was 1.56 (.22). This reversal in relative accuracy is consistent with the fact that some of the boundary colors in English have higher naming agreement among Himba speakers, i.e. they appear to be focal for speakers of that language. In fact, those color chips that were considered focal in Himba but not English (according to naming agreement patterns) were recalled significantly more accurately by Himba speakers (at the $p<.05$ level) than those considered focal in English but not Himba.

Interestingly, the patterns in the Himba data for this task closely resemble those obtained among the culturally and ecologically disparate Berinmo population that has a similar five-term naming system. This resemblance is evident in Figure 7.1, adapted from Roberson et al. (2005:391). The chart is based on their results for the task just described, as well as on results obtained among the Berinmo for Roberson, Davies, and Davidoff (2000). As evident in the figure, the results suggest that color recognition is facilitated not by a universal focal pattern, but by language-dependent focal patterns. People appear to recall best those colors that are easily and consistently named by speakers of their own native language.

In a separate but related task that involved the longer-term recall of supposedly universal focal and non-focal colors over a period of five days, Roberson et al. (2005) and Roberson, Davies, and Davidoff (2000) obtained similar results for Himba and Berinmo speakers. There was no significant disparity between the two groups' long-term abilities to recall so-called universal focal colors when contrasted with non-focals.

In another series of tasks, Roberson et al. (2005) investigated the categorical perception of colors among Himba speakers, much as Roberson, Davies, and Davidoff (2000) did for speakers of Berinmo. Specifically they sought to test whether cross-color discrimination was heightened at lexical boundaries in the Munsell array, or whether such discrimination was immune to linguistic influences and affected instead by boundaries between potentially innate color

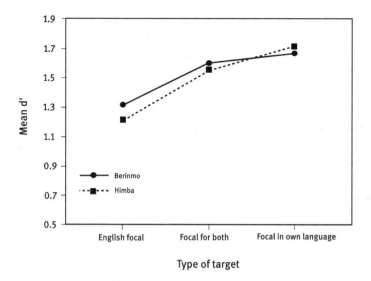

1.9
1.7
1.5
Mean d'
1.3
1.1
0.9
0.7
0.5

———●——— Berinmo
· · ·▪· · · Himba

English focal   Focal for both   Focal in own language

Type of target

Figure 7.1: Mean ratios of correct responses (in *d'* scores) of Himba and Berinmo speakers, according to focal status. Adapted from Roberson et al. (2005:391)

boundaries. Much as Roberson, Davies, and Davidoff (2000) tested for categorical perception effects across the blue-green and *nol-wor* boundaries, Roberson et al. (2005) tested for such effects across the blue-green and *nol-wor* boundaries (neither of which are linguistically salient in Himba), as well as across a boundary that is lexically codified in Himba: *burou* vs. *dumbu*. The latter distinction is similar though not isomorphic with the Berinmo *nol-wor* distinction. Here we will consider only one of three categorical perception tasks undertaken in Roberson et al. (2005).

For the task in question, nine triads of color chips were utilized. Each triad was mounted in triangular fashion on an off-white card 80 mm x 100 mm in size. The nine triads were presented in randomized orders to twelve Himba-speaking adults. Each of the triads contained three similar color chips, representing colors in the blue-green, *nol-wor*, or *burou-dumbu* ranges (the latter two ranges being similar). In some cases all three members of a triad represented one of the two categories (e.g. three different shades of green), in other cases two chips represented one category and a third represented a separate one (e.g. two green chips and one blue chip similar to the green ones). Speakers were asked to choose the two members of the triad that looked the most like each other, at the expense of the third. Each triad was presented to the speakers on four separate occasions, with the positions of the colors on the off-white cards being counterbalanced across presentations.

For triads involving the blue-green distinction, speakers of Himba and Berinmo differed significantly from speakers of English. That is, English speakers were more likely to perceive dissimilarities between the hues of the blue and green chips when they occurred on different sides of the lexically based "blue"/"green" boundary. The disparities between English and Himba speakers' responses and English and Berinmo responses were significant according to between-participants ANOVAs (at $p<.01$ and $p<0.05$, respectively). In other words, when contrasted with speakers of Himba and Berinmo, English speakers were more likely to perceive dissimilarities between blue and green hues. Crucially, though, Himba speakers were most likely (of the three populations) to perceive dissimilarities between *dumbu* and *burou* hues, while Berinmo speakers were most likely to perceive dissimilarities between *nol* and *wor* hues. In short, the data in Roberson et al. (2005) suggest unambiguously that native language affects participants' assessment of color similarity in triad discrimination tasks.

One potential criticism of a relativistic interpretation of the results of such a triad discrimination task is that it assumes that the patterns of discrimination are not experimental artifact. It is possible after all that Himba speakers, for example, use color names in an attempt to resolve what is to them a foreign and bizarre task. That is, their tendency to discriminate *dumbu* and *burou* colors may not be due to actual perceptual dissimilarities, when contrasted to English and Berinmo speakers, but to experimental strategy. A difficulty faced by such a criticism, however, is that speakers of all three languages were generally able to quickly and accurately complete the task even when colors did not cross color boundaries. For instance, when faced with triads containing two very similar varieties of *dumbu* and one dissimilar variety of *dumbu*, Himba speakers had no major difficulty discriminating the most dissimilar hue. None of the three groups analyzed in Roberson et al. (2005) faced pronounced difficulties in merely completing the task, and were capable of grouping colors without linguistic cues. Nevertheless, their patterns of perceptual discrimination hinted at consistencies between the linguistic reification of hues and the nonlinguistic discrimination of those hues.

This triad-discrimination task, along with two other categorical perception experiments with similar results described in Roberson et al. (2005), strongly suggest that Himba speakers, much like Berinmo speakers, are relatively adept at perceiving differences in colors that straddle lexical boundaries in their native language. Conversely, speakers of these languages struggle comparatively when attempting to discriminate colors across a boundary (green/blue) that is not lexically codified in their language. So the Himba and Berinmo data on categorical perception indicate that humans are particularly sensitive to color categories instantiated via linguistic praxis. The data in question are not consistent with the claim that there are universal neurophysiologically governed color categories that lead to the innate preferential discrimination of some focal colors. This does not imply necessarily that such innate color categories do not exist. It offers no evidence for them, however, and suggests that, if they do in fact exist, they are not particularly salient among adults that have had repeated exposure to color terms that do not match these supposedly focal colors. This finding is further supported by research with Russian speakers. Winawer et al. (2007) provide extensive evidence on the categorical perception of light blues and dark blues by speakers of Russian. These colors are represented via different terms in Russian, with *goluboy* denoting lighter blues and *siniy* denoting darker blues. As we might predict given the results in Roberson et al. (2005), the researchers found that Russian speakers' cross-category discrimination of *goluboy* and *siniy* colors was relatively rapid, when contrasted to a control group of English speakers who do not rely on such a basic lexical distinction. In addition, this categorical advantage was mitigated by verbal interference, indicating that the Russian speakers' heightened discrimination owed itself specifically to linguistic factors.

7.3.2 Hemisphere-variant categorical perception effects

Gilbert et al. (2006) presented a remarkable development in the study of color perception. The authors of that study tested the hypothesis that linguistic effects on the categorical perception of colors do not surface uniformly across cerebral hemispheres. The hypothesis posits that such categorical effects are the result of processes occurring principally in the left cerebral hemisphere, where the majority of linguistic faculties are housed in most adults. Therefore, the hypothesis suggests color stimuli should be more susceptible to categorical perception if the stimuli are presented to the left hemisphere. Given that the right visual field (RVF) feeds contralaterally into the left hemisphere, while the left visual field (LVF) feeds into right hemisphere, a simple testable prediction results from the hypothesis: categorical perception should surface more readily when subjects are forced to discriminate similar colors observed via the RVF when compared to those observed via the LVF. More specifically, the discrimination of similar colors indexed with different color terms should be temporally enhanced for stimuli presented in the RVF. On the other hand, the discrimination of similar colors indexed with the *same* color terms should be comparatively slow for stimuli presented in the RVF. Finally, a specific prediction of the hypothesis is that a verbal interference task should eliminate or reduce any observed categorical perception effects for stimuli presented in the RVF, if in fact such effects are due to the engagement of the linguistic faculties. Gilbert et al. (2006) conducted two related experiments with thirteen English speakers in order to test these predictions.

For each trial in the first experiment, speakers were presented with a ring of twelve colored squares surrounding a cross on which they were told to fixate. Those squares to the left of the fixation cross were therefore presented to the LVF (right hemisphere), while those squares to the right of the cross were presented to the RVF (left hemisphere). The hue of eleven of the squares was identical, while that of the twelfth square differed slightly from the others. In all cases the colors of the squares represented blue and green hues. In the case of some rings of squares, all twelve of the squares (including the one differing in color) represented the same lexical category. In the case of other rings, the divergent square represented a separate lexical category, i.e. it crossed the "green"/-"blue" boundary. The rings also varied in terms of the extent to which the hue of the divergent square differed from the remaining eleven squares. One of the rings used in a trial is depicted in grayscale form in Figure 7.2.

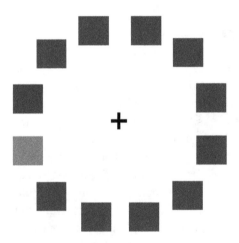

Figure 7.2: A grayscale representation of a ring of squares employed by Gilbert et al. (2006:490).

Subjects were asked to, as quickly as possible, judge whether the divergent square was located to the left or to the right of the fixation point. Their responses were made via keyboard depressions. In addition, in some instances participants made such judgments while performing a verbal interference task.

This task consisted of quietly recalling a sequence of eight numbers during the color discrimination trials.

The results obtained matched those predicted by the hypothesis that categorical effects surface disproportionately across the two cerebral hemispheres. The results for trials involving no verbal interference are depicted in Figure 7.3. As can be seen in the figure, speakers generally located the disparate color square most quickly when it was presented in the RVF and also represented a separate lexical category. When the disparate hue represented the same lexical category as the color of the other squares, this temporal enhancement of responses was not observed for the stimuli presented to the RVF. In fact, when all stimuli were denoted by the same color term in RVF-presented rings, subjects were slowest to locate the divergent square. The reaction times for RVF targets were an average of 24 ms faster for stimuli crossing lexical boundaries, when contrasted to those RVF targets representing the same lexical category. (t =2.78, p<0.02) In stark contrast, when stimuli were presented in the LVF, no significant disparity in reaction times for the two stimuli types was evident (t =0.19, p<0.85), i.e. response times were not significantly faster when the contrasted hues represented separate lexical categories. In short, between-category discrimination was more quickly arrived at, when contrasted to within category discrimination, but this hallmark of categorical perception only surfaced in the case of stimuli presented in the RVF, to the left hemisphere. This evidence for categorical perception in only the left hemisphere suggests

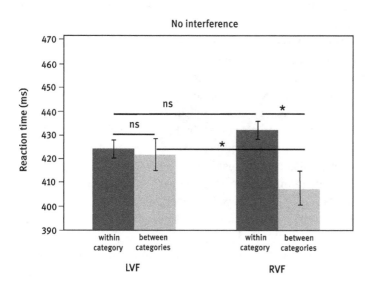

Figure 7.3: Reaction times for trials without verbal interference. Adapted from Gilbert et al. (2006:490).

strongly that color discrimination is motivated, at least in part, by linguistic factors. This conclusion is further supported by the fact that the categorical perception of colors in the RVF targets disappeared in those trials performed concurrently with the aforementioned verbal interference task. When the subjects' linguistic faculties were otherwise engaged, then, the relevant linguistic categories did not significantly impact their performance in the task. Categorical perception effects did surface for RVF-targets in the case of a similar second experiment when speakers were presented with *nonverbal* interference. Furthermore, Gilbert et al. (2006) replicated their results via a third experiment conducted with a single participant with a severed corpus callosum. In such a person interhemispheric cerebral communication is precluded by biological factors. Tellingly, this person more quickly discriminated hues representing two lexical categories, when compared to those within the same category. Once again, though, this categorical effect surfaced only for RVF targets.

Gilbert et al.'s (2006) innovative study offered evidence that some kinds of color discrimination may be universal and not linguistically mediated, viz. those occurring in the right cerebral hemisphere, while others are clearly mediated by language. This evidence suggests a new less dichotomous approach to the standard universalist/relativist debate surrounding the conceptualization of color categories. The methods utilized in their study have been adopted and adapted in subsequent work, notably in Drivonikou et al. (2007), Franklin et al. (2008), and Roberson, Pak, and Hanley (2008). In the former study the experiments were extended to other hues besides blue and green, namely purple and pink. Like Gilbert et al. (2006), Drivonikou et al. (2007) found that the categorical perception of colors surfaced in a strong fashion for RVF targets. Unlike Gilbert et al. (2006), though, they also found evidence for more modest categorical effects in the perception of colors presented in the LVF.

Roberson, Pak, and Hanley (2008) extended the general experimental paradigm in question to a language besides English. They tested for categorical effects associated with two color categories in Korean, *yeondu* and *choruk*. These terms reflect a distinction between light green hues – a distinction that does not exist in basic English color terms. Twenty Korean speakers and twenty English speakers participated in their perception task, which was remarkably similar in form to the task described above for Gilbert et al. (2006). Participants were asked to fixate on a cross in the middle of a screen in front of them. After one second, a ring of ten squares of light green hues was presented. One of the ten squares contained a lighter hue than the remaining nine squares, and the participants were instructed to respond whether the disparate hue was located to the right or to the left of the fixation point. Their response times were tabulated.

Overall accuracy on the task was quite high for both groups, at around 95%. The participants clearly had little difficulty actually locating the divergent hue. There was a difference in reaction times between the two populations, however, vis-à-vis within-category differences and cross-category color difference (i.e. those crossing the *yeondu-choruk* border). When the divergent square represented a separate lexical category in Korean, Korean respondents responded significantly more quickly ($p<.05$ according to a mixed ANOVA). No appreciable cross-category advantaged surfaced in the English speakers' responses, however. Like Gilbert et al. (2006) and Drivonikou et al. (2007), then, the results in Roberson, Pak, and Hanley (2008) pointed to linguistic effects on the reaction times associated with color discrimination. Unlike the two other studies in question, though, the results from the latter study did not contain gross differences between reaction times for stimuli presented to the RVF or the LVF, respectively. Instead, when the Korean data were examined as a group, the cross-category advantage surfaced regardless of whether the divergent square/target appeared in the RVF or the LVF. Interestingly, though, among the eight Koreans with the fastest reaction times, there was in fact a difference between response times for RVF targets and LVF targets. More specifically, the responses of these Koreans were more consistent with the findings of the two previous relevant studies, in that cross-category advantages surfaced only in the case of RVF targets processed first by the left hemisphere. Interestingly, the reaction times documented in Drivonikou et al. (2007) and Gilbert et al. (2006) were generally much faster, when contrasted to those in Roberson, Pak, and Hanley (2008). This fact led the authors of the latter study to a natural conclusion: In the case of fast respondents, lexical cross-category status benefits discrimination of RVF targets only. A potential explanation for this fact is that, for such fast respondents, categorical perception effects do not surface for LVF targets since in such cases the right hemisphere does not have sufficient time to process linguistic data originating in the left hemisphere. However, in the case of slow respondents, categorical perception effects were obtained for both RVF and LVF targets. This suggests perhaps that colors perceived by the right hemisphere (LVF) are affected by linguistic categories in such cases because there is sufficient time for the relevant linguistic information to be transferred across the corpus callosum. (Since eye movement was not monitored in these studies, however, it is possible that slower respondents simply scanned across the fixation point with both eyes.)

These studies offer a new kind of data that shed light on humans' discrimination and conceptualization of color. All three studies are remarkably consistent to the extent that they demonstrate that linguistic categories do affect the discrimination of colors in nonlinguistic tasks, and to the extent that all point to stronger categorical perception effects in the case of stimuli presented to the RVF (at least for faster respondents). They also demonstrate nonlinguistic disparities between speakers of two different languages, revealing that cross-categorical reaction time reductions vary in accordance with the lexical color categories participants are familiar with.

7.4 Discussion and conclusion

At the most basic perceptual level, human vision is capable of discriminating as many as two million colors. (Roberson and Hanley [2010]) This ability is clearly not language dependent. There is also some evidence that humans perceive some colors categorically from an early age, even in infancy. (Franklin and Davies [2004]) In some sense, then, we can be confident that there is a genetically driven aspect of color discrimination shared by all humans. The data presented in Section 7.3 suggest, though, that color terminology also impacts human color discrimination abilities. This conclusion is further supported by some work on the ontogeny of color discrimination. A study conducted with child speakers of Himba and English has demonstrated that variation in color discrimination begins at an early age. In a longitudinal study, Roberson et al. (2004) compared the color recall and naming abilities of Himba-speaking children in Namibia and English-speaking children in the UK. Twenty-eight British children participated in the study, as did 63 Namibians. The children were tested prior to learning color terms in school, and again three years later. Roberson and colleagues found that, at the age of three, the children were similarly unpredictable in terms of the color categories they were familiar with, and in terms of their ability to remember particular colors. After acquiring color terms, however, they exhibited superior recall for, in particular, colors that were considered independently good exemplars of color categories in their native language.

Regier et al. (2010) and Regier and Kay (2009) have noted that, in order for us to understand the role of language in color discrimination, two principal questions must be answered. First, are the color categories that exist in the world's languages just arbitrarily arrived at? Second, do crosslinguistic differences in color terms result in perceptual or cognitive differences for speakers of the relevant languages? We suggested earlier in this chapter that, with notable exceptions such as Rosch (1972) and Kay and Kempton (1984), the second question went largely unexplored in much of the relevant literature over the last few decades. Instead, most pertinent studies addressed the first question and offered evidence that color terminologies were far from random in their representation of the colors of the Munsell array. This evidence for universal patterns in color naming was taken by some as sufficient evidence for a universalist account of color conceptualization. Yet the issue is not that simple, since even if we accept that there are universal tendencies in the basic color categories of the world's languages, this does not preclude the possibility that extant crosslinguistic disparities nevertheless result in some dissimilarities in the discrimination of color categories. As we saw in the preceding section, the most recent experimental evidence leads unequivocally to the conclusion that linguistic disparities in the composition of color categories do yield nonlinguistic disparities in the categorical perception of colors. In other words, there is increasing evidence for a relativistically oriented response to the second aforementioned question: crosslinguistic differences do yield cognitive differences, at least during the online discrimination of colors.

With respect to the first question regarding the potential arbitrariness of color terms, the evidence from the World Color Survey points to implicational universals in the basic color terminologies of the world's languages, which like other linguistic "universals" are not exceptionless. In addition, as a number of anthropologists and linguists have argued, the data gathered for the World Color Survey are not completely unproblematic. Going forward, research on this topic may shed more light on the color terminologies of the world's languages by, for example, using a more diverse set of stimuli varying not just according to lightness and hue as in the Munsell array. For now, though, the patterns in the World Color Survey offer us the most comprehensive database available on basic color systems. They suggest that color systems, while variable, are far from arbitrary and are characterized by tendencies in the way they divide up the visible spectrum. The motivation(s) for these commonalities remains a matter of some debate, and could relate to innate neurophysiology, ecological factors, cultural factors, or some combination thereof. If they are simply due to some innate capacity, some explanation must be found for clear exceptions to the commonalities in question, for instance Karajá and Waorani. Further explanation must also be provided for those cases in which languages show little sign of a diachronic transition to larger basic color term inventories. To that end, future work could more substantively explore the relative functional load of color terms across languages, including those represented in the World Color Survey. As Levinson (2001:41) notes with respect to Yélî Dnye, for example, "Lack of functional load would help to explain the variability, the relative lack of standardized expressions, their failure to cover the domain, and the many supplementary, often ad hoc descriptive phrases." In other words, within the context of the Yélî Dnye's culture and ecology, there is apparently little need for an elaborate set of "basic" color terms. Similar claims have been made for a number of indigenous groups, and this issue must be explored more fully if we are to truly comprehend the extent to which the putative color term universals hold across human languages.[51]

Research among nonhuman primates suggests that they have similar abilities to perceive color differences, when contrasted to humans, even though there is no evidence that other primates discriminate colors into categories in a human fashion. (See Fagot et al. [2006] regarding the color discrimination abilities of baboons.) On some level, then, human color perception is uniform across our species and, in some respects, similar to that evident in other species. Yet clearly some aspects of color discrimination co-vary with linguistic features. In this way this discussion of the domain of color conceptualization leads us back to a familiar place: Much about color construal owes itself to biology shared within our species and even with others, and much of the relevant construal owes itself to linguistic factors. This is not to suggest that linguistic categories are the only non-genetic factors that yield differences in the perception and conceptualization of colors. For now we can be confident, though, that such differences owe themselves at least in large part to linguistic factors since a) they surface more readily in the left hemisphere where the language faculties primarily reside, b) they correspond neatly to crosslinguistic disparities such as "blue"/"green" vs. *nol-wor*, c) they disappear during tasks in which verbal interference (but not other interference) is utilized, and d) their ontogenetic appearance coincides with the acquisition of color terms.

Since the work surveyed in Section 7.3 suggests that color discrimination is comparably faster when hues cross lexical boundaries, such lexical boundaries could be understood to facilitate color discrimination. For instance, perhaps English speakers perceive differences between green and blue colors relatively quickly because the hues are denoted with separate terms. Yet as Roberson and Hanley (2010) point out, the categorical perception effects in question are quite plausibly due instead to the inhibition of color discrimination caused by similar lexical representation. Under such an interpretation of the phenomenon in question, slightly different hues of color categories like green are per-

---

51 According to the "emergence hypothesis" associated with the work of Lyons (1995), the functional load of color terms in some societies is so low that there is no fixed basic inventory of terms used merely for color denotation. From this perspective specific color terminologies emerge in large measure as they become culturally requisite. That is, many "basic" color terms may not be employed until a need arises. The low functional load of color words in many contemporary languages may be evidenced by traits such a lack of hyponyms (e.g. "dark-blue") or hypernyms (e.g. "color"), the inability of relevant terms to exhaustively refer to the Munsell array, the presence of few color references in linguistic corpora, and a large amount of intra-speaker variation in color naming.

ceived differently, but the discrimination of this difference conflicts with the hues' identical lexical labels (in this case "green"). The "incorrect" identical lexical representation in such cases could be interpreted as meddling or interfering with the basic discrimination of such colors.

As we noted in the introduction to this chapter, color discrimination was once considered a clear example of the way in which patterns in languages merely reflect universals of human cognition, rather than influencing that cognition. Oddly, while claims about colors were never a part of the pivotal claims made by Whorf, data associated with this domain were sometimes taken to provide robust evidence for strong anti-Whorfian positions. To those unfamiliar with the more recent work covered in this chapter, such an interpretation of the crosslinguistic color term data may still seem permissible. The paths that have now been tread in research on the categorical perception of colors make such an interpretation untenable. There are many other paths that could be taken in the future exploration of the manner in which color term differences impact nonlinguistic cognition. Some of these paths are now visible in large measure because of the work discussed above, which is at the vanguard of the contemporary exploration of this issue.

8 Objects and substances

8.1 Introduction

While the investigation of the perception of colors in different populations has played a major role in shaping discussions of linguistic relativity over the last few decades, color classification actually plays a relatively limited role in grammar. As we noted in the previous chapter, color is not a semantic category that is consistently indexed grammatically in the world's languages, as many other categories are (Lucy [1997]). One semantic notion that *is* commonly evident in grammars is that of object or substance classification. Take for example the English distinction between "count" and "mass" nouns. I can refer to "twenty-five cars" or "twenty-five men" but it is ungrammatical in most contexts to refer to "twenty-five muds" or "twenty-five sands". Clearly English grammar classifies nouns in accordance with whether they represent objects that are easily individuated, or substances that are less easily individuated. This bifurcated classification is evident in the permissibility (or impermissibility) of the plural suffix being attached to a noun. In many other languages, though, nouns are categorized according to a much wider variety of semantic parameters, as evident in formal gender systems or nominal classifier systems. Oftentimes classifier systems are particularly evident when objects or materials are quantified. A natural question is whether crosslinguistic disparities in such nominal classifier systems, or the mere presence/absence of such systems, yield dissimilarities in the way in which associated objects or materials are perceived or individuated by speakers' of the relevant languages. While this question has received less attention than many examined in the preceding chapters, there have nevertheless been a host of studies produced in recent years that address the way in which speakers mentally categorize objects and materials. Once again, the results of these studies hint at some language-dependent patterns in nonlinguistic cognition.

8.2 Initial findings among the Yucatec Maya

The most easily traceable genesis of work on this topic is a series of studies conducted by John Lucy among the Yucatec Maya. In 1992, Lucy produced two influential books on the topic of linguistic relativity. One of these (Lucy [1992a]), cited heavily in Chapter 1 of this volume, represented a synopsis of the history of the central ideas of the linguistic relativity hypothesis, as well as a detailed re-envisioning of the way in which research on this topic ought to be carried out. The second work (Lucy [1992b]) provided a detailed case study that illustrated the way in which Lucy felt empirically grounded research on the topic could be carried out in the field, by marrying experimental techniques with detailed linguistic analysis. With respect to linguistic analysis, Lucy (1992b) provided a comprehensive description of the object classifier system in Yucatec Maya and contrasted the ways in which number marking works in English and Yucatec Maya, respectively. With respect to experimental techniques, he provided the results of some simple experiments with picture and object stimuli. The relevant experiments were designed to test whether English and Maya speakers exhibit differences in their nonlinguistic categorization of physical entities, and whether any differences match predictions based on the pertinent crosslinguistic disparities. The results suggested in fact that object/ substance conceptualization differences between the populations exist, and that the differences in question quite plausibly owe themselves to dissimilarities in nominal classification between the two languages in question.

To speakers of languages like English, nominal classifier systems may seem esoteric. Such systems are common to many languages, though, including Mandarin, Japanese, southeast Asian languages, Austronesian languages, and many sub-Saharan African languages (see Aikhenvald [2000] for discussion). In languages with formal noun classes, nouns must be classified in particular grammatical contexts in accordance with some cohesive or quasi-cohesive set of semantic properties. Nominal classifiers tend to surface in numeral expressions, when the quantity of a particular noun is denoted. The ways in which nouns are categorized semantically vary tremendously in accordance with the classifier system in question. Typically, a nominal classification system groups nouns according to social function, biological sex, animacy, shape (or some other salient physical property), or some combination of these features. In addition, there are often intra-linguistic exceptions to classifier systems, so that individual nouns that might be predicted to fall into one class are actually categorized in a seemingly inconsistent way by the grammar in question.

Yucatec Maya has nearly 100 classes of nouns (Lucy [1992b:50]). Among other ways, these classes are denoted via suffixes attached to cardinal numerals in noun phrases. To get some idea of the specificity of some of these classes, consider that the suffix –*túul* is used when the head of the noun phrase is an "agricultural or other socially significant plant", or that the suffix –*tú'uk* is utilized when the noun is a "corner" or an "edge" of an object. Many Yucatec classifiers specify the way in which a given noun is measured, referring roughly to concepts such as "armful" and "stack". If the correct classifier is not used, a noun phrase becomes ungrammatical and potentially unintelligible. This is true in large part because classifiers are often required to denote the physical delimitation of a particular material being quantified, whose shape is not defined in the absence of the classifier. While English lacks a productive nominal classifier system, there are many cases in our language in which an amorphous substance requires analogous physical demarcation during quantification. Consider the following English phrases:

(8.1)   one clump of dirt
         *one dirt
(8.2)   one chunk of concrete
         *one concrete
(8.3)   two drops of water
         *two waters
(8.4)   two ounces of gold
         *two golds

In each of these examples, a classifier-like word occurs after the numeral, prior to the noun being classified. Without this word, which defines the shape of the amorphous material being classified, the expression is ungrammatical in most contexts.[52] (The expressions are not ungrammatical in those contexts in which the substance's shape is predefined, for instance when ordering "two waters" at a restaurant.) The classification of mass nouns in English is not morphologically productive, as evidenced by the absence of a formal set of nominal classifiers. Furthermore, whereas in English there are many "count" nouns that do not require categorization (in the way that "mass" nouns such as "water", "sand", or "dirt" do), in Yucatec Maya classifiers are generally obligatory in noun phrases with quantifiers. For one example of these classifiers, consider the -tz'íit suffix utilized in (8.5) and (8.6). This suffix is attached to cardinal numerals modifying noun, in these examples kib', 'wax'. (See Lucy [1992b, Chapter 2] for further examples.)

(8.5)   'un-tz'íit   kib'
         one-long.thin.CL wax
         'one long thin candle'

---

52 Like many formal noun class systems, the count/mass distinction is idiosyncratic in some cases. Some items of approximately the same size and shape are treated differently by English grammar. For instance "pebbles" and "beans" are treated as count nouns while "rice" is treated as a mass noun.

(8.6)   ká' a-tz'íit   kib'
               two-long.thin.CL wax
               'two long thin candles'

The classifier in these two examples is, like nominal classifiers often are, oriented according to the shape of the nominal referent. More specifically, it defines the shape of a given amorphous material. The term *kib'* can in fact be used for various types of wax, and is not used exclusively in reference to candles. In other words, we might say that the word *kib'* is undefined with respect to shape (much like English "mass" nouns), drawing attention only to a type of material that is then given shape by the classifier that surfaces during quantification.

Lucy (1992b) suggests that the inspection of the Yucatec Maya classifier system yields the following prediction: Yucatec Maya speakers should be comparatively attuned to the materials/substances of nominally denoted referents, when contrasted to speakers of languages like English in which the shape of such referents is not described via productive shape-oriented classifiers. Put differently, since English nouns generally refer to objects that are predefined in terms of shape, while Yucatec Maya nouns frequently refer to materials that are amorphous in the absence of classifiers, English speakers should rely to a greater extent on shape-based information when categorizing objects, even in nonlinguistic contexts. Conversely, Yucatec Maya speakers should rely to a greater extent on material-based information when categorizing objects. Lucy (1992b) and Lucy and Gaskins (2001) sought to test this relativistic prediction with a set of object-sorting tasks carried out with speakers of both languages.

In the first categorization task in Lucy (1992b:138), Yucatec and English speakers were presented with triads of objects. Each triad consisted of two objects that differed according to both shape and material, for instance a sheet of plastic and a book. In addition to these "alternate" objects, speakers were presented with a "pivot" object that matched one alternate in terms of shape, and matched the other in terms of material. In the example just cited, this pivot was a sheet of paper. Speakers were asked to group two of the three objects at the expense of the third, ostensibly revealing whether they chose similar shape or similar material as a basis for categorization. In the sample case mentioned, then, if the speakers grouped the sheet of paper with the sheet of plastic, they would apparently be basing their decision on a shape-based categorization. The other possible grouping would reflect a material/substance-oriented categorization. For this particular task, other triads included the following: 1) a strip of cloth (pivot), a strip of paper, and a shirt, 2) a stick of wood (pivot), a candle stick, and a block of wood, and 3) a cardboard box (pivot), a plastic box, and a piece of cardboard. A total of eight triads were used for this task.

The results of the triad-discrimination task were consistent with the linguistically based prediction offered above: speakers of Yucatec Maya tended to group objects according to material, while speakers of English grouped objects according to shape. In fact, 12/13 English speakers grouped the eight triads by shape in a majority of cases, while 8/10 Yucatec Maya speakers grouped the triads by material in a majority of cases. This cross-population disparity was significant ($p<.0007$, one-tailed Fisher exact test).

While Lucy's (1992b) results for the triad task in question were suggestive of a relativistic account, they were not dispositive. After all, the methods do not rule out the typical confound of some more general nonlinguistic cultural factor. One could of course argue that the triad-discrimination patterns of the Yucatec Maya speakers may be due to a cultural orientation to materials that also happens to surface in language. It is important to stress that Lucy's (1992b) results were consistent with the relativistic prediction made prior to the experiment. This prediction was made only after thorough examination of the relevant systematic linguistic disparity between the two languages in question.

Nevertheless, Lucy's (1992b) initial experiment also indicated a need for methodological refinement. This need owed itself not just to potential cultural confounds, but also to some other issues with the triad discrimination task. Consider for instance the triad containing a cardboard box (pivot), a plastic box, and a piece of cardboard. Since English speakers were more likely to group the cardboard box with the plastic box, we might interpret this discrimination as being shape-oriented. Another potential explanation, though, is that the discrimination is function-oriented, and that English speakers are more attuned to and familiar with the functions of boxes, when contrasted with Yucatec Maya speakers. Conversely, since Yucatec Maya speakers were more likely to group the cardboard box with the piece of cardboard, we might interpret this preference as being the result of heightened material-orientation. Since a cardboard box and a sheet of cardboard are generally the same color, though, the discrimination preference might simply reflect a heightened orientation towards color. We should stress that these alternate explanations are less satisfying since there is no discernible non-post-hoc reason why Yucatec Maya speakers should generally pay less attention to function or more attention to color across a large set of stimuli triads. Nevertheless, Lucy's (1992b) initial triad-based experiment was refined in order to better reduce the likelihood of such alternate motivations for the cross-population disparities in selection patterns.

Lucy and Gaskins (2001) utilized tasks that controlled for the color, function, as well as the size of stimuli. In a triad discrimination task, they contrasted English speakers' and Yucatec Maya speakers' categorization of objects in a way that controlled specifically for the function of the stimuli. For instance, in one triad a plastic comb with a handle (pivot) was grouped with either a plastic comb without a handle (material alternate) or a wood comb with a handle (shape alternate). When function was controlled for in this manner, the disparity in selection preferences between the two groups was reduced. Nevertheless, there was still a significant difference between the populations, such that Yucatec Maya speakers were more likely to discriminate triads according to material.

In addition, Lucy and Gaskins (2001) employed a novel nine-sort task in which subjects were presented with four objects of the same material, and four objects of the same shape, in addition to an object that matched the material of the former group as well as the shape of the latter one. The subjects were presented with the nine stimuli sequentially, and asked to sort them into two groups upon presentation. The pivot stimulus was presented last, once the two groups had naturally been formed according to shape and material, respectively. This sorting task was performed with five different sets of stimuli. For example one set contained a matchbox, needle envelope, cheese box, and a label, all made out of cardboard (the material group). The set also contained a copper pipe, a flashlight casing, a plastic pipe, and a bicycle handle grip, all cylindrical objects (the shape group). In addition, the set contained a toilet paper core, which was the pivot stimulus since it was made of cardboard but cylindrically shaped. In all sets the pivot stimulus could naturally be grouped with either of the two groups. By utilizing a nine-sort task, rather than a triad-based task, Lucy and Gaskins (2001) reduced the potential role of confounding factors such as the similar function, color, or overt linguistic similarity of two members of a triad. Despite the mitigation of such extraneous factors, Lucy and Gaskins (2001) replicated the general finding of Lucy (1992b). Yucatec speakers grouped the pivot stimulus with the material group in 73.6% of cases, while English speakers grouped the pivot with the material group in 23.6% of cases ($p<.001$, $n=12$, one tailed Kolmogorov-Smirnov two-sample test). (Lucy and Gaskins [2001:272]) As an illustration of the Yucatec speakers' focus on material during object sorting, consider the following anecdote offered by Lucy and Gaskins (2001:271–272):

> The Yucatec speakers were constantly evaluating the material composition of the test items before sorting them: feeling how heavy they were, poking their nails into them to test for malleability, scraping the surface to see what the material under the paint was, smelling and tasting the objects, and generally questioning or commenting on their material properties – and all this with familiar objects. The English-speaking Americans showed none of this sort of reaction – they could get all the information they needed by

sight alone. A particularly striking example of an alternative sorting occurred with one Yucatec woman during pilot work, where we could not make sense of the principle she was using. When we asked her about her reasons during the follow-up discussion, she replied that the things on one tray would melt if they were burned whereas the ones on the other tray would turn to ash. This was a level of attention to material properties that went much deeper than we had originally imagined.

In addition to their contrast of English-speaking and Yucatec Maya-speaking adults' discriminations of objects, Lucy and Gaskins (2001) compared the object/substance-discrimination strategies of seven and nine-year-old Maya or English-speaking children. In the case of both the triad task and the nine-sort task, they found that seven-year-old children tended to group objects according to shape, regardless of their native language. The discrimination disparities between the two populations of children were comparatively minor, though they were more pronounced among nine-year-old children. The disparity in discrimination preferences was most pronounced among the adult populations. The lessened differences between children cohorts, in particular the groups of seven-year-old children, is potentially explained by the comparatively modest command of the classifier system by the younger Yucatec Maya speakers. As Lucy and Gaskins (2001:277) note, the children "fall short of having command of the full range of classifiers in comprehension and their range in production is narrower still." One plausible explanation for these experimental findings, then, is that Yucatec Maya speakers become more attuned to stimulus material as a basis for sorting as they gain experience with their language's system of nominal classification. While the age-variegated results in Lucy and Gaskins (2001) are plausibly motivated by linguistic factors, though, it is still possible that they owe themselves to other lurking cultural factors. Such factors could, after all, also become more salient as children become more embedded in their native culture, irrespective of their heightened grammatical awareness.

One of the chief merits of the research described in Lucy (1992b) and Lucy and Gaskins (2001) is that it relates to a linguistic phenomenon that is relatively common in the world's languages. That is, the mere existence of a nominal classifier system in a given language is typologically unremarkable. Therefore, there are many candidate languages in which such research might be further explored. In the following section we consider some of the more recent work that has in fact addressed this topic, with speakers of languages besides Yucatec Maya.

8.3 Work with speakers of other languages

Research on the acquisition of nouns by English-speaking children suggests that the count/mass distinction may play an important role in their under-standing of the differences between substances and objects (Quine [1969], Gentner and Boroditsky [2001]), though this role is apparently constrained by universal ontological distinctions between substances and objects, which are evident even among toddlers (Soja, Carey, and Spelke [1991]). In order to better understand the role of count/mass nominal distinctions in the shaping of such ontological concepts, Imai and Gentner (1997) contrasted the substance/object discrimination abilities of English speakers with speakers of a language with a nominal classifier system (and without a count/mass distinction like that in English), namely Japanese. Since they tested for cross-population linguistically based disparities in the discrimination of materials and objects, their results are fruitfully contrastable with those in Lucy (1992b) and Lucy and Gaskins (2001). Nevertheless, the methods described in Imai and Gentner (1997) relied more heavily on language usage, and so they can only play a limited role in informing our discussion of nonlinguistic substance vs. object discrimination.

Imai and Gentner (1997) also employed a triad-discrimination task. Four age cohorts participated in the task, with the following ages represented: 2, 2 ½, 4, and adults. The subjects represented two populations: English speakers residing in a large urban area (Chicago) and Japanese speakers residing in a larger urban area (Tokyo). The triads in the task consisted of a pivot that was either an object with a defined shape (in some cases a complex object, in others a simple object) or a substance shaped in a particular manner. This pivot could be naturally grouped with either one of the two alternate members of the triad. One alternate was an object of identical shape but different mate-rial, when contrasted with the pivot, and the other alternate was a group of pieces or piles of the identical material as the pivot. For this second alternate, neither the individual pieces/piles nor the grouping of the pieces/piles had a cohesive shape. For example, in one of the triads utilized the pivot object was a kidney-shaped piece of wax. One of the other members of the triad was a kidney-shaped piece of plaster, and the third consisted of a number of irregu-larly shaped pieces of wax. In another case the pivot substance was a crescent-shaped portion of Nivea. One of the other members of the triad was a crescent-shaped portion of hair gel, and the other consisted of a number of irregularly shaped piles of Nivea.

The children and adults were asked to group the pivots with one of the alternates, much as in Lucy (1992b) and Lucy and Gaskins (2001). Crucially, though, their responses were given linguistically.[53] The subjects were given nonce labels for the pivot terms, e.g. told by the experimenter that "This is my dax". They were then asked which of the other items in the triad could also be called a "dax". The prediction was that English speakers should tend to group the pivots according to shape (in this case by labeling the similarly-shaped alternate a "dax"), since they treat substances as a cohesive group via count/mass distinctions, and since they rely on shape during nominal reference in a way that speakers of classifier languages like Japanese do not. Since the task was overtly linguistic, it is unclear whether the speakers' groupings were affected by the engagement of their linguistic faculties. For example, it is possible that such engagement made English speakers more attuned to the differences between countable and non-countable items, and that the resultant groupings did not simply reflect their nonlinguistic ontological categorizations. Nevertheless, it is worth underscoring that the task did not rely overtly on linguistic categorizations since the pivot items were labeled via nonce terms.

In the case of triads involving pivots that were either simple objects or substances, a clear difference between the responses of Japanese and English speakers surfaced. In both cases, English speakers were significantly more likely to group the pivot with an alternate that matched its shape. Furthermore, the disparities between the groups' discriminations of these pivot stimuli were highest among adult speakers. The relative reliance of English speakers on shape, and conversely the comparative reliance of the Japanese speakers on substance, fell in line with a relativistic account. Some patterns common to both groups also surfaced, though, particularly among the two-year-old cohort. So the results in Imai and Gentner (1997) parallel neatly those found in Lucy (1992b) and Lucy and Gaskins (2001) vis-à-vis English and Yucatec Maya speakers. They offer additional support for Lucy's (1992b) suggestion that languages with a numeral-classifier system habitually draw their speakers' attention to the material of objects, in a manner not observed among speakers of languages without such a system. It seems implausible that the age-variegated results in Imai and Gentner (1997) would parallel those of Lucy and Gaskins (2001) in the manner they do unless the results in the studies reveal similar disparities in object/substance conceptualization, for both English-Japanese and English-Yucatec contrasts, respectively. While American and Japanese two-year-old children similarly discriminate individuated objects and non-individuated substances, this discrimination is apparently subsequently impacted by linguistic

---

53 The goal of the study was ultimately to address a pressing issue in the field of language acquisition (see discussion in Gentner and Boroditsky [2001]), rather than to specifically address the role of classifiers in fostering crosslinguistic differences of thought.

factors. In the words of Imai and Gentner (1997:169): "We speculate that children universally make a distinction between individuals and non-individuals in word learning but that the nature of the categories and the boundary between them is influenced by language." Assuming for the moment this conclusion is correct, it suggests that this area of cognition, like others considered in this book, is shaped by universal factors and language-contingent factors.

Work on the acquisition of nominal classification among English and Spanish-speaking children further supports this claim. Spanish does not have an extensive nominal classification system. As in English, though, Spanish nouns may be categorized as count or mass nouns (with grammatical gender also impacting nominal classification) in expressions with numeral modifiers. Sera and Goodrich (2010) provide experimental data on the acquisition of nouns in both languages. While these data were also obtained through largely linguistic methods, they impinge directly on the discussion at hand.

While both English and Spanish have a clear count/mass nominal distinction, the boundary between count and mass nouns is not identical in the two languages. Some nouns that are classified as "mass" nouns in English are "count" nouns in Spanish, as evident in the following translational equivalents: 'furniture'-*muebles*, 'news'-*noticias*, and 'jewelry'-*joyas*. While there is malleability to the count and mass noun categories in both English and Spanish, another difference between the languages is that the Spanish categories are putatively more malleable than the English categories. (Stockwell, Bowen, and Martin [1977]) In other words, Spanish count nouns can under certain conditions be treated as mass nouns, and vice versa, with greater ease than in English. Put differently, the class of mass nouns is less "semantically powerful" (see discussion in Sera and Goodrich [2010:439–440]) in Spanish than in English. Still, both languages have a distinction between these noun types, and in both languages count nouns can be pluralized via an – s suffix. Furthermore, in both languages countable nouns do not maintain their identity when they are divided linguistically. For example, if I say "a piece of car" I am no longer referring to a car proper. Conversely, if one subdivides a mass noun in either language, object identity is maintained. For instance, if I say "a piece of furniture" then I am still referring to a cohesive unit of furniture. These correlations suggest that only count nouns are perceived as individuated entities. With this fact in mind, Sera and Goodrich (2010) sought to test whether Spanish speakers and English speakers differ in the extent to which they perceive certain objects to be individuated, and whether any difference in the perception of object-individuation correlates with grammatical factors associated with the count/mass distinction. In addition to conducting an object-naming task that helped establish which of thirteen nouns were count or mass nouns in Spanish and English, the researchers conducted a task to assess the perceived individuation of the objects associated with these thirteen nouns.

The individuation task proceeded as follows: Participants were presented with a set of three models of objects, displayed on three separate boards on a table in front of them. One of these boards had two objects on it, another had one object, and a third had a portion of the object. They were then asked to point to one of the boards via the instructions: "Show me a piece of _____". (In Spanish, "*Enséñame un pedazo de* _____".) For example, for one sample set of stimuli, they were asked to point to "a piece of furniture". The set included a board on which there was a model office chair and an adjacent model side table. On top of another board was a model sofa, and on the third board was a fragment of model sofa (literally a "piece" of furniture). The assumption underlying the task was that, if objects were typically perceived as being naturally individuated, participants would select the object fragment. Conversely, if objects were typically conceptualized as non-individuated, then participants would be more likely to select a whole object.

A total of 13 sets of object triads such as that just described were tested in Sera and Goodrich (2010). Forty-eight English speakers and 48 Spanish speakers participated in the task. These participants equally represented four age groups: 5-year-olds, 7-year-olds, 9-year-olds, and adults. In nearly 100% of the cases, Spanish speakers selected the object fragment (e.g. the piece of a model of a single item of furniture) when they were asked to point to a piece of something. Sera and Goodrich (2010:432) interpret this finding as suggesting that Spanish speakers conceived of all the objects as being individuated. It seems possible, though, that at least for some triads this selection pattern may have been an artifact of the linguistic nature of the task. That is, *pedazo* might well be taken more literally to mean a 'fragment' to the Spanish speakers, when contrasted to the English speakers, since there is no idiom directly comparable to e.g. "piece of furniture" in Spanish. Not all mass nouns are even felicitously referenced via "piece of" in English. The idiosyncratic nature of the word "piece" in such cases of mass noun reference is further evidenced by the fact that we can refer to "a nice piece" regarding singular tokens of some mass nouns, such as "art", but not others.

The age-variegated results obtained among English speakers are revealing, however. Five-year-old English speakers tended to select fragments when asked to find a piece of an entity, much like the Spanish speakers. The older English-speaking groups did not, however. In fact, older English speakers were more likely to treat *only* those objects denoted via count nouns as being individuated, as evidenced by their tendency to select fragmented objects only in such cases. In short, the results of the task suggest that speakers of both languages have an ontogenetically primal tendency to treat objects as being individuated. In the case of English speakers, however, this tendency towards the individuation of objects is subsequently impacted by the acquisition of a fairly rigid count/mass distinction (and possibly by the acquisition of idioms like "a piece of"). This interpretation was supported by an additional object selection task reported in Sera and Goodrich (2010), in which the authors relied on nonce terms in order to mitigate the influence of overt linguistic influences during the task.

The findings in Sera and Goodrich (2010) offer compelling evidence that the perceived individuation of physical entities changes as speakers become more familiar with the English language. As in the case of Lucy and Gaskins (2001), the changes in object/substance individuation and associated nominal classification surface among children between the ages of 5–9. It is worth noting that children face difficulties in acquiring the grammatical consequences of the count/mass distinction until the age of seven (Keil [1979]). So the linguistic acquisition of count/mass distinctions seems to help shape the perceptions of the relevant objects/substances between the ages of 5–9, as children's relevant grammatical competence increases. At least Sera and Goodrich's (2010) data are consistent with such a claim. Since their experimental methods are partially linguistic, though, the study is somewhat limited in what it can definitively tell us about the completely nonlinguistic construal or individuation of objects. Nevertheless, it is quite useful in highlighting the manner through which increased fluency in a language with count/mass distinctions impacts nominal categorization.

Mandarin has a number of nominal classifier types, including a range of classifiers used when referring specifically to animals. These include *tou*, used for large land animals, *zhi*, used for small animals such as insects and birds, and *pi*, used only for horses. This latter example is an excellent case of culture impacting language, as its existence apparently reflects the historically prominent role that horses have played in Chinese society. Another example of a Mandarin nominal classifier is *tiao*, which is used to refer to snakes as well as inanimate objects with snake-like physical features, for instance rivers, ropes, and roads.[54] Saalbach and Imai (2007) investigated whether these and other nominal classifiers in Mandarin affect speakers' perceptions of the entities in question. Significantly, they also investigated the possible influence of other types of object categorization on conceptual organization. In particular, they

---

54 As with most noun classes, there are exceptions. For instance, *tiao* is also used when quantifying pants.

considered as well the role of taxonomic relationships and thematic relationships.[55]

Using German speakers as a control group, Saalbach and Imai (2007) tested Mandarin speakers' default object categorization through a forced choice categorization task, a similarity judgment task, an inductive reasoning task, and a priming task. Results of the tasks were mixed, with only the similarity judgments and inductive reasoning tasks offering evidence that the Mandarin classifiers influence the nonlinguistic categorization of objects. Furthermore, the data gathered through the tasks suggested that taxonomic and thematic relations play a larger role in Mandarin speakers' object categorization, when contrasted to linguistic classifier effects. This led the authors to conclude that classifier systems do not completely restructure nonlinguistic object categorization (contra the findings in Lucy and Gaskins [2001]), but yield more mild relativistic effects. They suggest the following: "The classifier effect found among Chinese speakers is perhaps best characterized as a magnified sensitivity to semantic features underlying classifier categories developed through the habitual use of classifiers in association with the names of objects." (Saalbach and Imai [2007:499])

We do not focus extensively on Saalbach and Imai's (2007) results, since the methods they utilized relied very heavily on linguistic stimuli. In fact, for all of their tasks, judgments were based on stimuli presented as words in booklets. For instance, in the similarity judgment task, readers were asked, in German or Chinese, "Which of the [B] or [C] best goes together with [A]?" In such cases, only one of the alternates matched [A] in terms of nominal class. Given the comprehensively linguistic nature of the tasks in Saalbach and Imai (2007), which did not rely on nonce terms and did not test the perception of actual objects/substances via tactile or visual stimuli (as in the other experiments we have considered in this chapter), their results should be interpreted with some circumspection in the context of the current discussion. The results do suggest that the mental classification of words is impacted by classifiers, though to a lesser extent than by thematic and taxonomic relationships. But it is unclear whether and to what extent such categorization effects surface in the classification of the actual associated objects, by German and Mandarin speakers. (See Malt et al. [1999] for evidence that cross-population disparities in "object" cate-

---

55 A taxonomic relationship holds when one entity is a member of another set, e.g. a capuchin is a kind of monkey. A thematic relationship holds when objects have some spatiotemporal association, for instance a table and a chair, or an iPad and fingers. Both taxonomic relationships and thematic relationships have been shown to influence object categorization in nonlinguistic tasks. (Waxman and Gelman [1986])

gorization may surface more readily in a linguistic task than a nonlinguistic task.)

Thankfully the construal of objects and substances has also been explored in research that relied more heavily on completely nonlinguistic methods, when contrasted with Imai and Gentner (1997), Saalbach and Imai (2007) and Sera and Goodrich (2010). Some recent work addresses the issue at hand with such methods while also more directly controlling for confounding cultural factors, when contrasted with studies such as Lucy (1992b) or Lucy and Gaskins (2001).

As in Imai and Gentner (1997), Imai and Mazuka (2007) considered differences in object/substance classification between speakers of English and Japanese. Recall that the latter language has a classifier system and does not have a count/mass distinction in the manner that English does. Imai and Gentner's (1997) results suggested that English speakers relied more heavily on shape/individuation during a language-based classification task, in line with the predictions in Lucy (1992b) and elsewhere. Imai and Mazuka (2007) again tested the object discrimination strategies of the relevant populations through several tasks, one of which was completely nonlinguistic (apart from task instructions) and will be highlighted here. In the "no-word" task in question, English speakers and Japanese speakers were presented with triads of objects/substances. As in other tasks discussed above, one of the members of the triad served as the pivot, and the participants were asked to group one of the alternates with the pivot at the expense of the other alternate. Subjects were prompted with the following instruction: "Show me what's the same as this", where "this" referred to the pivot stimulus. (The Japanese translation used was *"Kore to onaji-mono wa docchi desuka"*.)[56] Fourteen monolingual Japanese-speaking 4-year-olds and 14 monolingual English-speaking 4-year-olds participated in the task. In addition, 15 monolingual Japanese-speaking adults and 15 monolingual English-speaking adults participated. Twelve triads of stimuli were used in the no-word task. Four of these triads involved a complex-object pivot, four involved a simple-object pivot, and four involved a substance pivot. For example, a clear plastic clip (complex-object pivot) was placed next to a metal clip (shape alternate) and a clear piece of plastic (substance alternate). In another triad, sawdust in the shape of an omega (substance pivot) was placed next to tiny pieces of leather in an omega shape (shape alternate) and two small piles

---

56 While verbal instructions are given for this task, as in nearly all experiments, the task itself does not require language. This is also true of the individuation task in Sera and Goodrich (2010). However, in that study the verbal instructions included the phrase "show me a piece of", which relates more overtly to the distinction between count and mass nouns.

of sawdust (substance alternate). As a final example, in one triad a piece of orange wax in a roughly kidney shape (simple object pivot) was placed next to a bit of purple plaster in the same kidney shape (shape alternate) and also next to three pieces of orange wax (substance alternate). This last example is depicted in Figure 8.1, where the manner of triad presentation is more clearly evident.

Figure 8.1: Sample of stimuli used in Imai and Mazuka (2007:391).
Copyright 2007 Wiley-Blackwell, reprinted with permission.

If the count/mass distinction does impact English speakers' nonlinguistic construal of substances and objects, we would predict that such speakers would be more likely to group pivots with shape alternates, particularly in the case of simple object pivots such as that in Figure 8.1. After all, in cases with simple objects the role of confounding factors, such as an object's function within a culture, would seem to be reduced. It is unlikely, for instance, that participants ever confronted a kidney-shaped piece of wax quite like the pivot in Figure 8.1 prior to the experiment. In contrast, they were quite familiar with complex objects such as plastic clips, and may therefore have been more likely to group complex-object pivots according to function, rather than shape or substance.

If language plays a role in nonlinguistic object categorization, we would predict not only that English speakers pay greater attention to shape (due to the count/mass distinction in English), but also that English-speaking four-year-olds would be less likely than adults to categorize according to this factor. After all, four-year-olds are much less familiar with the count/mass distinction. Put differently, we might predict that differences in object discrimination would surface for Japanese and English-speaking populations, and that these differences would be more readily apparent among adults. Both of these predictions were in fact borne out by the data gathered by Imai and Mazuka (2007).

In the case of all three triad types, English-speaking adults were more likely than Japanese-speaking adults to select alternates according to shape rather than substance. This disparity was particularly evident in the case of triads with simple-object pivots, as predicted by a relativistic account. English-speaking adults selected shape-based alternates at the expense of substance-based alternates in 73.3% of such cases. (This orientation to shape was significant $[t(14)=2.71, p<.02]$.) In contrast, Japanese-speaking adults selected shape-based alternates in only 26.5% of cases. (This reliance on substance was also not due to chance $[t(14)= -2.06, p<.03]$.) In stark contrast to the strategies evident in the adults' discriminations of the triads, the four-year-old children's strategies reflected random object grouping in most cases. English-speaking children did not consistently use the shape-based strategy or the substance-based strategy. This generalization held for all triad types, whether they involved pivots that were complex objects, simple objects, or substances. Japanese-speaking children also showed chance-level discrimination choices for triads involving pivots with complex objects and simple objects, though they did reliably choose alternates according to substance in the case of triads involving substance pivots (see Imai and Mazuka [2007] for discussion).

Given the nonlinguistic and abstract nature of the categorization tasks used by Imai and Mazuka (2007), the results in that study offer some of the most compelling evidence to date that dissimilarities in object/substance construal do surface across groups of speakers of different languages. The most obvious explanation for their finding is that English speakers rely heavily on shape in discriminating object triads because the English language so clearly demarcates amorphous substances from individuated objects, via the count/mass distinction. This interpretation is buttressed by the fact that the responses of English-speaking children less familiar with the grammar of count/mass distinctions pattern more similarly to Japanese speakers' responses. Nevertheless, it is once again possible (if unlikely) that some other cultural variable helps motivate the disparity across language and age groups.

After all, English-speaking children become more familiar with their surrounding culture as they age, not just more familiar with their language. It is unclear though what nonlinguistic cultural variables might motivate the disparities between English-speaking and Japanese-speaking respondents' object discrimination patterns, particularly since both sets of respondents are members of industrialized societies, residing in urban areas, and with nearly identical material cultures. The potential linguistic motivation for these disparities is on the other hand readily apparent.

Imai and Mazuka (2007:409) stress that their results should not be interpreted as suggesting that fluent English and Japanese speakers have incommensurable perceptions of objects and substances. The similarities between Japanese and American children suggest once again that there are universal aspects of object/substance categorization. Nevertheless, the results of the experiment suggest in part that "structural differences among different languages in marking individuation can affect the default construal for entities that are located in the middle of the individuation continuum." (2007:410) These entities "in the middle of the individuation continuum" include simple objects without clear functions. Since most objects confronted during daily experience cannot be so defined, caution should probably be exercised before extrapolating from such results to grander claims about speakers' perceptions of the world around them. Put differently, it is unclear from such results how much linguistic differences in nominal classification impact habitual cognition.

A more recent study employs a novel methodology to try to ascertain whether such linguistic differences impact more quotidian reasoning. Srinivasan (2010) provides data suggesting that the Mandarin classifier system impacts its speakers' cognition in a task that is more indicative of reasoning used in the everyday construal of objects. The study contrasts the discrimination abilities of Russian, English, and Mandarin speakers vis-à-vis common objects such as pants, brooms, and spatulas. The discrimination task in Srinivasan (2010) was time-pressured, unlike those in the studies discussed to this point in this chapter.[57]

---

[57] Time-pressured tasks prevent experiment participants from deliberately relying on language in order to resolve an unfamiliar task in an experimental context. This could have happened, for instance, during Lucy and Gaskins' (2001) sorting tasks in which Yucatec speakers grouped objects in line with their language's classifier system. The sorting patterns clearly reflect linguistic patterns, but this fact could have resulted from a deliberate subvocal yet linguistically based strategy employed merely to complete the non-time-pressured task. The use of such a strategy may seem unlikely, but is theoretically possible.

Like English, Russian lacks a nominal classifier system, and so speakers of these two languages were used as control populations in Srinivasan's (2010) experiment. As we have already noted, Mandarin does have a prominent classifier system used in statements of quantification (e.g. 'four flat-thing table'), though not during counting (Srinivasan 2010:187). Four of the pertinent classifiers and classes were mentioned above. In addition to the aforementioned *to, zhi, tiao,* and *pi,* other Mandarin classifiers include the following: *ba* (for graspable objects), *zhang* (for flat rectangular objects), *gen* (for slender objects), and *ke* (for small grain-like objects). Srinivasan (2010) explored whether objects are harder to discriminate from surrounding objects, for Mandarin speakers, when the target objects and the surrounding objects are matched in terms of nominal class. He employed a visual search task, in which participants had to discriminate specific objects on a screen filled with other objects. One of the guiding assumptions of this work is that attention is allocated to visible stimuli on a competitive basis in visual search tasks, with heightened similarity between objects resulting in greater competition for attention. In visual search tasks, then, distractor stimuli that are similar to target stimuli are more likely to inhibit the clear discrimination of those targets. For example, in a visual search task entailing the counting of images of a certain object type surrounded by images of another object type, we might expect that the classifier status of the two object types would impact the ability of subjects to quickly discriminate and count the target object type. According to Srinivasan (2010:181):

> Thus, if classifier categories predict differences in cognitive processing, distractors that share a classifier category with a target could also be distracting for Mandarin speakers. If this is the case, Mandarin speakers could take longer to count target objects (e.g. *snakes*) pictured among distractor objects that take the same classifier (e.g. *ropes*), compared to distractors that take a different classifier (e.g. *tables*).

Now, in general snakes and ropes are more similar to each other than snakes and tables, so this prediction would appear to hold for any subjects regardless of language. To be clear, then, the prediction is that Mandarin speakers would take longer to discriminate e.g. snakes pictured among ropes (when contrasted to snakes among tables), when contrasted to speakers of languages without a classifier system, that is, in which snakes and ropes are not treated grammatically as members of a quasi-cohesive semantic category. In other words, the classifier system of Mandarin should contribute additional confusability to the visual perception task, for speakers of that language.

A total of 104 speakers participated in Srinivasan's (2010) study. Most of these were graduate students. Each language was represented by a similarly sized group: there were 35 English speakers, 36 Russian speakers, and 33 Mandarin speakers. These speakers were presented individually with 80 sequential displays on a computer screen containing target objects and distractor objects. In the case of each display, speakers were expected to count the target objects (non-verbally), which were scattered among the distractor objects. For each display all of the target objects were of the same type of object, e.g. a spatula. All of the distractor objects represented the same type of object as well, e.g. a broom. In 40 displays the distractor objects and the target objects represented the same noun class in Mandarin, and in the remaining 40 they did not. The prediction was that Mandarin speakers' discrimination of the target stimuli would be negatively impacted by shared noun class membership of the objects.

For each display, 8–11 target stimuli were present on the screen, along with a comparable number of distractor stimuli. In addition, a number was presented on the bottom right of the computer display. Participants were asked to say whether that number accurately conveyed the quantity of target stimuli embedded among distractor stimuli. In some cases the number was correct, in others it was incorrect by one. Participants were expected to perform the discrimination task as quickly as possible, and reaction times were measured. While the task was generally non-verbal, it did involve the subvocal counting of stimuli. While Mandarin does not employ numeral classifiers in actual counting, it does require them in noun phrases with numeral modifiers. The clear association of classifiers with numerosity could have resulted in the conscious (though subvocal) reliance on language during the task. Nevertheless, given that the participants in this task were expected to respond as quickly as possible and without speaking, the results are not based on what might be properly considered a linguistic task. In addition, the study is noteworthy since it relates to the discrimination of common objects familiar to speakers of all three languages. In other words, the study's results may have more to say about everyday experience when contrasted to the results of the more rigorously non-verbal task of Imai and Mazuka (2007).

Srinivasan (2010) found that, for all three groups of speakers, delays resulted when the displays contained target and distractor objects of the same Mandarin noun class. This is unsurprising since nouns of the same class have a semantic cohesiveness based in part on the vague physical resemblance of the objects they denote, which are visibly similar in most cases. Crucially, though, Mandarin speakers' ability to discriminate targets from distractors of the same class was negatively impacted, as evidenced by slower reaction times, to an extent not evident in the responses of English and Russian speakers.[58] In

---

[58] There was no disparity between the groups in terms of ratio of correctness, with each group averaging 74% or 75% correct responses.

fact there was a pronounced disparity between the reaction times of Mandarin speakers for the two display types (a 2219 ms mean difference), as they were much slower in recognizing the number of target stimuli in displays with distractor stimuli of the same noun class. The disparity in their reaction times exceeded the Russian and English speakers' reaction time disparities across the two conditions (1528 ms and 1334 ms, respectively). Most significantly, perhaps, the Russian and Mandarin groups had nearly identical response times for displays involving targets and distractors of different Mandarin noun classes, yet Mandarin speakers were much slower than Russian speakers to discriminate target stimuli surrounded by distractors of the same grammatical class. ($p<.001$ according to a mixed ANOVA) In a similar vein, the disparity between response times for the English and Mandarin speakers was more pronounced in the case of displays with same-class targets and distractors, though English speakers' reaction times were faster under both conditions–likely due to the fact that the instructions were provided in English.

The results in Srinivasan (2010) suggest, then, that Mandarin speakers are comparatively poor at discriminating and counting target objects that are surrounded by different items represented via the same nominal class as the targets. More work is required to understand whether this difficulty of discrimination surfaces in contexts that do not require subvocal counting. Srinivasan's (2010) study offers a new sort of task researchers might refine as they seek to better understand the way in which nominal classification impacts nonlinguistic cognition.

8.4 Discussion and conclusion

Where then do these recent findings leave us? All of the studies discussed here suggest that noun classes, or a grammaticalized count/mass distinction, affect the nonlinguistic categorization of objects and/or substances by speakers of the pertinent languages. Each of the studies has some methodological shortcoming, typically minor, that obfuscates the extent of the effects in question. This point is not meant as a criticism of the studies, but is meant instead to highlight the seeming intractability of designing tasks that account for all confounding variables when examining an aspect of human cognition that is so clearly tied to linguistic *and* cultural factors. For instance, Lucy (1992b) and Lucy and Gaskins (2001) are fascinating studies that build on decades of Lucy's fieldwork in the Yucatan. Lucy's experimental work and his familiarity with the Yucatec Maya people and their language leave little doubt that cross-population differences exist in the object/substance discrimination strategies of

Yucatec Maya and English speakers. Furthermore, Lucy and Gaskins (2001) demonstrate that these differences become more pronounced as speakers age, perhaps due to their increased familiarity with the grammars of their respective languages. Yet, as was noted above, it is also possible that their increased familiarity with other facets of their native cultures plays a role in the creation of such differences. While Lucy (1992b) plausibly posits that language is the only clear cultural factor that might establish such differences, skeptics may remain unconvinced in the absence of more abstract tasks involving only objects and substances that are unfamiliar to the cultures, or tasks involving verbal training or verbal interference or some other mechanism that is now used to differentiate linguistic effects from other cultural effects on cognition. On the other hand, proponents of Lucy's experimental designs might point out that the elegance of the tasks utilized among the Yucatec Maya is that they demonstrate cross-cultural disparities in object/substance discrimination with respect to very common objects and substances. In other words, the cross-cultural effects that are evident in Lucy's work are far from trivial, as is apparent in the anecdote (quoted above) regarding the attention paid to material by an elderly Yucatec woman. In contrast, studies such as Imai and Mazuka (2007) offer more controlled evidence for cross-population differences in the construal of very abstract objects/substances. The use of such abstract stimuli helps to rule out cultural factors such as the social function of objects, more definitively establishing language as the causal factor in the obtained results. In addition, by testing Japanese and American populations from large urban industrialized cities, each with comparable levels of education, Imai and Mazuka's (2007) work further controls for nonlinguistic cultural variables in a manner that studies on Yucatec Mayas and Americans simply cannot, given the wider cultural gap between the latter two groups. Yet, in contrast to Lucy and Gaskins (2001), it is less clear what the results obtained in Imai and Mazuka (2007) reveal about the habitual, quotidian cognitive patterns of the speakers involved. Do the relevant differences in cognition only surface when speakers consider abstract stimuli in experimental contexts, or do they surface in the perception of day-to-day objects and substances in speakers' natural environments? It is clearly hard to resolve this issue without introducing other complicating variables into an experimental design.

It is still difficult to judge the magnitude of the sorts of relativistic effects for which evidence has been provided in this chapter. Studies like Lucy and Gaskins (2001) are suggestive of strong effects of classifier categories on the organization of object ontologies. Others, such as Saalbach and Imai (2007), suggest that classifier effects exist, but that they are somewhat weak and decidedly less pronounced than other sorts of influences, such as thematic or functional relationships. Which account is correct? One possibility is that both accounts are correct. Perhaps the particularities of the Yucatec Maya classifier system and the Mandarin classifier system yield cross-population disparities in the prominence of classifier effects on object categorization. Perhaps the interaction of classifiers with other cultural factors attenuates the relevant linguistic effects among Mandarin speakers, in a way it does not among Yucatec Maya speakers.

Going forward, research on this topic will no doubt benefit from the consideration of a wider sample of languages with and without count/mass nominal distinctions, and with and without nominal classifier systems. Perhaps more homogenous experimental methods will be applied to a number of people groups. Part of the present difficulty in ascertaining the extent of grammatical effects on the construal of objects/substances owes itself to the diversity of methods employed by the studies discussed above. Aside from a basic reliance on triad-discrimination tasks shared by several studies, the methods and stimuli are quite diverse. As we saw in previous chapters, some cognitive domains have now been explored in a variety of populations, but through a more standard set of methods that allows for the more direct contrast of the results obtained. In the case of spatial cognition, for example, some of the same spatial orientation tasks have been used in a number of cultures, e.g. natives of Holland and Namibia. In the case of numerical cognition, Nicaraguans, Amazonian indigenes, and Americans have been tested in different studies by different authors, yet using nearly identical tasks. Similarly, the color construal of Russians, New Guinean indigenes, and others has been examined via the same experimental paradigm. The uniformity of such tasks in some of the recent work on these topics allows us to more readily contrast the results across populations. (This is not to suggest that only uniform tasks are beneficial, since oftentimes studies must be crafted according to specific linguistic features familiar to the speakers being tested.)

At this point it is impossible to come to an empirically well-grounded conclusion regarding the issue at hand, beyond this: the evidence now on offer suggests that grammatical divisions of noun types do impact speakers' nonlinguistic discrimination of at least some objects and substances, in a variety of documented tasks and settings. The nature and extent of this impact remains nebulous, however.

9 Gender

9.1 Introduction

As we saw in the previous chapter, many languages classify nouns according to some set of semantic features. While there is generally a degree of inconsistency or malleability to the way in which nouns are grouped by such classifier systems, there is nevertheless some underlying discernible basis of nominal categorization. Classifier systems may be quite robust, with some languages exhibiting one hundred or more classes. Other classifier systems may contain only a handful of noun classes. In a large number of languages, an interrelated phenomenon surfaces in which nouns are grouped into only two or three categories. In such cases, which seem less exotic given that speakers of European languages are generally familiar with them, the two or three categories are related in some fashion to biological sex. Referred to typically as grammatical gender, this sort of nominal grouping strategy entails that nouns be classified as masculine, feminine, or (in the case of languages with a three-fold gender system) neuter. (See Corbett [1991] for a comprehensive typological treatment of this topic.) There is some overlap between grammatical gender systems and nominal classifier systems, since gender is one of the semantic features employed in the construction of nominal classes in many languages. Some languages have only a few noun classes that are based in part on biological sex. Perhaps the most well known example of this sort is the Australian language Dyirbal (Dixon [1972]), which has four noun classes – two of which are based in large measure on biological sex. One class is used when denoting men and most other animate entities. Another is used when speakers refer to women, some animals, fire, water, and violence-related entities. (This class served as motivation for the title to George Lakoff's 1987 book, *Women, Fire, and Dangerous Things*.)

Most readers are likely quite familiar with some system of grammatical gender, so a few examples of this sort of nominal categorization should suffice. In Portuguese, as in many languages, nouns are simply classified as being masculine or feminine. This classification holds for humans, of course, but also for non-human animates and inanimate objects. Gender is denoted via the usage of a pre-nominal article, which is *o* for singular masculine nouns and *a* for singular feminine nouns. So, for example, you could refer to *o homem* ('the man'), *o garoto* ('the young guy'), *o menino* ('the boy'), or *o jogador* ('the male player'). In contrast, you might refer to *a mulher* ('the woman'), *a garota* ('the young gal'), *a menina* ('the girl'), and *a jogadora* ('the female player'). Note as well that in the case of some nouns the final vowel alternates between *a* for female referents and *o* for male referents. (This system of grammatical gender obviously bears striking similarity to that evident in other Romance languages, particularly that of Spanish.) So there is some phonological cohesiveness to each grammatical gender category. Yet there are exceptions to the phonological generalization in question, since some feminine nouns end in *o*, and some masculine nouns end in *a*. An example of the former type is *a modelo* ('the female model'), and an example of the latter type is *o caixa* ('the cashier station/box office'). This sort of irregularity is common in languages that have grammatical gender categories reified in part through phonological patterns.

Perhaps more surprisingly, grammatical gender systems are also not completely regular with respect to noun semantics. Consider that German has three noun categories: masculine, feminine, and neuter. And while most human referents are categorized in a predictable manner, some are not. Most notably, *das Mädchen* ('the girl') is categorized as grammatically neuter, as evidenced by the use of the article *das*. If an exception to a grammatical gender pattern can crop up in the case of such an obviously gendered referent, this indicates clearly that linguistic gender systems are partially arbitrary in the way they group nouns.

The arbitrary way in which some nouns, particularly those with inanimate referents, are classified via grammatical gender systems is especially evident when one considers equivalent words in different languages. For instance consider that the word for "boat" in Portuguese, *barco*, is categorized as masculine. The same is true of *bateau* in French, but in Spanish *barca* is treated as feminine. In German the equivalent *Boot* is treated as neuter. So, despite the clear diachronic association between the words for boat in these four Indo-European languages, they represent three grammatical genders.

Even within one language there are often cases in which words with nearly equivalent referents fall into different grammatical gender categories. As Cubelli et al. (2011:450) note, in Italian the word for "stone" may be translated as either a masculine noun (*sasso*) or a feminine noun (*pietra*). Similarly the word for "door" may be translated as either masculine (*uscio*) or feminine (*porta*). One example pair that comes to mind from Portuguese is *o retrato/a foto*, both of which refer to 'the picture', but with different genders. In a similar vein, there are countless cases in which hypernyms and hyponyms are categorized dissimilarly. For instance, in Portuguese the word for "tree" is feminine (*a arvore*), while many kinds of tree are masculine, e.g. *o babaçu*, a common palm tree. Such cases also suggest that nominal gender is rather arbitrary, at least from a synchronic perspective.[59]

In the face of so many arbitrarily assigned nouns, we might be tempted to think there is no semantic basis underlying grammatical gender categories. Yet clearly there is some basis in meaning. In languages with grammatical gender systems, referents that are clearly female are typically denoted via grammatically feminine nouns, and referents that are male are in the vast majority of cases denoted via grammatically masculine nouns. Given the clear association between the grammatical genders and biological sex, it is natural to wonder whether such grammatical genders lead to the conceptual association between non-sexed nominal referents and the biological categories associated with the nouns' grammatical gender. Put differently, we might wonder whether grammatical gender influences the way in which speakers construe non-gendered entities. For example, are speakers of Portuguese more likely to think of referents such as *o carro* ('the car') as having more masculine characteristics, when contrasted with referents such as *a moto* ('the motorcycle')? As in the case of many other semantic domains considered in this book, intuition has led people to starkly different answers to such questions. To some, grammatical gender is unlikely to have any effects on speakers' nonlinguistic construal of objects, in part because the classification of nouns into gender categories is somewhat arbitrary to begin with. To others, grammatical gender *is* likely to impact the nonlinguistic construal of entities without natural gender. Those that maintain this latter position may point to translational difficulties that relate to grammatical gender patterns in different languages. Vygotsky (1962), for instance, drew attention to such difficulties. Consider the following remarks (also cited in Cubelli et al. [2011:449]):

> In translating the fable "The Grasshopper and the Ant," Krylov substituted a dragonfly for La Fontaine's grasshopper. In French, *grasshopper* is feminine and therefore well suited to symbolize a lighthearted, carefree attitude. The nuance would be lost in a literal translation, since in Russian *grasshopper* is masculine. [...] Tiutchev did the same in his translation of Heine's poem about a fir and a palm. In German *fir* is masculine and *palm* is feminine, and the poem suggests the love of a man for a woman. In Russian, both trees are feminine. To retain the implication, Tiutchev replaced the fir by a masculine cedar. [...] One grammatical detail may, on occasion, change the whole purport of what is said. (1962:221–222)

Such translation-based examples dovetail neatly with the intuition of some regarding this topic. In this case the assumption is that being lighthearted and

---

59 This arbitrariness has been noticed for some time. For example, Mark Twain drew attention to the non-systematic nature of German gender by noting that trees are male, their buds are female, and their leaves are neuter. (*A Tramp Abroad*)

carefree actually correlates somehow with femininity in French and Russian culture, and that grammatically masculine nouns cannot adequately convey such characteristics. Krylov and Vygotsky seemed comfortable making that assessment. They concluded that Russian speakers are less apt than French speakers to think of grasshoppers in feminine ways. In addition, they assumed that Russian speakers are predisposed to think of dragonflies as having feminine characteristics, when contrasted to grasshoppers. These are interesting ideas, but ones that require corroboration.

In the last two decades, and particularly in the last several years, researchers have begun to empirically address the potential influence of grammatical gender on the nonlinguistic construal of nominal referents. In the next section we focus on a number relevant studies that address the way in which speakers perceive inanimate objects. The studies offer evidence that some perceptions are in fact affected, at least during online cognitive processing, by grammatical gender.

9.2 Construal of non-human entities

Most of the experimental studies on the topic at hand are recent. Yet as Boroditsky, Schmidt, and Phillips (2003) note, there are some older attempts to test for grammatical-gender effects on the perception of inanimate entities. Jakobson (1971:265) describes such an attempt:

> A test in the Moscow Psychological Institute (1915) showed that Russians, prone to personify the weekdays, consistently represented Monday, Tuesday, and Thursday as males and Wednesday, Friday, and Saturday as females, without realizing that this distribution was due to the masculine gender of the first three names (*ponedel'nik, vtornik, cetverg*) as against the feminine gender of the others (*sreda, pjatnica, subbota*). The fact that the word for Friday is masculine in some Slavic languages and feminine in others is reflected in the folk traditions of the corresponding peoples, which differ in their Friday ritual. The widespread Russian superstition that a dropped knife presages a male guest and a dropped fork a female one is determined by the masculine gender of *noz* 'knife' and the feminine of *vilka* 'fork' in Russian.

It is unclear exactly what this personification task entailed, but to Jakobson its results reflect a fact that is evident more generally in Russian culture: the perceived characteristics of days of the week match their grammatical gender.

This topic attracted the attention of a fair number of scholars during the latter part of the twentieth century (Osgood, Suci, and Tannenbaum [1957], Clarke et al. [1984], Zubin and Köpcke [1986], *inter alia*). Studies using more experimental methods began to surface in the 1990's (Konishi [1993], Sera,

Berge, and Pintado [1994]). Konishi (1993) addressed the issue by examining the way in which Spanish and German speakers perceive certain inanimate entities. Forty native German speakers and 40 native Spanish speakers participated in the study. They were provided with a list of words in their native language and asked to rank the words according to a variety of scales. These included scales oriented according to a "potency" dimension. A guiding assumption of the study was that masculinity is perceived as being more potent, compared to femininity. A total of 54 words for inanimate entities were provided to the subjects. Crucially, 27 of these words were masculine according to Spanish grammar, and feminine according to German. These were "Type I" words. Conversely, 27 were masculine in German and feminine in Spanish. These were "Type II" words. "Type I" words included the translations of "air", "apartment", "sun", "tablecloth", etc., while "Type II" words included the translations of "apple", "ball", "moon", "rock", etc.

Konishi predicted that, if grammatical gender impacts the way in which the relevant entities are perceived, then Spanish speakers should rank Type I words as being more potent, on average, than Type II words. On the other hand, German speakers should rank Type II words as having greater potency, when contrasted to Type I words. This hypothesis was supported by the data. On a scale of 1–7, the mean potency rating of Type I words by Spanish speakers was 4.21. In contrast their mean potency rating of Type II words was 4.11. In the case of German speakers, however, Type II words were considered more potent, as evidenced by their higher mean potency rating (4.32 vs. 4.22). A mixed ANOVA revealed that this language/word-type interaction was significant ($F(1,76)=8.51$, $p<.01$.) Given that the speakers were unaware of the motivations for the study, these results are at least consistent with the hypothesis that grammatical gender categories influence the way in which associated entities are perceived.

Yet there are some methodological issues with Konishi's (1993) study that make the results difficult to interpret. One issue is that the task in question is clearly a linguistic one (conducted in the speakers' native languages), so it is unclear whether the results are simply due to linguistic priming, as opposed to being due to a more powerful linguistic effect on the general nonlinguistic conceptualization of entities. Another issue is that the differences in the perceptions of the word categories, while statistically significant, are extremely minor for both sets of speakers. That is, there were only very minor variations in potency ratings across grammatical genders. Furthermore it appears these differences were due to a subset of individual words, as the authors note that the results owed themselves primarily to perceptions of a few masculine nouns. Finally, given that the task was not time-sensitive, and given that it was unfamiliar to the speakers, it is possible that some participants merely relied on grammatical gender categories as part of a task-completion strategy. Clearly, then, Konishi's (1993) data do not resolve the issue, despite their consistency with the claim that grammatical gender affects the perception of inanimate entities.

In three interrelated tasks, Flaherty (2001) also explored the role of grammatical gender in speakers' perceptions of inanimate objects. These tasks involved Spanish and English speakers. For the tasks, native speakers of each language were asked to attribute qualities and names to objects depicted in a booklet. The number of participants in the tasks ranged from 64 to 144. The same booklets, depicting twenty non-human items, were employed for all tasks. Eleven of the items that were used are represented via masculine nouns in Spanish, while nine are referred to via feminine nouns. The former group was comprised of the Spanish words for "watch", "bird", "car", "tiger", "sun", "monkey", "airplane", "tree", "elephant", "fish", and "banana". The latter was comprised of the words for "snake", "bed", "cup", "teapot", "frog", "house", "candle", "flower", and "moon". Speakers were asked to decide whether the depictions represented male or female entities. In a separate task, they were asked to evaluate gender-related qualities of the items as well. Three age cohorts of Spanish speakers participated in the task: 5–7 year-olds, 8–10 year-olds, and adults. In the case of the 5–7 year-olds, there was not a strong tendency for the genders attributed to the objects to match the grammatical gender of their associated nouns. In the case of 8–10 year-olds and adults, however, the speakers were much more likely to categorize objects in accordance with their noun's grammatical gender. Furthermore, the objects were more often than not perceived as having attributes that matched their nouns' grammatical gender. Objects denoted with female nouns were more likely to be rated as beautiful or small, for example, when contrasted with objects denoted with male nouns. Such patterns were unsurprisingly not observed in the responses of the English speakers. Flaherty's (2001) findings are clearly consonant with the claim that grammatical gender impacts the perceived gender and gendered attributes of entities, including inanimate ones.

Again, though, there are reasons to be circumspect about these results. The first reason is that the gendered attributes of the objects in question did not always match the grammatical gender. For example, the older Spanish speakers typically considered a monkey to be male rather than female, when asked to choose. This selection matches the grammatical gender, yet the same speakers were also more likely to perceive the monkey as having more feminine attributes. Similar mismatches occurred with a few other objects as well. More problematically, though, the task instructions used in Flaherty (2001) explicitly addressed gender. That is, subjects were well aware that the gender of the described entities was relevant to their responses. Given this overt visibility of gender in the tasks, it seems possible and even plausible that speakers relied on grammatical gender simply as a means of completing the experiment. So the correlation between grammatical gender and the gender attributed to objects may not tell us much about the role of grammatical gender in general nonlinguistic thought. It may simply suggest that, when faced with such unordinary gender-based tasks, speakers turn to the grammar of their language for assistance. This is not an inconsequential finding, but it still leaves very open the question at hand: Does grammatical gender generally influence the way people perceive entities?

To some, another point of concern with these sorts of studies is that, in addition to relying on linguistic responses, participants in the studies were communicated with only via their native language. Boroditsky, Schmidt, and Phillips (2003) suggest that any cross-group disparities that surface through such methods may owe themselves to problems in translating the directions of the relevant tasks. Such disparities do not necessarily reflect deeper differences of conceptualization vis-à-vis the depicted entities. To Boroditsky, Schmidt, and Phillips (2003) it is helpful, when possible, to test speakers in a language besides their native language. If experimental cross-group disparities surface even when speakers are tested in a non-native language, yet those disparities are consistent with relativistic predictions based on their native languages, the disparities are more likely to be the result of deeper differences of conceptualization, rather than merely reflecting dissimilar online linguistic strategies adopted for task completion. With this assumption in mind, Boroditsky, Schmidt, and Phillips (2003) describe the results of an experiment they conducted for an unpublished study, in which native Spanish and German speakers' perceptions of 24 objects were tested. The experiment was carried out entirely in English. All 24 objects are referenced via nouns of opposite grammatical genders in Spanish and German. Subjects were asked to learn proper names for each of the objects. For example, an apple was named "Patricia" in some cases, and "Patrick" in others. Since the word for apple is feminine according to Spanish grammatical gender, in the former case the English name was consistent with Spanish gender, and in the latter case it was inconsistent. The reverse was true for German, since the word for apple is masculine in that language. The gender to which objects were assigned through such naming was consistent with each language in half the cases. Boroditsky and colleagues tested the rate at which Spanish and German speakers recalled the made-up names for non-gendered entities, and found that both German and Spanish speakers remembered the names for items better when the names given matched their native languages' grammatical gender, e.g. cases such as Patricia=apple for Spanish speakers and Patrick=apple for German speakers. Given that the participants had little reason to suspect the study related to gender, and given that they were tested in a non-native language, Boroditsky, Schmidt, and Phillips (2003) took the experiment's results as strong evidence that grammatical gender actually influences nonlinguistic thought.

Of course a by-now-familiar criticism might be made of this study also: it relied on a linguistic task to uncover evidence for a nonlinguistic pattern. While the findings do hint at differences in thought based on disparate patterns of grammatical gender, it is unclear how much they owe themselves to online language-related processes, for instance facilitated priming of concepts in cases of name/grammatical-gender matching. The demonstration of such processes is not insignificant, but uncovering such processes is not the same as uncovering deeper divisions between German and Spanish speakers' respective categorizations of the relevant entities.

In an even more language-based task carried out in English, Boroditsky and colleagues simply asked German and Spanish speakers to list the first three adjectives that came to mind when they were presented with the names of the 24 objects. They found that the adjectives used by the speakers had a tendency to match the grammatical gender of their native language. For instance, the word "key" was more likely to be described by German speakers as being hard, heavy, jagged, or serrated. In contrast, it was more likely to be described by Spanish speakers as golden, intricate, lovely, or shiny. While noteworthy, such patterns may owe themselves to task-specific conditions, in that speakers may have developed labeling strategies based on their native language simply to complete the task.

The results from studies like Konishi (1993), Flaherty (2001), and Boroditsky, Schmidt, and Phillips (2003) hint that grammatical gender plays a role in the categorization and recall of non-sexed entities. This is at least true in the case of tasks that rely on language, even if participants are not told the tasks relate to gender. Such studies also reflect how difficult it is to construct tasks in which speakers' perceptions of objects are explored while simultaneously preventing those speakers from relying on task-resolution strategies that may only incidentally rely on their native language's grammatical gender categories. To better prevent the implementation of such strategies, Boroditsky and colleagues also conducted a task in which English speakers were taught a made-up grammatical gender system in a made-up language, Gumbuzi. Subjects were taught the names of words for four male entities, four female entities, and twelve inanimate objects. These names were preceded by "grammatical gender" morphemes, as evidenced by the fact that female entities were always denoted via the same made-up morphological marker, while male enti- ties were treated as a separate group morphologically. Interestingly, the authors found that these made-up grammatical gender categories were suffi- cient to influence the way in which English speakers subsequently described the inanimate objects in a labeling task. Inanimate objects that were labeled with the masculine grammatical gender in Gumbuzi were more likely to be denoted via more masculine-like adjectives, and the reverse held of objects labeled with the feminine grammatical gender. Such results clearly do not owe themselves to task-resolution strategies based on the participants' native lan- guage, since English does not have a productive system of grammatical gender. They may still owe themselves to task-dependent strategies, however. Given that the task was not time-sensitive, and given the clear sex-based patterns in the nouns' made-up grammatical genders, speakers may have relied on the invented linguistic cues to provide lists of adjectives that they assumed matched the goals of the task. In short, while the pertinent linguistic effects on thought presented by Boroditsky, Schmidt, and Phillips (2003) are not inconsequential, they could be explained without appealing to deep-seated cross-population differences in nonlinguistic cognition.

Other studies have further explored these issues experimentally while attempting to refine our understanding of the way in which grammatical gen- der impacts thought (e.g. Sera et al. [2002], Vigliocco et al. [2005]). Vigliocco et al. (2005) note that there are in fact two related hypotheses that might account for the apparent influence of grammatical gender on thought. One of these, which they term "the similarity and gender hypothesis" (2005:501), stipulates that nouns of the same grammatical gender are perceived more simi- larly since their meanings are simply colored by the fact that they share similar phonological, morphological, and syntactic properties. For instance, as noted above, Portuguese nouns of the same gender tend to end in the same phoneme, *o* or *a*. This is a phonological property. Furthermore, Portuguese nouns of the same gender take the same definite article, which is also *o* or *a* (for singular nouns). This is a morphological property. In addition, adjectives in a given noun phrase may vary in form in order to show gender agreement with the head noun of that constituent. This is a morphological and syntactic property. For instance, speakers might say *a casa vermelha* ('the red house') but *o carro vermelho* ('the yellow car'). According to the similarity and gender hypothesis, words of the same gender might be construed as having somewhat similar meanings, simply because speakers assume that words with similar phonologi- cal, morphological, and syntactic properties should also have more similar meanings.

A second relevant hypothesis is termed the "sex and gender" hypothesis by Vigliocco et al. (2005). According to this hypothesis, potential similarities in the way speakers perceive certain objects are based on the correspondence of grammatical gender categories with actual features of particular sexes. Put differently, as humans acquire languages with grammatical gender, they begin to realize that many words of the same grammatical gender share some characteristic related to biological sex. In other words, there is a more overt association between biological sex and grammatical gender. This overt association then results in the extension of sex-based characteristics to non-sexed entities referred to via gendered nouns.

While the predictions of these two hypotheses are generally quite similar, they differ in some respects. Most notably, the sex and gender hypothesis predicts that grammatical gender effects on thought will be most prevalent among speakers of languages in which the correspondence between grammatical genders and sex categories is relatively transparent. According to Vigliocco et al. (2005), in languages of this type human referents are consistently indexed via one of two grammatical genders, which generally matches their biological sex. Romance languages such as Portuguese, Spanish, or Italian fall into this category. Conversely, in languages in which the correspondence between grammatical genders and sex categories is weak or unclear, such effects will be more difficult to uncover according to the sex and gender hypothesis. Languages in which humans may be represented via one of three genders and not always in a way that matches their biological sex, for instance German, fall into this category.

Vigliocco et al. (2005) conducted several experiments with English, German and Italian speakers. All but one of these tasks were entirely linguistic, and so they will receive limited attention here. For instance, two tasks were based on triad discriminations of words. In one experiment English and Italian speakers were presented with triads of words and asked to group the two words they judged to be most similar. In another task the same method was used, but with English and German speaking participants. In the case of the former inter-language contrast, it was found that Italian speakers were significantly more likely to group members of word triads that shared a grammatical gender. This difference between English and Italian speakers only surfaced for words with animate referents, however, in keeping with the sex and gender hypothesis. In the case of the latter contrast, there was no significant difference between the way in which German speakers and English speakers discriminated the triads of words. This finding was also consistent with the sex and gender hypothesis, according to Vigliocco et al. (2005), since the association between biological sex and grammatical gender is less transparent in German than in Italian.

Most tellingly, Vigliocco et al. (2005) describe a completely nonlinguistic task in which Italian and English speakers' construal of objects, rather than words, was tested. Thirty-six native speakers of each language participated in the task. Twenty pictures of animals and 24 pictures of inanimate objects were used in the task. These pictures were used to compose over 3,000 picture triads. Each participant examined a unique subset of these triads (just over 300 in number) and was asked to choose the two members of each triad that they found to be most similar. Crucially, at least two depicted objects in each triad represented words that are denoted via the same grammatical gender in Italian. Interestingly, the patterns evident in the English and Italian speakers' discrimination of the object triads were quite similar. Furthermore, the differences between them could not be explained in terms of grammatical gender, as no significant grammatical effects on the discrimination patterns surfaced.

In short, Vigliocco et al. (2005) provide evidence that grammatical gender affects the perceived similarity of words by Italian speakers, but not German speakers, in keeping with the sex and gender hypothesis. Notably, though, this influence of language on thought only surfaces in linguistic tasks, according to their results. Their findings are consistent with the conclusion that the influence of grammatical gender on thought is restricted to instances of "thinking for speaking" (Slobin 1996). Contra Konishi (1993), for example, their results are not consistent with the claim that grammatical gender impacts the nonlinguistic conceptualization of entities. In addition, they find no evidence, even in linguistic tasks, for grammatical effects on the perceptions of non-sexed entities. Vigliocco et al. (2005:513) are careful, however, not to draw more wide-ranging conclusions about the potential role of grammar on thought from their data for this particular domain.

Since the publication of Vigliocco et al. (2005), however, the issue at hand has been further explored in several detailed studies. For instance, Ramos and Roberson (2011) offer novel experimental data gathered among speakers of Portuguese – data that are in one fundamental way similar to those in Vigliocco et al. (2005), and in another way dissimilar. Ramos and Roberson's (2011) findings, like Vigliocco et al.'s, suggest that grammatical gender's influence on thought is restricted to contexts in which the linguistic faculties are actively engaged. However, their results suggest that the influence in question extends beyond animate entities to the perception of inanimate objects. While inconsistent with Vigliocco et al.'s (2005) claims, the latter finding is consistent with the conclusions offered in Boroditsky, Schmidt, and Phillips (2003), Konishi (1993), and Flaherty (2001).

Ramos and Roberson (2011) conducted four experiments with speakers of Portuguese and English. These experiments were designed to test whether grammatical gender plays a role in Portuguese speakers' discrimination of objects, and also whether any such role is restricted to tasks that are overtly focused on gender. In their first task, they tested the perceptions of 50 native Portuguese speakers and 50 native English speakers, vis-à-vis animate objects with obvious genders and inanimate objects without gender characteristics. Subjects were presented with eighty pictures of common inanimate objects. Forty of these objects are represented via feminine nouns in Portuguese, and 40 by masculine nouns. The subjects were also presented with eight pictures of gendered entities, including depictions of a boy, girl, king, and queen. Participants were told that the figures in the pictures would be personified in an upcoming cartoon, and were asked whether the voice of each figure should be male or female. In about 70% of cases, Portuguese speakers' decisions on the gender of the voice matched the grammatical gender of the relevant noun, regardless of whether the depicted figure actually represented a sexed entity. The difference in gender selection patterns between English and Portuguese speakers was significant, at both the by-item and by-participant levels ($p<.01$ and $p<.05$, respectively), according to an ANOVA. This sort of disparity reveals an effect of grammatical gender on thought, but in a linguistic task overtly referring to gender, in which Portuguese speakers may have appealed to grammatical gender as a task-resolution strategy.

In a related task, 42 Portuguese speakers and 42 English speakers were asked to rate the similarity of the meaning of words presented in pairs, on a scale of one to five. Thirty-five of these pairs contained words of the same grammatical gender, and 71 contained words of different genders. Here again grammatical gender impacted the responses of the Portuguese speakers, but only in the case of words with different grammatical genders was there a significant disparity between Portuguese and English speakers. In such cases, Portuguese speakers rated the nouns in question significantly more dissimilarly. Surprisingly, perhaps, Portuguese speakers did not rate words of identical gender to be significantly more similar to each other, when contrasted to English speakers. To Ramos and Roberson (2011), the results of this task suggest that grammatical gender was used as a task-resolution strategy in some cases only, and that grammatical gender does not impact the nonlinguistic conceptualization of inanimate objects since Portuguese speakers do not even perceive nouns of the same gender to be more alike than English speakers do.

In a third experiment, Ramos and Roberson (2011) tested the perceptions of Portuguese and English speakers with respect to object pictures and words. The task did not appeal to gender in any overt fashion. Fifty native English speakers and 50 native Portuguese speakers participated. For each of the two major tasks in this experiment, participants were presented with triads of stimuli and asked which of two alternate members of the triad "went best" with the pivot member of the triad. They made their selection via key press, and were asked to select as quickly as possible after the presentation of each triad. In the case of the "picture" task, 74 trials were conducted for each speaker, each trial with a unique triad of pictures. In the case of the related "word" task, 67 trials were conducted per speaker, each trial with a unique triad of words. Crucially, for all triads only one of the alternates of the triad matched the pivot in terms of grammatical gender.

No significant cross-population disparities surfaced for either triad-based discrimination task, though cross-group differences in the word-triad task did approach significance, and were in line with predictions based on grammatical gender. In other words, grammatical gender appeared to play a very minor role in Portuguese speakers' discriminations of the presented words. In the case of the nonlinguistic picture-discrimination task, however, grammatical gender did not seem to play any role in the Portuguese speakers' discriminations of depicted entities.

Based on their results and the results obtained in other relevant studies, Ramos and Roberson (2011) arrive at the following conclusion:

> Thus, grammatical gender effects on semantic judgments appear to vary along a continuum: strongest for tasks that involve both mandatory use of language (verbal modality) and overt reference to grammatical gender [...]; weaker for tasks where reference to gender categories is removed, but items are presented in the verbal modality [...]; and virtually absent for tasks with pictorial materials that do not require language processing [...]. (2011:109)

This conclusion is generally consistent with the work we have so far surveyed, as well as other recent work demonstrating that gendered language impacts thought appreciably only in linguistic tasks, or only when speakers are primed with gendered language. For instance, Imai et al. (2010) examined the performance of Japanese (a language without grammatical gender) and German speakers in a deductive reasoning task involving gender assessments of animal types. They found that German speakers' assessments of the sex of animals were influenced by German grammatical gender categories, but only when those categories were overtly referenced in the relevant task via the usage of a gendered definite article. (See Imai et al. [2010] for details.) Similar results were obtained in Saalbach, Imai, and Schalk's (2012) study on the perception of animals by German-speaking and Japanese-speaking children. The authors of that study conclude that German children use grammatical gender categories to inform their judgments about the properties of animals. The study is equivocal, however, as to whether this linguistic influence is of a relativistic or a "thinking for speaking" variety, since the tasks utilized relied heavily on language. Given the ubiquity of gendered language in everyday discourse, though, the authors conclude that either interpretation of their data suggests that the conceptual import of grammatical gender categories is non-trivial. (Saalbach, Imai, and Schalk [2012:1265])

Belacchi and Cubelli (2011) discuss the results of three experiments in which English and Italian speakers were asked to categorize pictures of animals as either male or female. In one experiment, 173 native Italian speakers were asked to classify 64 pictures. Eighty of the speakers were college students, and the rest were preschoolers. The animals in question included some that were sex-specific, e.g. *gallo*, 'rooster'. They also included some that were undefined for sex, but nevertheless are represented via a gendered noun in Italian, e.g. *delfino*, 'dolphin' (masculine) or *pantera*, 'panther' (feminine). Participants viewed pictures of these animals, which were not labeled, and then placed the pictures in a blue box if they considered the animal in question to be male, and in a pink box if they considered it to be female. Despite a slight bias for "male" responses, the authors observed that the responses accorded quite neatly with grammatical categories. That is, speakers tended to place the animal pictures in the female box if the noun describing the animal was feminine, and in the male box if the noun describing the relevant animal was masculine. This was true for both the young children and the adults. In the case of the adults, pictures of grammatically masculine animals were categorized as males 98.1% of the time, while pictures of grammatically feminine animals were categorized as females 96.2% of the time. This pattern was less robust among the preschoolers. It still surfaced, however. In the case of grammatically masculine animals, 81% were categorized as males. In the case of grammatically feminine animals, 60.3% were categorized as females. So, while preschool-aged Italian speakers were biased towards male responses (a common finding – see e.g. Boloh and Ibernon [2010]), the predicted pattern still surfaced in a significant manner for both adults and children. Similar results were obtained in a related experiment involving 3, 4, and 5-year-old children, with those results suggesting that the grammatical-gender bias increased with age among young Italian children.

In a separate experiment, Belacchi and Cubelli (2011) replicated the same task with 35 native English speakers. The same 64 pictures were utilized. In the case of pictures of animals without any obvious biological sex, the picture sorting was random. This further supported the claim that the Italian speakers' response patterns owed themselves to the role of their language's grammatical gender categories. One important point made by the authors, however, is that the influence of grammatical gender on Italian speakers' animal classification was much more apparent in cases in which grammatical gender was indexed through both a gendered article and a gendered noun-ending vowel (e.g. *il delfino, la pantera*), as opposed to cases in which only the article reflected grammatical gender. The study's authors take this fact as evidence that patterns in the Italian speakers' responses are due to lexical processing effects, rather than to major differences between the conceptualization of all grammatically masculine and all grammatically feminine nouns.

Consistent with a recurring theme in this chapter, it should be pointed out that it is unclear is how much the lexical processing effects uncovered in Belacchi and Cubelli (2011) owe themselves to the experimental set-up the researchers employed. For example, it is worth noting that the participants were asked to name the pictures prior to categorizing them. In addition, the task overtly referenced gender, since speakers were asked to place pictures in blue or pink boxes. Finally, the responses were not time-pressured. All of these factors indicate that participants, particularly adult speakers for whom the findings were most robust, may very well have relied on grammatical gender categories simply as a means of resolving the task. Nevertheless, the results suggest that Italian speakers naturally resort to grammatical gender categories in order to classify animals. It is difficult to say, though, whether such categorization effects reflect any differences in the way in which Italian and English speakers actually perceive animals.

Cubelli et al. (2011) further explored the effects of grammatical gender on thought via a series of tasks that more carefully controlled for the possibility that speakers could rely on grammatical gender simply as a task-resolution strategy. They controlled for this possibility by using several appropriate methodological tactics, some of which we have touched on at various points in this book. First, unlike Belacchi and Cubelli (2011), they did not overtly reference the grammatical categories related to the task. Second, they tested reaction times in a time-sensitive task to help reduce the speakers' metalinguistic reflections and their usage of language-consistent yet task-specific strategies. Finally, in one of their tasks they utilized verbal interference in order to test whether external engagement of the linguistic faculties impacted task performance. By employing these methodological tactics, they were better able to distinguish pervasive linguistic effects on thought from experimental artifact.

Three experiments are discussed in Cubelli et al. (2011). In the first, 32 English-speaking and 32 Italian-speaking speakers witnessed pairs of pictures and were asked to denote, via the pressing of keys, whether the two depicted objects belonged to the same semantic category. Through an independent task with other Italian speakers, the pairs used were reduced to those that were not found to be very dissimilar visually. In addition, the names of the pictured objects were controlled for in terms of their length, their frequency, the age at which they are typically acquired, their phonological similarity, and other factors. The pairs included pictures of objects and animals, some of which were clearly semantically related to each other and some of which were not. Sixty-four experimental picture pairs and 64 filler pairs were used in the task. Participants were asked to decide on the semantic congruence of the pair items as quickly as possible. Accuracy and response times were calculated. Once the response times were examined, a definite pattern emerged. Italian speakers and English speakers were faster at responding when the pictures in the pairs depicted semantically similar referents, for instance related animals. In the case of Italian speakers, though, the grammatical gender of the nouns denoting the relevant referents also played a role. Across all stimuli, Italian speakers tended to respond faster when both pictures in a pair denoted objects of the same grammatical gender. This response-time disparity was not great, averaging about 25 ms over most responses, which were generally in the 800–900 ms range. Nevertheless, the disparity was significant according to a by-subjects ANOVA ($F[1,31]=8.34$, $p=.006$).

In another similar experiment, the same general methods were employed with speakers of two languages with grammatical gender: Italian ($N=32$) and Spanish ($N=32$). Crucially, some of the pictures used are denoted by nouns with the opposite grammatical genders in the two languages. For example, a picture of a nose was used. The appropriate noun in Spanish, *nariz*, is feminine. In Italian the relevant noun, *naso*, is masculine. As in the first experiment, participants responded more quickly when the nouns associated with the depicted objects matched in terms of grammatical gender. Crucially, though, the actual gender-congruent image pairs that were responded to more quickly varied across populations, since the nouns depicted did not always represent the same grammatical gender in Spanish and Italian. This finding demonstrates pretty clearly that grammatical gender does in fact play a role in the rate at which Spanish and Italian speakers adjudicate the similarity of two objects, even when they are not given ample time to develop a metalinguistically based task-resolution strategy.

In a third and final experiment, Cubelli et al. (2011) once again conducted a picture similarity judgment task, this time with 16 native Spanish speakers. The methods of the first two experiments were replicated, with one fundamental difference. Participants were required to perform a verbal suppression task simultaneously while they made judgments of semantic similarity. Remarkably, once a linguistic interference task was added, the influence of grammatical gender congruity disappeared. In other words, for this experiment speakers did not select "yes" more rapidly when the grammatical gender of the stimuli matched. Two observations follow naturally from this finding. First, the effect of verbal interference suggests even more definitively that the results of the first two experiments in Cubelli et al. (2011) owe themselves to a linguistic influence. Second, the role of verbal interference indicates that this linguistic influence is not deep seated, but surfaces only during online processing. In the words of Cubelli et al. (2011:456), "It follows that grammatical gender does not alter conceptual representation; rather the grammatical gender effect in categorization judgments reflects that semantic and syntactic lexical representation are accessed spontaneously in accomplishing the task."

With this important disclaimer in mind, however, it is worth stressing that these results, like others so far considered, suggest that grammatical gender definitely plays some role in the way in which people spontaneously categorize objects in nonlinguistic tasks. Such a role is not necessarily minor in scope. Judging from the findings considered in this section, it seems quite possible that speakers of languages with grammatical gender are generally more attuned to gender categories during the online processing of relevant non-human entities, when contrasted to speakers without access to grammatical gender categories.[60]

9.3 Construal of human referents

The studies surveyed in Section 9.2 do not directly address whether grammatical gender impacts the categorization of human referents. Two recent studies have addressed the potential role of gendered grammatical categories on the perception of such referents. These studies considered the potential influence of gendered pronouns, rather than gendered nominal categories, on speakers' discrimination of such referents. Each of the studies offers some preliminary evidence for such pronominally based effects, which merit more detailed exploration. The evidence in question is suggestive of linguistic priming of certain kinds of nonlinguistic thought, rather than of general disparities of nonlinguistic conceptualization.

Chen and Su (2011) examined the way in which English and Mandarin speakers comprehend human referents, both at the discourse and sentence levels. Speakers of these languages were contrasted since English relies heavily on a gender distinction in 3rd person singular pronouns, i.e. "she" vs. "he" and "her" vs. "him". Mandarin, on the other hand, employs a gender-ambiguous pronoun *ta* to denote 3rd person singular referents. (In written Mandarin,

---

60 This possibility is consistent with associated claims in the language acquisition literature suggesting that children speaking languages with grammatical gender appear to recognize their own sex, and the sex of others, earlier in life than speakers of languages without grammatical gender (see Guiora [1982]).

fairly recent orthographic developments allow for gender marking of *ta*.) Chen and Su (2011) posited that the ubiquitous reference to gender in English 3rd person marking might have some indirect effect on the way that speakers process human referents. They generated two experiments. In the first, 25 Mandarin speakers and 25 English speakers listened to five target stories and five filler stories. The target stories all contained references to people with obvious gendered characteristics, for instance wearing a skirt. The target stories also included 3rd person pronominal reference to these gendered people. Of course in English this pronoun was gendered, while in Mandarin it was not. The speakers were then asked questions regarding the stories, some of which related to gender. The majority of questions were filler questions in which gender went unmentioned. By employing filler questions and filler stories, the authors prevented the participants from discovering the purpose of the task, and lessened the odds of them employing metalinguistic strategies when answering the questions.

For this first experiment, clear differences between the Mandarin and English speakers' question responses surfaced. For the filler questions not related to gender, Mandarin and English speakers' responses were each accurate in 93% of the cases. In the case of the target questions related to gender, however, English speakers were more accurate (94% vs. 81%). This language-based disparity in accuracy for gender-oriented questions was significant according to an ANOVA ($p=.0017$). Furthermore, the mean response time of English speakers was significantly faster when the questions related to gender (669 ms) than when it did not (1009 ms). In contrast, the disparity across these conditions was much less pronounced in the case of Mandarin speakers. This language/question-type interaction was also significant according to an ANOVA ($p=.0002$).

In a second experiment, Chen and Su (2011) tested the effect of pronominal gender on sentence comprehension. Fifty English speakers and 54 Mandarin speakers participated in the experiment, in which they listened to eighty sentences in their native language. Some of these sentences referenced human participants, and some sentences did not. After reading each sentence, presented one word at a time on a computer screen, participants were presented with a pair of pictures and asked to select, via key press, which picture matched the sentence just read. Crucially, picture pairs following sentences with human referents contained a picture of a female and a picture of a male. Note that, since sentences in this case were provided visually, Mandarin stimuli also denoted a distinction between masculine and feminine 3rd person pronouns. Nevertheless, the working hypothesis of Chen and Su (2011) was that, since Mandarin does not index pronominal gender verbally, cross-group disparities should surface in the experimental results. This proved to be the case. Mandarin speakers were generally less accurate than English speakers when choosing the picture referents to match sentences (83% vs. 97% accuracy, respectively), but only in the case of sentences with gender reference. This language/sentence-type interaction was significant according to an ANOVA (p<.0001). In addition, Mandarin speakers' response times following such sentences were greater than those of English speakers, particularly in contrast to control filler sentences. This difference across conditions was +187 ms (614 ms for filler sentences, 781 ms for sentences with gender) in the case of Mandarin speakers, but only +88 ms (644 ms for filler sentences, 732 ms for sentences with gender) in the case of English speakers. Once again, this language/sentence-type interaction was significant according to an ANOVA (p=.0011).

The results in Chen and Su (2011) suggest that English speakers are somewhat faster and more accurate at judging the gender of people depicted in discourse and individual sentences, when contrasted to Mandarin speakers, even when they are not necessarily aware that a task relates to gender. A plausible motivation for this fact is the dissimilarities between the pronoun paradigms of the two languages, namely the fact that gender denotation is obligatory in English 3rd person singular reference. According to Chen and Su (2011:200), this obligatory gender denotation maintains gender in the foreground of English speakers' general information processing, allowing them to more quickly respond to gender-based questions. It is important to stress though, that the information processing effects they provide evidence for are very much tied to linguistic behavior. So the relevant data do not actually demonstrate that gender is always foregrounded in English speakers' thoughts. They do suggest, though, that the English language covertly primes people vis-à-vis gender categories in a manner that facilitates responses to subsequent gender-based questions. This conclusion is similar to that arrived at in the final study considered in this chapter, Everett (2011b).

All of the studies on gendered thought so far examined are based on languages spoken in large, urban, industrialized societies. In Everett (2011b), I explored the potential interaction of linguistic gender categories and thought among members of such a society, but also among members of an Amazonian indigenous group. The study considered whether gender marking on English 3rd person singular pronouns impacts the way in which English speakers construe non-gendered depictions of humans. In order to explore this possibility, I ran two tasks with speakers of English and also with speakers of Karitiâna. As mentioned in Chapter 1, Karitiâna is a Tupí language spoken by approximately 300 people in southern Amazonia. Crucially for the present discussion,

the language lacks all gender marking. There is no system of nominal grammatical gender, and most pertinently gender is also not indexed in any way in
Karitiâna pronouns. There is only one third person pronoun in the language,
i (a high front unrounded vowel), which is not marked for gender or case. In
other words, in the place of "him"/"her" and "she"/"he", speakers employ *i*.
This sort of gender-ambiguous pronoun is called an epicene pronoun, and is
actually relatively common in the world's languages. As we saw in the preceding discussion, Mandarin employs an epicene 3rd person pronoun. Other
widely spoken languages that employ epicene pronouns include Cantonese,
Indonesian, Malay, Japanese, Bengali, Filipino, and Korean. The epicene pronoun in Karitiâna is evident in (9.1)–(9.3).

(9.1) i   na-aka-t   i-tepyk-Ø   ese-pip
       She/he   copula   dove   water-in[61]
       'She/he dove into the water.'
(9.2) ajja   na-okyt-Ø   i
       2PL   killed   him/her
       'You guys killed him/her.'
(9.3) i   a-taka-hit-Ø   an   i-ty
       she   gave   you   him/her-OBL
       'She/he gave you to him/her.'

There is a long history of attempts to introduce epicene pronouns like Karitiâna's *i* into the English language, and a variety of neologisms have been
drafted for this task only to fail to catch on. Part of the motivation for this
failure is that many grammarians have overtly questioned the possibility that
the reliance on a gendered 3rd person pronoun actually impacts the manner
in which people think about human referents. Attempts at epicene pronoun
introduction have been motivated by the opposite intuition, namely that gendered 3rd person pronouns cause people to think in gendered ways, even when
gender may be irrelevant to a given 3rd person reference. More specifically,
proponents of epicene pronouns cite evidence that speakers of English and
other languages tend to rely on masculine pronouns in cases of gender ambigu-
ity or opacity, and suggest that this reliance yields a male bias in thought and
discourse. (MacKay [1980])

Surprisingly, perhaps, there is relatively little experimental data in the literature pertaining to this issue. Everett (2011b) specifically addressed the way

---

61 See Everett (2011b:141) for more detailed glosses.

gendered pronouns might impact the construal of depictions of gender-ambiguous human referents, through two related tasks conducted with 25 adult native speakers of Karitiâna and 42 adult native speakers of English. For each task, participants viewed short cartoon-like videos of abstract gender-ambiguous faces. For one of these tasks, the faces were those of adults, and for the other they were those of babies. All of the figures used in the short videos (about 4 seconds each) were independently considered gender ambiguous by a number of English and Karitiâna speakers who did not participate in the experiment. Figure 9.1 contains one of the depictions used in the task. Crucially, this is a static representation of the face. Each of the faces was presented conducting some action in the video, such as opening his/her mouth, closing his/her eyes, or sucking on a pacifier as in Figure 9.1.

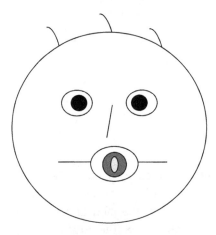

Figure 9.1: A static depiction of a gender-ambiguous face. Adapted from Everett (2011b).

Participants were unaware that the tasks in question related to gender, as evidenced by post-experiment interviews. Instead, if they had any ideas about the purpose of the tasks, they concluded that it related to the perception of actions. This belief was the result of a linguistic distractor exercise. Immediately after being presented with a short video clip of the cartoon-like humans performing an action, participants were asked to describe what they had just witnessed. The purpose of this exercise was not merely to distract the subjects, however. It was to prompt them to describe the images, and to test whether pronouns surfaced in such descriptions. In fact, pronouns did surface frequently in the descriptions. Sample English and Karitiâna descriptions are provided in (9.4)–(9.8).

(9.4)   The figure gasped.
(9.5)   He's shouting.
(9.6)   The baby frowned.
(9.7)   pyrynyrynan   i
          awakened   he/she
          'He/she woke up.'
(9.8)   pyrandyjn   i
          smiled/laughed   he/she
          'He/she smiled/laughed.'

The epicene pronoun was commonly found in the Karitiâna responses, as in (9.7) and (9.8). The gender-specific "he" occasionally surfaced in English descriptive phrases, as in (9.5), while "she" did not surface.

Following the presentation of each video and the elicitation of each subsequent descriptor phrase as in (9.4)–(9.8), speakers were asked to name the figure in the video. This naming exercise was used as an indirect means of assessing speakers' construal of the images' gender. Definite cross-language-group patterns in the naming strategies were uncovered. The results obtained for the task involving baby faces are summarized in Tables 9.1 and 9.2. Note that differences in the naming patterns also surfaced in accordance with the sex of the respondents, and for that reason the results are summarized in two tables.

As is apparent in the tables, there was a significant disparity across language groups in both cases. (In the case of the task involving adult faces, the significant pattern in question also surfaced, but only for male respondents.) These results suggest that Karitiâna speakers are less likely to provide masculine names for gender-ambiguous baby faces, when contrasted to English speakers. In that way they are consistent with the claim that epicene pronouns foster relatively gender-ambiguous thought. Of course, as I acknowledge in Everett (2011b), such results are not conclusive. One weakness of the results in Tables 9.1 and 9.2 is that they relate to only two languages. As a result, there remains

Table 9.1: Name choices for female Karitiâna and female English speakers. (Everett 2011b:147)

	Female names	Male names	Gender-neutral
Karitiâna	30	23	1
English	42	131	5
			Fisher's exact test: $p < 0.0001$

Table 9.2: Name choices for male Karitiâna and male English speakers. (Everett 2011b:147)

	Female names	Male names	Gender-neutral
Karitiâna	21	40	5
English	10	50	22
			Fisher's exact test: $p < 0.001$

the possibility that they owe themselves to some other cultural confound.[62] To better account for this possibility, Everett (2011b) provides the results of a pilot study carried out with ten speakers of Mandarin, which as we have noted has an epicene pronoun, and ten speakers of Portuguese, which like English obligatorily marks gender for 3rd person pronouns. The pilot study used the same stimuli employed in the experiment with Karitiâna and English speakers. Consistent with the findings of that experiment, the results of the pilot study suggest speakers of the language with epicene pronouns (Mandarin) are significantly less likely to give masculine names to the gender-ambiguous referents.

Of course the results in Everett (2011b), like those in Chen and Su (2011), are based on tasks that entailed language usage. Given that English and Karitiâna speakers used language to complete the task, it is unclear what the results say about cognition in completely nonlinguistic contexts. To be clear, though, the question addressed by such studies is not whether speakers of languages like Karitiâna or Mandarin generally see the world through lenses with less of a gender focus, or whether speakers of languages like English and Portuguese consistently see gender where none exists. Instead, the specific question addressed by these studies is whether cases of the actual usage of gendered language primes people to subsequently focus on gender, or make incorrect gender assumptions, in particular contexts. Both studies offer some evidence for an affirmative answer to this question. In the case of Everett (2011b), the results are at least suggestive that the default usage of masculine 3rd person pronouns may bias English speakers' perceptions of non-gendered representations of human referents. Maybe further work will address this issue with a greater range of methods.

Finally, it is worth highlighting that Chen and Su (2011) and Everett (2011b) are unusual studies in that they consider the potential role of gendered language on the way in which depictions of *human* entities are construed. In this way their findings pertain to a more socially relevant phenomenon than that addressed by the bulk of the work we have surveyed.

---

62 It is worth noting, though, that Karitiâna culture is far from egalitarian, and has pronounced gender roles. So it is unclear what nonlinguistic cultural factor would motivate the reduced androcentrism in the Karitiânas' naming habits.

9.4 Discussion and conclusion

Judging from the results of the studies we have examined, gendered language can prime or differentially induce certain kinds of thought. More specifically, when speakers use and hear grammatical gender categories, they are predisposed in some cases to think of associated nonlinguistic entities as having some characteristics of the gender with which they are indexed. In addition, the results considered in Section 9.3 suggest that speakers who use gendered pronouns are more apt to think of non-gendered depictions of humans in gendered ways.

Crucially, though, none of the results presented in this chapter offer convincing evidence that speakers of different languages think about gender differently in completely nonlinguistic contexts. All of the studies described above involved the utilization of language to one extent or another. Yet it is worth stressing that some of the tasks described above, while involving language, did not entail *gendered* language. In the case of Everett (2011b), for example, speakers were clearly unaware that the task even related to gender. The uncovered cross-group differences in gendered naming patterns did not result from subjects' metalinguistic awareness of gender categories. Instead, it appears that English speakers were primed to think about stimuli in gendered ways simply because they engaged their linguistic faculties.

One could justifiably conclude that the sorts of relativistic effects considered in this chapter are generally of a comparably weak variety, when contrasted to some of those surveyed in other chapters. Assuming this conclusion for the moment, it seems that there are two motivations why relativistic effects associated with linguistic gender might be somewhat tenuous. One potential motivation is that deeper linguistic effects on nonlinguistic cognition may surface more readily in thought associated with abstract phenomena such as temporal perception, color construal, and spatial orientation (see Boroditsky [2001]). Such cognitive processes relate to continuously perceived categories with no predefined physical boundaries, but with clearly defined linguistic boundaries. They may also relate to aspects of human experience that are reified linguistically through metaphors (e.g. "the future is forward") that do not surface in all languages. In other words, such abstract domains of cognition may be more susceptible to linguistic influence, whether via simple linguistic meddling or marked linguistic reorganization. Cognitive processes associated with more concrete stimuli, such as human beings and their (largely) discontinuous categories of biological sex, may be less susceptible to linguistic influence. After all, the categories of "male" and "female" exist in the actual world, and are salient to humans and other species regardless of the way in which they are instantiated linguistically. This is not true of some other categories touched on in this book. Consider that certain kinds of spatial orientation, for instance the left/right egocentric perspective, may not exist apart from linguistic reification. Color categories also do not actually exist if the relevant divisions of the color spectrum are not enforced linguistically or through some other mechanism. For most species, many quantity distinctions such as 7 vs. 9 are also meaningless, unlike male vs. female. And so on. So in some sense it is to be expected that the sorts of relativistic effects discussed in this chapter are weak compared to some of those relating to more abstract aspects of human cognition.

There is likely a second interrelated motivation for the comparative weakness of the relativistic effects discussed in this chapter: In many cases the information encoded in grammatical gender categories directly conflicts with concrete experience. For example, any Portuguese speaker is well aware that a fork has no actual biological sex. So on some level they must also be aware that the masculine gender of the associated noun *garfo* does not actually imply that forks are males. The same conclusion could of course be made for countless other nouns. In such cases, introspection reveals a disconnect between grammatical gender categories and biological sex categories. With this "conflict" in mind, it is not particularly surprising that grammatical gender seems to play a limited role in impacting the construal of non-gendered entities. In fact, it is somewhat remarkable that grammatical gender plays any role in habitual thought. Even if the role is simply to prime certain kinds of thought, then, it can hardly be dismissed. After all, from the perspective we are espousing based on the data offered above, grammatical gender induces certain kinds of thoughts, even though the thoughts in question relate to a concrete facet of human experience, and even though the thoughts may conflict with real-world knowledge regarding a given non-gendered entity. Furthermore, given the ubiquity of grammatical gender markers and gendered pronouns in actual discourse (in languages with such categories), such inducing effects may actually impact thought in a pervasive manner. At the least, this possibility warrants attention, and in fact it is currently being explored by a number of researchers.

10 Other kinds of effects

10.1 Introduction

So, what else? What other sorts of linguistic effects on nonlinguistic cognition might exist? So far we have considered evidence for relativistic effects associated with spatial orientation, the construal of time, quantity recognition, the perception of color, the categorization of objects, and the imbuement of gender into non-gendered objects. These topics have occupied most of our attention in large measure because of the volume of recent studies in which they are addressed. Yet there are various other sorts of potential relativistic effects, some of which have very recently been systematically explored. Work on such effects is discussed in this chapter. The research in question actually includes striking evidence for relativistic effects, suggesting that our knowledge of the range of extant linguistic effects on nonlinguistic cognition is inchoate.

This chapter is not meant as a "catch-all" for all remaining work on the linguistic relativity hypothesis, in part since there are numerous relevant ongoing studies not touched upon here. In addition, there are many potentially fecund areas in which the linguistic relativity hypothesis has yet to be explored. While there may prove to be strong limits on the kinds of relativistic effects that actually exist, there is at this point no clear upper limit on the potential sorts of effects meriting inquiry. The reason for this is simple: languages differ in innumerable ways. Randomly selected unrelated languages will always display a host of remarkably dissimilar formal properties. Hopefully we conveyed to some extent the range of such variation in our discussion of linguistic diversity in Chapter 2. Judging from the grammatical diversity evident in languages and the fact that various grammatical disparities have now been shown to motivate at least some variance in cognitive processes across populations, it is difficult to place limitations of the kinds of relativistic effects that could be explored in future research.

In addition to grammatical diversity, languages obviously exhibit extreme lexical diversity. That is, they often represent given semantic categories via different kinds and numbers of words. As we saw in Chapters 6 and 7, crosslinguistic lexical diversity associated with number words and color terms appears to motivate some clear differences in associated cognitive processes. In addition to the diversity associated with these well-explored semantic domains, though, there are numerous other kinds of lexical diversity that may motivate cross-group differences in thought – and here too it is difficult to place an upper limit on the kinds of diversity in question. For instance, in Chapter 1 we noted that Karitiâna has numerous words for monkey types, but no hypernym for the category of monkey. We suggested that this lexical difference between Karitiâna and English may (or may not) impact the way in which Karitiâna and English speakers think about monkeys. While admittedly this example is a bit inconsequential, it serves to illustrate the point that we cannot state *a priori* that lexical variation does not yield some nonlinguistic cognitive dissimilarity (however trivial) in such cases, particularly in the light of the evidence for lexical effects on thought associated with number words and color terms. And if we are willing to consider the potential for this kind of minor relativistic effect, then surely the potential effects to be explored are almost limitless.[63] These potential effects may be explored for instance in languages with typologically remarkable lexical diversity in specific semantic fields. For instance, the Hanunoo language of the Philippines is claimed to have dozens of basic words for "rice" (Conklin [1957]). In Shona, on the other hand, there are over two hundred words for types of "walking" (Comrie, Matthews, and Polinsky [2003:89]). Do such lexical patterns motivate differences in speakers' conceptualization of kinds of rice and types of walking? Maybe, maybe not, but such variation is at least suggestive of the many possible relativistic effects that have yet to be explored. In this chapter, though, we will focus primarily on several recently explored cases in which morphological and syntactic, rather than lexical, variation appears to motivate differences in thought. We will however draw attention to one case in which lexical variation may impact perception, specifically the perception of emotions.

10.2 Recalling accidents

When people talk about an event involving humans, they can depict the event in myriad ways. For example, speakers may choose to describe the event in a way that focuses on the human(s) who caused the event, i.e. the agent of an event. I can say, for instance, "LeBron James blocked Kobe Bryant's shot", drawing attention to the fact that it was LeBron James, as opposed to some other basketball player, who blocked the shot. In such a case I am highlighting the agency of James in the relevant action. Yet I can convey this same event in other ways, ways that may place less focus on James' agency. I might say

---

63 Many are likely to steer clear of such work given the way that associated claims on lexical diversity have been exaggerated in the past, as we noted in Chapter 1. See Lupyan (2012) for a detailed discussion of the mechanisms through which lexical diversity may impact nonlinguistic cognition.

instead "Kobe Bryant had his shot blocked", or simply "The shot was blocked". By employing morphosyntactic alternations associated with the passive voice, I could draw less attention to the person who initiated an action (Shibatani [1985]), in this case the blocking of a basketball shot. Interestingly, there is evidence that such a grammatical choice actually impacts how people perceive the roles of the humans involved in specific actions.

Fausey and Boroditsky (2010) presented experiment participants with a description of a short video clip of Janet Jackson's infamous "wardrobe malfunction". This event occurred during Jackson's halftime performance in the 2004 Super Bowl, in Houston, Texas. Justin Timberlake performed alongside Jackson. At the end of the performance, Timberlake reached over in an apparently choreographed maneuver and removed a portion of Jackson's outfit, partially revealing her right breast. Immediately following this event, there was a public outcry over this putatively obscene gesture. Timberlake claimed the exposure of the anatomy in question was accidental, coining the phrase "wardrobe malfunction" in order to exculpate himself. For the relevant experiment in Fausey and Boroditsky (2010), participants (N=589) were presented with either an agentive description of the event in question, or a non-agentive one. The former description included phraseology such as "He unfastened the snap and tore part of the bodice," in which the agent (Justin Timberlake) is referenced explicitly via "he". The latter description included "a snap unfastened and part of the bodice tore", and the agent was not mentioned though the same event was described. Some of the experiment participants were presented with a description prior to witnessing a video of the famous event, while others were presented with a description after witnessing it. Still others did not even view the event and were simply presented with a description. Fausey and Boroditsky (2010) found through a series of questions that participants were significantly more likely to ascribe blame to Justin Timberlake for the wardrobe malfunction if the event was described via agentive terminology such as "He unfastened the snap". This significant difference surfaced even in those cases in which participants viewed a video of the actual event and regardless of whether they saw the video prior to or after reading the description. In addition, participants who were provided agentive descriptions were significantly more likely to fine Justin Timberlake for his actions, if hypothetically given such powers, and to fine him a significantly higher dollar amount. The relative agency-focus of the phraseology chosen for the description impacted the speakers' actual perceptions of the event in question. More generally, agentively oriented language caused subjects to perceive a person as being more responsible for a given event, even when the subjects had witnessed the event in question. This finding was corroborated by other experimental work in Fausey and Boroditsky (2010), based on unrelated events.

Given the evidence that wording with high agency-salience impacts the construal of events for speakers of English, the natural question in the current context is whether languages differ with respect to how they denote agency, and, if they do, whether such differences yield cross-population differences in the construal of agents in witnessed events. Fausey et al. (2010) and Fausey and Boroditsky (2011) offer evidence for exactly these kinds of differences. Here we will focus on the results of the latter study.

When describing events in which agents deliberately performed a transitive action, English and Spanish speakers tend to use agentive language. For instance, if an English speaker witnesses someone deliberately breaking a vase, s/he might say "She broke the vase". A Spanish speaker might similarly state that *Ella rompió el florero*. Differences between English and Spanish surface in descriptions of accidental events, however. If a Spanish speaker views someone accidentally breaking a vase, they are likely to say something non-agentive like *Se rompió el florero*, best translated as "The vase broke itself". While English speakers may also use non-agentive language to describe such an event, they are much more likely to maintain agentive language such as "She broke the vase". This claim is supported by one of the tasks conducted in Fausey and Boroditsky (2011), in which the authors presented 68 English speakers and 29 Spanish speakers with 16 videos of intentional events and 16 videos of accidental events. In the case of the former sort of events (e.g. someone deliberately popping a balloon with a tack), speakers of both languages used agentive descriptions in over 90% of the cases, and there was no significant disparity between the groups vis-à-vis rate of agentive language usage. In the case of the latter kind of event (e.g. someone accidentally popping a balloon), however, there was a significant difference between the descriptions of the two groups. As predicted, English speakers relied on agentive language at a higher rate. In fact, the English speakers' descriptions of accidental events explicitly referred to the agent in about 75% of cases, while the Spanish speakers' descriptions only did so in about 60% of cases. The cross-group disparity was significant ($t[92]=3.31$, $p=.001$).

In a separate task with 113 English speakers and 109 Spanish speakers, Fausey and Boroditsky (2011) uncovered evidence that the heightened reliance on agentive language in English impacts the mere recall of people associated with accidental events. More specifically, English speakers were more likely than Spanish speakers to remember who accidentally popped a balloon, or who spilled water, or who dropped something. The task in question was conducted as follows: Participants viewed a set of 16 videos that had also been used in the description-elicitation task run with other participants. Each of the videos depicted an action that was either intentionally or accidentally performed by a human. Crucially, in half the videos the human performer involved was a male with a blue shirt, and in half it was a different male with a yellow shirt. Participants viewed the videos in succession, with one-second breaks between the videos. The order of videos was controlled for through pseudo-randomization. Participants were informed that their memory was being tested. Following a distractor task in which they were asked to count to ten, the participants were shown additional "probe" videos. Each of these probe videos replicated an event depicted in one of the 16 videos the participants had viewed in succession prior to the distractor task. In the probe videos, however, the human participant was a male they had not seen previously. After each probe video, the participants were asked "Who did it the first time?" (in their native language), while being prompted with separate pictures of the actors used in the initial 16 videos. In other words, participants were asked to recall whether the yellow-shirted man or the blue-shirted man had been involved in the first video depiction of the event in the probe video. During their individual sessions, participants also performed an unrelated recall task in which they memorized the way in which fifteen objects were oriented on a computer screen.

As we see in Figure 10.1, Spanish and English speakers recalled the agents of intentional events at roughly the same rate. Each group correctly recalled agentive actors in about 78% of the cases, with no significant difference between the populations. Crucially, though, English speakers accurately recalled the actors of accidental events at a higher rate. They did so in about 79% of cases, while Spanish speakers did so in slightly less than 74% of the cases. While this cross-group disparity was not as marked as the cross-group differences in rates of agentive phrasing evident in Fausey and Boroditsky's (2011) first "description" task, it was nevertheless significant ($t[208]=2.25$, $p=.01$). Clearly the hypothesis proposed by the authors was supported by their data.

The reliance of English speakers on agentive language appears to result in heightened focus on the human actors in accidental events, even when the events are not being described. This conclusion is at least consistent with the English speakers' facilitated recall of such actors evident in Fausey and Boroditsky's (2011) data. Note that the heightened recall of English speakers vis-à-vis such "accidental" actors was not due to some general recall advantage. After all, English speakers did not recall intentional agents at a significantly higher rate than Spanish speakers. Furthermore, in the control memory task based on the recall of the spatial orientations of fifteen objects, there was no disparity between the performance of the English-speaking and Spanish-speaking participants.

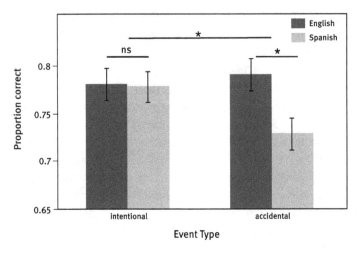

Figure 10.1: Proportions of correct recall for English and Spanish speakers. Adapted from Fausey and Boroditsky (2011:154).

The central finding in Fausey and Boroditsky (2011) is also supported by data from a related study, Fausey et al. (2010), conducted with speakers of English and Japanese. The latter language is similar to Spanish in that it relies less intensively on agentive language in the description of accidental events. The corroboration of this finding with speakers of Japanese suggests that the recall disparities evident in Fausey and Boroditsky (2011) do not simply owe themselves to some general cultural differences between the English-speaking and Spanish-speaking groups.

More work is required on this fascinating topic. One issue that is unclear from the discussion in Fausey and Boroditsky (2011), for instance, is whether English speakers were uniformly better at recalling the actors in accidental events, or whether they were particularly attuned to the actors in certain kinds of events, such as balloon-popping or water-spilling.

Fausey and Boroditsky's (2011) findings offer evidence for a fairly dramatic type of relativistic effect. The ramifications of the proposed effect are potentially quite serious. As the researchers themselves state, "We should note that in important real-world domains like eye-witness memory, even a small difference in performance can have serious consequences: it could make the difference between a life behind bars or getting away with murder, between being falsely accused or exonerated." (Fausey and Boroditsky [2011:155])

As of now it remains unclear how well the experimental effects uncovered by Fausey and Boroditsky (2011) represent speakers' actual perceptions of events in real-world contexts. In the light of the fascinating data in that study, though, one cannot discard the possibility of such "serious consequences" of the usage (or lack thereof) of agentive language.

10.3 Emotion

Some cross-cultural research suggests that human emotions, or at least some human emotions, are universal. Most notably, the research of Paul Ekman and colleagues (e.g. Ekman [1992], Ekman and Friesen [1971], *inter alia*) has demonstrated that there are some common patterns in human facial expressions. Based on these similarities, Ekman has helped popularize the notion that there are six fundamentally shared human emotions: anger, fear, happiness, surprise, sadness, and disgust. This claim is further supported by similarities between the facial expressions of seeing humans and those who are congenitally blind (Matsumoto and Willingham [2009]). Nevertheless, the claim for universal human emotions has led to criticisms, including claims of methodological shortcomings in the tasks employed by Ekman and colleagues (see for instance Wierzbicka [1999]). Even if we assume that there are six universal human emotions reflected in shared patterns of facial expressions, however, this assumption does not preclude the possibility of cultural variability in the way that human emotions are perceived. In fact, some work suggests there are differences in the way supposedly basic human emotions are experienced by members of different cultures (see Elfenbein and Ambady [2003], Russell [2003]). According to such research, a variety of factors may foster differences, sometimes minor, in the way basic emotions are perceived. These factors include basic facial characteristics of the humans whose expressions are being perceived (Weisbuch and Ambady [2008]) and the anxiety level of those perceiving the emotions (Bouhuys, Geerts, and Mersch [1997]). Furthermore, there is at least some cross-cultural variability in the facial expressions associated with emotions (Matsumoto, Kasri, and Kooken [1999]), as many ethnographers can attest. Given the existence of at least some variability in the way basic human emotions are displayed and construed, it is not unreasonable to wonder whether crosslinguistic disparities help foster differences in the production or perception of emotions. After all, languages do vary in terms of their number and types of emotion words, though the extent of that variability is a matter of some debate (see Wierzbicka [1999] for one perspective).

There is clear crosslinguistic variability in the way certain emotions are lexically encoded. For example, the way that love (which relates to several putatively basic human emotions) is encoded differs markedly across languages. Ancient Greek famously had four different words for emotions subsumed by the English word "love": *agápe, éros, philia,* and *storge.* These terms helped to differentiate feelings of deep forms of attraction and affection (*agápe*) from more passionate, sensual longing (*éros*), or from affectionate friendship-type feelings (*philia*), or from the emotion felt towards children and kin (*storge*). In the light of such lexical refinement, the word for love in English seems a pretty blunt instrument. I can, after all, say that I love my child or that I love burritos. In Karitiâna and many other languages this latter sort of usage would be impermissible since the word used for "loving" or liking food items differs from the word used for loving or liking other things.

Recent work by Debi Roberson and colleagues (Roberson and Davidoff [2000], Roberson, Damjanovic, and Pilling [2007]) indicates that language does impact the construal of emotions, at least among speakers of English. While the experimental paradigm exploited by the pertinent studies has not to my knowledge been extended to speakers of other languages, the basic findings are worth discussing in the context of the current discussion.

In the studies in question, participants were presented with many pictures of a man's face expressing happiness, anger, or fear – all supposedly universal human emotions. Through a visual morphing program, the man's face was presented in a number of pictures, and these pictures represented minute variations in his facial expression along an emotion "continuum". For instance, in one experiment an angry-happy continuum was utilized. The man's face looked extremely angry in one of the pictures used in this continuum, and in another picture his face looked extremely happy. The remaining pictures in the given continuum fell somewhere in between these two extreme variants. The pictures were controlled so that each only varied a minor amount from any adjacent pictures on the angry-happy continuum. Roberson and Davidoff (2000) and Roberson, Damjanovic, and Pilling (2007) observed that such pictures are perceived categorically, much like colors are. That is, when asked to judge whether a particular image represented a happy or angry face, speakers did not gradually alter their selections as they proceeded along the angry-happy continuum. Instead, at a given point on the continuum of facial images, the majority of participants' judgments changed from "angry" to "happy" and vice-versa. This was true even though all of the pictures varied to the same degree when contrasted to juxtaposed images on the angry-happy continuum. In other words, there was no physical basis for the categorical perception of the images. Instead, the motivation for the categorical perception appeared to be linguistic. Certain expressions were apparently subliminally labeled by the participants as "angry", while others were labeled "happy". This dichotomous labeling resulted in somewhat dichotomous perception, according to Roberson and colleagues. It appears, then, that the linguistic labels of emotions impact the nonlinguistic perception of actual expressions.

How, one might ask, do such findings suggest that the categorical perception of emotions owes itself to linguistic labels? After all, it is possible that linguistic labels are derived in accordance with more basic factors of emotion construal. The close mapping between linguistic labels and the categories through which emotions are construed could be epiphenomenal. Roberson and Davidoff (2000) and Roberson, Damjanovic, and Pilling (2007) offer strong evidence that emotion words do in fact motivate the categorical perception in question: results from tasks with verbal interference. When participants were asked to judge the facial expressions under conditions of verbal interference, the categorical perception of emotions disappeared. In other words, their perception of the emotion continuum between, say, angry and happy, became more gradual and less categorical when they viewed the faces during verbal interference tasks. Minor differences in expressed emotions were judged as minor differences, and there was no abrupt point at which an image crossed the threshold from e.g. angry to happy.

In addition, the studies in question suggest that the categorical perception of emotions disappears only under verbal interference, and not under other sorts of mental interference. In short, the findings in Roberson and Davidoff (2000) and Roberson, Damjanovic, and Pilling (2007) offer strong support for the notion that linguistic categories impact the way in which emotions are construed.[64]

Taken in concert with the well-known crosslinguistic variability in the lexical denotation of at least some emotions, Roberson and colleagues' findings suggest that such variability may foster differences in the perception of emotions. Future work might specifically address whether the categorical perception of emotions surfaces in different ways across speakers of languages that utilize non-equivalent words for particular emotions. At the least, the work of Roberson and colleagues draws attention to the possibility of such linguistically motivated variation in the construal of emotions.

10.4 Counterfactual reasoning

In two controversial studies, Alfred Bloom (1981, 1984) suggested that the language one speaks impacts his/her ability to reason counterfactually. This claim was based on findings among speakers of Mandarin and English. Bloom's

---

64 I refer the reader to the studies in question for a closer look at the experiments on which these claims are based. In addition, Roberson (2010) offers a succinct summary of these and associated studies.

results were almost immediately called into question by other studies (Au [1983, 1984], Liu [1985]) that failed to replicate his results because, according to the studies' authors, they corrected issues with the methods utilized by Bloom. While we do not wish to reproduce the entire dialectic here, the basic claims made by Bloom are worth reprising since related claims have been made in more recent work that hints at minor grammatically motivated cross-population differences in counterfactual reasoning patterns. (Yeh and Gentner [2005])

Counterfactual language refers to events or states of affairs that do not hold in actuality, i.e. are counter to actual fact. Suppose I state, "If I had been born with Messi's skills, I might have played for FC Barcelona too." This is a counterfactual statement. Both the antecedent ("If had been born with Messi's skills") and the consequent ("I might have played for FC Barcelona too") do not describe actuality since I do not possess Messi's skills and do not play for Barcelona. Counterfactual statements such as these allow us to convey thoughts about an alternate reality, contrasting it with our real experience. In English, counterfactual statements are typically indicated through the use of so-called "if-clauses", through the use of the past-perfect tense/aspect combination in the verb of the antecedent, and through intonation shifts. In some languages, though, counterfactual statements are not indicated so obviously. There is no clear syntactic, morphological, or prosodic marker of counterfactual statements in Mandarin, for instance, other than the use of the past tense particle *le* in the antecedent. (See discussion in Yeh and Gentner [2005:2411].) Since counterfactual statements are more grammatically distinct in English than in Mandarin, Bloom (1981) posited that English speakers rely more readily on counterfactual reasoning, when contrasted to Mandarin speakers. To test this hypothesis, he presented English and Mandarin speakers with translations of several versions of the same story about a fictional philosopher. One of the versions of the story could be interpreted as factual or counterfactual. Bloom found that English speakers were much more likely to interpret the story in question as counterfactual, when contrasted to Mandarin speakers. This result, however, may have been motivated by non-idiomatic translations in the case of the Mandarin materials used for the task. (Au [1983, 1984])

Yeh and Gentner (2005) returned to this topic by testing the way in which Mandarin and English speakers relied on counterfactual reasoning during an experimental time-sensitive task. Eighty-four Taiwanese Mandarin speakers and 30 English speakers participated in the experiment. Participants were presented with four counterfactually based stories of about 200–300 words, via computer screen. Two of the stories involved "non-transparent" counterfactuals that could hypothetically be true, i.e. they did not conflict with any real-world information familiar to all participants. In the other two stories "transparent" counterfactuals, which directly conflicted with participants' real-world knowledge, were presented.[65] For each story the first half contained factual information and the second half counterfactual information. After participants read the story, it disappeared from the screen and they assessed the validity of a series of eight randomly ordered true-false statements about the story, via key press. Half of the true-false statements pertained to the factually presented sections of the story, and half pertained to the counterfactually presented portions of the story. Yeh and Gentner (2005) sought to uncover potential differences in the accuracy and reaction times of the English and Mandarin-speaking respondents' true-false assessments.

There was no significant cross-population difference in the reaction times for the participants' assessments of the true/false statements. There was, however, a significant disparity in response accuracy. More specifically, English speakers' true/false assessments were significantly more accurate in the case of true/false statements pertaining to non-transparent counterfactual claims in the stories. On the other hand, there was no significant disparity between the groups' accuracy levels on the true/false statements pertaining to information presented via transparent counterfactuals. In other words, when Mandarin speakers and English speakers could rely on real-world knowledge while interpreting a counterfactually presented portion of a story, they comprehended that portion with the same degree of accuracy, and about 96% of each groups' true/false assessments were correct in such cases. In contrast, when participants could not rely on real-world knowledge while interpreting a counterfactually presented portion of a story, English speakers assessed the relevant true-false statements with higher degrees of accuracy than Mandarin speakers. English speakers were accurate in 92% of such cases, compared to 77% for Mandarin speakers.

Yeh and Gentner (2005) suggest that their results do not offer support for the claim that Mandarin speakers are simply less proficient at counterfactual reasoning, contra Bloom (1981, 1984). What their results suggest instead is that Mandarin speakers' counterfactual reasoning is comparatively compromised only when speakers' real-world knowledge does not usefully inform their interpretation of a given counterfactual statement. In such cases only, the authors

---

65 An example of a transparent counterfactual is "If antibiotics had never been discovered..." Even without the rest of the story one recognizes that this statement is counterfactual since s/he knows that antibiotics were in fact discovered. An example of a non-transparent counterfactual is "If Michael had gone out with his girlfriend that night..." In such a case, the reader must rely on linguistic cues, rather than real-world knowledge, to establish whether Michael went out on a particular night. S/he cannot know from the outset of the story about Michael's behavior, since it is not common knowledge. (See Yeh and Gentner [2005:2412].)

suggest, Mandarin speakers' comprehension of counterfactuality may suffer. Put differently, their data do not suggest that language determines people's ability to reason counterfactually, but do suggest that linguistic factors impact counterfactual reasoning in some contexts. They conclude that "Chinese speakers may be disadvantaged when counterfactuals must be detected with respect to specific current context." (Yeh and Gentner [2005:2415])

The results so far obtained on this topic relate to speakers of only two languages, Mandarin and English. Therefore, cross-population differences in performance on the counterfactual reasoning tasks may owe themselves to lurking cultural factors associated with these two groups. In addition, the results in this case are obviously based on tasks that are entirely linguistic– so their relationship to counterfactual reasoning in completely nonlinguistic contexts is unclear. (One wonders if it is even possible to test counterfactual reasoning with a completely nonlinguistic task.) Still, the findings in question offer some evidence for yet another way in which the language one speaks may subtly impact how s/he thinks.

10.5 Action construal

Crosslinguistically, actions are typically encoded via verbs. Yet languages vary remarkably in terms of how their verbs encode actions. One well-known example of this variation is a widespread difference in the encoding of the "manner" and "path" associated with motion verbs. (This phenomenon was touched upon in Chapter 4.) In so-called "satellite-framed" languages like English and other Germanic languages, the manner of motion is encoded in the verb but the path is generally encoded through a verb-external particle. For example, if I describe someone's motion into a building, I might say that s/he "walked into" or "ran into" or "jumped into" the building. In such cases the manner in which s/he moved is denoted verbally, and the direction of his/her motion's path is described via "into". In so-called "verb-framed" languages like Spanish and other Romance languages, the reverse is typically true: the path of the motion is encoded in the verb but the manner is generally encoded outside the main verb. For example in Portuguese, if I were to describe the same person's movement I could say that she *entrou andando* ('entered walking') or *entrou correndo* ('entered running') or *entrou pulando* ('entered jumping').

Given that languages vary in the way their verbs convey actions of motion, one might speculate whether such variation yields differences in the perception or construal of such actions. Do English speakers, for instance, perceive someone walking into a building differently than Portuguese speakers? Does the "satellite-framed" vs. "verb-framed" distinction have any impact on the nonlinguistic conceptualization of events? It is unclear how it might, though some work suggests that these verbal distinctions reflect important differences in the cognitive schemas associated with such verbs (Botne [2005]). Papafragou, Hulbert, and Trueswell (2008) present data on a nonlinguistic event perception task carried out with speakers of a satellite-framed language (English) and speakers of a verb-framed language (Greek). The eye-tracking results of this task suggest that speakers of these languages perceive events similarly, despite the differences in the way the languages encode motion events. Papafragou, Hulbert, and Trueswell's (2008) results did suggest, however, that members of these two groups study scenes in divergent manners after the completion of an event, indicating that the relevant linguistic differences do impact the way Greek and English speakers commit facts associated with events to memory. Regier and Zheng (2007) found evidence that speakers of English, Mandarin, and Arabic all pay similar attention to the endpoints of perceived events, even though the languages differ in the way they frame motion events. (English and Mandarin are satellite-framed languages, while Arabic is verb-framed.) In short, there has been some experimental work that investigated whether the verbal distinction in question impacts the way speakers construe actions, and the results of both studies on this topic do not offer support for the claim that the linguistic features in question actually impact event discrimination during the perception of actions. There are many other sorts of differences in verbal categorization across languages, however, and the absence of strong relativistic effects associated with the verb-framed/satellite-framed distinction does not imply the absence of other kinds of relativistic effects related to the discrimination of actions.

In Everett (2012c), I offer some tentative evidence for relativistic effects associated with the construal of action types. This work addressed the manner in which speakers of English and Karitiâna construe actions with one participant when contrasted with actions with two participants. Before delving into the experiment conducted for the study, some linguistic background is in order.

Typologically, one of the most common divisions between verb types is the distinction between semantically intransitive and semantically transitive verbs. In essence, semantically intransitive verbs are those that require only one participant or actor "on stage" during the event depicted by the verb. For instance, the verb "run" is semantically intransitive since in most usages there is only one actor required, the agent doing the running. This agent may be plural, as in "the people are running", but the only participant required is an agent running. In contrast, semantically transitive verbs typically require at least two participants, frequently one conducting an action and another undergoing an action. The verb "hit" is a prototypical semantically transitive verb since we frequently say that "*X* hit *Y*", i.e. we need someone/something doing the hitting and someone/something being hit. In many languages like English, the distinction between semantically intransitive and semantically transitive verbs is relatively fluid. That is, verbs can often be used in either an intransitive or a transitive sense. In some other languages, all verbs can be used in a semantically intransitive or semantically transitive manner, and so the distinction is not really evident grammatically. This is the case for example in Boumaa Fijian (Dixon [1988]). In some other languages, though, the distinction between these two basic verb types and associated kinds of events has important morphosyntactic consequences. This is true in Dyirbal (Dixon [1994]) or Karitiâna, for example. In the case of the latter language, the grammatical consequences of this distinction include variations in verbal prefixation. As we see in (10.1)-(10.3), semantically intransitive verbs in declarative clauses may be prefixed with *i-*. Semantically transitive verbs cannot be prefixed in this manner, though, and are instead inflected with the morpheme *naka-*, as we see in (10.4)-(10.6).

(10.1)	yn	i-hadnat	'I breathed'	
(10.2)	yn	i-mbik	'I sat'	
(10.3)	yn	i-kysep	'I jumped'	
(10.4)	yn	naka-yt	asyryty	'I ate the banana'
(10.5)	yn	naka-pydn	bola	'I kicked the ball'
(10.6)	yn	naka-mhip	him	'I cooked the meat'

There are numerous other pieces of grammatical evidence for the verbal distinction in question, but the relevant point is this: The Karitiâna language, like many others, reflects a division between two major types of actions, based on the number of participants the actions require. Actions requiring two or more participants are treated differently by the language, when contrasted to actions requiring only one participant. This grammatically reified distinction has a pervasive impact on the form of the language. After all, every time a Karitiâna speaker utters a verb, even a borrowed Portuguese verb, s/he must indicate whether the verb in question is semantically intransitive or semantically transitive.

Does this facet of Karitiâna grammar impact the way its speakers construe events, when contrasted to speakers of a language like English without a rigid verbal distinction of the same kind? In an attempt to answer this question, I conducted a pilot study involving a triad-discrimination task that forced speakers to group abstract actions with each other. Eighteen Karitiâna speakers and

28 English speakers, of various ages, participated in the pilot study. The purpose of the task was simply to test whether English and Karitiâna speakers construe the abstract actions differently, and in a manner that is consistent with the relevant verbal differences in the languages. To that end, the stimuli in the triads presented to the subjects consisted of abstract monochromatic depictions of basic events. The events depicted were of the basic action-chain/ billiard-ball model type that is commonly used to represent actions in cognitive linguistics (Langacker [1991]). For instance a triad might contain two separate depictions of two circles colliding and one depiction of a single circle moving. For each triad, the three separate events were presented on different portions of a computer screen. Two events were depicted in the top half of the screen, and a third event was centered in the bottom half of the screen. Each event was depicted via a video of 5–10 seconds. All three depicted events were of equal duration and were presented simultaneously. Participants were asked to view each triad of events, and to select which of the two top events most closely resembled the bottom event.

Figures 10.2 and 10.3 contain static representations of two of the fifteen triads used. For the triad in Figure 10.2, speakers could group the bottom action with the top-left action, in which case their decision would be based on the number of participants in the depicted action (since the bottom and top-left actions each have two participants). Alternatively they could group the bottom action with the top-right action, in which case their discrimination would be based on the shading of the circles in the depicted events. If the aforementioned Karitiâna verbal distinction impacts speakers' nonlinguistic discrimination of abstract events, we might predict that Karitiâna speakers would be more likely to group the bottom event with the top-left event, when contrasted to English speakers. After all, this sort of action discrimination would show a greater orientation towards the number of action participants. Put differently, it would be the "transitivity-oriented" choice.

For the triad in Figure 10.3, the actions involved black octagons, which moved across the screen alone or collided with another octagon. In this case, speakers could group the bottom action with the top-right one, if they relied on the number of participants to discriminate the depicted events. Conversely, they could group the bottom action with the top-left one, if they relied on octagon size as a basis for action discrimination.

Along with object shading (Figure 10.2) and object size (Figure 10.3), the distinctions between event-types in the fifteen triads were also based on object shape and object direction-of-movement. In all cases, the actions depicted in the triads could be discriminated according to these four factors, *or* according to event transitivity–the number of action participants. In addition to triads

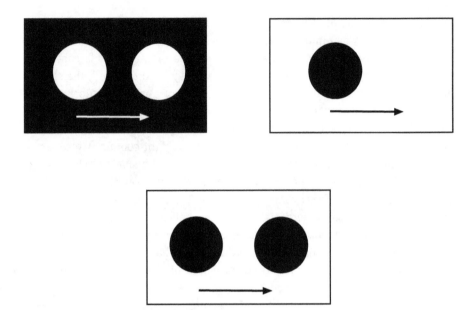

Figure 10.2: One of the fifteen triads employed in Everett (2012c), in which discrimination could be based on a "transitivity-oriented" choice or a color-oriented choice. Arrows here represent direction of movement of a circle in the actual videos.

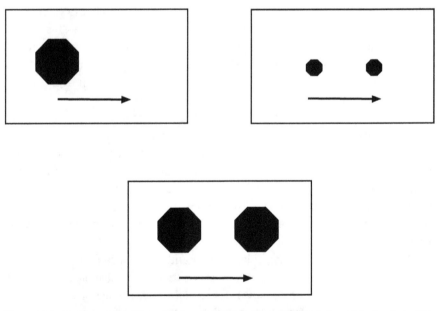

Figure 10.3: Another of the fifteen triads employed in Everett (2012c), in which discrimination could be based on a "transitivity-oriented" choice or a size-oriented choice.

such as those in Figures 10.2 and Figures 10.3, the pilot study subjects viewed multiple interspersed distractor triads of actions in which the number of event participants could not form a basis for discrimination. These filler triads were used to prevent the subjects from developing a task-resolution strategy that could be used for all the triads.

Is their evidence that the basic verbal categorization evident in Karitiâna grammar impacts speakers' discrimination of abstract actions? The results in Everett (2012c) suggested an affirmative answer to this question. For the 28 English speakers, 107 out of 420 discriminations (28 speakers x 15 triads) were based on transitivity, or number of action participants. For the 18 Karitiâna speakers, on the other hand, 103 out of 270 responses (18 speakers x 15 triads) were based on transitivity. In other words, the mean proportion of transitivity-oriented responses for the Karitiâna speakers was 39.3% (s.d. 29.6). The mean proportion of transitivity-oriented responses for the English speakers was 24.5% (s.d. 14.3). The disparity between the groups was significant at the $p<0.05$ level according to a two-tailed t-test contrasting individuals' proportions of transitivity-oriented responses ($t[44]=2.26$, $p =0.029$). Cross-group disparities in action discrimination surfaced for all triad types used. In addition, the results in Everett (2012c) indicated that older more monolingual Karitiâna respondents were particularly likely to discriminate actions according to transitivity, when contrasted with younger more bilingual Karitiânas. In short, the results were consistent with a relativistic account. This is not to suggest, of course, that this issue is resolved. The results simply offer preliminary evidence that the verbal distinction in question may yield disparities in nonlinguistic cognition. To offer more concrete evidence for this claim, results from a wider variety of tasks, conducted among a greater variety of language groups, are required. Replications with speakers of other languages would of course help to rule out the possibility of confounding cultural factors, even though it is unclear which nonlinguistic cultural factors could possibly motivate the divergent patterns of action discrimination we have just described. In contrast, the potential linguistic motivation for the patterns is readily discernible.

10.6 Other explorable topics

There are many potential sorts of linguistic effects on nonlinguistic cognition, aside from those associated with the cognitive domains touched upon in Chapters 4–9. Just a few of these other sorts of effects have been considered in this chapter. We have seen that recent work suggests that linguistic differences may foster nonlinguistic differences in the recall of accidents (Section 10.2), in the perception of emotions (Section 10.3), in some forms of counterfactual reasoning (Section 10.4), and even in the discrimination of certain action types (Section 10.5). This list does not exhaust the remainder of the recent and current work on linguistic relativity. Other recent examples of research related to this topic include Thibodeau and Boroditsky's (2011) work on the influence of linguistic metaphors on social problem-solving strategies and Danziger and Ward's (2010) work on the way in which speakers' implicit associations of others vary in accordance with the language in which the implicit association task is conducted. In the case of the latter study it was found that bilingual Arab Israelis valued Hebrew names more positively when they were surveyed in Hebrew than when they were surveyed in Arabic.

The topics touched on in this chapter have received less of our attention because the relevant research remains in its incipient stages. In the cases of all the topics covered in this chapter, pertinent studies have only been undertaken on three languages at most, and only in one or two languages in the case of some topics. This is in stark contrast to the bulk of the work covered in preceding chapters. Despite the modest number of studies devoted to the topics touched on in this chapter, however, the results of some of the work discussed offer preliminary evidence for striking kinds of relativistic effects. Most noteworthy perhaps is Fausey and Boroditsky's (2011) evidence for linguistic influence on the recall of actors in accidental events. Assuming it is borne out by future work, the effect in question arguably represents one of the more significant ways so far uncovered in which crosslinguistic variability can foster differences in thought.

In addition to offering tentative evidence for linguistic effects on nonlinguistic cognition, the studies discussed in this chapter also hint at the panoply of ways in which the linguistic relativity hypothesis can be explored going forward. Given the extreme diversity of the world's languages, there would appear to be no set upper limit on the potential kinds of relativistic effects. As noted at the outset of this chapter, there are many basic, common differences between the grammars of languages that, in theory anyway, could impact nonlinguistic cognition. As one prominent example of this sort of common difference, consider that languages differ markedly in the extent to which they have a "subject" category. There are many ergative languages in the world (see discussion in Chapter 2) in which the subject category, assuming it exists at all, is quite different from what we call subject in English. Countless articles and books have been written on the topic of ergativity, including many attempts at addressing the cognitive bases of the phenomenon (see Du Bois [1987], Everett [2009], *inter alia*). In contrast, there have been to my knowledge no attempts to examine the possible cognitive *effects* of the phenomenon, i.e. the possibility that ergativity impacts the nonlinguistic cognition of speakers of languages exhibiting the phenomenon. As McGregor (2009) notes in a survey of research on ergativity, future work will hopefully address this possibility.

In addition to straightforwardly grammatical sources, it would appear that one of the most potentially fertile sources of relativistic effects is the range of metaphors relied upon in languages. With the exception of work on temporal perception, most of the research discussed in this book does not tap into the way in which such metaphors potentially impact nonlinguistic thought. Many languages do not share some of the major metaphors so frequently relied upon in English, for example. This was evident when it was noted in Chapter 5 that Aymara does not share the FUTURE IS FORWARD metaphor with English. Yet this is only one of many pervasive metaphors in the English language. Others include UP IS GOOD, DOWN IS BAD, ACTIVITIES ARE CONTAINERS, IDEAS ARE ORGANISMS, THEORIES ARE BUILDINGS, etc. (For more on each of these metaphors, see Lakoff and Johnson [1980].) In fact, the study of metaphorical and metonymic reasoning is a vibrant area of research within cognitive linguistics, and crosslinguistic disparities in linguistic metaphors are surfacing at an ever-increasing rate. Given the growing role of such work, it seems natural that investigations of linguistic relativity might begin to rely more heavily on metaphorical variances across languages. After all, Chapter 5 suggested plainly that variant temporal metaphors influence speakers' nonlinguistic construal of specific stimuli associated with the perception of time.

Future experimental work may demonstrate that a variety of presently unexplored kinds of linguistic relativity exist, or that they do not, or that they exist in very qualified ways only. Only through such work on as-of-yet unexplored topics will we arrive at an adequate understanding of the range of ways in which linguistic features can impact nonlinguistic thought.

11 Conclusion

11.1 What this survey has demonstrated, and what it has not

The research covered in this book provides evidence of a number of kinds of relativistic effects. Some of these effects are of a comparatively weak variety, for instance the marginal effects of grammatical gender categories on the perception of inanimate nouns. Yet some effects could defensibly be judged to have a major impact on human cognition. Recall some of the phenomena that have been our principal foci throughout this book: Spatial relationships and spatial orientation, the construal of time, numerical cognition, the perception of colors, and the categorization of objects and other entities. All of these aspects of cognition are fundamental to human experience. With this fact in mind, any linguistically motivated differences in the way these domains are experienced could legitimately be interpreted as significant relativistic effects. That is, even minor effects on such major facets of cognition could justifiably be taken as powerful examples of the way in which human thought is impacted by linguistic factors.

Nevertheless, as we have stressed since the beginning of this work, it would be misleading to claim that any aspect of human cognitive processes is completely determined by one's native language. Numerous factors besides language shape our mental experience, and of course humans are capable of learning multiple languages and of adopting new linguistic features within their native language. Take the case of monolingual English speakers' default orientation towards time. While they tend to conceive of time as linear and horizontal, due to pervasive spatially based metaphors in their language, their lifelong monolingualism in English does not prevent them from learning to think of time in new ways. As we saw in Chapter 5, the data suggest that when English speakers are familiarized with vertical metaphors for time, their nonlinguistic conceptualization of time changes, at least in the short-term. Analogous arguments could be made for other relativistic effects we have discussed. People can learn new color terms, new number words, new patterns of grammatical gender, etc. And when they do, the way they think about associated concepts changes to some degree, though the magnitude of this degree varies in accordance with myriad factors. In other words, we may be accustomed to certain patterns of thought in part because of our native language, but we are not shackled to these patterns of thought – they are escapable.

The studies we have considered entailed work on a number of languages. These include Kuuk Thaayorre, Karitiâna, Kawahíb, Pirahã, Mundurukú,

Yucatec Maya, Himba, Dani, Tzeltal, Arrernte, Hai‖om, Tamil, English, Mandarin, Japanese, Korean, Yélî Dnye, Dutch, Portuguese, Italian, German, Aymara, Guugu Yimithirr, Longgu, Warwa, and Greek. This list includes the two most widely spoken languages in the world today, Mandarin and English, each of which has hundreds of millions of native speakers. It also includes languages spoken by only several hundred speakers or less, for instance Karitiâna and Kawahíb. The languages in question represent a variety of culture types, from western industrialized societies to small groups of hunter-gatherers autochthonous to Amazonia, Australia, and other regions. The languages are spoken on every continent, and the research we have surveyed includes fieldwork carried out in South American, Central American, North American, European, African, South Asian, Southeast Asian, and Oceanian sites. The languages in question also represent a number of major linguistic families, including Sino-Tibetan, Indo-European, Tupí, Pama-Nyungan, Austronesian, Maya, and Niger-Kordofanian.

While the languages touched upon in this book are diverse in terms of geographic, typological, and familial criteria, it is clear that only a very small fraction of the world's languages have been the focus of research related to the interaction of language and cognition. For that reason alone our knowledge of the extent of linguistic relativity remains inchoate. In addition, as was mentioned in the preceding chapter, there are a limitless number of potential kinds of relativistic effects that have yet to be systematically investigated. In short, the research considered in this book, while covering a number of languages and cognitive domains, likely only represents a starting point for empirically oriented research on this topic.

Some of the relativistic effects we have examined are the result of systematic lexical differences between languages, for instance vis-à-vis color terminology and number words. Others are based on morphosyntactic disparities, for instance the presence/absence of nominal classification systems. Others are based on linguistic disparities that entail both lexical and morphosyntactic factors, for instance differences between major kinds of spatial reference. Others are based on disparate linguistically reified metaphors related to time. Whether lexically, grammatically, or metaphorically based, the linguistic phenomena we have touched upon have been shown to have at least some impact on nonlinguistic thought besides the thought used specifically for the formulation of language. Put differently, we have found evidence for the "structural relativity" (Lucy [1992a]) described in Chapter 1.

As we also noted in Chapter 1, relativistic effects can be categorized according to the manner in which they impact thought, not just in accordance with the cognitive domains they are associated with. Various approaches to such a categorization could be taken. Reines and Prinz (2009) and Wolff and Holmes (2011) offer two compatible approaches, which we will rely on in this discussion.

Reines and Prinz (2009) posit the existence of four basic types of linguistic effects on thought, which they refer to as "Whorfianism". One of these types is a radical deterministic sort that suggests that thought is entirely dependent on language, and as we have noted this sort is not seriously entertained by most scholars. Another is a more modest sort according to which language effects thought only while words are being used. This sort of "online" relativity is akin to Slobin's (1996) "thinking for speaking", and as we have stated it is not considered linguistic relativity proper according to the framework being adopted here. Continuing with Reines and Prinz' (2009) list, there are two remaining sorts of linguistic relativity, which we might consider the two principal types of linguistic relativity proper ("structural relativity"). These are "ontological" and "habitual" linguistic relativity, respectively. The former category refers to linguistic effects that predispose speakers to "organize the world into categories" of a particular sort (2009:1029). In some cases these ontological effects could potentially allow reasoning of a particular kind that would be difficult or impossible to achieve without the categories in question. Such effects might be termed "augmenting" ontological effects (Wolff and Holmes [2011]). In other cases the categories could interfere with a given sort of cognitive processing, in which case we might refer to them as "meddling" ontological effects (Wolff and Holmes [2011]).

In the case of "habitual" linguistic relativity, the potential effects are less pronounced. Such effects are not expected to augment or meddle with basic thought processes in a deep-seated fashion. They *are* expected to result in tendencies or patterns of thought, however, as frequent linguistic patterns cause speakers to adopt habitual ways of thinking in relevant nonlinguistic cognitive domains. These habitual thought patterns could result in certain properties becoming relatively salient during thought, in which case language may function as a "spotlight" (Wolff and Holmes 2011). In other cases, linguistic habits could serve to prime certain kinds of thinking at the expense of others. Put differently, language might serve as an "inducer" for certain kinds of thought (Wolff and Holmes [2011]).

In the light of the categorizations of relativistic effects evident in Reines and Prinz (2009) and Wolff and Holmes (2011), we can retroactively classify the major effects surveyed in this book. In Chapter 7 we saw that color terms seem to hinder the perception of differences between similarly labeled hues. Such lexical effects might best be considered meddling ontological effects. In Chapter 6 we observed that number terms enhance the discrimination of numerical categories, and so such effects might be considered augmenting ontological effects. In contrast, in Chapter 5 we observed that dissimilar metaphors for time prime speakers to react to vertically and horizontally oriented images in disparate ways. Such priming effects might be termed inducing habitual effects. Other inducing habitual effects would include those observed in Chapter 9, where we saw that gendered language primes speakers to ascribe gendered characteristics to non-gendered items. Other effects could be considered spotlighting habitual effects. Based on the studies surveyed in Chapter 4, it appears that the habitual usage of geocentric language spotlights geocentric solutions to spatial orientation problems. In a related manner, we observed in Chapter 8 that nominal classification systems spotlight similarities between certain objects and substances.

While admittedly a bit reductionist, such a categorization is useful in drawing attention to certain patterns in the extant relativistic effects. For instance, the classification adopted in the preceding paragraphs suggests that the habitual effects are associated with concrete stimuli, as in e.g. the differentiated categorization of objects according to genders or nominal classifiers. Judging from our survey, abstract facets of cognition are more susceptible to stronger ontological relativistic effects. As we suggested in the conclusion of Chapter 9, one potential explanation for this tendency is that abstract aspects of human experience are more malleable and shapeable by external influences. They are apparently more susceptible to linguistic structuring or restructuring. For instance, the color spectrum can be broken up with only two basic color terms or with a dozen. Either choice does not conflict with the color stimuli abstractly extracted from physical entities actually interacted with by humans. In contrast, biological sex is much less abstract, and less continuously perceived. Most sexed entities can safely be categorized as being either male or female, and non-sexed entities clearly do not actually fall into one of these categories. We might expect then that the conceptualization of objects, while subtly influenced by the grammatical gender of associated nouns in some cases, would not be strongly impacted by the relevant grammatical gender categories. After all, speakers' actual experience with the objects in question can more concretely inform their conceptualization of the objects, even in the face of conflicting yet more abstract information provided by a system of grammatical gender.

Regardless of how one chooses to classify the kinds of documented relativistic effects, it is clear that they differ in essential ways. In addition, they differ in the extent to which they have been substantiated. The decision to dispute or discard one sort of effect does not require the rejection of others, and while the effects are clearly inter-related, they are not interdependent. The existence of each category of effect must be considered on its own merits. Acceptance of any of the kinds of relativistic effects, however, implies acceptance of the linguistic relativity hypothesis in one form or another, however weak.

Whether relativistic effects are of the ontological or habitual variety, their discovery and further exploration have much to teach us. While discussions of relativity are often centered on seemingly more dramatic ontological sorts of effects, we believe that habitual sorts of effects are at least as informative. Each sort of relativistic effect uncovered plays some role in the greater elucidation of human thought processes. Extreme ontological effects allow us to map the extremes of variation in human cognition, and help us to better understand the range of diversity of thought across human cultures. Less extreme habitual effects also play a role in illuminating this diversity of thought. Just as crucially, though, they enable us to better understand the way that nonlinguistic thought works, specifically what sorts of factors it is impacted by. As Casasanto (2008:76) suggests: "If people who talk differently form correspondingly different mental representations as a consequence, then mental representations must depend, in part, on these aspects of linguistic experience. If discovering the origin and structure of our mental representations is the goal, then cross-linguistic cognitive differences can be informative even if they are subtle and even if their effects are largely unconscious."

In sum, the understanding of radical and subtle relativistic effects can play a vital role in growing our understanding of the structure of human thought processes and in growing our understanding of the diversity of thought within our species.

The primary purpose of this book was to delineate in some detail cases of linguistic relativity that have been empirically corroborated in recent research. One of the consequences of this focus was the setting aside of many important yet tangential topics. Most notably, perhaps, we have not discussed in any substantive manner the mechanisms through which linguistic features may come to impact nonlinguistic cognition, though we have noted that it is difficult to envision how cross-cultural differences in thought could be transmitted and maintained across generations without being conveyed linguistically (see Chapter 4). While there are various potential mechanisms through which relativistic effects may be enacted, it is worth offering some basic remarks on how such effects may crop up.

Suppose someone speaks a language with default geocentric spatial reference. It follows that whenever s/he is observing a spatial relationship between some entities, s/he must pay some attention to the geocentric configuration of that relationship. For instance, if s/he is watching a soccer game, s/he should note where each team's goal is located cardinally with reference to the other –

north, south, east, west, or some other cardinal type of direction. The reason such an observer would be forced to pay attention to such facts is that, should s/he choose to speak about the game at any point, her/his language would require that the information be encoded verbally. More generally, linguistic requirements cause speakers of geocentric languages to mentally encode certain aspects of spatial relationships so that those relationships can be subsequently described in a fluent manner. If speakers did not adhere to these requirements, they would simply be unable to produce fluent descriptions regarding the witnessed events. Throughout their lifetime, such speakers will inevitably gain a lot of practice mentally encoding such geocentric relationships for the purpose of producing fluent language. Such relationships will inevitably become relatively salient for them, when contrasted to speakers of languages that do not rely on geocentric language to the same degree.

In the words of Levinson (2003:303), we might consider such linguistic effects on cognition to be cases of "experience for speaking", since one gains experience with certain ways of thinking, i.e. develops certain mental habits, because of the exigencies of one's native language. If features of a person's language create habitual patterns of focus or construal during everyday experience, it is not unreasonable to assume that these cognitive habits could then foster default patterns of conceptualization. In addition, if the linguistic features in question are not present in all languages, then we can assume that such crosslinguistic variance may yield cross-group disparities in the relevant default patterns of conceptualization. The evidence we have surveyed supports this assumption. Note that this is quite different from suggesting that members of different groups cannot think in the same ways. As Hanks (1996:234) perspicaciously notes in his discussion of linguistic relativity, "The key issue is not whether language form and use determine what people CAN think or experience, but rather the extent to which they influence what people usually DO think and experience." We assume that, with enough practice, all groups are capable of the same forms of thought. Simply put, though, some languages necessitate certain kinds of practice with given mental exercises, such as noting cardinal directions or recognizing differences between quantities, while other languages do not. This differentiated practice or experience leads to cross-group disparities in the performance of certain nonlinguistic cognitive endeavors.

Such cognitive effects resulting from the habitual practice of mental tasks required by one's language would surface first during ontogeny. As children grow up they are forced to pay selectively greater attention to certain facets of their experience, when contrasted to children speaking very different languages. By an early age they may have, for instance, already honed certain cognitive abilities due to the mental practice enforced by their native language. It is interesting to note, for example, that even young Kuuk Thaayorre children outperform English-speaking adults on dead reckoning tasks (Boroditsky [2011]), most plausibly because their language has frequently forced them to pay attention to cardinal directions.

The experience-for-speaking account addresses one of the major mechanisms that enables linguistic dissimilarities to yield nonlinguistic cognitive differences across populations. Other associated mechanisms are offered in the literature. (See Majid et al. [2004:113] for one take.) While there are a variety of proposals on the sorts of ways in which linguistic dissimilarities may gradually result in differences of thought, it is fair to say that more work needs to be done to clearly establish the processes through which relativistic effects come into existence. This is true, at least in part, because the way that such effects develop likely varies in accordance with the kinds of effects in question.

In addition to the more careful exploration of the potential mechanisms through which relativistic effects arise, future research will likely continue to explore the existence of a variety of such effects, in an ever-growing number of speech communities. Since relativistic effects owe themselves to differences in linguistic practices, they may prove to exist even among speakers of the same language, as long as some aspect of those speakers' linguistic practices varies significantly. For instance, in some languages several spatial frames of reference may be routinely used, yet individual speakers may vary in accordance with which frame of reference they most frequently rely on. In some cases, then, the exploration of relativistic effects may require the careful consideration of variation across speakers within the same speech community.[66]

In a related vein, researchers will likely continue to explore how cultural factors that are not associated with language or linguistic thought can foster cognitive variance. Of course language can be considered one manifestation of culture, and linguistic and nonlinguistic culture are intertwined.[67] To the extent possible, though, researchers may be able to more directly address the role of nonlinguistic cultural factors in fostering cross-population cognitive variation. Such work could help to more clearly establish the ways in which linguistic thought, nonlinguistic cultural thought, and other forms of thought,

---

66 In fact this sort of "inter-speaker" relativity has already been observed across sub-groups of a speech community (see Pederson et al. [1998:584]). There may also be cases of "intra-speaker" (Kay [1996]) relativity, according to which a given speaker's thoughts vary in accordance with the linguistic features they rely on, in context-dependent ways.

67 This perspective has been expressed in detail in D. Everett (2012). See in particular Chapter 10 of that work, in which the relationship between linguistic and nonlinguistic culture is explicitly addressed.

all interact. Surely this is an ambitious project with no set timetable, and in some ways the issue is intractable. Yet the results covered in this book offer some hope that we can in fact dissociate the role of linguistic effects on cognition from other sorts of cultural effects.

Debates regarding linguistic relativity have sometimes taken on simplistic tones in the past. People have in some cases assumed that the acceptance of linguistic relativity precludes the belief that there are shared fundamental aspects of human cognition that place pressures on the shape language takes. In fact, few would doubt such pressures, as evidenced by well-known crosslinguistic tendencies (see Chapter 2). Put differently, the view that nonlinguistic cognition impacts language is certainly not irreconcilable with the view that language impacts nonlinguistic cognition. Furthermore, neither of these views is incompatible with the notion that culture (or more precisely nonlinguistic aspects of culture) may impact nonlinguistic cognition and language, and may itself be impacted by facets of nonlinguistic cognition and also by linguistic factors. In this book we have simply considered one sort of interaction between these occasionally dissociable components of the human experience, namely the influence of language on nonlinguistic cognition. This focus does not imply, however, that other sorts of interactions between language, culture, and thought do not exist. Much work on these interactions has already been undertaken, and future work will likely more carefully detail the nature of these interactions.

One recurring theme that is evident in this discussion, and in this book in general, is the need for more research of the kind surveyed. As evidenced by the recency of most of the studies we have discussed, empirical work on the linguistic relativity hypothesis is both nascent and growing rapidly. At any given point there are numerous field linguists and anthropologists conducting studies of remote languages and cultures. As more of these field researchers become familiar with experimental methods, and also become equipped with tools such as software for running psychological tasks, they may be able to conduct important experiments on this fecund topic. Conducting such experiments is, after all, the easy part of this sort of work. The more laborious part is gaining the sufficient familiarity with a given language and culture required to generate testable hypotheses related to linguistic relativity. Hopefully more fieldworkers will begin to take a serious interest in these issues, to the point that they generate their own experimental work or collaborate with cognitive psychologists or other researchers familiar with the appropriate methods. And while it may seem quixotic to assume, it is possible that such experimental work could in fact come to represent a standard portion of fieldworkers' research agendas. Through such work, such researchers could play a vital role in more clearly establishing which facets of human cognition vary in accordance with, or are contingent upon, particular linguistic features. After all, this research must ultimately be informed by an in-depth awareness of the languages, cultures, and ecologies of the relevant people groups. Through the continued involvement of field researchers, we may be able to develop a rich vault of data gathered across numerous speech communities. These data could play a pivotal role in informing emerging ideas about the ways in which humans conceive of and perceive their world.

Throughout most of this book, we have maintained an arguably artificial distinction between language and thought. Like the aforementioned distinction between language and culture, this artificial division is probably unavoidable in such discussions, and is heuristically useful. It is worth mentioning, though, that this entire issue could be framed differently. Rather than being concerned with the influence of language on thought, we might frame the issue in manners such as the following: How inextricable are linguistic and nonlinguistic thought? How closely related are they? Which kinds of nonlinguistic thought are contingent upon which forms of linguistic thought? Now that it has been established that linguistic and nonlinguistic thought are in fact closely related, at least in some cases, we might claim that the goal of research on this topic is to better clarify the nature of the relationship between different kinds of thought. While we have maintained the tradition of speaking about the effects of language on thought, for the sake of convenience and consistency with the literature, alternate phrasing of the central issue in question is certainly possible. Regardless of the phraseology, however, at its core the issue itself remains the same: Does the language one speaks affect how s/he thinks, even when not using language?

11.2 The reality of linguistic relativity

The research we have discussed suggests that linguistic relativity is very much a reality, though we stress again that the acceptance of this fact by no means implies that speakers of different languages have incommensurable worldviews. Their thoughts are not completely determined by their native language(s). Yet it also seems fair to say that a number of relativistic effects we have considered represent major cognitive variation. Recall for example that Nicaraguan homesigners, Mundurukú speakers, and Pirahã speakers all struggle with the exact recognition of quantities greater than three, most likely for linguistic reasons. Even in such extreme cases, though, there is no evidence that the linguistically motivated challenges to numerical cognition cannot be circumvented, though circumvention may require a shift in the linguistic practices of the people in question.

While we believe the evidence surveyed points clearly to the existence of linguistic relativity, we should underscore one last time that this conclusion is by no means inconsistent with the acceptance of some universal features of human thought. In the light of the evidence covered in this book and elsewhere, it is reasonable to maintain that some aspects of human thought are relative and not governed by universal principles. Yet no influential contemporary researchers suggest that no aspects of cognition are universal. In our discussions of color perception and numerical cognition, for example, we saw ample evidence for both universal and relative patterns in the relevant data. From our perspective, though, it is only by understanding the extent of cognitive variation across human populations that we can better define which aspects of human cognition are truly universal. Rather than being mutually exclusive enterprises, then, the exploration of cognitive universality and linguistic relativity are synergistic endeavors. The exploration of each is not possible without the exploration of the other, and certainly the acceptance of one does not preclude the acceptance of the other unless one subscribes to some sort of radical cognitive universalism or radical relativism. Hopefully discussions of this issue have now progressed to the point that people will be less likely to espouse extreme views according to which language does not impact nonlinguistic thought outside of "thinking for speaking", or according to which language determines speakers' thoughts to the extent that speakers of different languages are incapable of thinking in similar ways.

We have seen evidence that cases of linguistic relativity may owe themselves to systematic lexical differences between languages, or to grammatical differences, or to disparate metaphors. In addition, other facets of linguistic practice such as co-speech gestures and orthographic patterns appear to impact thought. In short, not only is there evidence for linguistic relativity across a number of languages and cognitive domains, there is also evidence that relativistic effects may result from any number of kinds of variation in linguistic practice.

The central question addressed by this book is whether differences between languages affect the nonlinguistic cognition of their speakers. We have found strong evidence for a positive answer to this question. Nevertheless, many of relativistic effects we have discussed are subtle in nature. Still, the majority of the data we have examined suggest that systematic differences in linguistic practice can and do create divergent cognitive habits. And like all habits, they may be hard to break.

References

Aarsleff, Hans. 1988. Introduction. In Wilhelm von Humboldt (ed.), *On Language: The diversity of human language structure and its influence on the mental development of mankind* (Translated by Peter Heath), Cambridge, UK: Cambridge University Press.

Aarsleff, Hans. 1982. *From Locke to Saussure: Essays on the study of language and intellectual history*. Minneapolis: University of Minnesota Press.

Aikhenvald, Alexandra. 2004. *Evidentiality*. Oxford: Oxford University Press.

Aikhenvald, Alexandra. 2000. *Classifiers: A typology of noun categorization devices*. Oxford: Oxford University Press.

Arbib, Michael A. 2005. The mirror system hypothesis stands but the framework is much enriched. *Behavioral and Brain Sciences* 28 (2). 149–159.

Arnett, Jeffrey J. 2008. The neglected 95: Why American psychology needs to become less American. *American Psychologist* 63 (7). 602–614.

Astuti, Rita, Gregg Solomon & Susan Carey. 2004. Constraints on conceptual development: A case study of the acquisition of folkbiological and folksociological knowledge in Madagascar. *Monographs of the Society for Research in Child Development* 69 (3). 1–135.

Atkinson, Quentin D. 2011. Phonemic diversity supports a serial founder effect model of language expansion from Africa. *Science* 332 (6027). 346–349.

Atkinson, Quentin D., Andrew Meade, Chris Venditti, Simon Greenhill, J. Simon & Mark Pagel. 2008. Languages evolve in punctuational bursts. *Science* 319 (5863). 588.

Atran, Scott. 1993. Ethnobiological classification-principles of categorization of plants and animals in traditional societies. *Current Anthropology* 34 (2). 195–198.

Atran, Scott & Douglas Medin. 2008. *The native mind and the cultural construction of nature*. Cambridge, MA: MIT Press.

Atran, Scott, Douglas Medin, Elizabeth Lynch, Valentina Vapnarsky, Edilberto Ucan Ek' & Paulo Sousa. 2001. Folkbiology doesn't come from folkpsychology: Evidence from Yukatek Maya in cross-cultural perspective. *Journal of Cognition and Culture* 1 (1). 3–42.

Au, Terry K. 1984. Counterfactuals: Reply to Alfred Bloom. *Cognition* 17 (3). 289–302.

Au, Terry K. 1983. Chinese and English counterfactuals: The Sapir-Whorf hypothesis revisited. *Cognition* 15 (1–3). 155–187.

Baker, Robin. 1989. *Human navigation and magnetoreception*. Manchester, England: Manchester University Press.

Batschelet, Edward. 1981. *Circular statistics in biology*. London: Academic Press.

Beddor, Patrice & Winfred Strange. 1982. Cross-language study of perception of the oral-nasal distinction. *The Journal of the Acoustical Society of America* 71 (6). 1551–1561.

Belacchi, Carmen & Rorbert Cubelli. 2011. Implicit knowledge of grammatical gender in preschool children. *Journal of Psycholinguistic Research* 41 (4). 295–310.

Bender, Andrea & Sieghard Beller. 2011. Cultural variation in numeration systems and their mapping onto the mental number line. *Journal of Cross-Cultural Psychology* 42 (4). 579–597.

Bender, Andrea, Edwin Hutchins & Douglas Medin. 2010. Anthropology in cognitive science. *Topics in Cognitive Science* 2 (3). 374–385.

Berlin, Brent. 1992. *Ethnobiological classification*. Princeton: Princeton University Press.

Berlin, Brent & Paul Kay. 1969. *Basic color terms: Their universality and evolution*. Berkeley: University of California Press.

Bloom, Alfred. 1984. *Caution–the words you use may affect what you say: A response to Au. Cognition* 17 (3). 275–287.

Bloom, Alfred. 1981. *The linguistic shaping of thought: A study in the impact of language on thinking in china and the west.* Hillsdale, New Jersey: L. Erlbaum.

Boas, Franz. 1966. (1911.). *Handbook of American Indian languages.* Lincoln, NE: University of Nebraska Press.

Bohnemeyer, Jurgen & Christel Stolz. 2006. Spatial reference in Yukatek Maya: A survey. In Stephen Levinson & David Wilkins (eds.), *Grammars of space: Explorations in cognitive diversity*, 273–310. Cambridge, UK: Cambridge University Press.

Boloh, Yves & Laure Ibernon. 2010. Gender attribution and gender agreement in 4- to 10-year-old French children. *Cognitive Development* 25 (1). 1–25.

Boroditsky, Lera. 2011. How language shapes thought. *Scientific American*, February. 63–65.

Boroditsky, Lera. 2001. Does language shape thought? Mandarin and English speakers conceptions of time. *Cognitive Psychology* 43 (1). 1–22.

Boroditsky, Lera. 2000. Metaphoric structuring: Understanding time through spatial metaphors. *Cognition* 75 (1). 1–28.

Boroditsky, Lera, Orly Fuhrman & Kelly McCormick. 2011. Do English and Mandarin speakers think about time differently? *Cognition* 118 (1). 126–132.

Boroditsky, Lera & Alice Gaby. 2010. Remembrances of times east: Absolute spatial representations of time in an Australian aboriginal community. *Psychological Science* 21 (11). 1635–1639.

Boroditsky, Lera & Michael Ramscar. 2002. The roles of body and mind in abstract thought. *Psychological Science* 13 (2). 185–188.

Boroditsky, Lera, Lauren Schmidt & Webb Phillips. 2003. Sex, syntax, and semantics. In Dedre Gentner & Susan Goldin-Meadow (eds.), *Language in mind: Advances in the study of language and cognition*, 61–80. Cambridge, MA: MIT Press.

Botne, Robert. 2005. Cognitive schemas and motion verbs: Coming and going in Chindali (eastern Bantu). *Cognitive Linguistics* 16 (1). 43–80.

Bouhuys, Antoinette L., Erwin Geerts & Peter Paul A. Mersch. 1997. Relationship between perception of facial emotions and anxiety in clinical depression: Does anxiety-related perception predict persistence of depression? *Journal of Affective Disorders* 43 (3). 213–223.

Bowerman, Melissa. 1996a. Learning how to structure space for language: A crosslinguistic perspective. In Paul Bloom, Mary Peterson, Lynn Nadel & Merrill Garrett (eds.), *Language and Space*, 385–436. Cambridge: MA: MIT Press.

Bowerman, Melissa. 1996b. The origins of children's spatial semantic categories: Cognitive vs. linguistics determinants. In John Gumperz & Stephen Levinson (eds.), *Rethinking linguistics relativity*, 145–176. Cambridge, UK: Cambridge University Press.

Bowerman, Melissa. 1994. From universal to language-specific in early grammatical development. *Philosophical Transactions: Biological Sciences* 346 (1315). 37–45.

Bowerman, Melissa. 1978. The acquisition of word meaning: an investigation into some current conflicts. In Natalie Waterson & Catharine Snow (eds.), *The development of communication*, 263–287. New York: John Wiley.

Bowerman, Melissa & Soonja Choi. 2001. Shaping meanings for language: Universal and language specific in the acquisition of spatial semantic categories. In Melissa Bowerman & Stephen Levinson (eds.), *Language acquisition and conceptual development*, 475–511. Cambridge, UK: Cambridge University Press.

Bowerman, Melissa & Stephen Levinson (eds.). 2001. *Language acquisition and conceptual development*. Cambridge, UK: Cambridge University Press.

Bowerman, Melissa & Eric Pederson. 1992. Topological relations picture series. In Stephen Levinson (ed.), *Space stimuli kit 1.2*, 51. Nijmegen: Max Planck Institute for Psycholinguistics.

Boyd, Robert & Peter Richerson. 2005. *The origin and evolution of cultures*. New York: Oxford University Press.

Boyd, Robert, Peter Richerson & Joseph Henrich. 2011. The cultural niche: Why social learning is essential for human adaptation. *Proceedings of the National Academy of Sciences of the United States of America* 108 (Supplement 2). 10918–10925.

Brooks, Alison & Catherine Smith. 1987. Ishango revisited: New age determinations and cultural interpretations. *The African Archaeological Review* 5 (1). 65–78.

Brown, Penelope. 2001. Learning to talk about motion UP and DOWN in Tzeltal: is there a language-specific bias for verb learning? In Melissa Bowerman & Stephen Levinson (eds.), *Language acquisition and conceptual development*, 512–543. Cambridge, UK: Cambridge University Press.

Brown, Penelope & Stephen Levinson. 1993. "Uphill" and "downhill" in Tzeltal. *Journal of Linguistic Anthropology* 3 (1). 46–74.

Brown, Roger & Eric Lenneberg. 1954. A study in language and cognition. *Journal of Abnormal and Social Psychology* 49 (3). 454–462.

Brysbaert, Marc, Wim Fias & M. P. Noël. 1998. The Whorfian hypothesis and numerical cognition: Is 'twenty-four' processed in the same way as 'four-and-twenty'? *Cognition* 66 (1). 51–77.

Butterworth, Brian, Robert Reeve, Fiona Reynolds & Delyth Lloyd. 2008. Numerical thought with and without words: Evidence from indigenous Australian children. *Proceedings of the National Academy of Sciences of the United States of America* 105 (35). 13179–13184.

Bybee, Joan L. 2001. *Phonology and language use*. New York: Cambridge University Press.

Bybee, Joan L. 1985. *Morphology: A study of the relation between meaning and form*. Amsterdam: John Benjamins.

Carey, Susan. 2009. *The origin of concepts*. Oxford: Oxford University Press.

Carey, Susan. 1985. *Conceptual change in childhood*. Cambridge, MA: MIT Press.

Casasanto, Daniel. 2008. Who's afraid of the big bad Whorf? Crosslinguistic differences in temporal language and thought. *Language Learning* 58 (1). 63–79.

Casasanto, Daniel. 2005. Crying "Whorf". *Science* 307 (5716). 1721–1722.

Casasanto, Daniel & Lera Boroditsky. 2008. Time in the mind: Using space to think about time. *Cognition* 106 (2). 579–593.

Casasanto, Daniel & Lera Boroditsky. 2003. Do we think about time in terms of space? Proceedings of the 25th Annual Meeting of the Cognitive Science Society Conference, 216–221.

Casasanto, Daniel, Lera Boroditsky, Webb Phillips, Jesse Greene, Shima Goswami, Simon Bocanegra-Thiel, Ilia Santiago-Diaz, Olga Fotokopoulu, Ria Pita & David Gil. 2004. How deep are effects of language on thought? Time estimation in speakers of English, Indonesian, Greek, and Spanish. *Proceedings of the 26th Annual Cognitive Society Conference*, 575–580.

Chan, Ting Ting & Benjamin Bergen. 2005. Writing direction influences spatial cognition. *Proceedings of the 27th Annual Cognitive Society Conference*, 32–46.

Chen, Jenn-Yeu. 2007. Do Chinese and English speakers think about time differently? Failure of replicating Boroditsky (2001). *Cognition* 104 (2). 427–436.

Chen, Jenn-Yeu & Jui Jui Su. 2011. Differential sensitivity to the gender of a person by English and Chinese speakers. *Journal of Psycholinguistic Research* 40 (3). 195–203.

Chen, Keith. n.d. The effect of language on economic behavior: Evidence from savings rates, health behaviors, and retirement assets. Manuscript.

Chomsky, Noam. 1995. *The minimalist program*. Cambridge, MA: MIT Press.

Chomsky, Noam. 1980. *Rules and representations*. New York: Columbia University Press.

Chomsky, Noam. 1965. *Aspects of the theory of syntax*. Cambridge, MA: MIT Press.

Christiansen, Morten, Nick Chater & Florencia Reali. 2009. Restrictions on biological adaptation in language evolution. *Proceedings of the National Academy of Sciences of the United States of America* 106 (4). 1015–1020.

Christmann, Hans Helmut. 1967. *Beiträge zur Geschichte der These vom Weltbild der Sprache*. Wiesbaden: Franz Steiner.

Chun, L. 1997. A cognitive approach to UP metaphors in English and Chinese: What do they reveal about the English mind and the Chinese mind? Research degree progress report for Hong Kong Polytechnic University, 125–140.

Church, Timothy, Marcia Katigbak, Alicia del Prado, José Valdez-Medina, Lilia Miramontes & Fernando Ortiz. 2006. A cross-cultural study of trait self-enhancement, explanatory variables, and adjustment. *Journal of Research in Personality* 40 (6). 1169–1201.

Clark, Herbert. 1973. Space, time, semantics and the child. In Timothy Moore (ed.), *Cognitive development and the acquisition of language*, 27–63. New York: Academic Press.

Clark, Herbert & Eve V. Clark. 1977. *Psychology and language: An introduction to psycholinguistics*. New York: Harcourt Brace Jovanovich.

Clarke, Mark, Ann Losoff, Margaret McCracken & David Rood. 1984. Linguistic relativity and sex/gender studies: Epistemological and methodological considerations. *Language Learning* 34 (2). 47–64.

Cohen, Emma, Emily Burdett, Nicola Knight & Justin Barrett. 2011. Cross-cultural similarities and differences in Person-Body reasoning: Experimental evidence from the United Kingdom and Brazilian Amazon. *Cognitive Science* 35 (7). 1282–1304.

Comrie, Bernard. 1985. *Tense*. New York: Cambridge University Press.

Comrie, Bernard. 1981. *Language universals and linguistic typology: Syntax and morphology*. Chicago: University of Chicago Press.

Comrie, Bernard. 1976. *Aspect: An introduction to the study of verbal aspect and related problems*. Cambridge, UK: Cambridge University Press.

Comrie, Bernard, Stephen Matthews & Maria Polinsky. 2003. *The atlas of languages*. New York: Quarto.

Condry, Kirsten & Elizabeth Spelke. 2008. The development of language and abstract concepts: The case of natural number. *Journal of Experimental Psychology: General* 137 (1). 22–38.

Conklin, Harold. 1964. Hanunóo colour categories. In Dell Hymes (ed.), *Language in culture and society*, 189–192. New York: Harper & Row.

Conklin, Harold. 1957. Hanunóo agriculture, a report on an integral system of shifting cultivation in the Philippines. *United Nations Development Papers* 12, 209.

Corballis, Michael C. 2003. From mouth to hand: Gesture, speech, and the evolution of right-handedness. *Behavioral and Brain Sciences* 26 (2). 199–208.

Corbett, Greville G. 1991. *Gender*. Cambridge, UK: Cambridge University Press.

Croft, William. 2001. *Radical construction grammar: Syntactic theory in typological perspective*. Oxford: Oxford University Press.

Cubelli, Roberto, Daniela Paolieri, Lorella Lotto & Remo Job. 2011. The effect of grammatical gender on object categorization. *Journal of Experimental Psychology: Learning, Memory, and Cognition* 37 (2). 449–460.

Danziger, Eve. 2011. Distinguishing three-dimensional forms from their mirror-images: Whorfian results from users of intrinsic frames of linguistic reference. *Language Sciences* 33 (6). 853–867.

Danziger, Shai & Robert Ward. 2010. Language changes implicit associations between ethnic groups and evaluation in bilinguals. *Psychological Science* 21 (6). 799–800.

Dasen, Pierre & Ramesh Mishra. 2010. *Development of geocentric spatial language and cognition*. Cambridge, UK: Cambridge University Press.

Davidoff, Jules, Ian Davies & Debi Roberson. 1999. Colour categories in a stone-age tribe. *Nature* 398 (6724). 203–204.

Davies, Ian & Greville Corbett. 1997. A cross-cultural study of colour grouping: Evidence for weak linguistic relativity. *British Journal of Psychology* 88 (3). 493–517.

de Heinzelen, Jean. 1962. Ishango. *Scientific American*, June. 105–116.

Dehaene, Stanislas. 1997. *The number sense: How the mind creates mathematics*. New York: Oxford University Press.

Dehaene, Stanislas, Serge Bossini & Pascal Giraux. 1993. The mental representation of parity and number magnitude. *Journal of Experimental Psychology: General* 122 (3). 371–396.

Dahaene, Stanislas, Véronique Izard, Elizabeth Spelke & Pierre Pica. 2008. Log or linear? Distinct intuitions of the number scale in western and Amazonian indigene cultures. *Science* 320 (5880). 1217–1220.

Dehaene, Stanislas, Elizabeth Spelke, Philippe Pinel, R. Stanescu & S. Tsivkin. 1999. Sources of mathematical thinking: Behavioral and brain-imaging evidence. *Science* 284 (5416). 970–974.

Derbyshire, Desmond C. 1979. *Hixkaryana*. Lingua Descriptive Studies, Volume 1. Amsterdam: Croom Helm.

Deutscher, Guy. 2010. You are what you speak. *New York Times Magazine*, August 26.

Devitt, Michael & Kim Sterelny. 1987. *Language and reality: An introduction to the philosophy of language*. Cambridge, MA: MIT Press.

Dils, Alexia & Lera Boroditsky. 2010. Visual motion aftereffect from understanding motion language. *Proceedings of the National Academy of Sciences of the United States of America* 107 (37). 16396–16400.

Dixon, Robert M. W. 2004. *The Jarawara language of southern Amazonia*. Oxford: Oxford University Press.

Dixon, Robert M. W. 1994. *Ergativity*. Cambridge, UK: Cambridge University Press.

Dixon, Robert M. W. 1988. *A grammar of Boumaa Fijian*. Chicago: University of Chicago Press.

Dixon, Robert M. W. 1972. *The Dyirbal language of north Queensland*. Cambridge, UK: Cambridge University Press.

Dowker, Ann, Sheila Bala & Delyth Lloyd. 2008. Linguistic influences on mathematical development: How important is the transparency of the counting system? *Philosophical Psychology* 21 (4). 523–538.

Drivonikou, Gilda V., Paul Kay, Terry Regier, Richard Ivry, Aubrey Gilbert, Anna Franklin & Ian Davies. 2007. Further evidence that Whorfian effects are stronger in the right visual field than the left. *Proceedings of the National Academy of Sciences of the United States of America* 104 (3). 1097–1102.

Dryer, Matthew S. 2003. Significant and non-significant implicational universals. *Linguistic Typology* 7 (1). 108–128.

Dryer, Matthew S. 1997. On the 6-way Word Order Typology. *Studies in Language* 21 (1). 69–103.

Du Bois, John W. 1987. The discourse basis of ergativity. *Language* 63 (4). 805–855.

Dunn, Michael, Simon Greenhill, Stephen Levinson & Russell Gray. 2011. Evolved structure of language shows lineage-specific trends in word-order universals. *Nature* 473 (7345). 79–82.

Eastman, Carol M. 1975. *Aspects of language and culture*. San Francisco: Chandler & Sharp.

Eddington, David. 2009. *Quantitative and experimental linguistics*. Munich: Lincom Europa.

Ekman, Paul. 1999. Basic emotions. In Tim Dalgleish & Mick Power (eds.), *The handbook of cognition and emotion*, 45–60. Sussex: John Wiley & Sons.

Ekman, Paul. 1992. An argument for basic emotions. *Cognition & Emotion* 6 (3/4). 169–200.

Ekman, Paul & Wallace Friesen. 1971. Constants across cultures in face and emotion. *Journal of Personality and Social Psychology* 17 (2). 124–143.

Elfenbein, Hillary & Nalini Ambady. 2003. Universals and cultural differences in recognizing emotions. *Current Directions in Psychological Science* 12 (5). 159–164.

Enfield, Nick. 2009. *The anatomy of meaning speech, gesture, and composite utterances*. Cambridge, UK: Cambridge University Press.

Enfield, Nick. 2004. *Ethnosyntax: Explorations in grammar and culture*. Oxford: Oxford University Press.

Enfield, Nick. 2000. On linguocentrism. In Martin Pütz & Marjolijn H. Verspoor (eds.), *Explorations in linguistic relativity*, 125–157. Amsterdam: John Benjamins.

Epps, Patience. 2006. Growing a numeral system: The historical development of numerals in an Amazonian language family. *Diachronica* 23 (2). 259–288.

Epps, Patience, Claire Bowern, Cynthia Hansen, Jane Hill & Jason Zentz. 2012. On numerical complexity in hunter-gatherer languages. *Linguistic Typology* 16 (1). 41–109.

Evans, Nick & Stephen Levinson. 2009. The myth of language universals: Language diversity and its importance for cognitive science. *Behavioral and Brain Sciences* 32 (5). 429–448.

Evans-Pritchard, Edward E. 1939. Nuer time-reckoning. *Africa: Journal of the International African Institute* 12 (2). 189–216.

Everett, Caleb. In press. Linguistic relativity and numeric cognition: New light on a prominent test case. *Proceedings of the 37th Berkeley Linguistics Society*.

Everett, Caleb. 2013a. Independent cross-cultural data reveal linguistic effects on basic numerical cognition. *Language and Cognition* 5 (1). 99–104.

Everett, Caleb. 2013b. Without language, no distinctly human numerosity: Reply to Coolidge and Overmann (2012). *Current Anthropology* 54 (1). 81–82.

Everett, Caleb. 2012a. A closer look at a supposedly anumeric language. *International Journal of American Linguistics* 78 (3). 575–590.

Everett, Caleb. 2012b. Numeric cognition among speakers of the Jarawara language: A pilot study and methodological implication. *Proceedings of the 35th Annual Penn Linguistics Colloquium. University of Pennsylvania Working Papers in Linguistics* 18.51–59.

Everett, Caleb. 2012c. Linguistic effects on action discrimination strategies. Paper delivered at the *4th UK Cognitive Linguistics Conference*, London.

Everett, Caleb. 2011a. Variable velic movement in Karitiâna. *International Journal of American Linguistics* 77 (1). 33–58.

Everett, Caleb. 2011b. Gender, pronouns and thought: The ligature between epicene pronouns and a more neutral gender perception. *Gender and Language* 5 (1). 133–152.

Everett, Caleb. 2010. A survey of contemporary research on Amazonian languages. *Language and Linguistics Compass* 4 (5). 319–336.

Everett, Caleb. 2009. A reconsideration of the motivations for preferred argument structure. *Studies in Language* 33 (1). 1–24.

Everett, Caleb. 2008. Locus equation analysis as a tool for linguistic field work. *Language Documentation & Conservation* 2 (2). 185–211.

Everett, Caleb & Keren Madora. 2012. Quantity recognition among speakers of an anumeric language. *Cognitive Science* 36 (1). 130–141.

Everett, Daniel. 2012. *Language: The cultural tool*. New York: Pantheon.

Everett, Daniel. 2009. Pirahã culture and grammar: A response to some criticisms. *Language* 85 (2). 405–442.

Everett, Daniel. 2008. *Don't sleep there are snakes*. New York: Pantheon.

Everett, Daniel. 2005. Cultural constraints on grammar and cognition in Pirahã. *Current Anthropology* 46 (4). 621–646.

Fagot, Joël, Julie Goldstein, Jules Davidoff & Alan Pickering. 2006. Cross-species differences in color categorization. *Psychonomic Bulletin & Review* 13 (2). 275–280.

Fausey, Caitlin & Lera Boroditsky. 2011. Who dunnit? cross-linguistic differences in eye-witness memory. *Psychonomic Bulletin & Review* 18 (1). 150–157.

Fausey, Caitlin & Lera Boroditsky. 2010. Subtle linguistic cues influence perceived blame and financial liability. *Psychonomic Bulletin & Review* 17 (5). 644–650.

Fausey, Caitlin, Bria Long, Aya Inamori & Lera Boroditsky. 2010. Constructing agency: The role of language. *Frontiers in Cultural Psychology* 1. doi: 10.3389/fpsyg.2010.00162.

Fedorenko, Evelina & Nancy Kanwisher. 2009. Neuroimaging of language: Why hasn't a clearer picture emerged? *Language and Linguistics Compass* 3 (4). 839–865.

Feigenson, Lisa, Susan Carey & Marc Hauser. 2002. The representations underlying infants' choice of more: Object files versus analog magnitudes. *Psychological Science* 13 (2). 150–156.

Feigenson, Lisa, Stanislas Dehaene & Elizabeth Spelke. 2004. Core systems of number. *Trends in Cognitive Sciences* 8 (7). 307–314.

Fishman, Joshua A. 1982. Whorfianism of the third kind: Ethnolinguistic diversity as a worldwide societal asset. *Language in Society* 11 (1). 1–14.

Flaherty, Mary. 2001. How a language gender system creeps into perception. *Journal of Cross-Cultural Psychology* 32 (1). 18–31.

Flaherty, Mary & Ann Senghas. 2011. Numerosity and number signs in deaf Nicaraguan adults. *Cognition* 121 (3). 427–436.

Fodor, Jerry A. 1998. The trouble with psychological Darwinism. *London Review of Books* 20 (2). 11–13.

Fodor, Jerry A. 1983. *The modularity of mind*. Cambridge, MA: MIT Press.

Fodor, Jerry A. 1975. *The language of thought*. Cambridge, MA: Harvard University Press.

Frank, Michael, Daniel Everett, Evelina Fedorenko & Edward Gibson. 2008. Number as a cognitive technology: Evidence from Pirahã language and cognition. *Cognition* 108 (3). 819–824.

Franklin, Anna & Ian Davies. 2004. New evidence for infant colour categories. *British Journal of Developmental Psychology* 22 (3). 349–377.

Franklin, Anna, Gilda V. Drivonikou, Ally Clifford, Paul Kay, Terry Regier & Ian Davies. 2008. Lateralization of categorical perception of color changes with color term acquisition. *Proceedings of the National Academy of Sciences of the United States of America* 105 (47). 18221–18225.

Fryberg, Stephanie & Hazel Markus. 2003. On being American Indian: Current and possible selves. *Self and Identity* 2 (4). 325–344.

Fuhrman, Orly, Kelly McCormick, Eva Chen, Heidi Jiang, Dingfrang Shu, Shuaimei Mao & Lera Boroditsky. 2011. How linguistic and cultural forces shape conceptions of time: English and mandarin time in 3D. *Cognitive Science* 35 (7). 1305–1328.

Fuhrman, Orly and Lera Boroditsky. 2010. Cross-cultural differences in mental representations of time: Evidence from and implicit nonlinguistic task. *Cognitive Science* 34 (8). 1430–1451.

Gallistel, C. Randy 2002. Language and spatial frames of reference in mind and brain. *Trends in Cognitive Sciences* 6 (8). 321–322.

Gelman, Susan A. 2003. *The essential child: Origins of essentialism in everyday thought.* Oxford: Oxford University Press.

Gentner, Dedre. 2007. Spatial cognition in apes and humans. *Trends in Cognitive Sciences* 11 (5). 192–194.

Gentner, Dedre. 2003. Why we're so smart. In Dedre Gentner & Susan Goldin-Meadow (eds.), *Language in mind: Advances in the study of language and cognition*, 195–233. Cambridge, MA: MIT Press.

Gentner, Dedre & Lera Boroditsky. 2001. Individuation, relativity and early word learning. In Melissa Bowerman & Stephen Levinson (eds.), *Language acquisition and conceptual development*, 215–256. Cambridge, UK: Cambridge University Press.

Gentner, Dedre, Mutsumi Imai & Lera Boroditsky. 2002. As time goes by: Evidence for two systems in processing space time metaphors. *Language and Cognitive Processes* 17 (5). 537–565.

Gibbs, Raymond & Guy Van Orden. 2010. Adaptive cognition without massive modularity. *Language and Cognition* 2 (2). 149–176.

Gilbert, Aubrey L., Terry Regier, Paul Kay & Richard Ivry. 2006. Whorf hypothesis is supported in the right visual field but not the left. *Proceedings of the National Academy of Sciences of the United States of America* 103 (2). 489–494.

Givón, Talmy. 1984. *Syntax: A functional-typological introduction.* Amsterdam: Benjamins Pub. Co.

Glucksberg, Sam, Mary Brown & Matthew S. McGlone. 1993. Conceptual metaphors are not automatically accessed during idiom comprehension. *Memory & Cognition* 21 (5). 711–719.

Goldberg, Adele. 1995. *Constructions: A construction grammar approach to argument structure.* Chicago: University of Chicago Press.

Goldin-Meadow, Susan. 2003. *Hearing gesture: How our hands help us think.* Cambridge, MA: Harvard University Press.

Gordon, Peter. 2010. In Barbara Malt and Phillip Wolff (eds.), *Worlds without words: Commensurability and causality in language, culture, and cognition*, 199–218. Oxford: Oxford University Press.

Gordon, Peter. 2004. Numerical cognition without words: Evidence from Amazonia. *Science* 306 (5695). 496–499.

Greenberg, Joseph H. 1966. *Language universals: With special reference to feature hierarchies.* The Hague: Mouton.

Grossmann, Igor & Michael Varnum. 2011. Social class, culture, and cognition. *Social Psychological and Personality Science* 2 (1). 81–89.

Guiora, Alexander Z. 1982. Language environment and gender identity attainment. *Language Learning* 32 (2). 289–304.

Gumperz, John J. 1982. *Discourse strategies*. Cambridge, UK: Cambridge University Press.

Gumperz, John J. & Stephen Levinson (eds.). 1996. *Rethinking linguistic relativity*. Cambridge, UK: Cambridge University Press.

Hammarström, Harald. 2010. Rarities in numeral systems. In Jan Wohlgemuth & Michael Cysouw (eds.), *Rethinking universals: How rarities affect linguistic theory*, 11–60. Berlin: Mouton De Gruyter.

Hanks, William F. 2005. Explorations in the deictic field. *Current Anthropology* 46 (2). 191–220.

Hanks, William F. 1996. Language form and communicative practices. In John J. Gumperz & Stephen Levinson, (eds.), *Rethinking linguistic relativity*, 232–270. Cambridge, UK: Cambridge University Press.

Haspelmath, Martin. 2009. The best-supported language universals refer to scalar patterns deriving from processing cost. *Behavioral and Brain Sciences* 32 (5). 457–458.

Haspelmath, Martin. 2007. Pre-established categories don't exist: Consequences for language description and typology. *Linguistic Typology* 11 (1). 119–132.

Haspelmath, Martin, Mathew Dryer, David Gil & Bernard Comrie. 2011. *The world atlas of language structures online*. Munich: Max Planck Digital Library.

Haun, Daniel, Josep Call, Gabriele Janzen & Stephen Levinson. 2006. Evolutionary psychology of spatial representations in the hominidae. *Current Biology* 16 (17). 1736–1740.

Haun, Daniel, Christian Rapold, Gabriele Janzen & Stephen Levinson. 2011. Plasticity of human spatial cognition: Spatial language and cognition covary across cultures. *Cognition* 119 (1). 70–80.

Hauser, Marc, Susan Carey & Lilian Hauser. 2000. Spontaneous number representation in semi-free-ranging rhesus monkeys. *Proceedings of the Royal Society: Biological Sciences* 267 (1445). 829–833.

Hauser, Marc, Noam Chomsky & Tecumseh Fitch. 2002. The faculty of language: what is it, who has it, and how did it evolve. *Science* 298 (5598). 1569–1579

Haviland, John. 1998. Guugu Yimithirr caridinal directions. *Ethos* 26 (1). 25–47.

Haviland, John. 1996. Projections, transpositions, and relativity. In John Gumperz & Stephen Levinson, (eds.), *Rethinking linguistic relativity*, 271–323. Cambridge, UK: Cambridge University Press.

Haviland, John. 1993. Anchoring, iconicity, and orientation in guugu yimidhirr pointing gestures. *Journal of Linguistic Anthropology* 3 (1). 3–45.

Heine, Bernd. 1997. *Cognitive foundations of grammar*. Oxford: Oxford University Press.

Heine, Steven & Takeshi Hamamura. 2007. In search of east Asian self-enhancement. *Personality and Social Psychology Review* 11 (1). 4–27.

Henrich, Joseph, Steven Heine & Ara Norenzayan. 2010. The weirdest people in the world? *Behavioral and Brain Sciences* 33 (2–3). 61–83.

Hopper, Paul & Elizabeth Traugott. 2003. *Grammaticalization*. Cambridge, UK: Cambridge University Press.

Humboldt, Wilhelm. 1988. [1836.]. *On language: The diversity of human language-structure and its influence on the mental development of mankind* (Translated by Peter Heath). Cambridge, UK: Cambridge University Press.

Hurford, James R. 1987. *Language and number: The emergence of a cognitive system*. New York: Blackwell.

Hymes, Dell. 2001. On communicative competence. In Alessandro Duranti, (ed.), *Linguistic Anthropology: A Reader*, 53–73. Malden, MA: Blackwell.

Hymes, Dell. 1974. *Foundations in sociolinguistics: An ethnographic approach*. Philadelphia: University of Pennsylvania Press.

Hymes, Dell. 1966. Two types of linguistic relativity (with examples form Amerindian ethnography). *Proceedings of the UCLA Sociolinguistics Conference*, 114–167. The Hague: Mouton.

Imai, Mutsumi & Dedre Gentner. 1997. A cross-linguistic study of early word meaning: Universal ontology and linguistic influence. *Cognition* 62 (2). 169–200.

Imai, Mutsumi & Reiko Mazuka. 2007. Language-relative construal of individuation constrained by universal ontology: Revisiting language universals and linguistic relativity. *Cognitive Science* 31 (3). 385–413.

Imai, Mutsumi, Lennart Schalk, Henrik Saalbach & Hiroyuki Okada. 2010. Influence of grammatical gender on deductive reasoning about sex-specific properties of animals. *Proceedings of the 32nd Annual Meeting of the Cognitive Science Society*, 1160–1165.

Jaeger, Florian, Peter Graff, William Croft & Daniel Pontillo. 2011. Mixed effects models for genetic and areal dependencies in linguistic typology. *Linguistic Typology* 15 (2). 281–319.

Jakobson, Roman. 1971. *Selected writings*. The Hague: Mouton.

Jameson, Kimberly & Roy D'Andrade. 1997. It's not really red, green, yellow, and blue: An inquiry into cognitive color space. In C. L. Hardin & Luisa Maffi (eds.), *Color categories in thought and language*, 295–319. Cambridge, UK: Cambridge University Press.

January, David & Edward Kako. 2007. Re-evaluating evidence for linguistic relativity: Reply to Boroditsky (2001). *Cognition* 104 (2). 417–426.

Johnson, Keith. 2008. *Quantitative methods in linguistics*. Malden, MA: Blackwell.

Johnston, Judith R. & Dan Slobin. 1979. The development of locative expressions in English, Italian, Serbo-Croatian and Turkish. *Journal of Child Language* 6 (3). 529–545.

Jones, Edward E. & Victor Harris. 1967. *The attribution of attitudes. Journal of Experimental Social Psychology* 3 (1). 1–24.

Justice, David. *The semantics of form in Arabic in the mirror of European languages*. Amsterdam: John Benjamins.

Kant, Immanuel. 1988. [1798.]. *Kant Selections* (Translated by Lewis Beck). New York: Macmillan.

Kay, Paul. 1996. Intra-speaker relativity. In John Gumperz & Stephen Levinson (eds.), *Rethinking linguistic relativity*, 97–114. Cambridge, UK: Cambridge University Press.

Kay, Paul, Brent Berlin, Luisa Maffi, William Merrifield & Richard Cook. 2009. *World color survey*. Stanford: CSLI.

Kay, Paul, Brent Berlin & William Merrifield. 1991. Biocultural implications of systems of color naming. *Journal of Linguistic Anthropology* 1 (1). 12–25.

Kay, Paul & Willett Kempton. 1984. What is the Sapir-Whorf hypothesis? *American Anthropologist* 86 (1). 65–79.

Kay, Paul & Luisa Maffi. 1999. Color appearance and the emergence and evolution of basic color lexicons. *American Anthropologist* 101 (4). 743–760.

Kay, Paul & Chad McDaniel. 1978. The linguistic significance of the meanings of basic color terms. *Language* 54 (3). 610–646.

Kay, Paul & Terry Regier. 2003. Resolving the question of color naming universals. *Proceedings of the National Academy of Sciences of the United States of America* 100 (15). 9085–9089.

Keil, Frank C. 1979. *Semantic and conceptual development: An ontological perspective.* Cambridge, MA: Harvard University Press.

Keller, Charles M. & Janet D. Keller. 1996. *Cognition and tool use: The blacksmith at work.* Cambridge, UK: Cambridge University Press.

Kelly, Louis. 1979. *The true interpreter: A history of translation theory and practice in the west.* New York: St. Martin's Press.

Kenneally, Christine. 2007. *The first word: The search for the origins of language.* New York: Viking.

Kimball, Geoffrey. 1991. *Koasati grammar.* Nebraska: University of Nebraska Press.

Klein, Richard G. 2009. *The human career: Human biological and cultural origins.* Chicago: The University of Chicago Press.

Koerner, E. F. Konrad. 1992. The Sapir-Whorf hypothesis: A preliminary history and a bibliographical essay. *Journal of Linguistic Anthropology* 2 (2). 173–198.

Konishi, Toshi. 1993. The semantics of grammatical gender: A cross-cultural study. *Journal of Psycholinguistic Research* 22 (5). 519–534.

Labov, William. 2001. *Principles of linguistic change: Social factors.* Malden: MA: Blackwell.

Labov, William. 1966. *The social stratification of English in New York City.* Washington: Center for Applied Linguistics.

Ladefoged, Peter & Ian Maddieson. 1996. *The sounds of the world's languages.* Malden, MA: Blackwell.

Lakoff, George. 1993. The contemporary theory of metaphor. In Andrew Ortony (ed.), *Metaphor and thought*, 202–251. Cambridge, UK: Cambridge University Press.

Lakoff, George. 1987. *Women, fire, and dangerous things.* Chicago: University of Chicago Press.

Lakoff, George & Mark Johnson. 1980. *Metaphors we live by.* Chicago: University of Chicago Press.

Landau, Barbara & Ray Jackendoff. 1993. What and where in spatial language and cognition. *Behavioral and Brain Sciences* 16 (2). 217–238.

Langacker, Ronald W. 1991. *Foundations of cognitive grammar II: Descriptive applications.* Stanford: Stanford University Press.

Lantz, Delee & Volney Stefflre. 1964. Language and cognition revisited. *Journal of Abnormal and Social Psychology* 69 (5). 472–481.

Le Guen, Olivier. 2011. Speech and gesture in spatial language and cognition among the yucatec mayas. *Cognitive Science* 35 (5). 905–938.

Leavitt, John. 2011. *Linguistic relativities: Language diversity and modern thought.* Cambridge, UK: Cambridge University Press.

Lee, Demetracopoulou D. 1944. Categories of the generic and the particular in Wintu. *American Anthropologist* 46 (3). 362–369.

Lee, Penny. 1996. *The Whorf Theory Complex.* Amsterdam: John Benjamins.

Lenneberg, Eric & John Roberts. 1956. The language of experience: A study in methodology. *International Journal of American Linguistics* 22 (Memoir 13).

Levinson, Stephen. 2003. *Space in language and cognition.* Cambridge, UK: Cambridge University Press.

Levinson, Stephen. 2001. Yélî Dnye and the theory of basic color terms. *Journal of Linguistic Anthropology* 10 (1). 3–55.

Levinson, Stephen. 1997. Language and cognition: The cognitive consequences of spatial description in Guugu Yimithirr. *Journal of Linguistic Anthropology* 7 (1). 1–35.

Levinson, Stephen. 1996. Relativity in spatial conception and description. In Gumperz, John & Stephen Levinson (eds.), *Rethinking Linguistic relativity*, 177–202. Cambridge, UK: Cambridge University Press.

Levinson, Stephen, Sotaro Kita, Daniel Haun & Björn Rasch. 2002. Returning the tables: Language affects spatial reasoning. *Cognition* 84 (2). 155–188.

Levinson, Stephen, Sergio Meira & The Language and Cognition Group. 2003. 'Natural concepts' in the spatial topologial domain–adpositional meanings in crosslinguistic perspective: An exercise in semantic typology. *Language* 79 (3). 485–516.

Levinson, Stephen & David Wilkins (eds.). 2006. *Grammars of space: Explorations in cognitive diversity*. Cambridge, UK: Cambridge University Press.

Lewis, Paul. (ed.). 2009. *Ethnologue: Languages of the world*. Dallas: SIL International.

Li, Peggy, Linda Abarbanell, Lila Gleitman & Anna Papafragou. 2011. Spatial reasoning in Tenejapan Mayas. *Cognition* 120 (1). 33–53.

Li, Peggy & Lila Gleitman. 2002. Turning the tables: Language and spatial reasoning. *Cognition* 83 (3). 265–294.

Lieberman, Philip. 2007. The evolution of human speech: Its anatomical and neural bases. *Current Anthropology* 48 (1). 39–66.

Lindsey, Delwin T. & Angela Brown. 2006. Universality of color names. *Proceedings of the National Academy of Sciences of the United States of America* 103 (44). 16608–16613.

Liu, Lisa. G. 1985. Reasoning counterfactually in Chinese: Are there any obstacles? *Cognition* 21 (3). 239–270.

Loeweke, Eunice & Jean May. 1980. *General grammar of Fasu (Namo Me): Lake Kutubu, Southern Highlands Province*. Dallas: SIL International.

Lucy, John A. 2004. Language, culture, and mind. In Michel Achard and Suzanne Kemmer (eds.), *Language, culture, and mind*, 1–21. Stanford: CSLI Publications.

Lucy, John A. 1997. Linguistic relativity. *Annual Review of Anthropology* 26.291–312.

Lucy, John A. 1996. The scope of linguistic relativity: An analysis and review of empirical research. In John Gumperz & Stephen Levinson (eds.), *Rethinking Linguistic relativity*, 37–69. Cambridge, UK: Cambridge University Press.

Lucy, John A. 1992a. *Language diversity and thought*. Cambridge, UK: Cambridge University Press.

Lucy, John A. 1992b. *Grammatical categories and cognition: A case study of the linguistic relativity hypothesis*. Cambridge, UK: Cambridge University Press.

Lucy, John A. & Suzanne Gaskins. 2001. Grammatical categories and the development of classification preferences: A comparative approach. In Melissa Bowerman & Stephen Levinson (eds.), *Language acquisition and conceptual development*, 257–283. Cambridge, UK: Cambridge University Press.

Lucy, John A. & Richard Shweder. 1988. The effect of incidental conversation on memory for focal colors. *American Anthropologist* 90 (4). 923–931.

Lucy, John A. & Richard Shweder. 1979. Whorf and his critics: Linguistic and nonlinguistic influences on color memory. *American Anthropologist* 81 (3). 581–615.

Lupyan, Gary. 2012. Linguistically modulated perception and cognition: The label-feedback hypothesis. *Frontiers in Cognition* 3. doi:10.3389/fpxyg.2012.00054.

Lyons, John. 1995. *Colour in language*. In Trevor Lamb & Janine Bourriau (eds.), *Colour: Art and Science*. Cambridge, UK: Cambridge University Press.

MacKay, Donald G. 1980. Psychology, prescriptive grammar, and the pronoun problem. *American Psychologist* 35 (5). 444–449.

MacLaury, Robert E. 1997. Ethnographic evidence of unique hues and elemental colors. *Behavioral and Brain Sciences* 20 (2). 202–203.

Maddieson, Ian. 1984. *Patterns of sounds.* Cambridge, UK: Cambridge University Press.

Majid, Asifa, Melissa Bowerman, Sotaro Kita, Daniel Haun & Stephen Levinson. 2004. Can language restructure cognition? The case for space. *Trends in Cognitive Sciences* 8 (3). 108–114.

Malotki, Ekkehart. 1983. *Hopi time: A linguistic analysis of the temporal concepts of the hopi language.* Berlin: Mouton de Gruyter.

Malt Barbara, Steven Sloman, Silvia Gennari, Meiyi Shi & Yuan Wang. 1999. Knowing versus naming: Similarity and the linguistic categorization of artifacts. *Journal of Memory and Language* 40 (2). 230–230.

Malt, Barbara & Phillip Wolff (eds.). 2010. *Words and the mind: How words capture human experience.* New York: Oxford University Press.

Mathiot, Madeleine. 1962. Noun classes and folk taxonomy in Pagago. *American Anthropologist* 64 (2). 340–350.

Matlock, Teenie, Michael Ramscar & Lera Boroditsky. 2005. On the experiential link between spatial and temporal language. *Cognitive Science* 29 (4). 655–664.

Matsumoto, David, Fazilet Kasri & Kristie Kooken. 1999. American-Japanese cultural differences in judgements of expression intensity and subjective experience. *Cognition & Emotion* 13 (2). 201–218.

Matsumoto, David & Bob Willingham. 2009. Spontaneous facial expressions of emotion of congenitally and noncongenitally blind individuals. *Journal of Personality and Social Psychology* 96 (1). 1–10.

Matthews, P. H. 1981. *Syntax.* Cambridge, UK: Cambridge University Press.

McGregor, William. 2009. Typology of ergativity. *Language and Linguistics Compass* 3 (1). 480–508.

McNeill, David. 2005. Gesture and thought. Bristol: University Presses Marketing.

McNeill, David. 1992. Hand and mind. Chicago: Chicago University Press.

Medin, Douglas & Scott Atran. 2004. The native mind: Biological categorization and reasoning in development and across cultures. *Psychological Review* 111 (4). 960–983.

Mehl, Matthias, Simine Vazire, Nairán Ramírez-Esparza, Richard Slatcher & James Pennebaker. 2007. Are women really more talkative than men? *Science* 317 (5834). 82.

Miles, Lynden, Louise Nind, & C. Neil Macrae. 2010. Moving through time. *Psychological Science* 21 (2). 222–223.

Miracle, Andrew & Dios Yapita Moya (eds.). 1981. Time and space in Aymara. In *The aymara language in its social and cultural context.* Gainesville: University Presses of Florida.

Miura, Irene, Marcia Steere, Chih-Mei Chang, Chungsoon Kim, Michel Fayol & Yukari Okamoto. 1994. Comparisons of children's cognitive representation of number: China, France, Japan, Korea, Sweden, and the United States. *International Journal of Behavioral Development* 17 (3). 401–411.

Miyamoto, Yuri & Shinobu Kitayama. 2002. Cultural variation in correspondence bias: The critical role of attitude diagnosticity of socially constrained behavior. *Journal of Personality and Social Psychology* 83 (5). 1239–1248.

Monaghan, Leila. 2011. The expanding boundaries of linguistic anthropology: 2010 in perspective. *American Anthropologist* 113 (2). 222–234.

Müller-Lyer, F. C. 1889. Optische urteilstauschungen. *Archiv Fur Anatomie Und Physiologie, Physiologische Abteilung* 2. 263–270.

Nei, Masatoshi. 1995. Genetic support for the out-of-africa theory of human evolution. *Proceedings of the National Academy of Sciences of the United States of America* 92 (15). 6720–6722.

Nichols, Johanna. 1992. *Linguistic diversity in space and time.* Chicago: University of Chicago Press.

Niemeier, Susanne & René Dirven. 2000. *Evidence for linguistic relativity.* Amsterdam: John Benjamins.

Nuñez, Rafael, Kensy Cooperrider, D Doan & Jurg Wassmann. 2012. Contours of time: Topographic construals of past, present, and future in the Yupno valley of Papua New Guinea. *Cognition* 124 (1). 25–35.

Nuñez, Rafael & Eve Sweetser. 2006. With the future behind them: Convergent evidence from aymara language and gesture in the crosslinguistic comparison of spatial construals of time. *Cognitive Science* 30 (3). 401–450.

O'Meara, Carolyn & Gabriella Báez. 2011. Spatial frames of reference in Mesoamerican languages. *Language Sciences* 33 (6). 837–852.

Ochs, Eleanor & Bambi Schieffelin. 1983. *Acquisition of conversational competence.* London: Routledge, Kegan, & Paul.

Ohnuki-Tierney, Emiko. 1973. Sakhalin Ainu time reckoning. *Man* 8 (2). 285–299.

Oliveri, Massimiliano, Sonia Bonnì, Patrizia Turriziani, Giacomo Koch, Emanuele Lo Gerfo, Sara Torriero, Carmelo Vicario, Laura Petrosini & Carlo Caltagirone. 2009. Motor and linguistic linking of space and time in the cerebellum. *PloS One* 4 (11). e7933. doi:10.1371/journal.pone.0007933.

Osgood, Charles, George Suci & Percy Tannenbaum. *The measurement of meaning.* Urbana: University of Illinois Press.

Pagel, Mark. 2000. The history, rate, and pattern of world linguistic evolution. In Chris Knight, Michael Studdert-Kennedy & James Hurford (eds.), *The evolutionary emergence of language,* 391–416. Cambridge, UK: Cambridge University Press.

Papafragou, Anna, Justin Hulbert & John Trueswell. 2008. Does language guide event perception? Evidence from eye movements. *Cognition* 108 (1). 155–184.

Payne, Thomas. 1997. *Describing morphosyntax: A guide for field linguists.* Cambridge, UK: Cambridge University Press.

Pederson, Eric. 1995. Language as context, language as means: Spatial cognition and habitual language use. *Cognitive Linguistics* 6 (1). 33–62.

Pederson, Eric. 1993. Geographic and manipulable space in two Tamil linguistic systems. *Lecture Notes in Computer Science* 716. 294–311.

Pederson, Eric, Eve Danziger, David Wilkins, Stephen Levinson, Sotaro Kita & Gunter Senft. 1998. Semantic typology and spatial conceptualization. *Language* 74 (3). 557–589.

Piaget, Jean. 1977. *Epistemology and psychology of functions.* Boston: Reidel Publishing Company.

Piaget, Jean. 1955. Perceptual and cognitive (or operational) structures in the development of the concept of space in the child. *Acta Psychologica* 11 (1). 41–46.

Piaget, Jean & Bärbel Inhelder. 1956. *The child's conception of space.* London: Routledge & Paul.

Pica, Pierre & Alain Lecomte. 2008. Theoretical implications of the study of numbers and numerals in mundurucu. *Philosophical Psychology* 21 (4). 507–522.

Pica, Pierre, Cathy Lemer, Véronique Izard & Stanislas Dehaene. 2004. Exact and approximate arithmetic in an Amazonian indigene group. *Science* 306 (5695). 499–503.

Pierrehumbert, Janet. 2001. Why phonological constraints are so coarse-grained. *Language and Cognitive Processes* 16 (5/6). 691–698.

Pinker, Steven. 2007. *The stuff of thought.* New York: Viking.

Pinker, Steven. 1994. *The language instinct.* New York: Harper Collins.

Pinker, Steven & Ray Jackendoff. 2005. The faculty of language: What's special about it? *Cognition* 95 (2). 201–236.

Plank, Frans. 2009. Senary summary so far. *Linguistic Typology* 13 (2). 337–345.

Plato. 1892. *The Dialogues of Plato translated into English with Analyses and Introductions by B. Jowett, M.A. in Five Volumes.* 3rd edition. Oxford: Oxford University Press.

Platt, John R. & David Johnson. 1971. Localization of position within a homogeneous behavior chain: Effects of error contingencies. *Learning and Motivation* 2 (4). 386–414.

Polian, Gilles & Juergen Bohnemeyer. 2011. Uniformity and variation in Tseltal reference frame use. *Language Sciences* 33 (6). 868–891.

Port, Robert. 2007. How are words stored in memory? Beyond phones and phonemes. *New Ideas in Psychology* 25 (2). 143–170.

Port, Robert & Adam Leary. 2005. Against formal phonology. *Language* 81 (4). 927–964.

Prinz, Jesse. 2012. *Beyond human nature.* London: Penguin Group.

Pullum, Geoffrey. 1991. *The great Eskimo vocabulary hoax and other irreverent essays on the study of language.* Chicago: Chicago University Press.

Quine, William V. O. 1969. *Ontological relativity and other essays.* New York: Columbia University Press.

Ramos, Sara & Debi Roberson. 2011. What constrains grammatical gender effects on semantic judgements? Evidence from Portuguese. *Journal of Cognitive Psychology* 23 (1). 102–111.

Regier, Terry and Mingyu Zheng. 2007. Attention to endpoints: A cross-linguistic constraint on spatial meaning. *Cognitive Science* 31 (4). 705–719.

Regier, Terry & Paul Kay. 2009. Language, thought, and color: Whorf was half right. *Trends in Cognitive Sciences* 13 (10). 439–446.

Regier, Terry, Paul Kay & Richard Cook. 2005. Focal colors are universal after all. *Proceedings of the National Academy of Sciences of the United States of America* 102 (23). 8386–8391.

Regier, Terry, Paul Kay, Aubrey Gilbert & Richard Ivry. 2010. Language and thought: Which side are you on, anyway? In Barbara Malt & Phillip Wolff (eds.), *Words and the mind: How words capture human experience,* 165–182. New York: Oxford University Press.

Regier, Terry, Paul Kay & Naveen Khetarpal. 2009. Color naming and the shape of color space. *Language* 85 (4). 884–892.

Regier, Terry, Paul Kay & Naveen Khetarpal. 2007. Color naming reflects optimal partitions of color space. *Proceedings of the National Academy of Sciences of the United States* 104 (4). 1436–1441.

Reines, Maria Francisca & Jesse Prinz. 2009. Reviving Whorf: The return of linguistic relativity. *Philosophy Compass* 4 (6). 1022–1032.

Rennie, Léonie J. & Mairéad Dunne. 1994. Gender, ethnicity, and students' perceptions about science and science-related careers in Fiji. *Science Education* 78 (3). 285–300.

Roberson, Debi, Ljubica Damjanovic & Michael Pilling. 2007. Categorical perception of facial expressions: Evidence for a "category adjustment" model. *Memory & Cognition* 35 (7). 1814–1829.

Roberson, Debi & Jules Davidoff. 2000. The categorical perception of colors and facial expressions: The effect of verbal interference. *Memory & Cognition* 28 (6). 977–986.

Roberson, Debi, Jules Davidoff, Ian Davies & Laura Shapiro. 2004. The development of color categories in two languages: A longitudinal study. *Journal of Experimental Psychology: General* 133 (4). 554–571.

Roberson, Debi, Jules Davidoff, Ian Davies & Laura Shapiro. 2005. Colour categories in Himba: Evidence for the cultural relativity hypothesis. *Cognitive Psychology* 50 (4). 378–411.

Roberson, Debi, Ian Davies & Jules Davidoff. 2000. Color categories are not universal: Replications and new evidence from a stone-age culture. *Journal of Experimental Psychology: General* 129 (3). 369–398.

Roberson, Debi & Richard Hanley. 2010. Relatively speaking: An account of the relationship between language and thought in the color domain. In Barbara Malt & Phillip Wolff (eds.), *Words and the mind: How words capture human experience*, 183–198. New York: Oxford University Press.

Roberson, Debi, Hyensou Pak & Richard Hanley. 2008. Categorical perception of colour in the left and right visual field is verbally mediated: Evidence from Korean. *Cognition* 107 (2). 752–762.

Rock, Irvin. 1992. Comment on Asch and Witkin's "Studies in space orientation II." *Journal of Experimental Psychology: General* 121 (4). 404–406.

Rogoff, Barbara, Gilda Morelli & Cathy Angelillo. 2003. Cultural variation in young children's access to work or involvement in specialised child-focused activities. *International Journal of Behavioral Development* 27 (3). 264–274.

Rosch, Eleanor H. 1973. Natural categories. *Cognitive Psychology* 4 (3). 328–350.

Rosch, Eleanor H. 1972. Universals in color naming and memory. *Journal of Experimental Psychology* 93 (1). 10–20.

Ross, Lee, Teresa Amabile & Julia Steinmetz. 1977. Social roles, social control, and biases in social-perception processes. *Journal of Personality and Social Psychology* 35 (7). 485–494.

Ross, Norbert, Douglas Medin, John Coley & Scott Atran. 2003. Cultural and experiential differences in the development of folkbiological induction. *Cognitive Development* 18 (1). 25–47.

Russell, James A. 2003. Core affect and the psychological construction of emotion. *Psychological Review* 110 (1). 145–172.

Saalbach, Henrik & Mutsumi Imai. 2007. Scope of linguistic influence: Does a classifier system alter object concepts? *Journal of Experimental Psychology: General* 136 (3). 485–501.

Saalbach, Henrik, Mutsumi Imai & Lennart Schalk. 2012. Grammatical gender and inferences about biological properties in German-speaking children. *Cognitive Science* 36 (7). 1251–1267.

Sapir, Edward. 1949. [1929.]. *The selected writings of Edward Sapir in language, culture, and personality* (Edited by David G. Mandelbaum). Berkeley: University of California Press.

Sapir, Edward & Morris Swadesh. 1964. [1946.]. American Indian grammatical categories. In Dell Hymes (ed.), *Language in culture and society: a reader in linguistics and anthropology*, 101–107. New York: Harper and Row.

Sarnecka, Barbara W. & Susan A. Gelman. 2004. Six does not just mean a lot: Preschoolers see number words as specific. *Cognition* 92 (3). 329–352.

Saunders, Barbara & J. van Brakel. 1997. Are there nontrivial constraints on colour categorization? *The Behavioral and Brain Sciences* 20 (2). 167–179.

Scarf, Damian, Harlene Hayne & Michael Colombo. 2011. Pigeons on par with primates in numerical competence. *Science* 334 (6063). 1664.

Schoenemann, P. Thomas. 2004. Brain size scaling and body composition in mammals. *Brain, Behavior and Evolution* 63 (1). 47–60.

Scholz, Barbara, Francis Jeffry Pelletier & Geoffrey K. Pullum. 2011. Philosophy of linguistics. In Edward N. Zalta (ed.), *The Stanford Encyclopedia of Linguistics*. Stanford: CSLI. http://www.plato.stanford.edu/entries/linguistics.

Segall, Marshall, Donald Campbell & Melville Herskovits. 1966. *The influence of culture on visual perception*. Indianapolis: Bobbs-Merrill Co.

Sera, Maria, Christian Berge & Javier Pintado. 1994. Grammatical and conceptual forces in the attribution of gender by English and Spanish speakers. *Cognitive Development* 9 (3). 261–292.

Sera, Maria, Chryle Elieff, James Forbes, Melissa Clark, Burch Clark, Wanda Rodríguez & Diane Poulin Dubois. 2002. When language affects cognition and when it does not: An analysis of grammatical gender and classification. *Journal of Experimental Psychology: General* 131 (3). 377–397.

Sera, Maria & Whitney Goodrich. 2010. Who thinks that a piece of furniture refers to a broken couch? Count-mass constructions and individuation in English and Spanish. *Cognitive Linguistics* 21 (3). 419–442.

Seron, Xavier & Michel Fayol. 1994. Number transcoding in children: A functional analysis. *British Journal of Developmental Psychology* 12 (3). 281–300.

Shaki, Samuel & Wim Gevers. 2011. Cultural characteristics dissociate magnitude and ordinal information processing. *Journal of Cross-Cultural Psychology* 42 (4). 639–650.

Shibatani, Masayoshi. 1985. Passives and related constructions. *Language* 61 (4). 821–848.

Shusterman, Anna, Sang Ah Lee & Elizabeth Spelke. 2011. Cognitive effects of language on human navigation. *Cognition* 120 (2). 186–201.

Sidnell, Jack & Nick Enfield. 2012. Language diversity and social action: A third locus of linguistic relativity. *Current Anthropology* 53 (3). 302–321.

Silverstein, Michael. 1979. Language structure and linguistic ideology. In Paul Cline, William Hanks & Charles Hofbauer (eds.), *The Elements: A Parasession on Linguistic Units and Levels*, 193–247. Chicago: Chicago Linguistic Society.

Sinha, Chris, Silva Sinha, Jörg Zinken & Wany Sampaio. 2011. When time is not space: The social and linguistic construction of time intervals and temporal event relations in an Amazonian culture. *Language and Cognition* 3 (1). 137–169.

Slobin, Dan. 1996. From "thought and language" to "thinking for speaking". In John Gumperz & Stephen Levinson (eds.), *Rethinking linguistic relativity*, 71–96. Cambridge, UK: Cambridge University Press.

Smith, Andrew D. M., Kenny Smith & Ramon Ferrer i Cancho (eds.). 2008. *The evolution of language, Proceedings of the 7th International Conference (Evolang 7)*. Singapore: World Scientific Press.

Soja, Nancy, Susan Carey & Elizabeth Spelke. 1991. Ontological categories guide young children's inductions of word meaning: Object terms and substance terms. *Cognition* 38 (2). 179–211.

Soleé, Maria-Josep, Patrice S. Beddor & Manjari Ohala. 2007. *Experimental approaches to phonology*. Oxford: Oxford University Press.

Spaepen, Elizabet, Marie Coppola, Elizabeth Spelke, Susan Carey & Susan Goldin-Meadow. 2011. Number without a language model. *Proceedings of the National Academy of Sciences of the United States of America* 108 (8). 3163–3168.

Spelke, Elizabeth & Sanna Tsivkin. 2001. Language and number: A bilingual training study. *Cognition* 78 (1). 45–88.

Srinivasan, Mahesh. 2010. Do classifiers affect cognitive processing? A study of nominal classification in mandarin Chinese. *Language and Cognition* 2 (2). 177–190.

Stefflre, Volney, Victor Vales & Linda Morley. 1966. Language and cognition in Yucatan. A cross-cultural replication. *Journal of Personality and Social Psychology* 4 (1). 112–115.

Stockwell, Robert P., J. Donald Bowen & John W. Martin. 1977. *The grammatical structures of English and Spanish*. Chicago: University of Chicago.

Suddendorf, Thomas & Michael Corballis. 2007. The evolution of foresight: What is mental time travel, and is it unique to humans? *Behavioral and Brain Sciences* 30 (3). 299–313.

Sussman, Harvey, Celeste Duder, Eileen Dalston & Antonina Cacciatore. 1999. An acoustic analysis of the development of CV coarticulation: A case study. *Journal of Speech, Language, and Hearing Research* 42 (5). 1080.

Talmy, Leonard. 2000. *Toward a cognitive semantics*. Cambridge, MA: MIT Press.

Thibodeau, Paul & Lera Boroditsky. 2011. Metaphors we think with: The role of metaphor in reasoning. *PloS One* 6 (2). e16782. doi: 10.1371/journal.pone.

Tomasello, Michael. 2008. *Origins of human communication*. Cambridge, MA: MIT Press.

Tomasello, Michael. 2001. Cultural transmission: A view from chimpanzees and human infants. *Journal of Cross-Cultural Psychology* 32 (2). 135–146.

Tomasello, Michael & Josep Call. 1997. *Primate cognition*. Oxford: Oxford University Press.

Tse, Chi-Shing & Jeanette Altarriba. 2008. Evidence against linguistic relativity in Chinese and English: A case study of spatial and temporal metaphors. *Journal of Cognition and Culture* 8 (3/4). 335–357.

Turkheimer, Eric, Andreana Haley, Mary Waldron, Brian D'Onofrio & Irving Gottesman. 2003. Socioeconomic status modifies heritability of IQ in young children. *Psychological Science* 14 (6). 623–628.

Vigliocco, Gabriella, David Vinson, Federica Paganelli & Katharina Dworzynski. 2005. Grammatical gender effects on cognition: Implications for language learning and language use. *Journal of Experimental Psychology: General* 134 (4). 501–520.

Vygotsky, Lev. 1962. *Thought and language*. Cambridge, MA: MIT Press.

Wadley, Lyn, Tamaryn Hodgskiss & Michael Grant. 2009. Implications for complex cognition from the hafting of tools with compound adhesives in the middle stone age, South Africa. *Proceedings of the National Academy of Sciences of the United States of America* 106 (24). 9590–9594.

Wang, Ranxiao F. & Elizabeth Spelke. 2002. *Human spatial representation: Insights from animals*. Trends in Cognitive Sciences 6 (9). 376–382.

Wassmann, Jürg & Pierre Dasen. 1994. Yupno number system and counting. *Journal of Cross-Cultural Psychology* 25 (1). 78–94.

Watson, John B. 1913. Psychology as the behaviorist views it. *Psychological Review* 20 (2). 158–177.

Waxman, Sandra & Rochel Gelman. 1986. Preschoolers' use of superordinate relations in classification and language. *Cognitive Development* 1 (2). 139–156.

Weisbuch, Max & Nalini Ambady. 2008. Affective divergence: Automatic responses to others' emotions depend on group membership. *Journal of Personality and Social Psychology* 95 (5). 1063–1079.

Whalen, John, C. Randy Gallistel & Rochel Gelman. 1999. Nonverbal counting in humans: The psychophysics of number representation. *Psychological Science* 10 (2). 130–137.

White, Tim D., Berhane Asfaw, Yonas Beyene, Yohannes Haile-Selassie, C. Owen Lovejoy, Gen Suwa & Giday WoldeGabriel. 2009. Ardipithecus ramidus and the paleobiology of early hominids. *Science* 326 (5949). 75–86.

Whorf, Benjamin L. 1956. *Language, thought, and reality; selected writings* (Edited by John B. Carroll). Cambridge, MA: MIT Press

Widlock, Thomas. 1997. Orientation in the wild: The shared cognition of Hai‖om bushpeople. *Journal of the Royal Anthropological Institute* 3 (2). 317–332.

Wierzbicka, Anna. 2008. Why there are no 'colour universals' in language and thought. *Journal of the Royal Anthropological Institute* 14 (2). 407–425.

Wierzbicka, Anna. 1999. *Emotions across languages and cultures: Diversity and universals.* Cambridge, UK: Cambridge University Press.

Wierzbicka, Anna. 1992. *Semantics, Culture, and Cognition: Human Concepts in Culture-Specifc Configurations.* Oxford: Oxford University Press.

Winawer, Jonathan, Nathan Witthoft, Michael Frank, Lisa Wu, Alex Wade & Lera Boroditsky. 2007. Russian blues reveal effects of language on color discrimination. *Proceedings of the National Academy of the Sciences of the United States of America* 104 (19). 7780–7785.

Wittgenstein, Ludwig. 1922. *Tractatus logico-philosophicus* (Translated by Charles Kay Ogden). New York: Harcourt, Brace & Company.

Wolff, Phillip & Kevin Holmes. 2011. Linguistic relativity. *WIREs Cognitive Science* 2 (3). 253–266.

Wood, Guilherme, Klaus Willmes, Hans-Christoph Nuerk & Martin Fischer. 2008. . On the cognitive link between space and number: A meta-analysis of the SNARC effect. *Psychology Science Quarterly* 50 (4). 489–525.

Wrangham, Richard W. 2009. *Catching fire: How cooking made us human.* New York: Basic Books.

Wynn, Karen. 1992. Addition and subtraction by human infants. *Nature* 358 (6389). 749–750.

Xu, Fei & Elizabeth Spelke. 2000. Large number discrimination in 6-month-old infants. *Cognition* 74 (1). B1–B11.

Yeh, David & Dedre Gentner. 2005. Reasoning counterfactually in Chinese: Picking up the pieces. *Proceedings of the 27th Annual Cognitive Science Society*, 2410–2415.

Zebian, Samar. 2005. Linkages between number concepts, spatial thinking, and directionality of writing: The SNARC effect and the REVERSE SNARC effect in English and Arabic monoliterates, biliterates, and illiterate Arabic speakers. *Journal of Cognition and Culture* 5 (1/2). 165–165.

Zubin, David & Klaus Michael Köpcke. 1986. Gender and folk taxonomy: The indexical relation between grammatical and lexical categorization. In Colette Craig (ed.), *Noun classes and categorization*, 139–180. Amsterdam: John Benjamins.

Index